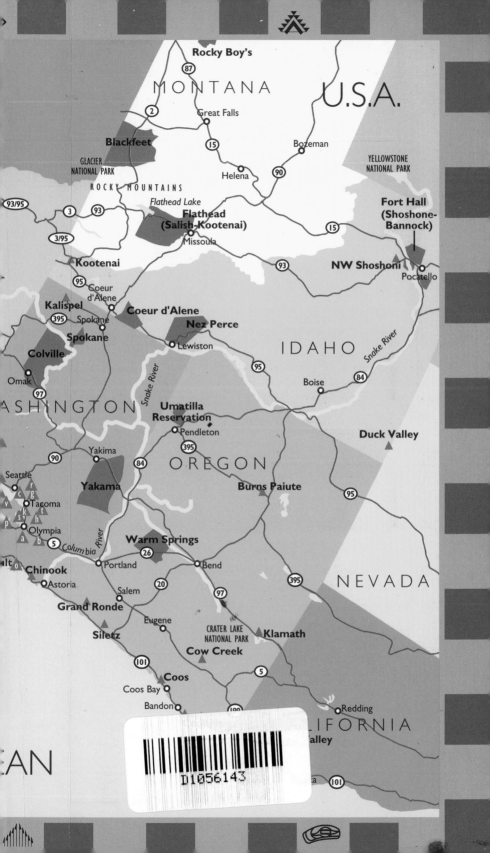

NATIVE PEOPLES OF THE NORTHWEST

NATIVE
PEOPLES OF THE
NORTHWEST

A TRAVELER'S GUIDE
TO LAND, ART, AND CULTURE

JAN HALLIDAY & GAIL CHEHAK

IN COOPERATION WITH THE AFFILIATED TRIBES OF NORTHWEST INDIANS

SECOND EDITION

SASQUATCH BOOKS
SEATTLE

Printed in the United States of America.
Distributed in Canada by Raincoast Books Ltd.

Second edition
07 06 05 04 03 02 01 00   5 4 3 2 1

Cover image: *The Raven and the First Men*, by Bill Reid (Haida). Courtesy of the University of British Columbia Museum of Anthropology, Vancouver, B.C. Photograph by Bill McLennan, UBC Museum of Anthropology. Courtesy of the photographer. Chapter opening art: Page 1: Detail of "Moon," by Calvin Hunt; courtesy of The Legacy. Page 45: Detail of "Helldiver, Sawbill, and Crane," by Andy Wilbur; courtesy of The Legacy. Page 119: Detail of a Wasco-Wishram–style twined bag; courtesy of Maryhill Museum of Art. Page 165: Detail of photograph of traditional dancer Tamara Arlene James (Yakama/Colville); copyright 1996 by Ben Marra, Photographer. Page 223: Detail of beaded vest by Maynard White Owl; courtesy of the artist. Page 237: Detail of beaded floral handbag by Maynard White Owl; copyright Marlene White Owl-Lavadour.
Cover and interior design: Lynne Faulk, Elizabeth Boyce
Foldout map: Barbara Dow
Interior maps: Karen Schober
Composition: Elizabeth Boyce
Copy editor: Amy Smith Bell

ISSN:1528-3062
ISBN: 1-57061-241-2

Sasquatch Books
615 Second Avenue
Seattle, Washington 98104
(206) 467-4300
www.SasquatchBooks.com
books@SasquatchBooks.com

CONTENTS

About the Cover Art

The Raven and the First Men, by Bill Reid (Haida, 1920–1998). Photograph by Bill McLennan, UBC Museum of Anthropology

Haida artist Bill Reid's acclaimed sculpture, *The Raven and the First Men*, is displayed in the University of British Columbia Museum of Anthropology, in Vancouver, B.C., along with four exhibit cases featuring a selection of Reid's smaller masterworks in gold, silver, argillite, and wood. With the assistance of several other artists, Reid created his massive sculpture out of a giant block of laminated yellow cedar. The sculpture depicts a moment in the ancestral past of the Haida people, when Raven, a wise and powerful yet mischievous trickster, has just found the first humans in a clamshell on the beach, and is coaxing them to venture out.

The Raven and the First Men was commissioned by Walter and Marianne Koerner and unveiled by HRH the Prince of Wales in 1980. Members of the Haida Nation were also present to celebrate the unveiling of the work. They brought the sand that is at the base of the sculpture from the beach where Raven is said to have made his discovery.

During his lifetime, Reid drew much from the traditions of his predecessors, including Charles Edenshaw (ca. 1839–1920), becoming internationally renowned for his extraordinary imagination and technical skill. His work continues to inspire new generations of Northwest Coast artists, such as Robert Davidson and Jim Hart, who are now masters in their own right. (For more about the University of British Columbia Museum of Anthropology see page 6.)

PREFACE

Gail Chehak and I met for the first time in 1994, in the offices of the Affiliated Tribes of Northwest Indians in Portland, Oregon. We spent a day together drinking lattes and brainstorming the ideas that eventually led to the first edition of *Native Peoples of the Northwest*. No one had written a book like this before—about the land, art, and culture of contemporary Native peoples—and at that time we encountered plenty of skeptics. We spent the next year visiting every tribe in the Northwest, collecting more information than we dreamed possible, and collaborating on the book. When the first edition was published in 1996, it was heralded as a long-overdue guide to the rich contemporary world of Northwest Natives. It was also an eye-opener to many people about how much there is to see, do, and learn in Indian Country.

The last several years have seen tremendous growth and changes not only in Indian tourism in the Northwest, but also in the interest in and appreciation of Native art and culture. During the time that we were researching the first edition, Gail was also dreaming of creating a large festival that would showcase the work of Northwest Indian artists. Within a year after the publication of the first edition and with virtually no funding in place, she produced Indian Art Northwest, a huge tented event in Portland's downtown that draws more than 200 exhibitors. As this new edition goes to press, the festival, held each Memorial Day Weekend, is in its third year. The rapid growth of the Indian tourism industry in the Northwest is also remarkable—new hotels, more guided tours, new museums, new wings being built to showcase collections long hidden in archival storage, the hiring of Indian curators, and the successes of a new generation of Indian artists. So welcome to the Native Northwest, a world of wonderful richness and diversity.

NATIVE AMERICAN, INDIAN, AMERICAN INDIAN, OR FIRST NATIONS?

The question that non-Natives ask most often is whether or not it's acceptable to call Native Americans "Indians." The word "Indian" is fine as long as you think of Indians as wonderfully diverse, sensitive, strong individuals with a fascinating, complex, and unique heritage. If you are still imagining the stereotypic version of Indians (as in Indians vs. cowboys), then "Indian" is not okay. The Affiliated Tribes of Northwest Indians, a group of 54 tribal governments in the Northwest, as well as the Ketchikan Indian Corporation and the Metlakatla Indian Reservation, use the term "Indian." They would not do so if the word had negative connotations.

Numerous other terms have come into use besides the word "Indian." The term "American Indian" is used in legal documents regarding the relationship between Native nations and the U.S. government. In Canada, the term "First Nation" is used in reference to sovereign Native peoples and their relationships to the Canadian government. The term "Alaska Native" is used to refer to the special status of the aboriginal people of Alaska. "Native American" came into common usage in the 1970s as a respectful way of grouping American Indians into one general category. The term "Native peoples" has gained more acceptance internationally. (And it's easier to say than "the indigenous peoples of the Western Hemisphere.") When greeting each other, Native people rarely use the words "Indian," "Native," "Native American," or "First Nation." Instead they describe themselves according to their tribal affiliation and ancestry. Someone who is an enrolled member of the Spokane Nation in Washington State might say: "I'm Spokane, with Coeur d'Alene and Welsh. My mother is Spokane, my father is Coeur d'Alene, and my grandfather is Welsh."

When you meet a Native person, just identify yourself as you would to anyone else. If you want to discuss heritage with a Native person, be prepared to know your own. For example, Jan Halliday might say "My family were lowland Scots who moved to Washington in the 1800s." What Jan is saying is that she descends from a long line of settlers. When Gail Chehak says, "I'm Klamath," she is saying that she descends from people who have lived for more than 500 generations on marshland in present-day southeastern Oregon. Encoded in both of these short introductions is a wealth of history and legend. What really matters, though, is the respect that individuals have for each other, and for each other's family history.

INTRODUCTION

Welcome to the Native Northwest. More than sixty Native tribes live in the Northwest, many of them on some of the most beautiful and protected lands in the world. This book, written in cooperation with the tribes themselves, is an invitation and a guide to you—to visit the tribes and their lands; to learn about their lives, history, art, and culture from them; and to see the wonders of the Northwest through their eyes.

Leave the Nineteenth Century and Meet Contemporary Native Peoples

You could spend your life studying Native American culture in libraries and museums, and never meet an Indian. Many museum exhibits about Northwest history begin with colorful displays of Native art, as a nod to the past, and then quickly segue into an exclusive focus on the 200 years of white settlement and development. They seem to ignore the fact that Indians continue to live, work, and create in the Northwest, very much tied to their traditional religions, cultures, and lands.

This book is a guide to the vital Native American culture that thrives today, both on and off tribally-held lands. We endorse Indian-guided tours and Indian-owned museums because we've discovered that Native people, whose families have lived for more than 10,000 years on these lands, tell great stories and present a side of history rarely voiced. There are creation myths, countless stories about Raven and Coyote, and hilarious tales of human error. Some are professionally told; many are shared casually. A story may begin with "See that rock up there?" and before you know it, your guide has covered centuries. Native people know their culture, their art, and their lands as no one else does.

Where and How to Buy Authentic Native Art

For those who wish to purchase authentic Native art, this book recommends more than fifty Northwest galleries, museum gift stores, and artist's studios. We introduce you to many of the Indian artists themselves—people who make everything from traditional dolls wrapped in buckskin to authentic Modoc bows and arrows and beaded cradleboards. You'll learn where you can buy authentic bead-work, watch totem poles being carved, and visit studios where you can see artists at work and perhaps purchase a piece from the very artist who created it. A special appendix, written by Gail Chehak, President of Indian Art Northwest, describes how to ensure that the art you buy is authentic Indian art. And we haven't limited our list-ings to visual arts: we also guide you to traditional performances with Native dancers and actors, give you guidelines for attending pow-wows, and list celebrations, rodeos, roundups, stick games, horse races, feasts, and powwows that are open to the public.

Museum Collections and Cultural Heritage Centers, Owned or Curated by Native People

In the Northwest, there are more than twenty-five museums that house spectacular Native art, much of it collected at the turn of the century. These include the Museum at Warm Springs in Eastern Oregon, named by the Smithsonian Institution as the top museum of its kind, and the University of British Columbia's Museum of Anthropology in Vancouver, B.C., one of the most visually stunning cultural museums in the world. In coastal museums, you'll find tall figures collected from abandoned villages, 30-foot-tall totem poles, cedar canoes, replicas of clan houses, ceremonial masks, and elaborate woven blankets. Inland museums display house styles such as tule mat, tepee, and wickiup, as well as hundreds of examples of beadwork.

In addition, during the past thirty years, Northwest tribes have built cultural heritage centers, some of them reconstructions of actual villages, and filled them with wondrous things—weathered totem poles, carved cedar house screens, elaborate masks, beaded cradle-boards, and baskets woven from cattail or cedar bark. On the Umatilla Reservation in Oregon is the handsome Tamastslikt Cultural Insti-tute, the only Indian-owned interpretive center on the Oregon Trail route, with more than 10,000 square feet of exhibits about life on the Columbia Plateau before white contact. The cultural center on the Makah Reservation in Washington houses one of the most impor-tant archeological finds in North America—the intact contents of an entire village that was buried in a mudslide more than 500 years ago.

The Most Beautiful and Protected Lands in the World

By visiting Native peoples and their lands, you can see and experi-ence the magnificent landscape of the West through the eyes of the people who have lived here for generations. First-time visitors to reservations often notice only the administration buildings, schools, and modern housing—none of which resemble archival photographs of beautifully decorated clan houses or tepee encampments. But there is far more than meets the eye. Tribal lands border magnificent national parks, such as Olympic National Park in Washington, Glacier National Park in Montana, and Crater Lake National Park in Oregon. Other tribal lands occupy parts of the isolated and rugged coasts of British Columbia, the rocky outcroppings of Hell's Canyon in Idaho, and vast stretches of hilly grassland between the Cascade Range and the Rocky Mountains. Many of the tribes offer first-class accommodations, resort hotels, and lake cruises, as well as fascinating eco- and cultural tours.

This guidebook also takes you into the Northwest's metropolitan areas, where just the faintest glimmer of Indian culture seems to remain. But here too there's far more then meets the eye. Descendants of Chief Seattle still live in and around the city that bears his name. A short ferry ride from downtown Seattle, on the Port Madison Reservation, you can visit Seattle's homeland, gravesite, and his tribe's cultural museum. In Vancouver, British Columbia, more than 100,000 aboriginal people live within the city limits. Their magnificent art is displayed in nearly every gallery in the city, as well as in a $4-million collection at the Vancouver International Airport, and at the University of British Columbia's Museum of Anthropology.

Native Guides Have a Unique Perspective

When you tour with a Native guide, it's like no other tour you've experienced. You see creation sites; hear legends, myths, and epic stories; and sometimes even meet the descendants of famous chiefs. On a guided raft trip with the Hupa Tribe in Northern California, you discover ancestral villages, learn about sacred dances, taste acorn soup, and watch how baskets are woven from maidenhair fern and wild grasses. In Montana, you can see buffalo, visit one of the first missions in the Northwest, attend a powwow with Salish guides, and stay in a first-class hotel overlooking the mountains and lake. In British Columbia, you can tour the old village where the tribe hosted Captain James Cook in the early 1800s.

The adventurous can kayak with the Kwakwaka'waka in British Columbia, ski with the Snohomish in Washington, or ride Appaloosa horses with the Nez Perce in Idaho. Or you can hike along a boardwalk through the oldest cedar grove in the world with the Nuu-chah-nulth on Vancouver Island, or enjoy a twilight cruise with the Salish-Kootenai on Flathead Lake in Montana.

We also take you to Native-owned fish hatcheries, where tribal biologists are raising salmon, trout, and even sturgeon—the historic backbone of tribal economy and culture in the Northwest. Situated amid beautiful surroundings, the hatcheries are a fascinating combination of technology and nature, where visitors are always welcome.

Visit Historical Sites

History buffs can visit historic Indian battlefields, missions, trails, and old fur-trading forts, and see petroglyphs and pictographs. On the Fort Hall Indian Reservation in Idaho, you can examine the traces of the nine emigrant trails that crossed through the valley; at Fort Clatsop near the mouth of the Columbia River, you can see the place where the Chinooks hosted explorers Lewis and Clark through a wet, rainy winter; and in Eastern Washington, you can visit the Whitman Mission, site of the Whitman massacre, to learn both sides of this grisly story. We've included tidbits of historical information throughout this book, along with recommendations for reading materials, videos, and Web sites that might be of additional interest.

Indian Givers: How the Indians of the Americas Transformed the World (1988, Ballantine Books), by anthropologist Jack Weatherford, is a must-read for people new to traveling in Indian Country. Weatherford traces, in an entertaining, easy-to-read format, contributions Indians have made to democracy, medicine, agriculture, ecology, farming, and trade.

Who Helped Us Write This Book

We wrote this guidebook with the help of the members of the Affiliated Tribes of Northwest Indians, a group of 54 tribes from Southeast Alaska, Washington, Oregon, Northern California, Idaho, and Western Montana. Based on their recommendations, we made on-site visits to nearly every place listed. Because the tribes themselves gave us their stamp of approval, you can be assured that you are welcome on reserves and reservations described in this book.

How to Use This Book

Take a Look at Our Map

The color foldout map at the front of this book is oriented on its side for a reason. It shows the Northwest from an unusual perspective, and reduces the visual impact of national borders and the familiar shapes of states and provinces. Prior to white contact, cultural affiliations and boundaries were determined by extended family groups who spoke similar languages. Intermarriage between clans strengthened trade relationships and ensured alliances. Travel along the coast was done primarily by water, to take advantage of ocean tides and currents. Overland travel was done by following streams and rivers, walking along the ridgetops of watersheds, or by using natural passes and openings in mountains and hills. Today, many of these ancient routes, created by aboriginal peoples and later used by explorers and pioneers, are now paved over as highways.

This Book is Driver-Friendly, Organized by Region

This is a driver-friendly guidebook, organized so that you can get from one place to the next easily. There are six chapters, each covering a different region of the Northwest: British Columbia, Western Washington, Western Oregon and Northern California, the Columbia River Gorge and Basin (which covers tribal lands in both Washington and Oregon), Central Oregon, and Idaho and Western Montana. Most often the parameters of a region are determined more by geography and natural features than by state boundaries, since it was geography that shaped tribal connections and similarities.

Appendixes on Powwow Etiquette, Sacred Sites, and Art

Be sure to check the appendixes at the back of the book for valuable and comprehensive information about sacred sites, attending powwows, annual events, buying Native art, Native-owned casinos, and tribal administrative offices.

Always Call Ahead

For every reservation, town, or city, we have listed numerous activities and destinations—everything from art galleries to powwows, Native-led walking tours to basket-weaving classes, houseboat rentals to tepee lodgings. For most of these, especially for those located in rural areas, we strongly suggest that you call ahead—to get directions, confirm hours or fees, or make appointments for tours. Remember that some of the businesses described in this book are operated out of private homes; many are run by tribal members who wear numerous hats. Use the phone number listed for the activity, or call the tribal office (tribal offices are listed in an appendix at the back of the book).

Check www.indianz.com, an American Indian e-zine with news reports of tribes and resources for students. The Talking Circle is the zine's chat room. Great links to other sites.

To Get More Information or Send in Your Comments

In this new edition, we've added Web sites whenever possible. Many of these have great links to other sites, where you'll find more information about Northwest Native peoples. Some are also linked to the author site, www.janhalliday.com, where you can order CDs and books, or email the authors with comments or questions.

About the Authors

We are co-authors. In 1995, when we were starting work on the first edition of *Native Peoples of the Northwest*, we met with the Yakama Tribal Council to ask their permission to write the book. Just before we walked into the meeting, a man in the hallway yelled, "Good Morning Full Bloods!" And so we are. Jan Halliday is Scot-Irish; Gail Chehak is Klamath Indian. We nicknamed ourselves Coyote and Raven because of the color of our hair, and laughed out loud when we spotted a real raven and coyote actually "dining" together (on venison) on writer Sherman Alexie's home turf, the Spokane Indian Reservation.

Jan Halliday has worked as a professional writer for twenty-five years. As a travel writer, she covers the region from Barrow, Alaska, to LaPaz, Mexico, for various regional and national publications. The great-granddaughter of pioneers who settled in the Northwest in the 1870s, Jan is the author of *Native Peoples of Alaska, A Traveler's Guide to Land, Art and Culture* (Sasquatch Books, 1998). She lives in Port Townsend, Washington. To learn more about Northwest Native peoples, order related CDs and books, or email the author with questions and comments, view Jan's Web site at **www.janhalliday.com.**

Gail Chehak worked for ten years in Washington, D.C., for the National Congress of American Indians, MorningStar Institute, and the Indian Arts and Crafts Shops. She is a Klamath Indian tribal member, founder and president of Indian Art Northwest, and editor of *Northwest Indian Magazine*. She lives in Portland, Oregon.

BRITISH COLUMBIA

BRITISH COLUMBIA

Along the thickly forested coasts of what is today British Columbia, Native villages of magnificently decorated cedar houses once lined the shores of sheltered inlets. The fire-lit interiors of the bighouses and longhouses were animated by the presence of massive carved and painted figures of wolves, bears, and other animals. Visitors would have been served delicacies from the sea and entertained by masked dancers accompanied by songs and pounding drums. Travelers journeying upriver into interior British Columbia would have been invited into the warmth (or shade) of insulated underground pithouses and offered feasts of fresh venison, huckleberries, nuts, roasted camas bulbs, and other bounty.

More than 170,000 aboriginal people reside today in British Columbia, both in urban areas and on more than 350 reserves on ancestral lands. Some of their number continue to live by hunting and fishing in isolated or remote areas. Like Native people throughout the Northwest, First Nations people have their feet firmly planted in both the traditional and the modern worlds.

For information and brochures on sightseeing, accommodations, and reservations in British Columbia, contact Tourism British Columbia, (800)663-6000. First-time visitors to British Columbia may be deceived by the distances between some destinations on the map. Vancouver Island's coastline is more than 400 miles long and nearly roadless. Both Prince Rupert and the Queen Charlotte Islands are about 600 miles north of Vancouver and just 100 miles south of Ketchikan in Southeast Alaska. Getting to the Queen Charlotte Islands by car requires a long drive and an expensive ferry crossing.

First Nations settlements are modern; many are fishing villages built on top of ancient village sites along the coastlines. Historic traditional structures, such as weathered totem poles and longhouse remains, are few in number. Skungwaii (Ninstints), an abandoned Haida village on the southern end of Haida Gwaii (the Queen Charlotte Islands), is one such site; protected as a United Nations world heritage site, its fragile beauty is guarded by the Haida Gwaii Watchmen.

All of the bighouses and longhouses that once lined the shores are gone now, except for those newly constructed for Native heritage centers, such as the seven longhouses of the 'Ksan Historical Indian Village, which is open to the public near the town of Hazelton. There are also exceptional First Nations—owned museums in the province, such as the Kwagiulth Museum and Cultural Centre on Quadra Island, which houses Winter Ceremony and potlatch items that were returned to the community by the Canadian government in the 1970s. Some First Nations sites and attractions are in or close to major cities and towns and are easily visited. Other locations, such as the islands of Haida Gwaii, are less easily reached. The Royal British Columbia Museum, in Victoria, and the University of British Columbia's Museum of Anthropology, in Vancouver, house significant collections of totem poles and

"Indians who remained by 1861 had been bullied and enticed into the life pattern devised by Sir William Johnson, the first British superintendent of Indians. It was Johnson who devised the treaties of surrender and the reserves which shaped the Indian policies of both Canada and the United States for two centuries. As a means of easing consciences and removing Indians, treaties and reserves were a success; as a basis for equality between Europeans and native people or as fair compensation, Johnson's system would prove a failure."
—Desmond Morton, *A Short History of Canada (McClelland & Stewart, 1998).*

artifacts, which have been brought together from many different places in the province. A mere 45-minute drive on the scenic highway north of Victoria's Royal British Columbia Museum is the Native Heritage Centre in Duncan, where you can meet people of the Cowichan Nation in person, watch totem-pole carving (and talk to the carver), sample traditional Coast Salish culture, and purchase a warm, hand-knit Cowichan sweater.

Just a few more miles north are two places where you can learn about extravagant pot-latches from the people who still practice them: the Kwagiulth Museum and Cultural Centre on Quadra Island, and the U'Mista Cultural Centre at Alert Bay. Within 3 hours of Victoria, at Tofino, you can go whale watch-ing across Clayoquot Sound with the Nuu-chah-nulth and take a tour of an old village site. Just a few hours east of Vancouver, you can visit the Secwepemc Native Heritage Park and discover the comfortable lifestyle of the Inland Salish people, as well as stay in a modern hotel designed to resemble the *kekuli* (winter house) of the Little Shuswap Band, who own and operate the lodging.

> For two good reads on Canada's First Nations history, try Arthur J. Ray's I Have Lived Here Since the World Began: An Illustrated History of Canada's Native People *(Key Porter Books, 1998) and* Indians and the Fur Trade: Their Roles as Trappers, Hunters, and Middle-men in the Lands Southwest of Hudson Bay 1660–1870 *(Univer-sity of Toronto, 1998). Ray, a history professor with the University of British Columbia, special-izes in the historical and cultural geography of First Nations people.*

Vancouver Area: *Coast Salish*

Several **FIRST NATION RESERVES** lie within the city limits of cos-mopolitan Vancouver, which is home to a large Native population. The University of British Columbia's Museum of Anthropology is one of the **FINEST MUSEUMS OF ITS KIND** in the world. In Vancou-ver you'll find Northwest Coast art in abundance in such public

Take the tram up the side of 4,100-foot Grouse Mountain to see the stunning view and to watch Our Spirit Soars, a 35-minute video presentation about Vancouver and its First Nations cultures; shown every hour on the hour, year-round. Grouse Mountain, 6400 Nancy Greene Wy, N Vancouver, BC V7R 4K9; (604)984-0661. Admission fee.

spaces as the Vancouver International Airport, built on Musqueam ancestral lands along the mouth of the Fraser River (with more than $4 million of Native art inside its terminals), and in Stanley Park, which houses a circle of totems. In addition, fine art is sold in most Vancouver galleries. The city is also home to the only restaurant in the Pacific Northwest featuring **AUTHENTIC (AND BEAUTIFULLY PRESENTED) NATIVE CUISINE.**

University of British Columbia Museum of Anthropology: *Stunning Art and Artifacts*

This modern museum is internationally renowned for its stunning collection of **COAST SALISH** and **NORTHWEST COAST NATIVE ART**, beautifully illuminated with natural light from three-story windows overlooking the sea. The effect is one of quiet grandeur and sanctuary, as if you were in an ancient cedar grove in a rain forest. The pride of First Nations and of British Columbia, this is a museum for people who hate museums.

You pass from the street through massive carved doorways sculpted by 'Ksan master carvers, as though passing through an opening in an elegant bentwood box. Northwest Coast art and artifacts fill the broad corridors and high-walled galleries. Magnificent Haida, Tsimshian, Gitxsan, and Kwakwaka'wakw totem poles, house posts, canoes, and monumental ceremonial potlatch vessels repose behind glass and tower to the high ceiling.

In this museum the archives are open to the public. Similar items, such as several examples of a single type of basket or dozens of bird-beaked transformation masks, are grouped together on glass shelves. Items are numbered and you can look up interpretive information for each piece in an accompanying log.

Haida carver Bill Reid's renowned cedar sculpture *The Raven and the First Men* (pictured on the cover of this book) sits alone under a rotunda. It shows Raven releasing mischief (humankind) from a giant clamshell. Outside, full-size Haida longhouses and totem poles face the water.

Call for the museum's calendar of events, including First Nations lectures and performances. A small gift store is on the premises. The museum is built on traditional Coast Salish (Musqueam band) territory. The Musqueam Reserve is about 3 miles south of the museum.

University of British Columbia Museum of Anthropology, 6393 NW Marine Dr, Vancouver, BC V6T 1Z2, (604)822-3825, 24-hour recorded message or (604)822-5087, museum office.

The museum is on the UBC campus, west of downtown Vancouver. Open most days year-round. Call for hours. Admission fee; family rates available; group rates with guided tours if booked in advance.

Vancouver International Airport:
First Nations Art

If you fly into Vancouver, you can't miss the extraordinary collection of Northwest Coast art displayed in the Vancouver International Airport, one of the city's best public areas to view First Nations art. In a small park near the airport's entrance are three **40-FOOT-TALL TOTEM POLES**, carved and restored by Gitxsan carvers Earl Muldon and Walter Harris. Inside the amphitheater in the main terminal is Haida carver Bill Reid's masterpiece bronze **THE SPIRIT OF HAIDA GWAII, THE JADE CANOE**, an astounding 19-foot-long canoe filled with totem spirits and paddlers. (Its only other casting, *The Spirit of Haida Gwaii, the Black Canoe*, is in front of the Canadian embassy in Washington, D.C.) The $3-million *Jade Canoe*, purchased by the Vancouver International Airport Authority, was the largest public art transaction ever made in Canada.

In the International Terminal, behind the security/customs gate, the airport houses a rare collection of **COMMISSIONED COAST SALISH ART**. There are two austere, 17-foot-tall traditional Musqueam welcoming figures carved by Shane Point, an artist of Musqueam ancestry. Honoring the Musqueam tradition of fine weaving is a **17-FOOT-HIGH SPINDLE WHORL**, carved from a single piece of red cedar by Musqueam tribal member Susan Point. Four large tapestries, woven in traditional patterns, hang from the ceiling. Banners, prints, carved disks, eagle posts, bears, thunderbirds, model totem poles, and two more welcoming figures are at various gates throughout the airport.

The airport authority has established a foundation to promote **AWARENESS OF ABORIGINAL ART** and to commission work from aboriginal artists for display in public buildings. It has also purchased First Nations artists' work in other media, such as copper, glass, wood, bronze, and paper. In the future the airport authority hopes to offer tours of the collection, led by Musqueam guides. Much of Vancouver and its airport (which is perched on an island in the mouth of the Fraser River) is built on traditional Musqueam territory.

Vancouver International Airport, PO Box 23750, Airport Postal Outlet, Richmond, BC V7B 1Y7; (604)276-6101. The airport is midway between the cities of Richmond and Vancouver on Hwy 99 or the southern end of Granville St.

Gold and silver jewelry carved with Northwest Coast designs is perhaps the best high-quality souvenir visitors can buy—attractive and easily portable. Such carved bracelets were a favorite giveaway at traditional potlatches. To see some early examples of this craft, visit the University of British Columbia's Museum of Anthropology (6393 NW Marine Dr, Vancouver; (604)822-3825).

Native-Owned Art Galleries

Photographer, writer, and artist **DAVID NEEL** showcases his work in the showroom that adjoins his studio. A nephew of Mungo Martin, a famous Native artist whose dedication to his culture and its art-forms helped keep its conventions alive through this century, Neel carves totems, dug-out canoes, and both traditional and contemporary masks. He also makes jewelry, incorporating traditional patterns and designs. Look for Neel's books *The Great Canoes, The Revival of a Northwest Coast Tradition,* and *Our Chiefs and Elders: Words and Photographs of Native Leaders.* (David Neel Studio, 441 W 3rd St, N Vancouver, BC V0M 1G9; (604)988-9215); www.neel.org/dneel.)

SUSAN A. POINT's studio and gallery (which exhibits only her work) are both on the Musqueam Reserve, a few minutes from the University of British Columbia. Point works in various media, including glass, wood, and stainless steel, and she uses such printing techniques as intaglio aquatint. (Susan A. Point's Coast Salish Arts, 3917 W 51st Ave, Vancouver, BC V6N 3V9; (604)266-7374. Open daily, 10am–5pm. Phone first for directions and to confirm hours.)

Located in the Granville Island shopping area, the **WICKANIN-NISH GALLERY** specializes in authentic Northwest Coast carved silver and gold jewelry made by carvers throughout British Columbia. This is the place to compare various carving styles. (Wickaninnish Gallery Ltd., 1666 Johnson St, Ste 14, Vancouver; (604)681-1057.)

The **CEDAR ROOT GALLERY** is a small, community-based gallery that draws its artwork from the more than 65,000 aboriginal people living on Vancouver's east side. The gallery, adjoining the Vancouver Aboriginal Friendship Centre, exhibits work by new young artists, as well as experimental pieces that combine tradition with contemporary art. (Cedar Root Gallery, 1607 E Hastings St, Vancouver; (604)251-6244.)

KHOT-LA-CHA, located on the Capilano Reserve, sells Coast Salish handicrafts, including yellow and red cedar carvings, totem poles, ceremonial masks, silver and gold jewelry, Cowichan sweaters, moccasins, and prints. (Khot-La-Cha, 270 Whonoak St N, Vancouver; (604)987-3339.)

CANOE PASS GALLERY is 30 minutes from downtown Vancouver in the historic fishing community of Steveston, within the city of Richmond. The gallery is on the wharf overlooking the mouth of the Fraser River. (Canoe Pass Gallery, No. 115, 3866 Bayview St, Richmond; (604)272-0095; open daily.)

COGHLAN ART, off Highway 13, south of Vancouver, is a fine arts gallery and collection of artists' studios housed in a historic electric railway substation. Its cofounder is one of Canada's best-known First

Nations painters, Norval Morrisseau. Look here for a dozen of Canada's finest First Nations artists, including George Hunt Jr., Gary Meeches, Stan Hunt, Tom Patterson, and Terry Starr. Masks, paintings, vessels, and textiles are also for sale on the upper level, in a lofty three-story room with large clerestory windows. Outside, there's a covered area for artists to work on such large commissioned pieces as totem and house poles. (Coghlan Art, 6835 256th St, Aldergrove; (604)644-5285.)

Vancouver also boasts many non–Native-owned galleries; all of them are listed in the Vancouver telephone directory. Among those recommended by First Nations artists are **EAGLE SPIRIT GALLERY**, Granville Island (1814 Maritime Mews; (604)801-5205); **HILL'S INDIAN CRAFTS** in Gastown (165 Water St; (604)685-4249); **IMAGES FOR A CANADIAN HERITAGE** in Gastown (164 Water St, Vancouver; (604)685-7046, specializing in Northwest Coast and Inuit art); **LEONA LATTIMER GALLERY**, Granville Island (1590 W 2nd Ave; (604)732-4556, reflecting Lattimer's 45 years of collecting and selling First Nations art in British Columbia); and **SPIRIT WRESTLER GALLERY, LTD.** in Gastown (8 Water St; (604)669-8813).

As companions to this book, two guidebooks are highly recommended: Pat Kramer's **Native Sites in Western Canada** *(Altitude Publishing, 1994), and Cheryl Coull's* **A Traveler's Guide to Aboriginal BC** *(Whitecap Books, 1996). Both are available from most western Canada booksellers for less than $20.*

Dorothy Grant, Ltd.: *Haida-Inspired Designer Clothing*

Dorothy Grant's boutique, in Vancouver's fashion district, is the most unusual clothier you'll find anywhere. It's located in Sinclair Centre, a historic post office building that has been converted to gallery and retail space. With its high ceilings, peeled cedar-log columns, and carved wood panels, Grant's stunning showroom is designed in traditional **HAIDA ARCHITECTURAL STYLE**, in the grand fashion of a pre-contact clan house.

First known for her interpretation of **HAIDA CEREMONIAL ROBES** (which are in major museum collections throughout Canada), Grant has contemporized Haida clothing embellishment and design with her line of women's **FINELY TAILORED CLOTHING**. Garments range from expensive wool cashmere coats, skirted suits, and vests to polar-fleece jackets and T-shirts, all tastefully embellished, either by appliqué or embroidery, with distinctive Haida clan symbols. For example, Raven buttons were designed exclusively for Grant's clothing line by artist Alvin Adkins.

Dorothy Grant, Ltd., Sinclair Centre Boutique #R250, 757 W Hastings St, Vancouver, BC V6C1A1; (604)681-0201. On the corner of Granville and Hastings St, near historic Gastown. Open Mon–Fri 10am–5:30pm, Sat 10am–5pm. Closed Sun and Canadian holidays. For a preview of this season's line, visit her "virtual boutique" at www.dorothygrant.com.

Capilano Suspension Bridge and Park:
Totem Poles and Carving Center

Stretching across a steep, narrow canyon is the 450-foot-long Capilano Suspension Bridge, which sways gently 230 feet above the Capilano River. Perched on the edge of the canyon is Capilano Park, one of Vancouver's first tourist attractions, established in the 1930s as a public facility with an Indian theme. Today the park features authentic **TOTEM POLES**; the Big House Carving Centre, with First Nations wood carvers at work; and a web of trails winding through a rain forest.

The park's more than 25 totem poles have been collected since the 1930s from local carvers. Newer poles, erected along the cliff at the park's south end, were all carved by Wyne Carlick (Tlingit/Taltan), who was raised on the Taku River in northern British Columbia. His poles include the Salmon Creek Pole, Wolf Guardian Pole, Human Peace Pole, a totem dedicated to Mary Capilano, and one depicting the legend of how Raven stole the sun. Carlick also leads a **TRADITIONAL DANCE** group, whose members don Native regalia and headdress masks he has carved and perform two or three dances each day at the park.

When there aren't too many visitors, **BIG HOUSE CARVING CENTRE** is a great place to strike up a conversation with the Native carvers; they will gladly discuss their techniques and traditions. In front of Big House is an honor pole, which recognizes all carvers who have worked at the center and celebrates the future generation.

Throughout the park are life-sized wooden statues of Indians that resemble the cigar-store-style Indian statues that were popular before the 1970s. The clothing and headdress style of these statues is typical of Plains Indians (hence the feathered bonnets). These statues were carved in 1935, in exchange for room and board, by two hungry Danes, who created them from memories of pictures of Plains Indians they had seen as children. The statues are kept in the park perhaps because they reflect the attitudes and unfavorable stereotypes of a less-enlightened time.

Authentic **FIRST NATIONS ART** from the region—including gold and silver Haida jewelry, masks, totem

The Great Canoes: The Revival of a Northwest Coast Tradition (University of Washington Press, 1995) contains 70 color photographs of the great cedar dugout canoes of the Coast Salish of British Columbia, Haisla, Kwaguitl, Nuu-cha-nulth, Tlingit, and Tsimshian, and interviews with canoe builders, elders, paddlers, and chiefs about the reemergence of the "Canoe Nations" in the past decade. Author and photographer David Neel, a Fort Rupert Kwaguith, has also published Our Chiefs and Elders: Words and Photographs of Native Leaders (University of British Columbia Press, 1995). Books are available from booksellers throughout the Northwest and from the online bookstore Amazon.com. For details, visit Neel's Web site at www.neel.org/dneel/.

poles, and carvings—is sold in Capilano's historic log cabin "tea house," which is perched on the edge of the canyon.

Capilano Suspension Bridge and Park, 3735 Capilano Rd, N Vancouver, BC V7R 4JI; (604)985-7474; www.capbridge.com. Ten minutes from downtown Vancouver through Stanley Park over Lions Gate Bridge, then north 1 mile on Capilano Rd. From Trans-Canada Hwy take the Capilano Rd exit, travel half a mile. 9am–5pm, daily, winter; longer summer hours. Wheelchair accessible. Restaurant, gift shop.

Liliget Feast House: *Authentic Northwest Dining*

Inspired by the public's renewed interest in First Nations culture, Dolly Watts and her family offer a unique experience in authentic Pacific Northwest dining in their Liliget Feast House. The subterranean dining room reflects traditional **LONGHOUSE-STYLE DESIGN**, with cedar walls and house posts, and has the same feeling as a Japanese tatami room, with seats flush to the floor. The most popular item on the menu is a huge **POTLATCH PLATTER**, heaped with alder-smoked salmon, oysters, mussels, prawns, and venison and served with wild rice, steamed ferns, and sweet potatoes. Appetizers include crab cakes with honey-garlic sauce, pan-fried eulachon (candlefish), and steamed herring roe. Soups range from clear salmon broth to thick corn and crab chowders. The Liliget also serves a "Caesar Goes Wild" salad, topped with your choice of smoked salmon, duck, or venison. The house specialty is a smoked salmon entrée; other entrées include barbecued duck, alder-grilled rabbit, and pan-fried rainbow trout served with hazelnuts. Bannock bread is served with all meals. Unusual condiments, such as crunchy toasted seaweed and eulachon oil for dipping, are examples of the extensive menu of **NORTHWEST COAST DELICACIES** that Native peoples once served guests during traditional feasts. Local wines are served; those originating from vineyards owned or managed by First Nations people get top billing (try Inniskillin or Dark Horse). Desserts include a sweetened berry juice folded into whipped soapberries, fresh berry tarts, and gourmet cookies. Liliget owner Watts is Gitxsan, from the village of Kitwanga on the Skeena River. She grew up in the Port Alberni area, which is Nuu-chah-nulth territory.

Liliget Feast House & Catering, 1724 Davie St, Vancouver, BC V6G 1W; (604)681-7044. Located near Vancouver's Stanley Park. The Feast House is open for dinner daily, 5pm–10pm. Reservations strongly recommended. Entrées range from $17.95 to $29. Catering menus are available by calling the restaurant during the day.

Sunshine Coast:
Sechelt & Sliammon

British Columbia's impressive coastline is broken by hundreds of inlets and channels, making road building an almost impossible task. The mainland's only coastal road, Highway 101, ends at Lund, about 100 miles north of Vancouver. To travel the length of Highway 101, you must first cross Horseshoe Bay and Jervis Inlet, both 45-minute journeys on BC Ferries (or longer, if you count the wait in line at the ferry terminal). Ferries are equipped with restaurants, bookstores, and comfortable seating, making for a pleasant ride. Some development has occurred on a narrow strip of coastline along Highway 101, but the rest is mostly untouched, deeply forested wildlife habitat. **TWO FIRST NATIONS** are easily accessible on what hardy British Columbians call their Sunshine Coast. On the northern side of Horseshoe Bay, at the town of Sechelt, the Sechelt Nation has a **MUSEUM, GIFT SHOP, AND FISH HATCHERY** open to visitors. The Sliammon Nation is near the end of the road, between the town of Powell River and Desolation Sound Provincial Marine Park. It is worth the drive to their fish hatchery just to talk with proud tribal members who have slowly nursed the salmon back to the small stream adjacent to their reserve.

For a list of parks and a map of British Columbia's Sunshine Coast, contact the District Manager, Garibaldi/Sunshine Coast District, PO Box 220, Brackendale, BC V0N 1H0; (250)898-3678.

Wind Spirit Gallery: *Haida Art Displayed*

This pretty gallery and restaurant, located in a remodeled bungalow-style house overlooking Malaspina Strait, contains the watercolor paintings, serigraphs, and limited-edition prints of **APRIL WHITE**. A direct descendant of **CHARLES EDENSAW**, the renowned Haida artist of the Eagle clan whose early work is housed in the University of British Columbia's Museum of Anthropology, White was born on Haida Gwaii. Her work as a geologist in remote areas of the Canadian West and her marriage to a commercial fisherman give her paintings an authentic Northwestern feeling. This is evident in her screenprint *Balance*, which depicts a glacial erratic nested on the shale beach of Haida Gwaii and superimposed with images of Eagle and Raven. The gallery is just up the street from her workshop, **WIND SPIRIT PRINTMAKERS**.

Wind Spirit Gallery, 4643 Marine Ave, Powell River, BC V8A 2K8; (604)485-7572. Call for hours.

Sechelt Nation's House of Hewhiwus: *House of Chiefs*

On Highway 101, at the town of Sechelt, is the Sechelt Nation's House of Hewhiwus. The modern complex includes the Sechelt Nation's administrative offices. Open to the public are **TSAIN-KO GIFTS**, (604)885-4592, a privately owned gift shop selling art from all over British Columbia; the Sechelt Nation's **TEM-SWIYA MUSEUM;** and the Raven's Cry theater.

If for no other reason, you should stop to see the highlight of the museum's small collection of Native artifacts, **A RARE STONE CARVING** of a mother and child, which was excavated from nearby Davis Bay. The gift shop keeps the same hours as the museum, and its staff will answer questions about the museum collection.

Sechelt Nation's House of Hewhiwus (House of Chiefs), 5555 Hwy 101, PO Box 740, Sechelt, BC V0N 3A0; (604)885-2273. Open daily. The Sechelt Nation's hatchery, with fish-rearing pens right in McLean Bay, is open daily, 6am–2pm. For free tours and directions contact the Sechelt resource manager; (250)885-5562.

Sliammon Fish Hatchery: *Native-Owned*

This modest little fish hatchery on the grassy bank of Sliammon Creek, below the highway bridge, is easy to pass by—but take care to check it out. First Nations–owned fish hatcheries are one of the best places to **MEET ABORIGINAL PEOPLE**. The experience can include sighting eagles perched in the trees, eyeing both the salmon running upstream and the hatchery workers dipping fish from the stream with nets. To allow visitors to see salmon spawning naturally, a shallow channel has been dug around a tree-covered island and the bottom filled with the size of gravel in which salmon prefer to lay their eggs. Holding tanks full of fry and fingerlings are interesting, but the best part of this fish nursery is the cheerful people who run it. There is usually time for a **FREE TOUR** and lots of free salmonid literature. Donations to the hatchery crew's doughnut and coffee fund are much appreciated.

Sliammon Fish Hatchery, RR 2, Sliammon Rd, Powell River, BC V8A 4Z3. On Hwy 101, north of Powell River. Open daily.

Kamloops: *Secwepemc & Little Shuswap Bands*

Secwepemc Native Heritage Park

About four hours east of Vancouver, at Kamloops, on the main highway to Alberta, is Secwepemc Native Heritage Park, which interprets the traditional culture and lifestyle of the interior Salish Secwepemc. Located on one of the major routes to the Rocky Mountains, Jasper, and Banff National Park, this is a great place to stop.

Built on a **1,200-YEAR-OLD VILLAGE SITE** overlooking the Little South Thompson River, the park features a full-scale replica of a winter village with several kekuli (subterranean traditional winter homes with a central fire pit), a few summer lodges, and a fish weir. Park guides explain the various traditional foods, medicines, and plants.

In summer there are **NATIVE SONG, DANCE, STORYTELLING, AND LIVE THEATER PRESENTATIONS** along with pit-cooking demonstrations and salmon barbecues in a traditional summer lodge. In winter visitors can view indoor museum exhibits and traditional Native art and crafts. The guides also discuss contemporary Native issues.

All guided tours begin with a 20-minute video. Summer tours extend to 1 hour when they include the outdoor heritage park. The gift shop carries locally published materials about Secwepemc life and culture.

Secwepemc Native Heritage Park, 355 Yellowhead Hwy, Kamloops, BC V2H 1H1; (250)828-9801. About 4 hours east of Vancouver, on the Coquohalla Hwy (Hwy 5). Northwest of Okanogan Lake on Hwy 97. The museum is open year-round; outdoor exhibits are closed in winter. Call for hours. Admission fee; group rates.

St. Joseph's Church: *Historic Church on Native Village Site*

Regular Catholic services continue to be held in this landmark church, which is more than 100 years old. The church was built on the village site of the Kamloops Indian Band, and they have restored the building. Visitors are welcome to tour the church or join the congregation for services.

St. Joseph's Church, Kamloops Indian Band, 315 Yellowhead Hwy, Kamloops, BC V2H 1H1; (250)828-9700. Open Wed–Sun, 12:30pm–7:30pm, Jul 2–Sept 1.

Quaaout Lodge: *Native-Owned Lodging*

This lakefront lodge, built in the early 1990s and owned by the Little Shuswap Band, features a 40-foot-high lobby designed to resemble a kekuli, a traditional winter house. The lobby doors are ornately carved with Interior Salish designs, and the floor is decorated with reproductions of **ANCIENT SHUSWAP PICTOGRAPHS** from a nearby site. From its location overlooking Little Shuswap Lake, the 72-room lodge offers fishing, swimming, and proximity to a sandy beach, with 3.7 miles of jogging trails and an indoor pool, exercise area, sauna, and whirlpool spa. The lodge will also arrange sailing, golf, trail riding, and other family activities. Some rooms have fireplaces and hot tubs. Guests may also stay in tepees and experience bathing in a **TRADITIONAL SWEAT LODGE.** The lodge restaurant, which also overlooks the lake, features First Nations cuisine in addition to North American fare.

Quaaout Lodge, PO Box 1215, Chase, BC V0E 1M0; (800)663-4303 or (250)679-3090. Located about 20 minutes east of Kamloops on Hwy 123, just outside Chase, on the way to Banff National Park. Cross the Squilax Bridge over the Little South Thompson River. Open year-round. Room rates $150. The lodge dining room is open daily for breakfast, lunch, and dinner, as well as Sun brunch. Reservations required for dinner. Wheelchair accessible.

Vernon: *Interior Salish*

Overlooking Okanagan Lake, Vernon is north of Penticton in central British Columbia, about 4 hours from Vancouver, and north of Washington State's Colville Indian Reservation. Highway 97 parallels the Okanogan River. The tribes and bands who live on reserves in southeastern British Columbia are related to the interior Coast Salish of Idaho, Montana, and Washington. For the tribes, the Canada–United States border is an artificial boundary, arbitrarily created and now dividing extended families.

Sen'Klip Native Theatre Company

In little more than a decade, Sen'Klip has grown from a community-based local theater to an award-winning, internationally recognized performance group. The company is known for its unique adaptations of **TRADITIONAL INTERIOR-SALISH LEGENDS,** as well as for its original plays that blend traditional themes and contemporary issues. They perform each summer on an impressive 100-foot-long earthen stage, featuring an indigenous plant garden and distinctive tepees of the Interior Salish. Cultural and Native art and craft tours in the area are available for groups of 12 or more by request. Sen'Klip is based in Vernon, in the heart of British Columbia's wine country.

Sen'Klip Native Theatre Company, 2902 29th Ave, Vernon, BC V1T 1Y7; (250)542-1247. Located at Newport Beach RV Park, Westside Rd in Vernon.

VANCOUVER ISLAND

Vancouver Island, almost 400 miles long, is home to three distinctly different First Nations cultures: the Nuu-Cha-Nulth (or Nootka) bands, who live along the Pacific Coast; the Coast Salish (related to the Puget Sound tribes) in the south; and the Kwakwaka'wakw on the eastern shore, whose carvings may be most familiar to the public as "Northwest Coast" style. These groups differ linguistically, and their art forms are stylistically different. The best place on Vancouver Island to learn generally about the three cultures is at the British Royal Museum in Victoria. Coast Salish culture is best represented at the Cowichan Native Village in Duncan; Kwakwaka'wakw culture, particualarly the explanation of potlatch and winter ceremonies, is best explained by their private museums at Alert Bay and on Quadra Island. While the Nuu-Cha-Nulth people have no museum championing their culture, traveling exhibits have been making the rounds of British Columbia museums for the past few years. One of the best places to see Nuu-Cha-Nulth art is at Tofino at the House of Himwitsa, a modern art gallery dedicated to promoting Nuu-Cha-Nulth artists.

Nearly 50,000 people attend the First Peoples Festival, a three-day event coordinated by the Victoria Native Friendship Centre, (250)384-3211, each August. The festival is held at Thunderbird Park (with its huge totem poles and bighouse), located on the Royal British Columbia Museum grounds and in Victoria's picturesque Inner Harbor. See traditional masked dances, storytelling, dugout cedar canoe races, and art exhibits, and sample great food, including baked salmon.

Victoria: *Coast Salish*

Royal British Columbia Museum:
First Nations Art and Artifacts

A person could visit this museum for years and never cease to be impressed by its showcase of **NORTHWEST COAST ART**, dominated by a full-scale bighouse installed on the second floor. Totem poles, towering Salish welcoming figures, and other monumental sculpture of the Haida, Heiltsuk, Nuxalk, Kwakwaka'wakw, Nuu-chah-nulth, and Tsimshian/Gitxsan/Nisga'a are installed alongside the escalators. While rising to the second floor, visitors can examine the totems at close range. The second floor's **FIRST PEOPLES EXHIBIT** begins with a full-scale replica of a kekuli, the traditional subterranean winter house used by the Nlaka'pamux and Okanagan interior tribes. Household goods (such as Nlaka'pamux looms and woven garments) bentwood boxes, canoes, and ceremonial objects are also displayed. Two scale models—one of a Ktunaxa encampment of tepees, the other a Skedans village—provide useful distinctions between interior and coastal tribal lifestyles. Narrated by the late Haida artist Bill Reid and supplemented by a small gallery of **EVOCATIVE PORTRAITS** is a moving account of the smallpox epidemic of the 1860s, which killed almost 90 percent of residents in these Native communities.

Also impressive is the museum's collection of nineteenth-century Northwest Coast **CARVED MASKS**, many of which are associated with the sky, earth, and undersea worlds. A darkened gallery allows visitors to sit and listen to stories as masks are illuminated one at a time. Another gallery, which replicates a supernatural cave where animal powers are said to have originated, exhibits the work of the well-known Kwakwaka'wakw carver Mungo Martin. The museum's Jonathan Hunt House is a recreation of a **TRADITIONAL BIGHOUSE**, complete with carved house posts, screens, benches, and a mock-glowing fire inside and the recorded caws of ravens overhead. The centerpiece of the First Peoples exhibit, the bighouse, is named for the late Chief Kwakwabalasami (Jonathan Hunt), a Kwakwaka'waka chief who lived in the Tsaxis (Fort Rupert) community. The crests shown in the house were validated by Hunt in the traditional manner, through potlatching. The Hunt family still uses the bighouse for ceremonial occasions. The house and the carvings inside were created by the chief's son, Henry Hunt, and grandsons, Tony and Richard Hunt. The Hunt family includes at least **30 ARTISTS** (for more about the Hunts, see the Port Hardy section of this chapter).

For one of the largest **OPEN-AIR DISPLAYS OF TOTEM POLES** anywhere in British Columbia, visit Thunderbird Park, which adjoins the museum. There is a full-sized replica of a **TRADITIONAL HAIDA HOUSE** (the Wa'waditla House), carved by Mungo Martin, which is also used for Native ceremonies.

Royal British Columbia Museum, 675 Belleville St, Victoria, BC V8V 1X4; (800)661-5411, (250)387-370, or (250)387-5822, recorded message. Located across from the Empress Hotel and the city's Inner Harbour. Open summer 9:30am–7pm; winter 10am–5:30pm. Admission fee. Groups of 10 or more should prebook their visit.

First Nations Art Galleries

Most Victoria galleries selling First Nations art are located along Government Street, anchored at the eastern end by the Royal British Columbia Museum. Across the street from the museum, in the famous Empress Hotel, is the **ART OF MAN GALLERY** (721 Government St; (250)383-3800), representing some of the region's top First Nations and Native Alaska artists. Even if the prices are out of reach, some of the finest artwork produced in the region is represented here.

If you can't make the hourlong drive to the **NATIVE HERITAGE CENTRE** in Duncan to buy an authentic Cowichan sweater, walk west along Government Street to find four Cowichan sweater outlets: **SASQUATCH TRADING LTD.** (1233 Government St; (250)386-9033); **COWICHAN TRADING LTD.** (1328 Government St; (250)383-0321); **CANADIANA GIFTS AND SOUVENIRS** (1012 Government St; (250)384-3123); and the **INDIAN CRAFT SHOPPE** (905 Government St; (250)382-3643).

Lloyd and Frances Hill began selling Cowichan sweaters in 1946 from their Koksilak/Duncan General Store and post office, paying the knitters with groceries and wool. Today the Hill family has one store in Vancouver's Gastown shopping district and four stores on Vancouver Island. In Victoria, **HILL'S INDIAN CRAFTS** (1008 Government St; (250)385-3911) offers a wide assortment of masks and other Native items. Check with the Victoria store for other store locations. Masks are for sale at **CHINOOK TRADING COMPANY** (1315 Government St; (250)381-3224); **RAVENSONG NATIVE ART GALLERY** (1221 Wharf (250)382-2787); **SANUUKWA GALLERIES** (1211 Wharf (250)480-5515); **ANCESTRAL JOURNEY GALLERY, LTD.** (665 Fort (250)383-6787); **RICHARD HUNT KWA-GULTH ARTS LTD.** (250)383-9531; **THUNDERBIRD GALLERY** (3105 Grace Pt. Square, north of Victoria on Salt Spring Island in Ganges, (250)537-1144).

Duncan: *Cowichan*

Cowichan Native Heritage Centre

One of the most interesting First Nations attractions in British Columbia, the Cowichan Nation's Native Heritage Centre, about an hour north of Victoria, includes a **TOUR THROUGH A BIGHOUSE**, and a carving shed, a multimedia show, an exhibit on the famous Cowichan knitters, and several galleries, one of which sells expensive **FIRST NATIONS FINE ART** from throughout the region. Spread over 6 lovely acres on the north bank of the Cowichan River, the complex is filled with totem poles, carved screens, canoes, and artists working in studios. A visit typically begins in the Longhouse Story Centre with a viewing of the film *Great Deeds*, about the Cowichan Nation. Resident carvers demonstrate their skills while they carve works for the center and for private and corporate clients. Local carvers have made the **MORE THAN 60 TOTEM POLES** that stand in the city of Duncan. During the summer, a fascinating 4-hour Feast and Legends program inside the bighouse features **TRADITIONAL DANCES**, storytelling, and a lavish six-course feast. Kids are encouraged to work with staff to make beaded name badges, headbands, and friendship bracelets on tanned moosehide, or try their hand at carving in the carving shed. This is also the place to buy an **AUTHENTIC COWICHAN SWEATER.** Made of undyed wool and knitted without seams, these are world-famous sweaters. If you don't find one that fits, knitters will custom-make one for you and mail it.

Cowichan Native Heritage Centre, 200 Cowichan Wy, Duncan, BC V9L 4T8; (250)746-8119. A 1-hour scenic drive north of Victoria on Hwy 1. The center is open daily, year-round. Guided tours are every hour on the half-hour, year-round. Admission includes guided tours. Midday salmon barbecues are held year-round (call ahead to confirm) with elders as guides, and there are masked dance performances. The longer Feasts and Legends program is held Fri only, in summer. Please call to confirm dates, times, and prices.

Judy Hill Gallery: *First Nations Carvers*

Judy Hill Gallery and Gifts carries the work of the region's top Native carvers, including Joe David, Robert Davidson, Richard Krentz, and David Neel.

Judy Hill Gallery and Gifts, 22 Station St; Duncan, BC VpL 4T8; (250)746-6663.

Tofino: *Nuu-chah-nulth*

The entire west side of Vancouver Island is Nuu-chah-nulth territory. For years in the Northwest the Nuu-chah-nulth Nation was referred to as the Nootka, a name mistakenly bestowed in the 1700s by Captain James Cook, who completely misunderstood his first introduction to a Nuu-chah-nulth chief. Sprinkled north to south on Vancouver Island's Pacific Coast are 14 VILLAGES AND BANDS: the Kyuquot, Ehattesaht, Nutchatlaht, Mowachaht, Hesquiaht, Ahousaht, Tla-O-Qui-Aht (Tofino), Ucluelet, Toquaht, Uchucklesaht, Ohiaht, Opetchesaht, Sheshaht, Pacheenaht, and Ditidaht. The Nuu-chah-nulth claim the Makah, on the northern tip of Washington state's Olympic Peninsula, as one of their own as well.

Look for Nuu-chah-nulth baskets, obsidian microblades traded from Oregon, gambling bones made from beaver teeth, and button blankets at the Alberni Valley Museum, 4255 Wallace St (in the Echo Activity Centre), Port Alberni, BC V9Y 3Y6; (250)723-2181. Open 10am–5pm, Tues–Sat.

There are only three paved roads to Vancouver's west side. Most of the villages on this rugged coast are reached only by gravel logging road or by boat or floatplane. One of the paved roads, a two-lane highway from Port Alberni in the middle of Vancouver Island, forks as it reaches the Pacific Ocean. One fork leads south to UCLUELET, the closest mainland town to the Broken Group islands. The hundreds of small islands that make up the BROKEN GROUP ISLANDS archipelago, at the mouth of Barkley Sound, were once home to an estimated 10,000 Nuu-Chah-nulth.

Pacific Rim National Park comprises three separate areas: Long Beach, the Broken Group islands, and the West Coast Trail. The park information center— offering maps, videos, and brochures—is off Highway 4, between Ucluelet and Tofino. For information, contact Pacific Rim National Park, PO Box 280, Ucluelet, BC V0R 3A0; (250)726-4212.

The other fork leads north along the beaches of Pacific Rim National Park to the resort town of Tofino, which is at the end of a very long and narrow spit. It's well worth the effort to get there, however. One side of the spit faces the rugged Pacific Ocean, offering miles of public beach; the other side faces gorgeous CLAYOQUOT SOUND, a safe harbor and feeding ground for migrating whales. Islands in the Sound are covered with 1,500-YEAR-OLD CEDAR TREES—some of the last old-growth cedar forests in the world.

Tofino is a real jewel. It offers a first-class FIRST NATIONS–OWNED HOTEL with its own private stretch of Pacific beach as well as several extraordinary galleries, great feasts of cracked crab and salmon caught in the Sound, tours of a nearby First Nations village, salmon-fishing and WHALE-WATCHING excursions, isolated hot springs, ancient rain forests, and even a 3-mile-long trail through a grove of ancient cedars, reached by a skiff that skims across the Sound.

To get to Tofino, take Highway 1 to Parksville, then head west on Highway 4 to Tofino on a two-lane paved road that, during heavy rains, is drenched with spray from roadside waterfalls. It's a pretty drive along the lakeshore and across roaring mountain streams, despite some severely clearcut slopes. At the coast, you travel either south to Ucluelet or north to Tofino. The route to Tofino parallels Long Beach in Pacific Rim National Park. For summer visits it's best to make hotel reservations months in advance. In midwinter you'll have your choice of rooms, but tours may be limited. Plan on taking about 4 hours from Victoria to Tofino, or about 2 hours from the ferry landing at Nanaimo.

Boat Trip to Barkley Sound: *Land of the Nuu-chah-nulth*

At Port Alberni, halfway between Parksville and Tofino, you can board the 100-passenger MV *Lady Rose* or 200-passenger MV *Frances Barkley* to the Pacific Coast and the Broken Group islands, a 5-hour trip each way. From the ship's deck, you'll see the landscape as the Nuu-chah-nulth have observed it for centuries—from the water—and pass several **FIRST NATIONS RESERVES** that are accessible only by boat. The working freighters make round-trips from Port Alberni to the oceanside towns of Ucluelet and to the Broken Group islands in Barkley Sound from June to September, and to Bamfield year-round. Ucluelet and Bamfield are both **ANCIENT VILLAGE SITES**—modern, with cafes and accommodations. Ucluelet is about 30 minutes south (by car) of Tofino; Bamfield can be reached only by boat, plane, or trail. The Broken Group is a cluster of about 100 islands. They have only campsites, best explored by kayaking after the freighter drops you off (kayak rentals are available at the Port Alberni dock). Those wishing to hike the West Coast Trail disembark at Bamfield. The 45-mile (72-kilometer) West Coast Trail is a 4- to 5-day hike over a challenging wilderness trail to Port Renfrew.

Alberni Marine Transportation (Barkley Sound Service), 5425 Argyle St, PO Box 188, Port Alberni, BC V9Y 7M7; (800)663-7192 for reservations, Apr–Sept; or (250)723-8313. Fares are under $50.

At Port Renfrew, Roy (Butch) Jack, a member of the Pacheedaht Band of Nuu-Cha-Nulth, ferries hikers across the Gordon and San Juan Rivers to the southern terminus of the West Coast Trail. He also offers 4- to 6-hour sightseeing tours (weather permitting) in his 28-foot aluminum skiff in San Juan Bay and out in the Pacific Ocean to see wildlife and the sea caves at Camper Creek, pointing out several old village sites along the way. His narration is based on your questions. For more information, contact him at (250) 647-5571 or bjferry@islandnet.com.

Meares Island Big Cedar Trail:
Tla-O-Qui-Ahts Protecting Trees

In Clayoquot Sound the fight is on to protect the **BIG CEDARS** and other **OLD-GROWTH TREES** from logging. In 1984 the Tla-O-Qui-Aht Nation and other local residents stood on the shores of Meares Island and declared their intention to stop logging by MacMillan Bloedel Ltd., proclaiming the entire island a tribal park. A handful of Tofino residents first built the Big Cedar Trail on the island in 1981 so the public could see the ancient cedars growing there. In 1993 the Western Canada Wilderness Committee provided funding for Tla-O-Qui-Aht carpenters to build a mile-long boardwalk over the spongy forest floor, one of several **"WITNESS TRAILS"** now in the area.

The Nuu-chah-nulth tribe recommends **Wisdom of the Elders: Native Traditions on the Northwest Coast,** *by Ruth Kirk (Douglas & McIntyre, 1986), as the best book on the Nuu-chah-nulth, Southern Kwakwaka'wakw, and Nuxalk cultures.*

A skiff takes you from the 4th Street Dock in Tofino across Clayoquot Sound (a 10-minute ride, unless you pause to look at whales or nesting eagles) and drops you off at the trailhead, barely visible through the overhanging branches of hemlock trees and salal. The boardwalk, which looks like something out of a Swiss Family Robinson movie, threads through the grove of absolutely astounding cedars. They are each so old (1,200 to 1,500 years) and gnarled that every one of the **17 NAMED TREES** seems to have a personality of its own. The boardwalk ends with a circle around the Hanging Garden Tree, British Columbia's **FOURTH-LARGEST WESTERN RED CEDAR.** The trail continues on bare ground for several more miles before looping back to the beach. It's too wet to walk the bare trail in winter, but the boardwalk on a rainy day under the forest canopy is delightful if you're dressed for it. Bring rain gear and wear nonslip-soled shoes. There are no handrails on some ramps.

To hike the Meares Island Big Cedar Trail, take the water taxi from the 4th St Dock in Tofino, about four blocks east of the House of Himwitsa; (250)725-2902.

Walk on the Wild Side: Heritage Trail to Ahousaht

Take a 45-minute boat ride from Tofino on the heated, enclosed 31-passenger *Spirit of Marktosis* seabus to the **NUU-CHAH-NULTH VILLAGE** of Ahousaht on Flores Island. The boat slows down so passengers can see sea lions, sharks, gray whales, orcas, and eagles. On Flores Island passengers disembark for a 2-hour, **FULLY GUIDED "SPIRIT WALK,"** to learn the history of the village, explore traditions, and see "culturally modified" trees in which signs of the Ahousaht's earliest occupation are carved. Guides also take you to uninhabited Ball Beach, where you'll learn about foraging for edible sea plants and shellfish, such as crab and gooseneck barnacles. There's a longer tour (about 5 hours) that includes a salmon barbecue.

Walk on the Wild Side, General Delivery, Ahousaht, BC V0R 1A0; (888)670-5986, (250)725-3342, or (250)670-9586. Adults $75; children 12 and under $60. Custom tours available for two or more people, and for schools and large groups by special arrangement.

House of Himwitsa: *First Nations Art, Restaurant, Lodging*

The House of Himwitsa, a handsome building over-looking Tofino's wharf and seaplane dock, boasts a first-rate **NATIVE ART GALLERY**, a restaurant, and three classy **VIEW SUITES** for rent. All of the artists represented in the gallery are First Nations people, and many are of the Nuu-chah-nulth Nation. The personable owners, Lewis and Cathy George, are Nuu-chah-nulth, and they and their staff are well acquainted with the artists and know the cultural history behind each piece.

In Ahousaht visitors might recognize scenes and faces from I Heard the Owl Call My Name, a 1973 film based on the book by Margaret Craven. The story is about a Catholic priest transformed by his stay in a Nuu-chah-nulth village. Footage includes a brief part of the Ahousaht Maquinna families' most sacred dances. The book is available at the House of Himwitsa in Tofino.

The gallery collection includes beautifully carved and painted **NORTHWEST COAST MASKS**, engraved silver and gold jewelry, cedar bark baskets, limited-edition prints, totem poles, and pottery, as well as coats, capes, and distinctive Maquinna hats. You can also preview and order selected merchandise from the gallery's Web site.

The restaurant, called the Sea Shanty, has a 180-degree view of the island-filled Clayoquot Sound and specializes in pasta and local seafood, including the **OYSTERS AND STEAMED CRAB** for which Tofino is famous. It's open for breakfast, lunch, and dinner most of the year.

On the top floor, overlooking the wharf and Clayoquot Sound, are three luxurious, spacious suites, all with fully stocked kitchens, large tiled baths, and decks with private hot tubs. Rooms are decorated with Native art prints from the gallery downstairs.

House of Himwitsa, 300 Main St, PO Box 176, Tofino, BC V0R 2Z0; (800)899-1947 or (250)725-2017; himwitsa@island.net; www.himwitsa.com. The gallery is open daily, year-round. Restaurant reservations, (250)725-2902; open Feb–Oct. Cappuccino and ice cream bar, open May–Sept. Suite rates vary according to season, $80–$165.

Tin Wis Resort Lodge: *Native-Owned Lodging*

The name Tin Wis means **"CALM WATERS,"** and every room in this 86-room, **TWO-STORY LODGE** faces a broad lawn overlooking the Pacific Ocean, as does the dining room with patio seating outside.

The resort is owned by the Tla-O-Qui-Aht First Nation Band of Nuu-chah-nulth and managed by Best Western. Nestled in the trees off the Pacific Rim Highway, it is private and quiet, with its own quarter-mile of **BROAD SANDY BEACH**. All rooms have queen- or king-size beds; some have fireplaces. There's a spa and exercise room. The resort's boardrooms hold up to 40 people; the convention center accommodates 200 to 300 people. The dining room, open for two meals a day, offers such items as grilled chicory salad, steamed crab and clams, a sampler of smoked fish, and venison.

Tin Wis Resort Lodge, 1119 Pacific Rim Hwy, Tofino, BC V0R 2Z0; (800)661-9995 or (800)528-1234 for the Best Western reservation line. Room rates $110–$240, depending on season. Children under 12 stay free with parents. Open year-round.

Wilp Gybuu (Wolf House) Bed and Breakfast:
Native-Owned Lodging

Hosts Wendy and Ralph Burgess offer large, delicious breakfasts and sparkling conversation in their spotless, contemporary home overlooking Clayoquot Sound—all within walking distance of Tofino's many attractions. Rooms have comfortable beds, private bathrooms, and all the amenities (slippers, candles, magazines, and thoughtful toiletries). Each room has its own private entrance; several rooms have fireplaces. Ralph, a Gitxsan Tsimshian who grew up in a village near Prince Rupert, is also a first-rate gold and silver carver. The house has a well-stocked **LIBRARY ON FIRST NATIONS PEOPLE**. The Burgesses are wonderful hosts, who thoughtfully leave a tray with early morning coffee outside your door. Make reservations months in advance.

Wilp Gybuu (Wolf House) Bed and Breakfast, 311 Leighton Wy, PO Box 396, Tofino, BC V0R 2Z0; (250)725-2330; wilpgybu@island.net; www.island.net/~wilpgybu/. From Campbell St in Tofino, turn left onto First, right on Arnet Rd, left onto Leighton Wy. Room rates $85–$95, including breakfast. Nonsmoking; cat in residence.

Whale-Watching and Salmon-Fishing Charters:
First Nations Guides

More than 22,000 gray whales pass close to Vancouver Island's western shore during their spring (March–April) and fall (September–October) migrations, and dozens of whales stay all summer in Clayoquot Sound, just a short boat ride from Tofino. During the last two weeks in March, Tofino and Uculet celebrate the whales' return with a **GRAY WHALE FESTIVAL**, with more than 100 events. The Nuu-chah-nulth once hunted whales from their canoes and still are the most competent guides in the area. They tell some of the best whale tales you've ever heard, as well as stories of growing up on Vancouver Island's remote west side. The listings that follow are all whale-watching charter boats owned and operated by First Nations people.

The 35-foot MV *Clayoquot Whaler,* owned by Cindy Dennis of Ahousaht and her husband, Steve, leaves Tofino's wharf five times daily for a 2- to 2.5-hour **ECO-TOUR** of Clayoquot Sound. You can also book their open-air 25-foot, 12-passenger Zodiak for tours or for trips nearby. (Seaside Adventures, (250)725-2292. Prices vary. Operates February through November.)

Al Keitlah Jr. and his son, Neil, operate the 19-foot, six-passenger, open-cockpit *Raven Dancer* for whale-watching, sportfishing, and customized tours.

Felix Thomas has an enclosed, 12-passenger Cougar Island water taxi for **WHALE-WATCHING** as well as transportation to such local destinations as Flores Island, Meares Island, and Hot Springs Cove.

Daybreak Charters offers a 26-foot Tolly Craft with an enclosed cabin and command bridge, and a skipper with 40 years experience, for fishing charters (tackle supplied), whale-watching, and water taxi service.

For information about whale-watching and other charters in the Tofino area, call SuperNatural British Columbia, (800)435-5622, or Tofino Tourist Information, (250)725-3414.

The Clayoquot Valley Witness Trail Map and Recreation Guide *describes wilderness hikes, lakes, and camps in the Clayoquot River valley, as well as fern meadows, boardwalks, old-growth Sitka spruce groves, rock slab caves, cliffhanger log walks, rock gardens, and limestone sculptures—all in an area earmarked for logging by MacMillan Bloedel Ltd. Volunteers opposed to the clearcuts have donated 15,000 hours to build "witness trails" through the forest. This guide is available from Tla-O-Qui-Aht First Nations, PO Box 18, Tofino, BC V0R 2Z0; (250)725-3233. Call for cost.*

First Nations Art Galleries

Tsimshian graphic artist Roy Henry Vickers, from Kitkatla near Hazelton, British Columbia, has built the **EAGLE AERIE GALLERY**, a replica of a traditional Tsimshian longhouse, complete with carved house posts and screens. The gallery displays Vickers' original serigraphs. He also owns the Eagle Moon Gallery in Victoria. (350 Campbell St, Tofino; (800)663-0669 or (250)725-3235; open daily, year-round.)

William Barr's hand-engraved silver and gold Native jewelry is sold at **BARR'S NATIVE JEWELRY & ART.** (346 Campbell St, Tofino; (250)725-4482.)

The **DU QUAH GALLERY**, built like a cedar longhouse, is on the main street of the charming little port of Ucluelet, about 14 miles south of Tofino. Chief Bert Mack and his wife, Lillian, sell masks, totem poles, silver, turquoise, Cowichan sweaters, leatherwork, and prints from all over British Columbia. (1971 Peninsula, Ucluelet; (250)726-7223.)

Courtenay: *Comox*

Queneesh Native Gallery and Gift Shop

Centrally located in the heart of Vancouver Island, this gallery shows the work of the **THREE MAJOR FIRST NATIONS GROUPS** who live on the island: the Coast Salish, the Kwakwaka'wakwa, and the Nuu-cha-Nulth. The gallery carries the work of Calvin Hunt, Mark Henderson, Marvin Child, George Hunt Jr., Richard Hunt, and Susan Point, among others. It's Queneesh Band–owned and –operated, next to the band's bighouse. Visitors are welcome to tour the bighouse, accompanied by someone from the gift shop—just ask.

Queneesh Native Gallery and Gift Shop, 3310 Comox Rd, Courtenay, BC V9N 3P8; (250)339-7702. In front of the Comox Band Big House. Open daily, 10am–5pm.

Campbell River: *Kwakwaka'wakw*

You'll see a number of totem poles in the town of Campbell River, but the most photographed are at the Heritage Pavilion at Foreshore Park, overlooking Discovery Passage, next to the ferry landing. Campbell River, best known for its salmon fishing, boasts a community museum with a display of masks by contemporary carvers, as well as older ethnographic materials. From Campbell River, take the ferry to Quadra Island, to the Kwagiulth Museum and Cultural Centre at Quathiaski Cove, or take Highway 28 across Vancouver Island to Gold River, where you can board a boat bound for Nootka Sound and stop at the Yuquot village for a tour with the Mowachaht Band.

Museum at Campbell River: *First Nations Stories*

The Museum at Campbell River, located on a hillside overlooking the Inside Passage, is a regional museum telling the story of First Nations on the east and west coasts of British Columbia as well as on the mainland inlets as far north as Bella Coola. The museum negotiated with a Gwawa'enuxw family, on the mainland, for permission to tell the family story of a young man's adventures in the undersea world. The resulting **MASKS** are the work of 20 Kwakwaka'wakwa artists. Many masks have moving parts, depicting Komegwey (the king of the undersea), sea monsters, spring salmon, octopus, and other sea creatures. These contemporary masks are outstanding proof that the **FIRST NATIONS ARTISTIC TRADITION** and culture continue to thrive. The museum's gallery is co-curated with First Nations, whose cultural history is represented by the museum's **ETHNOGRAPHIC COLLECTION**. Videos about First Nations history, based on archival materials, are shown in the museum's 30-seat theater, including Edward Curtis's short fictional account of Kwakwa̱ka'wakwa culture, *In the Land of the War Canoe*. First Nations played a huge role in developing the commercial fishing industry on Vancouver Island, a story that is also exhibited in the museum. A small museum store sells First Nations art and books.

Museum at Campbell River, 470 Island Hwy, PO Box 70, Station A, Campbell River, BC VPW 1Z9; (250)287-3103. Call for hours. Admission fee; family group rate.

Quadra Island: *Kwagiulth*

Quadra Island sits smack-dab in the middle of the Inside Passage, and for centuries the Kwagiulth living on the island were the gatekeepers of the passage. There are two good reasons to visit Quadra Island, which is accessible by a short ferry ride from the town of Campbell River: the Kwagiulth Museum and Cultural Centre at Quathiaski Cove, which houses the Potlatch Collection and offers one of the best explanations of the potlatch available; and Tsa Kwa Luten Lodge (pronounced "saw-kwa-looten"), tribally owned and operated, which is designed like a Kwagiulth bighouse and overlooks Discovery Passage.

Ferries leave Campbell River for Quadra Island once an hour, daily, year-round. For schedule and fare information, call BC Ferries, (604)386-3431.

Kwagiulth Museum and Cultural Centre

Shaped like the spiral shell of a moon snail (a fist-sized mollusk common to Pacific Northwest waters), the Kwagiulth Museum and Cultural Centre was built in 1979 specifically to house the returned portion of the Kwagiulth's **POTLATCH COLLECTION**. Masks, headdresses, coppers (large objects of hammered copper and a monetary unit that represented enormous wealth to the Kwagiulth), and other objects were confiscated by a zealous Indian agent in the early 1900s, when a law banning the potlatch was enforced. The Kwagiulth were forced to surrender ceremonial objects and regalia used in Winter Ceremonies and potlatches or face imprisonment. The agent earmarked objects for the personal collection of Duncan Campbell Scott (Canada's superintendent general of Indian Affairs), sold some of the items to George Heye, a New York collector, and packed off the rest to museums in Ottawa, Ontario. Objects from these private collections are in every major museum in the world today. After more than 60 years of negotiations, a portion of the Potlatch Collection was returned to the Kwagiulth Nation, an emotional event documented on a videotape shown at the museum.

Look here also for **PHOTOGRAPHS OF KWAGIULTH VILLAGES** in the late 1800s and early 1900s, fiberglass casts of **PETROGLYPHS** found on rocks on nearby beaches, and large wooden ceremonial flutes that visitors to the museum can pick up and play. The museum, overseen by the Kwagiulth's Nuyumbalees Society, also houses a well-stocked bookstore and gift shop featuring contemporary Kwagiulth masks, prints, wooden plaques, hand-crafted fine silver and gold jewelry, and handmade dolls.

Kwagiulth Museum and Cultural Centre, 34 Weiway Rd, Cape Mudge Village, PO Box 8, Quathiaski Cove, BC V0P 1N0; (250)285-3733. From the ferry landing on Quadra Island, take Green Rd to Wei Wy Rd (gravel road), and turn right into Cape Mudge Village; continue along the beachfront, past the community center and cemetery. The museum is located next to the cemetery. Open daily, year-round; closed Sun in winter. Admission fee. Gift shop.

Tsa Kwa Luten Lodge: *Native-Owned Lodging*

Located on a 1,100-acre forest overlooking Discovery Passage on the south end of Quadra Island, Tsa Kwa Luten Lodge's "great room" is designed in the architectural style of a traditional **KWAGIULTH BIG-HOUSE**. The lodge offers 26 deluxe suites with ocean views and four waterfront cabins. Some have private verandahs, fireplaces, and Jacuzzis. Overnight guests are welcome, but most people come for a couple of days of salmon fishing in the fast tidal currents of Discovery Passage, at the mouth of the Campbell River. The lodge offers fishing packages that include lodging and meals. Fishing trips include boat, tackle, bait, all-weather gear, and a professional guide. Catches are cleaned, packaged, fast-frozen, and shipped for guests. The concierge also arranges boat cruises of the outer islands and Seymour Narrows, whale-watching, scuba diving, and kayaking. Conference rooms accommodate up to 80 people and include fax, photocopying, and secretarial services.

Tsa Kwa Luten Lodge, The Resort at Cape Mudge, PO Box 460, Quathiaski Cove, BC V0P 1N0; (250)285-2042. Located on the southern tip of Quadra Island on Lighthouse Rd. The lodge is open Apr–Oct 15. Room rates vary. Seaplane flights can be chartered from Seattle, Vancouver, and Victoria (the lodge will help with arrangements).

Yuquot: *Nuu-chah-nulth*

From Gold River board the MV *Uchuck*, a working freight boat. With a Mowachaht guide, travel through the narrow inlets, passages, and channels of Nootka Sound to the oceanside village of Yuquot on Nootka Island. Also known as Friendly Cove, Yuquot has been the **ANCESTRAL HOME** of the Mowachaht/Muchalaht people for thousands of years and has been designated as a **CANADIAN NATIONAL HISTORIC SITE**. Among the mariners the tribe hosted in the late 1700s at Friendly Cove was Captain James Cook, who spent a month with the Mowachahts while his ship was being retrofitted, shortly before his death in the Sandwich Islands (Hawaii). When the Mowachahts traded otter pelts with the British in the late 1700s, Spain jealously responded by building Fort San Miguel at Yuquot in 1789 and seizing a number of British ships. This "Nootka Controversy" nearly ignited a war in Europe.

At Yuquot, the hourlong tour of the village, the ruins of Fort San Miguel, and the site of the Mowachahts' sacred whaler's shrine is enriched with details of **MOWACHAHT CULTURE**. In an old church, you'll also see historic photographs of the village, as well as a fallen original totem pole and several sets of **CARVED HOUSE POSTS**. The tribe also maintains six new rustic cabins and a wilderness campground in Nootka Island's old-growth forest. Five cabins overlook the freshwater lake, just a few hundred feet from the Pacific Ocean; one overlooks the ocean beach. Cabins are equipped with kitchens and wood stoves. The campground has 18 tent sites, with fire pits, picnic tables, potable water, and pit toilets. To get to Gold River, take scenic Highway 28 from the town of Campbell River, west across Vancouver Island. At Gold River turn left at the BC Information Centre, and follow the main road through Gold River toward the mill. Ahaminaquis—from which the 100-passenger MV *Uchuck*, water taxi, and floatplanes depart—is about 8.1 miles (14 kilometers) outside of Gold River. The Ahaminaquis Tourist Information Centre, open June through September, has a **PHOTO EXHIBIT OF NUU-CHA-NULTH HERITAGE** and history, as well as art, Maquinna hats, prints, and carvings for sale. The MV *Uchuck* Mowachaht tour leaves from Ahaminaquis every Wednesday during July through August. The daylong roundtrip, with a 1-hour stop and tour in Yuquot and other stops in Nootka Sound, is less than $50. If you arrive by plane, water taxi, or personal craft, the hourlong village tour is $7.

Yuquot can also be accessed year-round from Gold River by Native-owned Maxi's Water Taxi, (250)282-2282, a 12-passenger enclosed boat (the 1-hour trip is $180 one way for one to eight people); or by Air Nootka charter floatplane, (250)283-2255, about $125 per person each way.

Book tours through the Ahaminaquis Tourist Information Centre, PO Box 1137, Gold River, BC V0P 1G0; (800)238-2933. Call the Mowachaht Band's office in Gold River for package rates that include transportation, tour, and accommodations; (250)283-2015. Cabins, campgrounds, and ground tours are open year-round; fees vary according to season and whether you go by boat. The MV Uchuck III has regularly scheduled tours Jul–Aug, also available on demand from May–Sept. The Information Centre is open 10am–6pm, daily, Jun–Sept.

POTLATCHES

Since time beyond recollection, the Kwakwala-speaking groups have expressed their joy through the potlatch. The word "potlatch" comes from Chinook jargon, a trade pidgin formerly used along the West Coast, meaning "to give." The term came to designate a ceremony common to peoples on the Northwest Coast and parts of the interior. The potlatch ceremony marks important occasions in the lives of the Kwakwaka'wakw: the naming of children, the advent of marriage, the transferral of rights and privileges, and the mourning of the dead. Guests witnessing the potlatch are given gifts. The more gifts distributed by the potlatch host, the higher the status achieved. It is a time for pride— a time for showing the masks and dances owned by the family hosting the potlatch.

Although there was no immediate opposition to the potlatch at the time of initial contact with the white man, opposition began to grow with the coming of missionaries and government agents. People refused to give up the potlatch, leading officials, teachers, and missionaries to pressure the federal government into enacting legislation prohibiting ceremonies. The first version of the law was passed in 1884, but was difficult to enforce because of the vagueness of its wording. Later, the law was revised and following a large potlatch held at Village Island in December 1921, 45 people were charged under Section 149 of the Indian Act. Of those convicted of offences, including making speeches and dancing, twenty-two people were given suspended sentences. The sentencing was based on the illegal agreement that if entire tribes gave up their potlatch paraphernalia, individual members of those tribes who been found guilty would have their sentences suspended. Three people were remanded for appeal and twenty men and women were sent to Oakalla Prison to serve sentences of two months for first offenders and three months for second offenders.

Alert Bay: *Kwakwaka'wakw*

Alert Bay, one of Vancouver Island's **MOST VISITED COMMUNITIES,** is located on Cormorant Island, 40 minutes by ferry from Port McNeill, several hours north of Campbell River. Best known for its U'Mista Cultural Centre, Alert Bay was formerly used as a burial ground by the Namgis people. **HANDSOME MEMORIAL TOTEMS** still stand today in the cemetery along the waterfront, and Alert Bay totems include

The ceremonial gear, including coppers, masks, rattles, and whistles, was gathered up by William Halliday, the Indian agent in Alert Bay, who had been largely responsible for the mass arrest. Inventoried and crated, the artifacts were sent to Ottawa. There, the collection was divided between the Victoria Memorial Museum, now the National Museum of Man in Ottawa, and the Royal Ontario Museum in Toronto. Some objects were set aside for the personal collection of Duncan Campbell Scott, then super-intendent general of Indian Affairs. Approximately 30 objects had been sold to George Heye, a collector from New York, before the material left Alert Bay.

For some years the potlatch went "underground" to evade further pros-ecution under the law. In Fort Rupert, for example, people favored stormy weather as a suitable time to hold potlatches, knowing that neither the police nor the Indian agent could travel in such weather. When the Indian Act was revised in 1951, Section 149 was simply deleted rather than repealing the antipotlatch act.

Since 1921 those who had lost their treasures had not forgotten their loss. The first real efforts to repatriate these objects were started in the late 1960s. Their return, in the late 1970s, was conditional on the con-struction of museums in Cape Mudge (see Quadra Island section in this chapter) and Alert Bay.

The only permanent exhibit in Alert Bay's U'mista Cultural Centre is that of the Potlatch Collection in the Big House. The first objects shown are a group of coppers (large objects made of copper that represented units of wealth). It should be noted that when the collection was shipped to Ottawa, the Department of Indian Affairs paid token compensation of $1,495 for the entire collection, while the owners of the coppers had val-ued these alone at more than $350,000.

—Courtesy of the U'Mista Cultural Centre

the **WORLD'S TALLEST TOTEM POLE.** Europeans settled in Alert Bay in 1870 and built a small fish saltery. Today the little town, with its centerpiece Anglican church dressed in gingerbread trim, numbers about 1,400. Alert Bay is in the heart of orca territory, and there are a number of **WHALE-WATCHING AND SPORTFISHING** tours, as well as kayaking and scuba diving opportunities. The long drive from Victoria (about 6 hours) is well worth it. You'll find plenty to do here. Accommodations on the island are limited, and reservations should be made far in advance of your visit.

For general information, contact Alert Bay Tourism, (800)690-8222 or (250)974-2260. For ferry schedule information, call (250)956-4533.

U'Mista Cultural Centre

A large number of confiscated **POTLATCH ITEMS** were returned from Canada's National Museum of Man and the Royal Ontario Museum in 1979 and 1988, respectively, to the Kwakwaka'wakw community at Alert Bay. These items are now safely ensconced in the U'Mista Cultural Centre, along with nine pieces that were recently returned from the Smithsonian Institution in Washington, D.C. The center, located a few feet from the rocky beach, is built in the style of a **CEDAR BIGHOUSE.** Upon arrival, visitors watch *Box of Treasures,* a video explaining the long and fascinating journey of the confiscated ceremonial items from the village and back. The items, many elaborately **CARVED AND PAINTED MASKS,** are displayed around the inside walls in the order they would appear at a potlatch. Browse the collection on your own or join a **NATIVE-GUIDED TOUR** that takes about an hour (recommended). Many other videos are available at the center for visitors to watch. Among these are *Mungo Martin: A Slender Thread/The Legacy* and *Potlatch: A Strict Law Bids Us Dance,* both produced by U'Mista Cultural Centre. During summer months there are regularly scheduled traditional **KWAKWAKA'WAKW DANCE PERFORMANCES.** The center will arrange private dance performances for groups of 50 or more. The gift shop sells lovely carved jewelry, masks, silk-screened prints, and other items made by local artists, some of whose work is internationally known.

U'mista Cultural Centre, Front St, PO Box 253, Alert Bay, BC V0N 1A0; (250)974-5403. Open year-round. Call for hours. Admission fee; tours and dance performances cost extra. Wheelchair accessible.

Port Hardy: *Kwakwa̱ka'wakw*

At the northern end of Vancouver Island, literally at the end of Highway 19, sits Port Hardy, nestled above a snug harbor on the island's east side and protected by several barrier islands from the often stormy Queen Charlotte Strait. One of the oldest village sites found on Vancouver Island, dating to **8,000 YEARS OLD,** was discovered a few miles from Port Hardy at Bear Cove. Local Kwakwa̱ka'wakw descendants offer **KAYAK EXPEDITIONS** of Quatsino Sound, a protected inland waterway west of Port Hardy with at least a dozen **ABANDONED VILLAGE SITES** on its shores. A visit to Cape Scott Provincial Park via a gravel road, on Vancouver Island's most northwesterly point, provides an idea of what Vancouver Island looked like before white contact and the twentieth century's rapacious timber harvesting. The park offers nearly 15,070 hectares of **UNTOUCHED COASTAL WILDERNESS,** resplendent with old-growth cedar, and 20 miles of Pacific Ocean waterfront. Port Hardy is the gateway for ferries heading from the end of Vancouver Island to remote Bella Coola on the mainland, with stopovers at the equally remote villages of Klemtu, Bella Bella, Ocean Falls, and Shearwater, located on islands and peninsulas in the Inside Passage. Or, from Port Hardy, take the 15-hour BC Ferries trip all the way north to Prince Rupert, a small coastal town just south of the Alaska–British Columbia border. Prince Rupert is the departure point in northern British Columbia for Haida Gwaii (the Queen Charlotte Islands) and to roads leading to the northern interior of British Columbia. From Prince Rupert you can fly on to Ketchikan, Alaska, and continue your understanding of Northwest Native culture.

Park maps for Cape Scott Provincial Park are available from the Port Hardy and District Chamber of Commerce, PO Box 249, Port Hardy, BC V0N 2P0; (250)949-7622.

The Copper Maker Carving Studio and Gallery

Hunt family progeny have included some of the **FINEST CARVERS** in the world as well as more than 30 artists working in other mediums. This prodigious outpouring by the past three generations of Hunts began in the 1850s, when Englishman Robert Hunt, a Hudson's Bay Company employee, married Mary Ebbets, the Tlingit daughter of a Tongass tribal chief. In the early nineteenth century, their offspring collaborated with anthropologist Franz Boas and photographer Edward Curtis.

Calvin Hunt and his wife, Marie, own the Copper Maker Carving Studio and Gallery just outside of Port Hardy. His work and that of other Hunt family members—from **POTTERY, PRINTS, JEWELRY,**

AND CARVING—is for sale at the gallery. Family members often work on larger commissions in the gallery's carving studio. Commissions for ceremonial robes, as well as scheduling for dance exhibitions, are booked through the Copper Maker.

The Copper Maker Carving Studio and Gallery, 112 Copper Wy, Fort Rupert Village; (250)949-8491. Open 9am–5pm year-round. The gallery is just south of Port Hardy. Call first; the gallery closes when the family travels to major exhibitions.

Ancient Voices: *Native Cultural Kayak Expedition*

A five-day kayak exploration of inner Quatsino Sound, **TRADITIONAL TERRITORY** of the Quatsino Band of Kwakwaka'wakw, is offered several times during the summer months. As a guide drums and sings a traditional song intended to calm the waters and provide for a safe journey, you depart from the historic whaling town of Coal Harbour and paddle through the Quatsino Narrows to meet Fran "Jsinau" Hunt-Jinnouchi at the abandoned village site of Old Quatsino. As you sit on the beach and eat lunch, Hunt-Jinnouchi points out landmarks, bringing the old village alive with stories. Then it's back into the kayaks and paddling up the sound, with overnight camping at Drake Island, and in subsequent nights, at Mahatta Creek, Koskimo Bay, and Oya-Kumla. The last night includes an evening of **FEASTING AND TRA-DITIONAL KWAKWAKA'WAKW SINGING AND DANCING**.

This dinner is a major event. It begins with a Native seafood soup called *usa*, which is served into wooden bowls and sipped with hand-carved wooden spoons. Guests are seated around an 8-foot-long **POT-LATCH FEAST DISH**, and offered plates heaped with traditionally prepared feast foods: halibut, prawns, crab, smoked and barbecued salmon, eulachon (a small oil-rich fish), herring eggs, venison, steamed wild sea asparagus, and fresh berries, all—in contemporary style—downed with fine wine. As in the old days, when potlatch feasts for hundreds of guests were planned for months and lasted for days, guests are seated around a fire after dinner under the gaze of the 15-foot Sisiutl (a double-headed sea serpent, carved from cedar) and are entertained by dancers wearing carved wooden masks and ceremonial robes. Dancers and drummers sing songs passed down over the centuries through generations of families. The journey ends at Winter Harbour, and paddlers are water-taxied or driven by van back to Port Hardy. Guides and entertainers on the expedition include Fran Hunt-Jinnouchi, of Kwaikiutl ancestry and owner of North Island Boat, Canoe, and Kayak Rentals; Kaleb Child, a singer and drummer; and Mervyn Child, an extraordinary carver and storyteller.

Ancient Voices Kayak Tours, North Island Boat, Canoe, and Kayak Rentals and Tours, 8600 Granville St, PO Box 291, Port Hardy, BC V0N 2P0; (250)949-7707; kayak@trinet.bc.ca;. www.trinet.bc.ca/~kyak/. Included in the cost are double or single kayaks, cultural and kayak guides, gear (bring your own sleeping bag), all meals and snacks. Summers only. Please call for current rates and schedule. Discounts are available for groups and school education trips. Private tours for 8–12 people can be arranged.

Port Hardy Museum: *Prehistoric Artifacts Interpreted*

This small, local museum exhibits artifacts and accompanying interpretation that describes the oldest **PREHISTORIC SITE** found on Vancouver Island. The Bear Cove site, dated to 8,000 years old, is located on the shoreline about 2 miles from Port Hardy, where the BC Ferry terminal now sits. The site was examined by archeologists in 1978, and the artifacts were moved to storage rooms of the Royal British Columbia Museum for safekeeping. Stone and bone tools that were once used for fishing and carving, and obsidian spear points recovered from the site are on loan to the Port Hardy Museum. Also displayed are donated stone tools, wooden dishes, and basketry from the local area made in the 1800s. The museum's gift shop carries a large selection of nonfiction books on British Columbia First Nations culture, and a substantial collection of carved jewelry, wood carvings, and other locally crafted items for sale.

Port Hardy Museum, 7110 Market St, PO Box 2126, Port Hardy, BC V0N 2P0; (250)949-8143. Located on the ground level of the Port Hardy Library. Call for hours.

Prince Rupert: *Tsimshian*

An **EXCEPTIONAL MUSEUM** and harbor tour is offered in Prince Rupert, a coastal town and ancient Tsimshian village site near the Southeast Alaska border, at the mouth of the Skeena River. The Skeena River is the mythical birthplace of Raven, protagonist of the Raven stories of the Northwest Coast. Tsimshians have occupied the area for at least 10,000 years, and Prince Rupert has the highest concentration of **ARCHAEOLOGICAL SITES** anywhere in North America. Today many Tsimshians live in Prince Rupert and along the Skeena River.

Getting to Prince Rupert can be daunting, although it's **A SCE-NIC TRIP** no matter how you get there. BC Ferries, (604)669-1211, leave from Port Hardy, on Vancouver Island's northern end, cross Queen Charlotte Strait, and thread their way through the islands of the narrow Inside Passage to Prince Rupert, a 15- to 18-hour trip.

From the city of Vancouver, on the mainland, the Yellowhead Trans-Canada Highway 16 to Prince Rupert is about 935 miles (1,500 kilometers), or two very long days on the road. Greyhound Bus, (604)662-3222, makes the trip twice a day from Vancouver. The Canadian railway VIA Rail, (800)561-3949, goes from Vancouver to Prince Rupert via Jasper (Alberta), where passengers change trains. The trip takes two days and nights, with arrival on the third day. The quickest route to Prince Rupert is by Air Canada, (800)776-3000, which flies 68-passenger jets twice a day from Vancouver to Prince Rupert.

For assistance with lodging and car rentals, contact Prince Rupert Visitor Information Centre, (800)667-1994. From Prince Rupert, you can continue to Southeast Alaska on the Alaska State Ferry (it's best to leave your car behind), (800)642-0066, or visit the Queen Charlotte Islands on BC Ferries, (604)669-1211.

Museum of Northern British Columbia: *Tsimshian Culture*

The Tsimshian name of this museum is Na Xbiisa Lagigyet, which means **"TREASURE BOX OF THE ANCIENT ONES,"** and indeed this is. The museum is built in the style of a huge Northwest Coast longhouse, and is filled with treasures that portray Tsimshian and other Northwest culture dating back to the last ice age. Look here for petroglyphs, bone and stone tools, extraordinary **CARVED RATTLES, CHILKAT ROBES, AND ARGILLITE FIGURES**. The Great Room, filled with **MONUMENTAL TOTEMIC ART** such as house posts and totem poles, has a spectacular view of Prince Rupert's harbor. There are four other galleries in the museum, with exhibits on more recent history. The First Nations **CARVING SHED** is open to the public when artists are working.

Museum of Northern British Columbia, 100 First Ave W, PO Box 669, Prince Rupert, BC V8J 1A8; (250) 624-3207. On the waterfront at the foot of McBridge St (Hwy 16). Admission fee.

Laxspa'aws, Pike Island: *Tsimshian-Guided Tours*

With a Tsimshian guide, you can visit three **ANCIENT VILLAGE SITES,** dating back nineteen centuries, on Pike Island, near the Tsimshian village of Metlakatla. Inhabited until the 1800s, the island has five of 150 identified village sites in the Prince Rupert area. Once the center of Tsimshian culture, the present city of Prince Rupert is thought to have been the most densely populated area in North America (north of Mexico) prior to European contact. What you'll see on Pike Island are house depressions in the alder and salal, and **DOZENS OF PETRO-GLYPHS** chipped into the rocks along the shoreline. Travel is by water taxi across Venn Passage from Prince Rupert. During the five-hour tour, guides discuss the traditional uses of trees, shrubs, and plants.

Metlakatla Development Corp., PO Box 224, Prince Rupert, BC V8J 3P6; (250) 628-3201; www.citytel.net/library/pike. Buy tickets from the Museum of Northern British Columbia (listed above). Tours available summer months only, or by special arrangement.

Guided Archaeological Harbor Tours:
Exploring Tsimshian History

Visitors begin with a slide show at the Museum of Northern British Columbia, then board a covered boat in Prince Rupert's harbor for a **MULTICULTURAL TOUR**. Museum guides take you to a historic Finnish fishing village at Dodge Cove, built on the site of a **5,000-YEAR-OLD TSIMSHIAN VILLAGE**. Back onboard the boat, guides pass around artifacts for visitors to handle while pointing out more than 200 archaeological sites along the shore, including **ROCK CARVINGS**. At the modern village of Metlakatla, the site of a thousand-year-old Indian village, learn about its brief history as a Christian utopian community. The entire village moved to Annette Island in Southeast Alaska in the late 1800s. Tours are co-sponsored by the Metlakatla Band of Tsimshians and the Museum of Northern British Columbia.

Tours daily, mid-Jun–Aug 31. Adults, $20; children 16 and under, $12; children under 5, free. Purchase tickets at the Museum of Northern British Columbia (see above); get them early in the day, as the tours are popular. Tours may be canceled on short notice due to sudden storms; in which case money will be refunded.

First Nations Art Studios

MARIE OLDFIELD weaves cedar bark and spruce root vessels, baskets, and garments at her home studio; call (250)627-1665.

On the Prince Rupert waterfront look for **EAGLE WIND NATIVE ARTS**, where the Adams family carves traditional Nisga'a art from the Nass River. They also sell popular lathe-turned birch, alder, and yellow cedar carved bowls and 1- to 8-foot-tall totem poles, moon and sun masks, silk-screened prints, and carved gold and silver jewelry. Also look for handwoven natural wool sweaters knitted by Nisga'a elders. (203 Cow Bay Rd, Prince Rupert. There is no phone number for this one, so you're on your own in locating them.)

'Ksan Village Cultural Centre

For thousands of years Gitxsan villages have occupied this site at the junction of the Skeena and Bulkley Rivers. Its narrow canyon made it a desirable spot to trap salmon as they made their way upriver to spawn. East of Prince Rupert, the **'KSAN HISTORICAL INDIAN VILLAGE**, one of the most popular First Nations attractions in British

Columbia, includes totem poles and reconstructions of seven traditional longhouses. It stands where the old villages once stood.

Three longhouses are named after Gitxsan clans and furnished with cultural items. The Fireweed House of Masks and Robes contains contemporary masks and robes belonging to the 'KSAN PERFORMING ARTS GROUP. The Frog House of the Distance Past is furnished with everyday household goods that would have been used before white contact. The Wolf House of Feasts reflects a 1920s-era potlatch. Guided tours (about 45 minutes long) of these three longhouses are available only during the summer, and there's a fee to view them.

The other longhouses are used as a gift shop, museum, and carving school and are open year-round to visitors. The museum contains Gitxsan and Wet'suwet'en objects collected from sites within a 50-mile radius of 'Ksan. Often on Friday nights in July and August, awe-inspiring **"TRANSFORMATION MASKS"** are worn and "danced" (to "dance a mask" is to bring the spirit it represents to life) as part of the Breath of Our Grandfathers performance by the 'Ksan Dancers. The gift shop sells outstanding carved masks, housescreens, totem poles, and jewelry that have been collected from all over British Columbia as well as from local artists perfecting their skills at the 'Ksan Historical Indian Village's KITANMAAX CARVING SCHOOL.

'Ksan Village Cultural Centre, PO Box 326, Hazelton, BC V0J 1Y0; (250)842-5544. 'Ksan is 180 miles east of Prince Rupert. Admission fee. Open year-round. Tours are mid-Apr–Sept 30. Due to severe weather, the three furnished longhouses normally on the tour are closed in winter, but the gift shop, the Kitanmaax carving school, and the Treasure Room and Exhibition Centre are open daily, year-round. Please call for hours.

Totem Poles on the Skeena River

Prince Rupert has a number of **CARVED TOTEM POLES** raised throughout town. Gitxsan villages along the Skeena River have totem poles as well, some of which are the oldest still standing in British Columbia. Look for them especially at the villages of Kitwanga and Kitwancool (between Hazelton and Prince Rupert, on Highway 37); at Kispiox (north of Hazelton); and at Kitsegyukla (south of Hazelton on Route 16). There are also totems at the 'Ksan Village Cultural Centre near Hazelton.

Maps and books are available from the Museum of Northern British Columbia or the Prince Rupert Travel Information Centre, at the junction of Hwys 16 and 62, PO Box 340, New Hazelton District, BC V0J 2J0; (250)842-6571.

Queen Charlotte Islands:
Haida Gwaii

The archipelago of Haida Gwaii, known as Dida Cwaa in the Haida Raven stories, was named the Queen Charlotte Islands by the Canadian government in 1878. The islands are also often referred to as the **CANADIAN GALAPAGOS** because of their unique flora and fauna. The archipelago lies about 60 miles off of the northern British Columbia mainland. The 180-mile-long necklace of **150 ISLANDS** (some of them no larger than a seal's nose) is the **HAIDA'S ANCESTRAL HOME**. The Haida, a nation legendary for its art, frequent raids on other bands, and fierce domination of the inland waters all the way to Vancouver Island, have never ceded the islands to Canada. Many of their villages, now overgrown with moss-covered rain forests, were abandoned in the 1800s, when smallpox epidemics forced the few remaining Haidas to consolidate in two central locations on Graham Island: Skidegate, on the southern end, and Old Masset, on the northern end.

Some people come to Haida Gwaii to visit and photograph the **ABANDONED VILLAGES** on the southern end of Moresby Island known as Gwaii Haanas. It's very expensive to get here, however, and you must make a reservation with the Canadian Park Service before visiting any of the protected villages.

A car ferry links Graham and Moresby Islands, but south Moresby Island is roadless, accessible only by personal watercraft, private charter, floatplane, or helicopter. The majority of visitors fly or ferry to Graham Island and drive to Skidegate, Old Masset, and other small towns on the island, to buy **HAIDA ART** in several galleries. In Skidegate (population 650), the **HAIDA GWAII MUSEUM** houses Haida carvings of argillite (a type of slate), a totem pole carved by master carver Bill Reid, and longhouses. Highway 16 links the towns of Skidegate, Old Masset, Port Clements, Tlell, and Queen Charlotte City. In Old Masset seven poles have been carved and raised in the past 20 years. To get to the Queen Charlotte Islands, take the BC Ferry, (250)386-3431, from Prince Rupert across the Hecate Strait to Skidegate. The 6-hour crossing costs about $125 each way for car and driver. Ferries depart once daily, May to September. From October to April, ferries travel across the Strait three times a week. Flights from Prince Rupert to

There are two Visitor Reception Centres on the Queen Charlotte Islands—one at Sandspit, in the airport building, the other in Queen Charlotte City. Both centers carry marine charts and topographic maps for sale and own a marine VHF radio to check weather forecasts. The Observer, a Queen Charlotte weekly newspaper, sells an 80-page Guide to the Queen Charlotte Islands, updated annually, for less than $5; call (250)559-4680 for a copy.

Skidegate take about 45 minutes. You can also fly to Graham Island from the city of Vancouver.

HAIDA ART AND ARTISTS

The Haida own the world's only known quarry of argillite and retain the exclusive right to carve it. The rare black argillite, a fine, easily carved slate material, is sculpted into miniature totem poles, jewelry, plaques, boxes, and pipes. The work of well-known argillite carver Charles Edensaw is shown prominently in Vancouver's University of British Columbia Museum. Edensaw's great-nephew, the recently deceased Bill Reid, is one of the most famous Haida artists, known for his monumental art and jewelry. Renowned Haida artist Robert Davidson, brought up in the north coast village of Old Masset, began carving argillite as a young boy. His brother, Reg Davidson, also a fine carver, lives in Masset year-round. Many Haida artists carve wood, silver, and gold as well as argillite. Their distinctive artwork is housed in major museums and private collections all over the world. **HAIDA ARGILLITE CARVINGS** *can be purchased throughout the Pacific Northwest and in Southeast Alaska, but the best place to buy them is in Haida Gwaii. For names of local carvers from whom you can buy directly, contact the Haida Gwaii Museum, RR1, Second Beach Rd, PO Box 1373, Skidegate, VC V0T 1S1; (250)559-4643; or the Council of Haida Nations, (250)626-5252.*

Haida Gwaii Museum: *Preserving Haida Culture*

Located just outside Skidegate, on Graham Island, is a fine museum dedicated entirely to Haida culture and history and the natural history of the Queen Charlotte Islands. Built on Qaykun (Sea Lion) Point, on the site of an old Haida village, the museum is constructed entirely of cedar posts and beams, echoing Haida **TRADITIONAL BIGHOUSE** style. Inside are four **HISTORIC TOTEM POLES** preserved from the abandoned villages of Tanu and Skedans as well as recently deceased Haida carver Bill Reid's first totem pole, which was commissioned by Shell Canada and donated to the museum. Reid's 50-foot Haida canoe *Lootaas* (wave eater), carved for Canada's Expo '86, stands adjacent to the museum. The museum houses more than **500 ARGILLITE MINIATURES**, including totem poles and carved plates, pipes, sculpture, and jewelry. Haida

Tours of the Skidegate Inlet in the Lootaas canoe are offered sporadically during the summer. For information, contact the Haida Gwaii Watchmen Native-Operated Tours, PO Box 609, Skidegate, BC V0T 1S0; (250)559-8225.

carver Robert Davidson, who began carving argillite as a boy and later expanded his work into other media, donated nine major pieces of his art to the museum. **CONTEMPORARY ART** is for sale in the museum's gift shop, along with an extensive inventory of books on Haida art and culture. The museum's multilevel decks overlook Skidegate Inlet. This is one of the world's best places to see migrating gray whales in the spring and fall; drawn close to shore, they feed in eelgrass meadows.

Haida Gwaii Museum, RR 1, Second Beach Rd, PO Box 1373, Skidegate, BC V0T 1S1; (250)559-4643. The museum is just south of town on Hwy 16, on the Skidegate Reserve. Open daily in summer; in winter, shortened hours and some closed days. Call for hours. Admission fee.

Gwaii Haanas National Park Reserve and Haida Heritage Site

Dotting the southern end of Moresby Island are the Northwest's largest number of known **ABANDONED HAIDA VILLAGES**. The villages were set aside in the 1980s as a national park preserve. Just off the southernmost tip, on Anthony Island, is the site of Skungwaii (Ninstints), today designated a **UNITED NATIONS WORLD HERITAGE SITE**. From Skungwaii the powerful Kunghit Haida once ruled Gwaii Haanas. The Kunghit, who numbered in the thousands in their most powerful era, were hit hard by smallpox epidemics, and by the late 1800s only 30 to 40 survivors were left.

The old Haida village sites were documented by Victoria artist **EMILY CARR**, who journeyed here alone in the early 1900s to paint the remains of Skungwaii and other villages. Chief Ninstints, one of the last three or four surviving Kunghits at that time, guided and informed Charles F. Newcombe, who left a written record of the sites; in 1901 they circumnavigated and mapped the southern portion of the islands.

In the late 1950s, 11 of the best-preserved totem poles were removed from the area. Today they are exhibited at the University of British Columbia Museum of Anthropology in Vancouver and at the Royal British Columbia Museum in Victoria. Skungwaii today, which is about 95 nautical miles from any town, has only **LEANING MORTUARY POLES, FRAGMENTS OF LONGHOUSES, AND SHELL MIDDENS.** The site adjoins a wildlife reserve, home to nesting puffins and petrels

VISITING GWAII HAANAS PARKS
Canada will send you a free travel planning guide covering the basics for visiting Gwaii Haanas on Moresby Island—from checklists, maps, and information about accommodations to boat and plane charters and guided tours. This guide also contains a list of references, guidebooks, and marine charts, and reports where to purchase these items on the mainland. Contact Parks Canada; PO Box 37, Queen Charlotte, BC V0T 1S0; (250)559-8818. Many tours are offered in the area of non-Native charter companies who do not employ Haida guides. To find tours or special events led by members of the Haida Nation, contact the Council of Haida Nations, (250)626-5252, or the Skidegate Band Office, (250)559-4496.

and herds of seals. Other villages on Gwaii Haanas, such as Skedans on Louise Island, are guarded by the **HAIDA GWAII WATCHMEN**, tribal members who contract with the Canadian Park Service as guides and caretakers. To protect the sites, only a limited number of tourists are allowed to visit south Moresby Island each year. There are no facilities or roads in Gwaii Haanas National Park Preserve. Travel must be arranged by private charter, floatplane, or helicopter. Visitors must leave the reserve by dusk.

Gwaii Haanas National Park Reserve and Haida Heritage Site, Parks Canada, PO Box 37, Queen Charlotte City, BC V0T 1S0; (250)559-8818. To make arrangements to see abandoned villages, contact the Haida Gwaii Watchmen, PO Box 609, Skidegate, Haida Gwaii, BC V0T 1S0; (250)559-8225. Jun–Aug 15 are the best months to visit. The area is often foggy in Jul–Oct.

British Columbia First Nations Events

QUEEN CHARLOTTE ISLANDS

- Singaay Laa (Skidegate Days), Community Grounds; (250)559-4496; Skidegate.

VANCOUVER ISLAND

- Yuquot Spirit Summerfest, Gold River/Yuquot; (250)283-201; mid-Aug.
- Native Heritage Annual Art Show & Sale, Native Heritage Centre; (250)746-8119; 200 Dowichan Wy, Duncan; Nov.

VANCOUVER AND COAST

- Chilliwack Native Powwow, Ag-Red Centre; (250)858-0662 or (250)858-6661; Chilliwack; mid-May.
- Seabird Island Indian Festival; (604)796-2177; Seabird Island, 5 km east of Agassiz on Hwy 7; end of May.
- Indian Festival, main beach; (604)858-3334; Cultus Lake; Jun 1.
- Annual International Powwow, Mission; (604)826-1281; mid-Jul.
- Whey-ah-wichen Canoe Festival; (604)929-3454; Cates Park, North Vancouver.
- Aboriginal Cultural Festival "Bringing People Together," Pacific National Exhibition Hall; (604)251-4844; Vancouver; mid-Sept.

INTERIOR

- Cathedral Lakes Powwow; (250)499-5528; Rodeo Grounds, Keremeos; mid-May.
- Canadian Rodeo Association Rodeo; (250)679-8868; Neskonlith Lake, Chase; Jun.

- Annual Kamloops Powwow, Kamloops Powwow Days, Chief Louis Centre; (250)828-9700; Kamloops; mid-Aug.
- Canim Lake Band Art Show; (250)397-2227; Canim Lake; mid-Aug.
- West Moberly First Nations Days; (250)788-3345; Moberly Lake, Chetwynd; Aug.
- Friendship Barbecue, Parkinson Recreation Centre; (250)763-4905; Kelowna; mid-Sept.
- Remembrance Day Powwow; (250)397-2227; various locations, Lytton; Nov.
- Friendship Centre Native Awareness Days, Springs Feast, Summer Feast, and Fall Feasts; (250)785-8566; from May–Sept.

WESTERN WASHINGTON

WESTERN WASHINGTON

Most of the rivers in Western Washington are named after the tribes who live near them today: the Nooksack, Sammish, Skagit, Snoqualmie, Snohomish, Skykomish, Duwamish, Puyallup, Nisqually, Skokomish, Quileute, Hoh, Quinault, Queets, Chinook, Cowlitz, and Chehalis. The Lummi, Makah, Muckleshoot, Sauk-Suiattle, Shoalwater Bay, S' Klallam, Swinomish, Squaxin Island, Stillaguamish, Suquamish, and Tulalip Tribes live in Western Washington as well. Some of these tribes, such as the Quinault, are actually confederations of tribal people who were uprooted from their ancestral villages and forced to relocate together to designated areas. Many Quinault tribal members, for example, are actually descendants of Chinook-speaking bands who were removed from their villages along Washington's southern coast and the mouth of the Columbia River to the Quinault Reservation, after treaties were signed.

Washington State has 27 federally recognized Indian tribes with a combined population of 91,000. The tribes employ around 14,400 Washington citizens full time, including nontribal employees. The tribes contribute $1 billion annually to the state's overall economy; in 1997 their tribal enterprises spent $865.8 million for supplies, equipment, and services and $51.3 million in federal employment and payroll-related taxes. —The Governors Office of Indian Affairs Economic Study Group

From 1854 through 1855, most of the tribes in Western Washington signed treaties with the U.S. government. Territorial governor Isaac Stevens established only a few reservations, with the plan to later round up all of the Indians in the Puget Sound region to a single location on the

Olympic Peninsula. The treaties stated that in exchange for signing away ownership to their land, the tribes could reserve forever the right to fish, hunt, and gather roots and berries at all of their traditional (usual and accustomed) places.

The Puget Sound Indian Wars of 1855–56 followed as a result of the refusal of the Puyallup and Nisqually Tribes to move to the useless reservation lands assigned to them. Battles pitted Indian warriors from both sides of the Cascade Mountains against American volunteers recruited by Stevens, as well as against the professional army stationed at Fort Steilacoom on southern Puget Sound. On August 5, 1856, Stevens met again with Indian leaders to adjust details of the reservations and consider the Natives' objections. Today's reservations are the result of those negotiations.

It is difficult now to imagine Native American life as it once existed in Western Washington. Modern cities, highways, and industries dominate the landscape, particularly on Puget Sound's eastern shore. Most of the original bands of Coast Salish Indians, such as the Duwamish (who lived in what is now Seattle), were long ago moved to reservations or (presumably) assimilated into the dominant white culture. A closer look reveals that tribal people in Western Washington have remained strongly identified with their roots, however. Empowered by both federal recognition of treaty rights, self-determination, casino revenues, and cultural resources, the tribes are once again commanding visibility in contemporary metropolitan culture.

Coast Salish art, long hidden in the shadow of Northwest Coast totems and totemic masks, has been resurrected in the past 25 years by artists such as the James family blanket weavers, numerous basket weavers, and Skokomish woodcarvers such as Pete Peterson and Andy Wilbur, all of whom are determined to give this art form its due.

This chapter explores the rim of Puget Sound and the Olympic Peninsula, directing you to tribally owned museums such as the Makah Cultural and Research Center in Neah Bay; to historic sites such as Chief Seattle's grave in Suquamish; to art installations such as the Salish Ravens and Crows at the University of Washington; and to contemporary Native events such as the Lummi's Stommish Water Festival and the Swinomish Annual Blues Festival. The chapter begins in southern Puget Sound, the southern end of the 1,000-mile-long Inside Passage, an island-filled waterway that stretches from the shellfish-laden tideflats in Washington's Nisqually Delta all the way north to the glacier-filled bays in Southeast Alaska.

Puget Sound and Olympic Peninsula tribes are committed to restoration of natural resources. They employ more fish and wildlife biologists (both Indian and non-Indian) than any other agencies in the state.

PUGET SOUND

Olympia Area: *Coast Salish Tribes*

Evergreen State College: *House of Welcome*

On the Evergreen State College campus, outside Olympia, is a full-scale adaptation of a **TRADITIONAL SALISH LONGHOUSE**. At one time a huge boulder, incised with Salish bear symbols, marked what is now

More than 35,000 people attend the Native Arts Fair, held each mid-June at the House of Welcome at Evergreen State College during the Super Saturday campuswide festival. Artists sell their work and provide demonstrations. Native dancers and storytellers perform. There are also a salmon bake and several Indian taco stands. Sat, 11am–7pm. For the next festival date, call (360)866-6000, ext. 6413.

the Evergreen campus as a gathering place for all the Coast Salish nations.

A vision of Lummi elder and founding Evergreen faculty member Mary Ellen Hillaire, the longhouse was built for **CULTURAL EXCHANGE AND NATIVE AMERI-CAN EDUCATION**. It was designed by Johnpaul Jones, of Choctaw descent, with the Seattle architectural firm Jones & Jones. Indian elders advised on the design. In keeping with the Northwest Indian tradition of naming significant buildings, in 1997 Puget Sound spiritual leaders and elders named the longhouse the House of Welcome, and it was sanctified with traditional ceremonies. It is open to the public.

Over the longhouse entrance perches a massive Thunderbird, carved and painted by Greg Colfax (Makah) and Andy Wilbur (Skokomish). Window covers are woven cedar-bark **CEREMONIAL SCREENS**, illustrated with creation stories by Skokomish artist Bruce Miller. Other figures from Native American mythology adorn screens surrounding two fireplaces. The hoods over the fireplace are finished with hammered copper, the most common metal extracted and used by Pacific Northwest tribes prior to European contact.

In its display cases, the longhouse features art by some of the Northwest's most **PRESTIGIOUS NATIVE ARTISTS**, such as Lillian Pitt (Warm Springs), John Hoover (Aleut), Pat Courtney-Gold (Warm Springs/Wasco), Larry Avakahna (Inupiat), Hazel Pete (Chehalis), and David Boxley (Tsimshian).

With a $325,000 grant from the Northwest Area Foundation, and in conjunction with the South Puget Sound Intertribal Planning Agency and the Port Gamble S'Klallam Tribe, the longhouse administers a far-reaching arts initiative. Not only do they have an **ARTIST-IN-RESIDENCE PROGRAM**, but they also provide mini-grants to six tribes supporting Native art and act as an art sales broker between artists and buyers. The House of Welcome publishes a directory (soon to be online) of 150 Native artists living in the Northwest region—from story tellers to visual artists, traditional to contemporary, with another 350 artists on the mailing list. The House of Welcome hosts an International Gathering of Indigenous Visual Artists of the Pacific Rim in August 2001.

House of Welcome, Evergreen State College, 2700 Evergreen Pkwy NW, Olympia, WA 98505; (360)866-6000, ext. 6718; moomaht@evergreen.edu; www.evergreen.edu. Take the Hwy 101 exit from I-5 at Olympia; follow 101 to the Evergreen State College exit. Tours should be arranged in advance.

Washington State Capitol Museum: *Salish Art and Artifacts*

The Washington State Capitol Museum in Olympia houses collections of Native art and artifacts from seven tribes living in the southern Puget Sound region: the Chehalis, Cowlitz, Nisqually, Puyallup, Skokomish, Steilacoom, and Squaxin Island. Its installation "**TRADITIONS AND TRANSITIONS**: The American Indians of South Puget Sound" is the only thorough **EXPLANATION OF SALISH CULTURE** on display in the Northwest. Elders and cultural leaders helped design the hands-on exhibit, which includes the interior of a winter house furnished with household items, baskets, and tools. The exhibit also explores the transition of tribal culture from its original state to the European model first introduced to the region by the Hudson's Bay Company in 1833. An adjoining gallery displays **MASTERWORKS BY CONTEMPORARY NATIVE ARTISTS**. The archives contain a large number of Salish baskets, which are publicly displayed from time to time.

Washington State Capitol Museum, 211 W 21st Ave, Olympia, WA 98501; (360)753-2580. Seven blocks south of the state capitol grounds, off Capitol Wy. Open Tues–Fri; Sat and Sun afternoons. Admission fee.

Yelm: *Nisqually Tribe*

The woodlands, prairies, and adjacent marine waters of the Nisqually River drainage were the **TRADITIONAL TERRITORY** of the Nisqually bands. Today Interstate 5 passes over the Nisqually River, where it flows and floods into the wide, fertile Nisqually Delta between Olympia and Tacoma. Fishing was central to the Nisqually economy and culture, and families lived in villages along the river and its tributaries. They hunted game and gathered roots and berries in the upland prairies and foothills around Mount Rainier.

Under the treaty terms presented by Territorial governor Isaac Stevens at Medicine Creek in 1855, the Nisqually were ordered to relinquish their fishing grounds for 160 acres of barren rocky ground. Led by their war chief, **LESCHI**, the tribe engaged in a two-year armed conflict against the territorial government, which resulted in the tribe's receiving a more suitable 5,000-acre reservation along the banks of the Nisqually River and retaining fishing, hunting, and gathering rights. The reservation was divided into allotments in the 1880s, with each tribal family receiving a 60- to 150-acre parcel for farming.

Seventy years after the treaty was signed, more than two-thirds of the **NISQUALLY RESERVATION** (3,300 acres) was "condemned" and transferred to the U.S. Department of War in preparation for the creation of the sprawling Fort Lewis military base. Tribal families were evicted from their homes and farms in the dead of winter and relocated to the remaining portion of the reservation or moved to other reservations in the region. Over the next 50 years the Nisqually lived in the shadow of the Fort Lewis military base. Most of this "condemned" land served as an artillery impact area.

Over the years the tribe continued to endure devastating encroachments on their resource base, culture, and way of life. During World War II more lands were condemned, and the Department of Defense made repeated attempts to take possession of the remaining portion of the reservation up until the 1970s. Today the reservation is less than 2,000 acres in size, a combination of tribal ownership, individually owned parcels, or lots owned by non-Indians.

In the early 1970s, however, the tribe began fighting back to reestablish the Nisqually Reservation as a viable community. They continue to acquire more land today, and the tribe has been able to provide their members with much needed housing as well as education, health, and social services. There are no tours of the reservation at the time of this writing.

Nisqually Delta: *The Medicine Creek Treaty*

You can still see the site in the Nisqually Delta where the Medicine Creek Treaty of 1855 was signed by the tribes of southern Puget Sound. Under a tree in a grove next to Medicine Creek (called She Nah Num by the Nisqually and now known as McAllister Creek), the terms of the treaty were presented to the assembled tribal leaders by Territorial governor Isaac Stevens. Known by the local tribes as the "**TREATY TREE**," the old spar is in a closed, no-access area on the Nisqually Wildlife Refuge but visible from trails in the refuge and from the freeway. A kiosk displays information about the Medicine Creek Treaty. The refuge itself is a must-see: protected wetlands rich in bird and plant life.

Assigned by presidential mandate to obtain title to all Indian lands in the Pacific Northwest as quickly as possible, Stevens made several

Before the Port of Tacoma filled the Puyallup River estuary for industrial development, the river's mouth was a lush fish and shellfish nursery, rivaling the Nisqually Delta farther south, producing huge quantities of Dungeness crab, among other species. Today the river's mouth and Commencement Bay, earmarked for two Superfund cleanups, are contaminated with arsenic, heavy metals, and agricultural runoff. The Puyallup Tribe does not own any tidelands on their reservation that are clean enough to farm shellfish for human consumption. More than 60 tribal members work as divers in the tribe's commercial geoduck clam harvest in offshore waters up to 70 feet deep, a million-dollar-a-year fishery. The giant clams are sold primarily to the Asian market.

mistakes when he appeared for the treaty signing. He failed to dress ceremonially for the occasion, deeply offending the tribes. He also failed to fully translate the terms of the treaty into Salish dialects, instead choosing to use limited Chinook jargon, which masked the treaty's full intent. And he misjudged the innate intelligence of the Nisqually leader, **CHIEF LESCHI**, who refused to sign the treaty. Leschi crossed the Cascade Range on horseback to warn the Yakama and other tribes in Eastern Washington of Stevens's intentions. The **INDIAN WARS** followed, and Leschi was captured and sentenced to hang. Neither the U.S. Army at Fort Steilacoom nor the British at Fort Nisqually approved of this sentence, however. They refused to have gallows built at their forts and attempted to save Leschi during a second trial. They failed in those efforts, though, and Leschi was eventually hanged.

Two monuments to the Medicine Creek Treaty are in the Nisqually area: One can be seen at the crossroads in the town of Nisqually; the other, marking the very spot where Chief Leschi was hanged, is at Thunderbird Square in nearby Lakewood.

Nisqually National Wildlife Refuge, 100 Brown Farm Rd, Olympia, WA 98516; (360)753-9467. From I-5, take exit 114, and follow signs to the refuge. Wildlife viewing trails (5½ miles of trail) through the delta are open to the public during daylight hours, year-round. The education center is open 10am–2pm, Saturdays only. Trails are open dawn to dusk, daily. No pets, no bicycles. Entrance fee per family.

Steilacoom: *Steilacoom Tribe*

Steilacoom Tribal Cultural Center and Museum

The **OLDEST TOWN IN WASHINGTON**, the little waterfront burg of Steilacoom was incorporated in 1854 by white settlers. Today the historic town, named after the tribe whose largest village was at the mouth of nearby Chambers Creek, still includes the original town hall and a 1903 church, which is now owned by the Steilacoom Tribe and houses the their Cultural Center and Museum. Nearby (where Western State Hospital now stands) is the former site of Fort Steilacoom, a U.S. military fort built in 1849. The old "Indian Trail," which extended from the fort to the mouth of Chambers Creek, is still visible. Like the Chinooks, Cowlitz, and others who have repeatedly applied for federal recognition but have been denied, the Steilacoom Tribe is currently not recognized by the federal government. Nonetheless, they have continued to elect tribal leaders.

The first floor of the two-story museum is dedicated to the **STEILACOOM TRIBE'S EARLY HISTORY**, with a replica of an archaeological dig that was conducted in the Chamber Creek village site. Charcoal from fire pits and petrified bone recovered from a butchering site date to the early 1400s. Buttons, trade beads, nails, and ceramics found at the site date to the early 1800s, when Europeans settled in the area and began trading with village members.

Upstairs is an exhibit of how one Steilacoom family maintained its cultural identity through eight generations. A gallery exhibits **NATIVE AMERICAN ART AND ARTIFACTS** that are on display for six months to a year.

A small cafe serves traditional clam chowder (made without milk or tomatoes), smoked salmon–stuffed croissants, and other treats. The gift shop features unique handcrafted items made by local Indian artists. Proceeds from the gift shop support the all-volunteer museum and cultural center activities.

Steilacoom Tribal Cultural Center and Museum, 1515 Lafayette St, PO Box 88419, Steilacoom, WA 98388; (253)584-6308. One block from the Steilacoom ferry landing. Admission fee for adults; children free. Museum memberships at $15 a year include a newsletter. Guided tours and catered lunches for groups are available on request. Open 10am–4pm Tues–Sun, year-round.

ORIGINAL FORT NISQUALLY SITE

The site of the original Fort Nisqually was on the fields overlooking the present-day Nisqually Delta Wildlife Refuge, near the small town of Du Pont between Olympia and Tacoma. It is one of the most important historic sites on Puget Sound. Established by the Hudson's Bay Company in Nisqually Indian territory in 1833, Fort Nisqually operated briefly as a fur-trading post but soon developed into a completely different kind of enterprise employing Native people.

As the demand for furs decreased, the demand for other Northwest resources, most notably gold, became insatiable. In the late 1840s the Hudson's Bay Company, began supplying animal and grain products to the developing Northwest. The company's new enterprise was centered in the Nisqually Delta and was renamed the Puget Sound Agricultural Company. Cattle driven from Mexico were fattened on the rich grassland, hundreds of sheep were tended at several sheep stations between the Nisqually and Puyallup Rivers, and acres of potatoes, corn, peas, and wheat were grown in present-day Pierce County. These British-born agricultural practices were in opposition to Native management of natural resources, which included burning to keep camas-bulb meadows free of encroaching vegetation, seasonal harvesting of wild plants and their fruit, and careful harvesting and

Tacoma: *Puyallup Tribe*

The word *spwiya'laphabsh* means "generous" or "welcoming" in Salish. It's the original name of the tribe now known as the Puyallup. Legends say the Puyallup came into being in the foothills of Mount Rainier, behind what is now Sumner, Washington, many thousands of years ago. At the time the waters of Puget Sound and the glaciers merged in the valleys. As the ice melted and river valleys were formed, the Puyallup settled the region along Commencement Bay in the industrial district of present-day Tacoma and fished for salmon in the Puyallup River and in Puget Sound. They speared halibut and flounder and dug clams from the bay. The rich Puyallup River valley became a **TRADING CENTER FOR MANY TRIBES**. The Puyallup prospered under the watchful spirit of Tacobet, who (it is said) still lives within the snowy peaks of the mountain they called Tahoma.

In 1855 the Puyallup were among the many bands who signed the Medicine Creek Treaty. The **PUYALLUP RESERVATION** was established in 1856, when the tribe refused to move to other reservations.

preparation of fish, shellfish, and game. Farm managers were recruited from England and Scotland; day laborers consisted of Native Hawaiians brought to the Pacific Northwest on Hudson's Bay ships, and local Squaxin, Nisqually, Chehalis, Cowlitz, Steilacoom, and Puyallup Indians.

The Hudson's Bay fleet shipped grain and products from the farm's creamery as far south as San Francisco during the California gold rush and as far north as Sitka, Alaska, to the Russian American Trading Company's headquarters. The farming operation also supplied nearby Fort Steilacoom and traded food for cedar shingles with new settlers clearing land in the Northwest. This food supply was critical to the success of resource extraction in the west, and contributed to the extermination or displacement of Native Alaskans, California Indians, and tribes of the Pacific Northwest.

The farm era ended in 1869. Pieces of the farmland were sold off; the buildings languished unused. In the 1930s the DuPont Power Company, which had purchased the original Fort Nisqually site to manufacture explosives, donated the last two original buildings to the public. In 1940s the factor's house and the granary were moved to Tacoma's Point Defiance State Park, 17 miles to the north (see the description of Fort Nisqually on the following pages).

Washington State History Museum: *Coast Salish Exhibits*

Both contemporary and historic Native American perspectives are included at the Washington State History Museum in Tacoma, housed adjacent to the city's restored historical train station (and echoing the train station's dome design elements). Enter the museum through a southern **COAST SALISH WINTER HOME** built by Lance Wilkie, a Makah longhouse builder. In the longhouse, visitors "hear" the conversations of family members as they mend nets and cook fern cakes in a basket. Another room includes a recreation of a **PETROGLYPH WALL OUTCROPPING** and videos of traditional stories told by contemporary Indian elders. A gallery addresses the devastation caused by epidemics—from the smallpox outbreaks of the early 1800s to this century's tuberculosis among Indians; contemporary Indian masks made by Native artists who were asked to express the feelings that emerged as they thought about these catastrophic events represent an unusual approach. A computer module allows you to hear greetings in different **INDIAN LANGUAGES**, such as an example of Chinook jargon, an early wax-cylinder recording of Chief Joseph's voice, and a Nez Perce elder speaking about her life, partially in her Native language. Historical photographs appear throughout the exhibits and include pictures of the Cushman Indian School in Puyallup and portraits of Indians on the Olympic Peninsula, taken by Indian agent Samuel G. Morse in 1896. If you've seen where the Medicine Creek Treaty was signed in the Nisqually Delta, this is the next place to visit—an exhibit explains both the event and issues surrounding it.

Published by the tribe, Puyallup Tribal News covers local tribal news as well as national Native issues. Subscriptions are $10 a year; for single-issue fees, contact Puyallup Tribal News, 202 E 28th St, Tacoma, WA 98404; (206) 593-0174.

Special collections feature **NATIVE ARTIFACTS** from all of Washington's tribes and include a handsome display of basketry, as well as a rare set of bone tools and points, more than 11,000 years old, uncovered in an Eastern Washington apple orchard. Contemporary Indian perspectives are also incorporated in the many exhibits in a variety of ways, such as taped interviews with nationally known Indian leaders. There is a museum shop and a cafe, which offers outdoor dining on the plaza with views of Mount Rainier (Tahoma), historic Union Station, and Commencement Bay.

Washington State History Museum, 1911 Pacific Ave, Tacoma, WA 98403; (253)272-9747. Open 10am–5pm, Tues–Sat; longer summer hours. Admission fee.

Fort Nisqually Historic Site: *Local Native Interpretation*

Fort Nisqually Historic Site, reconstructed from the 1830s-era Hudson's Bay Company trading post and farm that was originally located in the Nisqually Delta, is in Tacoma's 800-acre **POINT DEFIANCE PARK**. Six fully furnished buildings recreate life at the fort from 1833 through 1869. Two of the original buildings, the factor's house and the granary, were moved to Point Defiance in 1940 from the original site. Self-guided tours include a fully furnished trade-goods store, a laborer's dwelling, a blacksmith's shop, the granary, a clerk's house, and the factor's home. Special events include candlelight tours in October, several "living-history days" during the summer, and lectures about local tribes.

Fort Nisqually Historic Site, 5400 N Pearl St, #11, Tacoma, WA 98407; (253)591-5339. From I-5 near Tacoma, take the Bremerton exit and continue west to the 6th Ave Point Defiance Park exit. Follow signs on 5-Mile Dr, within the park, to the site. Open 11am–6pm, daily, summers; in winter only the museum and gift shop are open, Wed–Sun. Docent-led group tours and educational programs by reservation year-round. Admission fee, summer; free, winter.

Puyallup Tribal Museum

In 1900, Thomas Stolyer, presiding chief of the Puyallup Tribe, gave his land to build a government school. The boarding school buildings included dormitories, a church, and a health clinic. In 1929, because of mounting deaths in the Northwest Indian community from tuberculosis, the buildings were transformed into the **CUSHMAN INDIAN HOSPITAL**, located on the outskirts of what is now Tacoma.

Many Indian families were separated by prolonged stays in the hospital's sanitarium, which isolated patients for years at a time. "I remember looking up to the third window from the corner to see my mother," one guide recalled, looking up at the second floor of the hospital. "I was 3 years old. It was the first time I remember seeing her, my first memory."

A new hospital was built in 1942 and still dominates the entire hilltop. It now serves as the tribal administration office. A **TOTEM POLE** at the entry softens the hard edges of the institutional setting.

On the first floor, in a small room that opens into the reception area, is the small Puyallup Tribal Museum. The collection—some items permanent, some for sale—was originally put together with contributions from tribal members. From floor to ceiling are baskets, several hundred years old, as well as contemporary artwork. The museum has a good selection of **LOCAL NATIVE ART** for sale, including cedar-plaited dresses and baskets.

Puyallup Tribal Museum, 2002 E 28th St, Tacoma, WA 98404; (253)597-6200. From I-5, take exit 135. Open 9am–3pm, weekdays.

Medicine Creek College: *Native Art and Culture Classes*

Familiarize yourself with Native culture by taking **BASKET-MAKING OR BEADWORK CLASSES** at the Puyallup Tribe's Medicine Creek College, a 2-year community college open to the public. The school emphasizes outreach to other tribes and non–Native people. More than 28 tribes are represented in the student body. Curriculum includes art classes **TAUGHT BY NATIVE ARTISTS** from throughout the Northwest region. "We want the students to see the differences in art from other areas," says college president Kay Rhoads. "For example, each region made their baskets a little differently. We want our students to appreciate them all."

Medicine Creek College, 2002 E 28th St, Bldg 18, Tacoma, WA 98404; (253)593-0171.

Puyallup Fish Hatchery: *Tribally Sponsored Habitat Restoration*

The Puyallup received monies and land in a 1990 settlement, which also gave them more clout in demanding **ENVIRONMENTAL CLEANUP** of the Puyallup River watershed, degraded by industrial waste, hydroelectric dams, and flood–control projects. The terms of the agreement stated that local governments must take steps to modify their land-use plans to protect fish habitat, and that land traded by the Port of Tacoma in lieu of cash had to be decontaminated before the tribe would accept it. Monies from the settlement and other sources also have funded a number of fisheries habitat restoration projects. The hydroelectric Electron Dam has blocked 26 miles of fish-spawning habitat on the Puyallup River since 1904. In their settlement with the electric company that owns the dam, the tribe has built a downstream fish bypass for smolt, is building a fish ladder, and has installed acclimation ponds for coho and chinook salmon above the dam. The tribe has also worked with the U.S. Forest Service in a cooperative project to restore a wild run of spring chinook to the White River, up to 1,200 returning salmon from a low of 10 fish in the mid-1980s. Stop for a tour at the **TRIBE'S FISH HATCHERY** and ask for their site restoration catalog—a wish list of locations, such as Oxbow Lake and remnant wetlands, along the rivers the tribe would like to see restored.

Puyallup Fish Hatchery, 6824 Pioneer Wy, Puyallup, WA 98371; (253)573-7926. Open 8am–5pm, weekdays, year-round. Tours. Call first.

Jack Curtright and Sons: *Tribal Art*

Gallery owner Jack Curtright's father and paternal grandmother were Jamestown S'Klallam tribal members. Curtright remembers going to tribal meetings with his father when he was a kid, and he also remembers his grandmother's stories about her years in a Catholic orphanage and at the old Indian boarding school between Milton and Fife. Most of the items in his shop are **NATIVE ANTIQUITIES**—Haida argillite carvings; Inupiat ivory carving and scrimshaw; Plains beadwork; a large inventory of handwoven baskets from the Northwest, California, and Arizona; and historical photos.

Curtright and Sons Tribal Art, 759 St Helens Ave, Tacoma, WA 98405; (253)383-2969; jcurtri286@aol.com. Call for hours.

Chinook Landing: *Tribally Owned Marina*

In 1993 the Puyallup Tribe built the 219-slip Chinook Landing Marina on the south shore of Commencement Bay to accommodate **TRIBAL FISHERS** as well as the public. The facility includes a convenience store, 24-hour security, pump-out station, electricity, shower, and laundry. Guest moorage is available. Waterfront restaurants are a short drive away. There are no lift, launch, or fuel facilities.

Chinook Landing Marina, 3702 Marine View Dr, Tacoma, WA 98422; (253)627-7676.

Auburn: *Muckleshoot Tribe*

The Muckleshoot Tribe consists of **DESCENDANTS OF BANDS** who once occupied the Puyallup and Kent Valleys, located between the northern flanks of Mount Rainier and the shores of Lake Washington. Bands lived in villages along parts of the Black, Carbon, Cedar, Green, Puyallup, Stuck, and White Rivers—all of which originate in the Cascade Mountains and flow into Puget Sound, and all of which were once rich with salmon. Ancestral hunting, fishing, and gathering grounds included much of modern King, Pierce, and Snohomish Counties, including areas in what is now Seattle.

The Muckleshoot have occupied this abundant ecosystem for about **9,000 YEARS**, probably since the recession of the last sheet of glacial ice that once covered Puget Sound. The bands called themselves by such names as the Skopamish, Smulkamish, Stkamish, Tkwakwamish, and Yilalkomish, and had in common a dialect of the Coast Salish language. They were active traders with inland tribes through well-used trail systems crossing over the Cascade Mountains.

Throughout the early and mid-1800s, white settlers rushed to claim the fertile farmland of the Kent and Puyallup Valleys. They were assisted by the Hudson's Bay Company's Puget Sound Agricultural Company, located in the Nisqually Delta and at Fort Vancouver on the Columbia River. When veins of coal and other minerals were discovered in the Black Diamond, Enumclaw, and Renton triangle in the mid-nineteenth century, European immigrants moved into company towns to work in the mines.

During the 1800s, Northwest tribes were forced to move to small reservations, relinquishing their vast territory for settlers to claim. The bands around Puget Sound fought together in armed resistance in what are now known as the Puget Sound Indian Wars. Ancestors of today's Muckleshoots played an active role in resistance. Defeated, however, they were relocated to the small **MUCKLESHOOT RESERVATION** set aside pursuant to the treaties of Point Elliott and Medicine Creek, which were signed in the mid-1850s.

The reservation, between the Green and Black Rivers, is located on and named after the site of **ONE OF THE LARGEST ORIGINAL VILLAGES**, the Muckleshoot Prairie, near the present-day town of Auburn. As more settlers and industrialists moved into the Seattle region, landless Native peoples such as the Duwamish and the Snoqualmie moved to the Muckleshoot Reservation, along with people from such federally recognized tribes as the Tulalip and the Suquamish.

In recent history one of the most protracted and determined battles the Muckleshoot and other Northwest tribes have fought is for recognition of their inherent rights as the original peoples of the Puget Sound and the Strait of Juan de Fuca ecosystem. In particular, they have fought to claim the fishing rights explicitly guaranteed in nineteenth-century treaties. Their struggles culminated in what were called the Fish Wars of 1960 and 1970. The resulting **BOLDT DECISION** gave the tribes the right to claim their share of the state-allotted fish quota and the opportunity to serve as comanagers of regional salmon resources.

Vi Hilbert, an Upper Skagit tribal member who has lectured throughout the world, is one of only a few fluent Lushootseed speakers alive today. She started Lushootseed Research, a nonprofit organization with the mission to teach, preserve, and archive the language and literature of the Puget Salish tribes.

Today the Muckleshoot's 6-square-mile reservation consists of several diamond-shaped land parcels strung along Highway 164, between Enumclaw and Auburn. The Muckleshoot Tribe, like its neighboring Puyallup Tribe, sits in one of the Northwest's most rapidly developing urban areas. A proposed performing arts amphitheater is currently going through the county review process; a retail mall has been constructed, and the tribe is considering other practical means, such as light manufacturing, to provide employment for its members.

For more information about the Muckleshoot Tribe, visit their Web site at www.muckleshoot.nsn.us.

Seattle: *Suquamish and Duwamish Tribes*

The city of Seattle is named after the famous orator **CHIEF SEATTLE**, son of a Duwamish mother (Scholitza) and Suquamish father (Schweabe). The Duwamish Indians were Lushootseed speakers, as were the other Coast Salish Bands who lived on the eastern shores of Puget Sound.

Seattle is built on the **CEDED LANDS** of the Suquamish and the Duwamish Indian Tribes, who shared Seattle's waterfront. The Duwamish were primarily freshwater-oriented, living in settlements along the lower reaches of the Duwamish River, Elliott Bay, and the land around Lake Washington, including present-day Bellevue. Traces of winter longhouses have been found along the former channel of what was the Black River (which no longer exists), in the city of Renton.

According to Mary Lou Slaughter, a descendant of Chief Seattle and member of the Duwamish Tribe, during the Indian Wars of 1855–56, with no treaty in place, most Duwamish were relocated from their homes to various reservations. Many returned to the sites of their **ORIGINAL WINTER VILLAGES** near the then small city of Seattle, most often finding employment as domestics and laborers. During the 1860s and 1870s traditional living areas along the city's waterfront were backfilled for development, and the Indians were displaced again. One spot they found was called Ballast Island, an artificial island created from ships' ballast dumped onto the waterfront, at the intersection of what is today First Avenue and Washington Street.

In the late 1800s the Duwamish worked in local mills and looked for whatever niche they could find to survive in the new cash economy—selling firewood, clams, and woven baskets. (It was in this period that photographer **EDWARD S. CURTIS**, whose studio was in what is now called the Pioneer Square area, asked Chief Seattle's daughter Kick-is-om-lo, or, as whites called her, Princess Angeline, her hair wrapped in a printed scarf, to sit for her now well-known portrait.) Today about

One of Chief Seattle's descendants is Duwamish weaver and public speaker Mary Lou Slaughter (Sla 'Da), who lives in Port Orchard. Born to a Duwamish mother and Swedish father, her great-great-grandmother was Mary Talasia, the daughter of Princess Angeline. Slaughter remembers being taunted, whooped at, and spit on as a younger girl when classmates discovered she was Indian. She did not embrace her Indian heritage until years later, when she picked up an eagle feather on the beach and felt a jolt of awareness. Slaughter took basket-weaving classes from Tsimshian weaver Loa Ryan, Suquamish weaver Ed Carrier, and others. For a current list of where her work is exhibited or to make an appointment with the artist, call (360)876-6271; slaughter@wvin.com.

450 people can trace their lineage to **DUWAMISH ANCESTORS**. The Duwamish have no reservation and no formal relationship with the federal government.

Seattle's major institutions, like those of other Northwest metropolitan cities, reflect very little of the city's original Coast Salish heritage. Except for an exhibit about **LUSHOOTSEED LANGUAGE** at the University of Washington, most collections and public art purchases have been focused on the colorful art of more northerly tribes, those in British Columbia and Southeast Alaska. Likewise, most of the carved totems adorning Seattle, the Native art in the galleries, and the Native collections displayed in the city's major museums are not Coast Salish, but Haida, Kwakwaka'wakw, Nuu-chah-nulth, Tlingit, and Tsimshian of Canada and Southeast Alaska. In shops you'll also find a lot of Alaska Native stone and ivory carving from the Arctic. Even Tillicum Village, a major tourist attraction located on a former Suquamish fishing camp on Puget Sound's Blake Island, offers entertainment based primarily on Southeast Alaska and northern British Columbia tradition. Why? One reason is that Seattle, with its train routes to the east and enormous shipping port on the waterfront, has been the North American gateway to and from ice-locked Alaska ever since the Alaska gold rush in the 1800s. The souvenir trade of Native Alaskan art and trinkets has been ongoing in Seattle for more than 100 years.

Just because Seattle hasn't trumpeted its Coast Salish heritage doesn't mean there isn't an enormous underground wealth of knowledge. To learn more about the region's Salish history, visit the Northwest Manuscript Collection on the second floor of the Suzzallo Library, University of Washington, (206)543-1879.

Today more than 26,000 Native Americans live in the Seattle metropolitan area: a third are Alaska Natives; a large majority are from tribes throughout the Puget Sound region and Eastern Washington. The best place to meet the descendants of Seattle's Duwamish and Suquamish Tribes is on the **SUQUAMISH RESERVATION**, about 45 minutes from downtown Seattle. There you can visit the Suquamish Tribal Center and Museum and Chief Seattle's grave in the old churchyard in Suquamish (see the Suquamish section in this chapter). You might also want to meet Duwamish basketmaker Mary Lou Slaughter, a **GREAT-GRANDDAUGHTER OF CHIEF SEATTLE** (fourth generation), living and working in her Port Orchard studio, across Puget Sound from Seattle. The more subtle and equally lovely Coast Salish art has at long last become visible to the general public, thanks to contemporary artists such as Susan Point (Musqueam), Pete Peterson and Andy Wilbur (Skokomish), and Ed Carriere (Suquamish), all of whom display their art in various Seattle galleries.

Daybreak Star Indian Cultural Center

Daybreak Star Indian Cultural Center, located in Discovery Park north of downtown Seattle, is named after a vision that came to Oglala Sioux holy man Black Elk more than 100 years ago: "I saw the daybreak star falling far and when it struck the earth, it rooted and grew and flowered, four blossoms on one stem." The center is divided into four wings, in observance of the four blossoms, the four directions, and the four races of humankind.

Built in Seattle's Discovery Park, on 20 acres overlooking Puget Sound, Daybreak Star is a Northwest Native American Grand Central Station, coordinating **SOCIAL SERVICES AND EVENTS FOR INDI-ANS** living in the metropolitan area. The exterior of the concrete and cedar shake building is modest. But inside, among massive lodgepoles donated by the Colville Tribe, is a permanent collection of **NATIVE ART** by some of the country's most esteemed Indian artists, including Chippewa artist George Morrison, Caddo-Kiowa painter T. C. Cannon, and Aleut sculptor John Hoover. An entire wall is carved and painted in the style of a **TLINGIT HOUSESCREEN** by famed Tlingit artist Nathan P. Jackson. Self-guided pamphlets explaining the building's art collection are available at the door, and the center's Sacred Circle Gallery staff also lead narrated tours (see the Sacred Circle Gallery listing in this section).

Indian dinner theater, featuring fresh salmon and authentic **NATIVE DRUMMING, DANCING, AND SINGING**, is available for groups of 100 or more, by advance reservation.

One of the largest **INTERTRIBAL POWWOWS** in the Northwest, the annual Seafair Indian Days Pow Wow, held in July on the grounds of the Daybreak Center, draws up to 500 dancers and 15,000 spectators, with salmon bakes, arts and crafts, and food concessions. Grandstands and powwow grounds are adjacent to an alder grove behind the center.

Daybreak Star Indian Cultural Center, United Indians of All Tribes Foundation, Discovery Park, W Government Wy at 36th Ave, PO Box 99253, Seattle, WA 98199; (206)285-4425. Take Elliott Ave west from downtown Seattle to Emerson St (south of the Ballard Bridge), turn west on Commodore Wy, and follow signs to Daybreak Star. Open 10am–5pm, Mon–Sat; Sun afternoons. Free.

Sacred Circle Gallery: *Contemporary Native Art*

The Sacred Circle Gallery at Daybreak Star Indian Cultural Center in Discovery Park is on the cutting edge of **CONTEMPORARY INDIAN ART**. It hosts traveling exhibitions throughout the year that are often provocative, sometimes deeply disturbing, and always first-rate. Director and curator Steve Charles has proven to be a powerful force in bringing contemporary Native art to Seattle. The gallery draws internationally exhibited artists from throughout the Northern hemisphere, such as Conrad House (Navaho artist), James Lavadour (Umatilla painter and founder of the Crow's Shadow Institute), Juane Quick-to-See Smith (Salish activist), and Edward Poitras (Canadian Metis installation artist).

Group shows address such issues as the ramifications of colonialization and the commodification of Native spiritual and cultural life by mainstream Western media. Traditional art reworked in new media, such as glass and steel, is often showcased. Receptions for the artists feature performing artists such as the Cape Fox Dancers (Tlingit), the Bering Sea Heritage Dancers, and others.

Sacred Circle Gallery, Daybreak Star Indian Cultural Center, Discovery Park, W Government Wy at 36th Ave, PO Box 99253, Seattle, WA 98199; (206)285-4425. Take Elliott Ave west from downtown Seattle to Emerson St (south of the Ballard Bridge), turn west on Commodore Wy, and follow signs to Daybreak Star. Open 10am–5pm;, Mon–Sat; Sun afternoons.

EDWARD S. CURTIS PHOTOGRAPHY

Best known for his turn-of-the-century North American Indian images, photographer Edward S. Curtis's original studio was located in what is now Seattle's historic Pioneer Square district. One of his first portraits was of Princess Angeline, daughter of Chief Seattle, digging clams on the Seattle waterfront. In 1899 he was the official photographer on a scientific expedition to the Bering Sea and coastal Alaska with naturalist John Muir. Curtis photographed Chief Joseph and other great Indian leaders in the late 1800s. After Joseph's death, Curtis attended the Joseph Potlatch, at Nespelem, where Joseph had been exiled on the Colville Reservation in Eastern Washington. His 20-volume, 2,500-image masterwork The North American Indian, was financed in part by industrialist J. P. Morgan and took nearly 30 years to complete. Costing nearly $1 million to produce, the collection was limited to 500 sets and priced at $3,000. Determined to preserve what he mistook for the vanishing race, Curtis staged many of his portraits—taken more than 80 years after white contact—with props, including wigs and such clothing as cedar-bark capes that were no longer worn. He carried these items with him in several oversized trunks.

Seattle Native Art Galleries

FLURY & COMPANY sells original photographic works by Edward S. Curtis, including vintage silver and platinum print photographs, goldtones, and vintage photogravures from Curtis's 20-volume masterwork, *The North American Indian*. Adjacent is Flury's Jackson Street Gallery, (206)447-0102, selling Indian antiquities dated from the mid-1800s to 1960. (Flury & Company, 322 1st Ave S, Seattle, WA 98104; (206)587-0260.)

THE LEGACY, specializing in historic and contemporary Indian and Eskimo Art since 1933, is one of Seattle's best sources for authentic Native arts. The gallery showcases the work of British Columbia's Hunt family (more than 34 family members are totem and mask carvers, printmakers, and jewelers), Andy Wilbur (Skokomish) and Greg Colfax (Makah). Owner Mardonna Austin-McKillop knows her artists personally; she also buys contemporary work from the now grown children of the Native artists the gallery represented in the 1970s. (The Legacy, 1003 1st Ave, Seattle, WA 98104; (206)624-6350.)

THE SNOW GOOSE carries the work of more than 200 Native artists, mostly Canadian Inuit and Alaska Inupiat and Yup'ik carvers of ivory, whalebone, and soapstone. Also look for work by Northwest artists such as Warm Springs basket weaver Pat Courtney Gold and Inupiat sculptor Lawrence Ulaaq, who lives in Suquamish. (The Snow Goose, 8806 Roosevelt Wy NE, Seattle; WA 98115; (206)523-6223.)

THE STONINGTON GALLERY carries monumental art such as totem poles carved by the top Northwest Coast carvers and regional Native artists, including Robert Davidson, John Hoover, George Hunt Jr., Tony Hunt Jr., Joe David, and Susan A. Point, as well as Alaska Native artists such as Thomas Stream and Melvin Olanna. There are frequent one-person shows and artist lectures throughout the year. Non-Native carvers working in the Northwest Coast tradition, such as Bill Holm, Steve Brown, and Duane Pasco, are also represented. (The Stonington Gallery, 119 S Jackson St, Seattle, WA 98104; (206)405-4040. In Pioneer Square between First and Occidental.)

The **JEFFREY MOOSE GALLERY** shows the work of Larry Ulaaq Ahvakana, an Inupiat sculptor whose studio is on the Suquamish Reservation. (The Jeffrey Moose Gallery, 1333 5th Ave, Rainier Square, Seattle, WA 98101; (206)467-6951.)

BEN MARRA STUDIO carries Marra's dazzling formal portraits of Native dancers. For the past decade, Marra has taken such portraits in a makeshift studio he sets up adjacent to powwow arenas throughout the West. Signed copies of Marra's calendars and his book, *Powwow: Images Along the Red Road* (Abrams, 1997) are available through his Pioneer Square studio in the historic Globe Building, just a few blocks from the studio where Edward S. Curtis produced some of his finest portraits of Native Americans in the past century. (Ben Marra Studio, 105 S Main, Ste 333, Seattle, WA 98104; (206)624-7344; www.halcyon.com/benmarra/.)

Boxley and Vanderhoop Studios: Tsimshian and Tlingit Art

Artist David Boxley (Tsimshian) carves **TOTEMIC ART** and teaches apprentices in his Kingston studio 45 minutes northwest of Seattle on the Kitsap Peninsula. Boxley is also the leader of Tsimshian Haayuuk, one of the most dynamic Native dance groups in the region. The dancers use huge resonant box drums and enormous masks. Evelyn Vanderhoop (Tlingit) is one of a handful of weavers making **CHILKAT TAPESTRY ROBES**; she demonstrates her work throughout the region.

Boxley is usually at his studio unless he's working on a commissioned piece on site. In 1998, when he carved a 30-foot Raven story pole at the Canadian Pavilion in Epcot Center, Florida (carving a hidden Mickey Mouse into the pole).

Other commissions have included a totem erected at Port Ludlow on the Olympic Peninsula (this one includes a man holding a cell phone), and working as a consultant with four carvers to create a dazzling Killer Whale housescreen and four totem poles for the Port Gamble S'Klallam Tribe's longhouse on the Kitsap Peninsula.

David Boxley and Evelyn Vanderhoop; by appointment only through the Snow Goose Gallery, Seattle; (206)523-6223.

Shotridge Studios: Tlingit Totem Carver

Israel Shotridge has carved a number of **TOTEM POLES** that now stand throughout Southeast Alaska. Shotridge is of the Brown Bear clan (Teikweidee Taantakwan). His Tlingit clan name, "Kinstaadadl," means "the bear who is standing up." Named by the Alaska State Council on the Arts as a **MASTER IN ARTS** of Carving and Engraving, Israel Shotridge carved the 55-foot replica of the **CHIEF KYAN POLE** that stands in downtown Ketchikan. One of his recent commissions was to carve a house post on site for a clan house in a Native American theme park near Vienna, Austria.

Today Shotridge's home and studio, where he carves commissioned artwork, is on the south end of Vashon Island, about a 25-minute ferry ride from West Seattle. Visitors to the studio can easily while away an hour, watching Shotridge and his apprentices carve while sipping a cup of fragrant herbal Hudson's Bay tea, or settling into a chair to view a video made for public television about Shotridge's mother, Esther Shea, an elder of the Tongass Bear clan. Shotridge and his wife, Sue, also offer **NATIVE ARTS WEEKEND WORK-SHOPS** at their studio.

Shotridge Studios, PO Box 2508, Vashon, WA, 98070; (206)463-7677; www.shotridgestu-dios.com. Take the Fauntleroy ferry from West Seattle to Vashon Island, follow the main road to Dockton on the south end of the island. By appointment only, afternoons and evenings.

Marvin Oliver Gallery: *Northwest Coast Art On-Line*

Native artist Marvin Oliver's monumental metal, bronze, glass, and wood sculpture, and framed, embossed serigraphs are now sold on-line. He closed his Fremont Gallery in 1999 after the birth of his son Owen. **DIRECTOR OF INDIAN STUDIES** at the University of Washington, curator of contemporary Native American art at the Burke Museum, and an educator at the University of Alaska in Ketchikan, Oliver presents new forms of **TRADITIONAL NORTHWEST COAST ART**. Considered one of the region's foremost sculptors and print-makers, Oliver (of Quinault and Isleta Pueblo heritage), fuses ancient forms with modern aesthetics. For example, his bronze–cast towering, **STYLIZED WHALE FINS** and his cedar totem poles have been installed throughout Canada, Japan, and the United States. Check his Web site for more affordable art, such as his series of handsome wool blankets based on several of his serigraphs and woven by Pendleton Woolen Mills. There are also gold-foil embossed cards, stationery, and other items, such as a white stationery box embossed with leaping salmon, with a graceful paper Salish canoe perched on top. Also look for embroidered sportswear and tote bags.

Marvin Oliver Gallery, www.marvinoliver.com. For commissioned art, call (206)633-2468.

Betty David Studio: *Spokane Tribe Clothing Designer*

Clothing designer Betty David, an enrolled member of the Spokane Tribe, makes high fashion and impeccably **TAILORED SHEARLING JACKETS** using soft Icelandic lamb suede and finished leathers. The jackets are imprinted with **NATIVE AMERICAN IMAGES**, including horses, handprints, adaptations of Northwest Coast clan designs, and tattoos. Jackets are custom made to fit, in both adult and children's sizes. Clothing is available at David's downtown Seattle studio.

Betty David Studio, 105 S Main, Seattle, WA 98104; (206)624-7666; www.bettydavid.com. By appointment only.

Burke Museum of Natural History and Culture: *Northwest Coast Art and Artifacts*

Located on the University of Washington campus north of downtown Seattle, the Burke Museum is a treasure trove of **NORTHWEST COAST SALISH ART**, with some of its most dedicated proponents, such as author and carving teacher Bill Holm and Marvin Oliver (Quinault), on the museum's staff. Many budding anthropologists and traditional artists have cut their teeth in the archives of this museum. The **NORTHWEST ARTIFACT COLLECTION**, which is one of the largest in the United States, is part of the museum's 3-million-piece collection. Upstairs are rotating exhibits and a hands-on walk through **NORTHWEST NATURAL HISTORY**. Downstairs, in the permanent **PACIFIC VOICES EXHIBIT**, artifacts are combined with videotapes of people from around the Pacific Rim speaking about their cultures, illustrating the diversity of 18 regional cultures.

Ongoing is a project to put on videodisc and catalog 25,000 slides of Northwest Coast artifacts that currently reside in more than 200 museums and 100 private collections worldwide. For example, one videodisc shows both front and back views of more than 80 Plateau cornhusk bags from the Burke collection, describing when the bags were made, where they were collected, what materials were used, and other useful information. The museum frequently sponsors **EVENTS, LECTURES, AND TOURS**, such as a weeklong tour of Haida Gwaii (the Queen Charlotte Islands) with Robin Wright, museum curator of Native American art.

The museum's impressive gift shop carries a large selection of books on **PACIFIC NORTHWEST CULTURE, ART, AND NATURAL HISTORY**. Keep an eye out for original art pieces by Northwest Coast artists, such as masks. Sold through the gift shop, most masks are purchased as soon as they are displayed.

Burke Museum of Natural History and Culture, University of Washington, PO Box 353010, Seattle, WA 98195; (206)543-5590; www.washington.edu/burkemuseum. On the northwestern corner of the UW campus at NE 45th St and 17th Ave. Park on campus. Admission fee. Open 10am–5pm, daily. Gift shop and cafe.

Seattle Art Museum: *Native American Collections*

The Native American exhibits of the Seattle Art Museum are based on the collection of John H. Hauberg, who spent four decades collecting **INDIAN MASKS, SCULPTURE, TEXTILES, AND HOUSEHOLD OBJECTS** from the northern tip of Washington to Southeast Alaska.

A Tlingit screen depicting Raven highlights a favorite tribal story told from the coastal areas of Washington to Alaska. Haida art, from British Columbia's Queen Charlotte Islands, is represented in a small

group of jet black argillite carvings from the nineteenth and twentieth centuries, including works by Haida master carver and jeweler
Charles Edensaw. Four elaborately carved full-scale interior house
posts, carved by Arthur Shaughnessy around 1907, as well as Makah
masks and ceremonial regalia, are part of the collection.

Another gallery showcases fiber arts of Northwest Coastal
weavers (primarily women), who used mountain goat and dog wool,
cedar bark, spruce roots, and other plant fibers in their weaving.

The museum uses Native language terms whenever possible to
help illuminate their creators' sense of the objects' identity. Native
scholars and writers work with the museum to provide authoritative
interpretation for the exhibits. The interactive computer-audio installation in the performance gallery allows visitors to hear **TRADITIONAL
SONGS, ORATORY, AND STORYTELLING** in a sampling of various
Native languages.

*The Spirit Within: Northwest Coast Native Art from the John H.
Hauberg Collection* (Seattle Art Museum, 1995), a 304-page volume
with full-color photos and essays by contemporary Haida carver
Robert Davidson and Tlingit poet and writer Nora Dauenhauer, is
available in the museum gift shop.

*Seattle Art Museum, 100 University St, Seattle, WA 98122; (206)654-3100; www.seat-
tleartmuseum.org. Downtown, between 1st and 2nd Aves, 2 blocks south of the Pike Place
Market. Admission fee. Open Tues–Sun, year-round. Gift shop, cafe, library.*

Museum of History and Industry: *Indian Exhibits*

This museum, located near the University of Washington, owns one
of the Northwest's largest historic photo collections and is one of the
largest private heritage organizations in the state. It has a permanent
exhibit about the importance of salmon to the Pacific Northwest, and
from time to time it carries exhibits about **NATIVE AMERICAN
REGIONAL HISTORY**.

*Museum of History and Industry, 2700 24th Ave E, Seattle, WA 98112-2099; (206)324-
1126. Admission fee.*

Tillicum Village: *Longhouse-Style Performance Center*

Boats leave daily from Piers 55 and 56 in Seattle for lunch and dinner theater at Tillicum Village, a longhouse-style performance center
built on the northern point of **BLAKE ISLAND** in Puget Sound. All
473 acres of tree-covered Blake Island, an ancestral fishing camp of
the Suquamish Indians, are now a state park with views of the
Olympic and Cascade Mountains and towering Mount Rainier.

The boat ride to Blake Island takes about an hour. Native people, costumed in the **TRADITIONAL BLUE AND RED BUTTON CAPES** and headpieces worn by tribes in Southeast Alaska, British Columbia, and Puget Sound, greet passengers with cups of **STEAMING CLAM BROTH** on the walkway to the longhouse. Inside, diners line up at the buffet to load up plates with **FRESH SALMON**, new potatoes, salad, and warm bread. Salmon is cooked in the traditional style on alder skewers in front of open fire pits. After everyone is seated, **"DANCE ON THE WIND,"** a choreographed stage performance showcasing legends, masked dancing, and song, begins with a drumbeat.

Tillicum Village was the brainchild of restaurateur Bill Hewitt in the early 1970s. A Boy Scout leader at the time, Hewitt was looking for a way to combine traditionally prepared fresh salmon and Indian crafts with Boy Scout "Indian" dancing. This dancing was all the rage in the 1950s and 1960s, when mostly non–Native Boy Scouts competed nationally for dance titles. Over the years this dancing and the attraction itself has become more authentically Native. Today, Tillicum Village hires Native staff to manage, greet visitors, cook, and perform in the stage show. The attraction reflects mostly Southeast Alaska, British Columbia, and Northwest Coast art and tradition.

Tillicum Village and Tours, Inc, 2200 6th Ave, Ste 804, Seattle, WA 98121; (206)443-1244. Call for a schedule, reservations, and brochures. Ticket stands are on the Seattle waterfront between Piers 55 and 56. Boats leave twice a day almost year-round; tours are 4 hours long. Adults $55; children 5–12, $22.

Annual Salmon Homecoming Festival:
Affirming Native Beliefs

In 1999 more than 30,000 people congregated at Seattle's Waterfront Park, Pier 62/63, and at the Seattle Aquarium for the eighth annual Salmon Homecoming—a celebration of salmon and a tribute to life and the Native American belief that all things are connected. The three-day event honors the cultural, spiritual, and economic significance of salmon to the Northwest through **NATIVE MUSIC, DANCE, AND ART**, a potlatch-style gathering, canoe ceremonies, storytelling, a powwow, and a 3½-mile "salmon run." Inside the Seattle Aquarium, there's an educational salmon forum, kid's corner, a salmon habitat exhibit, and opportunities for involvement in hands-on Northwest watershed restoration projects. Sponsored by the Indian Tribes of the Pacific Northwest, the Seattle Aquarium, the City of Seattle, the Northwest Indian Fisheries Commission, the Seattle Aquarium Society, and corporate sponsors such as the *Seattle Times*, the annual event kicks off a coastwide commitment to saving the salmon, now included on the endangered species list.

The Annual Salmon Homecoming Festival occurs in late summer (Aug or Sept) on Seattle's waterfront at Pier 62/63, Waterfront Park, and at the Seattle Aquarium, located side by side on Alaskan Wy. Free; donations accepted. For dates and a schedule of events, contact the Seattle Aquarium, 1483 Alaskan Wy, Pier 59, Seattle, WA 98101; (206)386-4320; or Northwest Indian Fisheries Commission, 6730 Martin Wy E, Olympia, WA 98506; (360)438-1180.

Marysville: *Tulalip Tribes*

The Tulalip Tribe's ancestral home, Hebolb, is at the mouth of the Snohomish River. The present-day Tulalip Tribe is a confederation of tribes from the northern Puget Sound area. The 22,000-acre **TULALIP RESERVATION**, once home of one of the largest Indian boarding schools in the Puget Sound area, is adjacent to Everett. The mostly undeveloped reservation possesses areas of cultural and spiritual significance, scenic views, magnificent waterfront, and freshwater streams and lakes. The Tulalips' location next to the major metropolis and sprawling developments of Everett poses a headache similar to that with which many tribes in the Puget Sound region must contend.

As the metropolis expands and develops, wildlife—such as bears and cougars—flees to the reservation's undeveloped lands. To protect the sensitive areas and watershed, the tribe limits development by tribal members living on the reservation to one house per 80 acres.

Some of the reservation's most **SENSITIVE WETLANDS**, watershed, and woodlands are now owned by non-Indians, however; about 55 percent of the reservation, in fact. The tribe has no zoning jurisdiction over development of non-Indian-owned lands within their reservation (according to a 1989 U.S. Supreme Court ruling that forbids any tribes from having such zoning authority). At press time, the City of Everett was planning to build a 395-unit housing development and two golf courses on 906 acres of woodlands on the reservation. Everett bought the land for $2.4 million from Unocal, an oil company that purchased the land in the 1950s from the tribe. (The tribe sold it to Unocal only because the oil company promised to build a refinery on the land, which would have provided desperately needed jobs for tribal members. After the company purchased the land, however, they scuttled the deal.) Without the power to enforce zoning laws on the land, the tribe can only try to raise enough money, perhaps with casino revenues, to buy back its land to protect fish habitat and conserve open space. See the Tulalip Tribes Web site at www.tulalip tribes.com and tulalip.nsn.us/.

Tulalip Museum: *Work in Progress*

In 1988 the Tulalip carved their FIRST TRADITIONAL CANOE in more than 100 years. Made of a single cedar trunk, it holds 20 people and more than a ton of cargo and is paddled with the aid of a sail woven of cedar or tule reeds. The canoe, stored in the tribe's CARVING SHED, is part of a small exhibit of PHOTOMURALS, CARVINGS, TOTEMS, BASKETS, AND BLANKETS, all housed in one of a group of modules. This little exhibit has attracted members of the British Parliament and a delegation from Nigeria, among other high-profile visitors. When a new museum building is completed, the tribe will be able to display ceremonial items long absent from view. Plans include a boardwalk into adjoining wetlands where tribal members gather traditional basket-weaving materials. Be sure to ask to see the tribe's Lushootseed language videos.

Tulalip Museum, 6410 Ave NE, Marysville, WA 98271; (360)651-4000. Open weekdays, year-round. Call in advance for tours. Admission is by donation. All proceeds go to the new museum building fund.

Tulalip Fish Hatchery and Stream Restoration

Catching spawning salmon in fish ladders and broomstick weirs in March and May, the Tulalip Fish Hatchery raises and releases more than a million coho, a million chinook, and 4 million chum salmon each year. The hatchery is a few miles inland from Tulalip Bay. Protection of these salmon resources and their watershed is the priority for the tribe. INDIAN-MANAGED FISH HATCHERIES are among the best places to visit on reservations, and this one is no exception. Visitors are welcome; large groups are asked to make arrangements in advance.

Tulalip Fish Hatchery, 10610 Waterworks Rd, Marysville, WA 98270; (360)651-4550. Located a few miles from Tulalip Bay, at the confluence of Battle Creek and Tulalip Creek. Open weekdays, year-round. Free.

Historic St. Anne's Roman Catholic Church: *Tulalip Congregation*

On the National Register of Historic Places, St. Anne's, a white, LATE-VICTORIAN GOTHIC-STYLE CHURCH, overlooks Tulalip Bay. Built in 1867 in a cedar grove, the original church burned down in 1902 and was replaced in 1904. A statue of the Virgin brought from France was rescued from the fire and still stands in the church today. Most of the congregation are Tulalip tribal members; Natives and non-Natives alike are welcome to attend Sunday services.

St. Anne's Roman Catholic Church, Mission Beach Rd, Marysville, WA 98271. Worship service times are posted on the church door.

Indian Shaker Church: *Preserving History*

Although it's on the National Register of Historic Places, the inside of this site is not open to the public except during services, but its outside is also interesting. This active church was built in 1924 (the sign says "1910" because that's the date the government sanctioned the Indian Shakers as a bona fide religion) and is one of the **BEST-PRESERVED CHURCHES** in the region. When an episode of the TV show *Northern Exposure* was filmed here in the early 1990s, the film company put a new roof on the building and reinforced the steeple as a gift to the church membership.

Indian Shaker Church, N Meridian Ave, Marysville, WA 98271. From Marysville, pass the casino and go west on Marine Dr about 2½ miles to N Meridian; turn right (the sign may say Shaker Creek Rd) about ½ mile.

La Conner: *Swinomish Tribe*

The picturesque little town of La Conner, located north of Seattle and built on the east bank of the Swinomish Channel, was first a trading post, founded in 1867 by John Conner before railroads came to Washington. The town's historic waterfront is as picturesque as it gets. Its small shops and restaurants are a favorite tourist destination, especially in the spring when the adjacent Skagit Valley tulip and daffodil fields are in full bloom.

Across the narrow channel from La Conner, on Fidalgo Island, is the **SWINOMISH RESERVATION**, home to the descendants of the four tribes who lived in what are now the lower Skagit River valley, coastline, and estuary. Their 7,000-acre reservation was assured by executive order in 1873.

Throughout the early and mid-1800s, the Swinomish traded with Russian and British traders who arrived in the area in the 1830s. It's estimated that 85 percent of the Native population died from ensuing smallpox epidemics. La-hail-by, son of Huah-le-tsa ("He of the Magic Robe") was one of the few who survived to carry on the religious practices of the Swinomish longhouse. La-hail-by became known as "The Prophet."

On the reservation's small Swinomish dock is a carved eagle totem and a wooden cross. Each year when the salmon return, Indian fishers gather there for the blessing of the fleet. The public is welcome to attend. For information, call the Swinomish Indian Tribal Community, (360)466-3163.

The Swinomish Reservation can be reached by crossing the Rainbow Bridge (named for its bow shape), which connects La Conner and the Swinomish Reservation at the south end of La Conner.

In La Conner the Swinomish Tribe owns a small **OPEN-AIR MARKET** on a waterfront pier, where you can buy smoked salmon and a seafood lunch and sit at picnic tables overlooking the channel and the reservation's undeveloped beach. Below the pier are a fishing dock and a couple of spots for boaters to tie up. The Kikallious, Lower Skagit, Samish, and Swinomish Tribes were (and still are) primarily commercial fishers.

Years ago, the Swinomish used a number of methods to fish: drift netting and tidal traps, weirs, hook-and-line troll fishing, gill nets, trawl nets, beach seines, dip nets, harpoons, leisters, and gaff-hooks. Nets longer than 100 feet, made of nettle fibers, were used to trap ducks. Deer were hunted on what is now Whidbey Island. Seals, sea lions, and other marine mammals were taken in the exposed reefs and rocky headlands. Beaver, muskrat, otter, mink, elk, and bear were hunted in the fall. The meat was used fresh or was dried for storage. Traditional homes were large cedar buildings up to 1,000 feet long that housed several extended families.

In winter the village community gathered in longhouses around the fire pits, with smoke rising through holes in the roof. Benches surrounded the fire, serving as seats by day and beds by night. During mild summers temporary camps were constructed, some with A-framed structures made of woven cattail mats called wickiups.

Swinomish Smokehouse: *Practicing Traditional Religion*

There's a special silence found only in churches and other sanctuaries, such as the Swinomish Smokehouse, located on the reservation, right across the channel from La Conner. As you walk through the large wooden doors hand-carved with eagles, the sounds of youngsters playing baseball in the field below are left behind. All you can hear is the rustle of wings from birds perched on beams high overhead. The Swinomish practice their traditional religion in this **200-FOOT-LONG LONGHOUSE.**

Built in traditional longhouse style and situated in a cedar grove, the Smokehouse seats up to 1,200 people on bleachers set on an earthen floor. It is easy to imagine a time when the trio of fires, with smoke curling through the openings in the roof, warmed the tribe, who in the old days would have slept comfortably here. **EIGHT FLOOR-TO-CEILING POLES** are placed around the hall. Some poles signify the great spirits of Eagle or Salmon; others depict shamans and such important stories as the "Maiden of Deception Pass."

For centuries traditional Coast Salish Indian religions were practiced in smokehouses. And for years traditional Indian religions have been closed to outsiders, forced into secrecy by federal regulations outlawing Indian prayer and ceremony. Money to build the Smokehouse came from a settlement negotiated by three Skagit River tribes that had been affected by three dams licensed to Seattle City Light. The Smokehouse includes a kitchen and dining hall and a smaller room used for local gatherings. Outside, a barbecue pit under the trees is used to cook salmon—a staple at all Swinomish gatherings.

Tours of the Swinomish Smokehouse are by appointment only for groups, usually offered in the spring, summer, and early fall. A donation is requested. For tours, call Larry Campbell, (360)466-1236, or Linda Day, (360)466-1058.

Paul Carvings: *Coast Salish Studio*

When the doors of Native artist Kevin Paul's carving shed are thrown open, visitors should certainly stop by. Paul and his father have carved a number of poles for the Swinomish community, including those inside the casino and a replica of a pole carved by Charlie Edwards that formerly stood on Pioneer Way. In Paul's studio are 4-inch **TOTEMS, LARGE POLES, AND CARVED SCREENS** for sale. One of the best-known carvers from Swinomish, Paul learned his craft from his relatives in Canada.

Paul Carvings, PO Box 1147, La Conner, WA 98257; (360)466-3906. His studio, surrounded by piles of raw cedar and totems, is on Pioneer Wy, a few doors down from St. Paul's Catholic Church. By appointment only.

Legends Art Gallery: *Northwest Coast Art*

With a sales gallery in the front and exhibit space in the back, Legends Art Gallery, on La Conner's waterfront, is first-rate. Owned by a Swinomish tribal member, Legends carries mostly **NORTHWEST COAST ART**, including the work of Canadian carvers. Look for Simon Charlie's gorgeous Coast Salish cod lures as well as such items by other Native artists as masks, cards, stationery, engraved silver and gold jewelry, and silkscreened ties and scarves. There's also an excellent book selection. The gallery is easy to spot among the other shops on La Conner's 1st Street: You can't miss the carved **WHALE TOTEM** outside.

Legends Art Gallery, 705 1st St, La Conner, WA 98257; (360)466-5240. Open daily, year-round.

Skagit County Historical Museum: *Native Artifacts*

In addition to interpreting vignettes on early 1900s farming, fishing, logging, mining, and pioneer life, the Skagit County Historical Museum carries the only exhibit of **LOCAL NATIVE HISTORY** in the area. See basketry, fishing spears, early tools, horn spoons, historical photographs, and a 39-foot **SHOVEL-NOSED CANOE** found by the Boy Scouts in 1948 buried in mud near the Skagit River bank.

Skagit County Historical Museum, 501 S 4th St, La Conner, WA 98257; (360)466-3365. Open afternoons, Wed–Sun, year-round. During the annual Skagit Valley Tulip Festival, generally in early April, the museum is open daily. Admission fee. Reserve tours in advance.

Swinomish Annual Blues Festival: *Native Drums and Dancers*

In August the Swinomish Reservation is transformed as it hosts the Swinomish Annual Blues Festival. **NATIVE DRUMS, DANCERS, AND SINGERS** are joined by such groups as Roy Rogers & the Delta Rhythm Kings, Burnin' Chicago, Little Bill & the Blue Notes, Rantin & Raven, and many others during a weekend of music, culture, food, and fun. Proceeds from the event—first held in 1991 and nominated as one of the best blues festivals in the state—support the Swinomish Smokehouse.

The Swinomish Annual Blues Festival is held in the John K. Bobb Ballpark, below the Smokehouse, the third weekend in August, Fri–Sun. Tickets are available at a number of outlets in La Conner, Mount Vernon, Seattle, and Bellingham. Children 15 and under, free. For information, call Jimmy Sam Williams and Ava Goodman, (360)466-3052.

Swinomish Pier in La Conner: *Traditional Smoked Salmon*

Several vendors serve food and espresso on the Swinomish Pier, the only property owned by the Swinomish in La Conner (across the street from the Native-owned Legends Art Gallery) on La Conner's waterfront. **PUGET SOUND SMOKERS** offers free samples of delicious peppered, garlic, and traditional honey-smoked salmon, prepared according to owner Vern Mcleod's grandmother's recipe. **LEGENDS SALMON BAR** sells large portions of fresh barbecued salmon, fried oyster sandwiches, Indian fry bread served with fresh berries, jam, and butter, **SALMON INDIAN TACOS**, and other fast foods for less than $7. If they have time, some vendors may point out the differences between gill-netters, purse seiners, and other fishing vessels tied up at the La Conner docks.

Swinomish Pier, 708 1st St, La Conner, WA 98257; Legends Salmon Bar, (360)466-5240; Puget Sound Smokers, (360)466-4129.

St. Paul's: *Historic Catholic Church*

Built in 1868, picturesque St. Paul's Catholic Church is the second oldest church in Washington. Behind it is the Swinomish Spiritual Center, used jointly by other religious denominations. Stained-glass windows incorporate orca, deer, and feather designs.

St. Paul's Catholic Church is on Pioneer Wy, on the Swinomish Reservation. The church faces La Conner and is usually open. For more information, call Beverly Peters, director of the Swinomish Spiritual Center, (360)466-7257, at the tribal office.

Walk Along the Swinomish Channel: *Tribally Owned Wetlands*

A short paved walkway follows the Swinomish Channel, accompanied by interpretive signs about the area wetlands and beaches. The welcoming plaque says "Gwu'sh-book-wahk-beyou sjool-eel": "For all people to enjoy." The project was started when the tribe built its seafood processing plant. They wanted to make sure that displaced plants would grow farther upstream and original Native wetlands would be reestablished. This is a great picnic spot, with a picturesque view of La Conner.

To reach the Swinomish Channel, follow Pioneer Wy to the cedar-shake-covered Community Services buildings. Follow the driveway toward the water and the path along the water.

ARCTIC RAVEN GALLERY ON SAN JUAN ISLAND

On San Juan Island, a ferry ride away from Anacortes (just northwest of La Conner), is the Arctic Raven Gallery, overlooking Friday Harbor's boat-filled waterfront.. This lovely light-filled gallery displays some of the best Native art around. Owner Lee Brooks represents work by such Native artists as Susan A. Point (Musquem), Andy Wilbur (Twana, Squaxin Island), Fran James (Lummi), Willie Dan (Musqeum), Greg Colfax (Makah), Marvin Oliver (Quinault, Isleta Pueblo), and Arthur Vickers (Tsimshian). Look here also for masks and silver and gold jewelry from British Columbia, Southeast Alaska, and Washington State, as well as Inuit sculptures and limited edition prints from the Arctic and Northwest. Five or six shows for visiting artists are offered March through September. All work is guaranteed to be authentic. (Arctic Raven Gallery, One Front St., 2nd Floor, PO Box 2139, Fri Harbor, WA 98250; (360)378-3433. The gallery is located one block north of the ferry landing, overlooking Spring St Landing. To get to San Juan Island, take the Washington State Ferry from Anacortes.)

Padilla Bay National Estuarine Research Reserve:
Traditional Lands

The land spreading from the foot of the ridges to Padilla Bay, north of the Swinomish Reservation, was once a huge salt marsh that was fed by the rushing Skagit River—a haven for juvenile salmon, shellfish, and waterfowl. In the 1800s, however, settlers began diking the river, changing its course to the south. By 1900 almost the entire estuary and salt marsh was diked and filled, creating the agricultural lands and tulip fields evident today in the Skagit Valley. Very little natural salt marsh is left in the area.

The **BREAZEALE INTERPRETIVE CENTER**, on the ridge overlooking the old salt marsh, houses a few small exhibits and a resource library, where you can learn more about the old marsh as it was in the days when 11 tribal bands subsisted on its bounty. The **PADILLA BAY** shore trail, 2½ miles long, has many interpretive signs describing the area's history, waterfowl, tidal marsh, and sloughs.

Padilla Bay National Estuarine Research Reserve and Breazeale Interpretive Center, 1043 Bayview-Edison Rd, Mount Vernon, WA 98273; (360)428-1558. From I-5, take exit 230 to Anacortes on Hwy 20; 15 miles west on Hwy 20, at the Farmhouse Inn Restaurant, turn north on Bayview–Edison Rd and watch for signs. Open Wed–Sun, year-round. Free.

Bellingham: *Lummi Indian Nation*

The **LUMMI INDIAN RESERVATION** is on a peninsula, 10 miles west of Bellingham, jutting out into the Strait of Georgia. From here, a small car ferry crosses the channel to Lummi Island. The island today is not part of the reservation and its land is all privately owned, but it is part of Lummi ancestral territory, which stretched across the foothills of Mount Baker and present-day Bellingham and included portions of the nearby San Juan Islands.

Having control of traditional territory has helped the Lummi preserve several areas in the region, such as Madrona Point on Orcas Island in the San Juans and, in an unusual partnership with several private foundations, the Arlecho Creek Forest near Mount Baker. In a lovely **BASIN WITH OLD-GROWTH TREES** more than 500 years old, which the Lummi call T'sak, the forest was saved from clearcutting with a $3.75-million grant from the Paul G. Allen Forest Protection Foundation and $4.25 million from the Nature Conservancy. Saved were 2,240-acres—an area the Lummi have fought to protect for more than a decade. The land sellers, Crown Pacific, a timber company, deeded the land to the Lummi Nation, who must raise $2.85 million, their share of the land price, by 2001. In the meantime, T'sak is assured of protection as a cultural area and a nature preserve for such species as the marbled murrelet, which requires old-growth forest to nest. (Contributions to help the Lummi meet their share of the land price can be made to the Lummi Tribal Government.)

One of the **LARGEST GROUPS OF BASKET WEAVERS** in the Puget Sound area lives on the Lummi Reservation, as do the James family, who weave traditional black, brown, and white Coast Salish–style blankets using sheep's wool. Lummi artists are active in celebrating and teaching Salish culture and art through classes offered at Northwest Indian College. Visitors are welcome to attend the tribe's annual Stommish Water Festival, held each June on Gooseberry Point (see listing later in this section).

Wexliem Community Center House:
Traditional Longhouse

Two carved frogs welcome visitors to the Wexliem (Place of the Frogs) Community Center House, overlooking Hale's Pass from the top of a wooded hillside on the Lummi Reservation. The **TRADITIONAL LONGHOUSE-STYLE BUILDING** accommodates up to 2,000 people. Designed by Richard Jefferson, a tribal member and mechanical engineer, the 17,000-square-foot longhouse, the first of its kind to be constructed in more than a century, was built with logs from the Quinault Reservation by the Colville Tribe construction company. The center has a large commercial kitchen, restrooms, and three cupolas that provide natural light, as smokeholes did in original structures. The floor is dark concrete, stained to represent the packed-earth floors that were once covered with densely woven cedar mats. The **HOUSE OF TEARS CARVERS**, led by Jewell James (Lummi), provided artwork for the building's interior: four unpainted 20-foot housepoles, which have traditionally provided support for roof beams, and monumental carved watchmen, placed at the end of each seating section. The longhouse is used by traditional societies for large gatherings, such as memorials and naming ceremonies, and is also available for non-Native groups to rent. Visitors are welcome.

Wexliem Community Center House, 2220 Lummi View Dr, Bellingham, WA 98226. Contact the Lummi Tribe administration office for a tour, (360)384-1489.

"My brother said that if he was going to paint his carvings, he'd do it the traditional way. 'Okay, I'll head down to the fish house,' I told him. 'What for,' he asked. 'Well, if you are going to paint the traditional way,' I told him, 'you'll need to chew up salmon eggs and spit them on cedar bark. The bark will pull the transparent shell away from the eggs, and your saliva will dissolve the water-soluble omega-3 oil in the fish eggs so that when you paint it on your carving, the wood fibers will absorb the pigment you have mixed with it: ochre (red), charcoal (black), cattail pollen (yellow) or plant ash (white). If you lived up north, you'd mix copper with salt water and young boy's urine to oxidize the copper, mix that with fish egg oil and that would give you that pretty blue-green.'"
—Jewell James

Stommish Water Festival: *Honoring Veterans*

Every June the Lummi Nation and the American Legion host the Stommish Water Festival, open to the public, to honor **NATIVE AMER-ICAN VETERANS** of all wars. (Native Americans have consistently had the highest number of volunteers for U.S. military service of any minority group in the United States; 80 percent of all Lummi men have been involved with the military through the years.) The festival features **CANOE RACES**, with 11-person teams from throughout the Northwest racing 55-foot war canoes through Hales Passage. Other events include foot races, tugs-of-war, traditional dancing, salmon barbecue, traditional bone-game tournaments, and arts and crafts sales.

For information about the Stommish Water Festival, contact the Lummi Indian Nation, 2616 Kwina Rd, Bellingham, WA 98226; (360)384-1489. Stommish grounds are located 1 mile east of the Lummi casino at Gooseberry Point. Dates for the June festival depend on the tides. Admission fee.

Lummi Art and Artists

Many talented Lummi artists produce their carvings, weavings, and sculpture on the reservation, which is also home to one of the largest basket-weaving groups in the Puget Sound area. Lummi art is showcased in one of the area's most celebrated exhibitions, **SHARING OF THE CULTURE**, which is held each June in conjunction with Allied Arts of Whatcom County in the Bellingham area. Lummi artists include wood carvers Jewell Praying Wolf James and Harry Cooper. Salish basket weavers include Anna Jefferson, Joyce Tommy, Ted and Marina Plaster, and Fran and Bill James, who also weave traditional Coast Salish wool blankets, sculptor Yvonne Thomas, and drum maker Joe Page.

For information about Lummi art and Sharing of the Culture exhibition, contact the Lummi tribal office, 2616 Kwina Rd, Bellingham, WA 98226; (360)384-1489.

Lummi Basket-Weaving Classes

Wild cherry, red-cedar bark, and beargrass are some of the materials used in Lummi woven baskets. Salish weaver Anna Jefferson teaches basket weaving at the **NORTHWEST INDIAN COLLEGE** and other institutions, such as the **NORTH CASCADES INSTITUTE**'s weekend seminars. Classes are open to the public.

Northwest Indian College, 2522 Kwina Rd, Bellingham, WA 98226; (360)676-2772. North Cascades Institute, 2105 State Rt 20, Sedro Woolley, WA 98284; (360)856-5700. Call for free course catalogs.

Whatcom Museum of History and Art: *Local Native Art*

The Whatcom Museum of History and Art, in downtown Bellingham, includes a fine collection of local Native art consisting primarily of baskets donated by University of Washington linguist Melville Jacobs, who worked with Northwest tribes in the 1930s. The museum also houses a private collection of 50 to 60 unidentified **NORTHWEST BASKETS**. Contemporary Lummi weavers helped the museum identify individual weaving styles and designs, which are family-related trademarks, passed down through generations. Traveling exhibits and group shows of contemporary Native artists also pass through the museum. The museum is housed in Bellingham's historic former city hall (built in 1892) and three adjoining buildings.

Whatcom Museum of History and Art, 121 Prospect St, Bellingham, WA 98225; (360)676-6981. Open afternoons, Tues–Sun. Free.

Northwest Indian College

Accredited by the Northwest Association of Schools and Colleges, this land-grant college was founded at the Lummi Reservation in 1978. As a Lummi-chartered tribal community college, it provides on-reservation higher education in Idaho, Oregon, Southeast Alaska, and Washington. The **CULTURALLY BASED CURRICULUM** offers an associate of arts college transfer degree, and four-year teacher education and natural resources management programs.

Reflecting community needs, the college has been central to preserving **LOCAL NATIVE LANGUAGES** and such traditional skills as basket weaving and carving. More than 350 students attend the school and at least 1,000 others take classes offered at 24 reservation sites throughout the Northwest. Distance education centers linked via satellite are at the Makah, Nez Perce, Nisqually, Nooksack, Swinomish, and Upper Skagit Reservations. The college hosts workshops and conferences. Natives and non-Natives alike are welcome to enroll.

Northwest Indian College, 2522 Kwina Rd, Bellingham, WA 98226; (360)676-2772; foundation@nwic.edu; www.nwic.edu

St. Joachim's Catholic Mission Church: *Lummi Historical Landmark*

A **HISTORIC LANDMARK**, St. Joachim's Catholic Mission Church is one of the oldest churches still standing in Washington. After the 1855 signing of the Treaty of Point Elliott at present-day Mukilteo, which established the Lummi Reservation, the Roman Catholic Church sent the Reverend Eugene Casimir Sheroise to set up a mission among the Lummi. The church, built in 1861, has been used continuously since that time and is now open only during Sunday Mass.

St. Joachim's Catholic Mission Church, Kwina Rd, Bellingham, WA 98226. From I-5, take Haxton Rd to the Lummi Reservation and follow it to the shoreline. Turn left on Kwina Rd to the corner of Kwina and Lummi Shore Rd S. For mass hours, call St. Joseph's Church in Ferndale, (360)384-3651.

Eagles Haven RV Park: *Native-Owned Business*

Privately owned by tribal members Dean and Sherry Williams, Eagles Haven is approximately 1 mile from the Lummi Island ferry landing. This well-kept park includes full-service hookups with cable TV, hot showers, laundry, security, and a convenience store. The Williamses are nice, generous folks and their store carries books, snacks, and gifts. Sherry Williams has an affinity for nostalgic prints and other kitschy items featuring romanticized images of Native peoples, produced in abundance in the 1950s. These prints decorate the store and can be purchased (although these pieces sell like hotcakes). In addition to the usual hot dogs and donuts, you'll find espresso and salmon jerky. A public trail across the road leads to the waterfront and public beach.

Eagles Haven RV Park, 2924 Haxton Wy, Bellingham, WA 98226; (360)758-2420. From I-5, 12 miles west of Bellingham, take the Slater Rd exit.

Deming: *Nooksack Tribe*

Thirteen miles east of present-day Bellingham, the Nooksack people lived in about **13 VILLAGES** near the Nooksack and Sumas Rivers on the west flank of Mount Baker. Fishing grounds extended from Bellingham Bay to British Columbia, but the Nooksack also gathered hazelnuts, huckleberries, and bracken fern roots ("Nook" means "people"; "sa'ak" means "bracken fern root"). The fern roots were baked in hot ashes, ground into a fine powder, and used as thickening or cereal. Forced to abandon villages near present-day Lynden, Washington, in the mid-1800s, the Nooksack then settled into one traditional village and five settlements made up of homesteads adapted from the European model, with garden plots and domestic animals.

Unlike other Northwest tribes, the Nooksack had a friend in an **EARLY WHITE SETTLER,** John Bertrand, who helped them collect recommendations from whites and file the lengthy applications for homesteads. To file a claim for a homestead, however, the government required that individual tribal members promise to sever ties with their tribe. Other settlers provided assistance and served as witnesses to help defeat later attempts to oust the Natives from their lands.

Today in Deming you can walk on one of the **ORIGINAL FAMILY HOMESTEADS**, pioneered by the Nooksack Williams family, who own it still. In 1993 the family granted the tribe permission to use their land to bring the salmon back to the creek that runs through the homestead's meadow. Choked by canary grass that had been brought in by settlers and planted for hay, the creek had nearly disappeared. To kill the grass by shading it rather than using herbicides, the Nooksack Fish and Wildlife Department planted weeping willows along the creek. The willows' shade also cools the water for salmon. Tribal young people helped build two short walking trails that cross the secluded stream on wooden bridges and benches overlooking the water, made of alder entwined with vine maple. The **SALMON HATCHERY**, a mere 6 feet square, is fed by clear springwater and has replenished the creek with chum salmon, coho, and steelhead. It's an inspiring spot. Trails end at a little park with a picnic table.

For directions and to obtain permission to visit (or tour), contact the Nooksack Tribe Administrative Offices, 5048 Mount Baker Hwy (Hwy 542), PO Box 157, Deming, WA 98244; (360)592-5176.

CLANCY'S SKI SCHOOL: SNOHOMISH

Snohomish tribal member Francine Long and her staff instruct all ages and all levels in downhill skiing and snowboarding near the top of 4,061-foot Stevens Pass off Highway 2, which winds over the Cascade Mountains between Everett and Leavenworth. Ask Long anything about the Snohomish Indians who once used the slopes and river valleys in the mountains as their summer hunting, fishing, and gathering territory. Clancy's Ski School, 5031 27th Ave W, Everett, WA 98203; (425)348-3622 or (360)973-2634.

North Cascades National Park:
Ancient Native Settlements

For the past decade, archaeologists have worked with the Upper Skagit and Snoqualmie Tribes east of Everett and Bellingham to piece together evidence about what was obviously an extensive network of **NATIVE SETTLEMENTS, HUNTING CAMPS, AND TRADE ROUTES** up the rivers and through the mountains. Some rock shelters in the Cascades have been dated to 8,000 years old, and quarried stone from this region has been found as far south as California, evidence of extensive trade routes.

One **1,300-YEAR-OLD ROCK SHELTER** is part of an interpretive exhibit at North Cascades National Park's visitors center in Newhalem, about 50 miles east of Sedro-Woolley on the Skagit River. The shelter floor covers about 10 by 20 feet; the naturally formed wall and ceiling consist of boulders that were probably left here by retreating glaciers. When the site was excavated, it yielded a treasure trove of information about Upper Skagit subsistence in the mountain wilderness. There were hunting points, flakes from tool-making, and bones of mammals including a set of mountain goat legs arranged in a ritualistic way that is thought to have protected the site against "stick" Indians (spirits). According to an Upper Skagit elder, the shelter was typical of those where hunters stashed their gear well into the twentieth century.

The shelter is less than a quarter mile from the road and the trail is handicapped accessible (with assistance) through an old-growth Douglas fir forest. The interior of the shelter is visible from a boardwalk and viewing deck.

North Cascades National Park, 502 Newhalem St, Rockport, WA 98283; (360)856-5700. From Hwy 20, take the Visitor Center Rd to milepost 119 into the Newhalem campground: take Loop D until you reach gravel. The trail is on the right side of the first bridge you cross. Park down the road in the turnaround area. The trail is about 0.3 miles, round-trip.

KITSAP PENINSULA

Suquamish: *Suquamish Tribe*

The traditional territory of the Suquamish Tribe comprises much of present-day metropolitan Seattle, the Kitsap Peninsula, and most of Puget Sound's larger islands—Bainbridge, Blake, Vashon, and Whidbey. The Suquamish's **PORT MADISON RESERVATION** and the town of Suquamish, where the great orator Chief Seattle is buried, are about 45 minutes from downtown Seattle, including the 30-minute ferry ride from Seattle's waterfront. (Take the Winslow ferry across Puget Sound, then follow the highway across Bainbridge Island toward Poulsbo. The Port Madison Reservation boundary is on the north side of the Agate Pass Bridge.) The name *Suquamish* comes from the tribe's ancient village, D'Suq'Wub, on the shores of Agate Pass, a narrow waterway that separates Bainbridge from the Kitsap Peninsula. In the village of D'Suq'Wub ("the place of clear saltwater") stood "Ole Man House," a longhouse 60 feet wide and more than 500 feet long, surrounded by madrona, cedar, and fir trees. The village site is memorialized with a small park in the Port Madison Reservation.

The annual Chief Seattle Days festival is the third weekend in August and open to all. First celebrated in 1911, the festival features a salmon bake, canoe races, traditional dancing, Indian arts and crafts, a powwow, a baseball tournament, and a graveside memorial service to Chief Seattle. For information, call the Suquamish Tribe, (360)598-3311.

The most famous of the Suquamish people is **CHIEF SEATTLE**. Born on Puget Sound, perhaps on Blake Island, he witnessed the arrival of the first white explorers in the region, led by Captain George Vancouver, in 1792. He gave an eloquent speech during treaty negotiations in 1854, a masterpiece of mature observation and oratory. Known as a peacemaker with the whites and chief of Puget Sound's allied tribes, Chief Seattle's vision and negotiating skills are the reason there were fewer successful wars or skirmishes during this period as white settlers began to claim Native lands. An old man by the time his tribe was relocated from their homelands to the Port Madison Reservation, Chief Seattle died in 1866, shortly before his worst fears for his people were realized.

Pressure on the Suquamish Tribe began when the tribe refused to accept destructive European models of farming or to accept the meager variety of commodity food provided by the army on the Port Madison Reservation. The Suquamish insisted on retaining their hunting and fishing rights, as promised by the treaty they had signed in 1854. After Seattle's death, and while families were gathering food during the summer of 1870, **OLE MAN HOUSE**, of great spiritual significance to the Suquamish community, was burned to the ground by the U.S. military. The military's goal was to force the Suquamish to give up their traditional lifestyle; yet the military claimed the lodge was burned to keep epidemics from spreading. Either way, the house was destroyed without the Suquamish people's consent. The village that surrounded Ole Man House continued to thrive for 20 years, until the army forced the tribe to relocate to individual allotments upland. The remainder of their land was sold by the U.S. government to a real estate and advertising agency, which then resold the land for summer homes. Real estate advertising from that era is on display in the Suquamish Museum.

In 1998 a pod of orca whales left their normal feeding grounds in northern Washington and British Columbia in pursuit of salmon. When they entered the Suquamish Tribe's commercial fishing sites in Puget Sound, the tribe chose to sacrifice their fishing for the entire season, stating that "the whales must eat too." The cost in lost revenue to the tribe was more than $100,000.

The Port Madison Reservation today comprises about 7,800 acres, half of which is Indian-owned. The rest of the land, most of it valuable Puget Sound waterfront, is owned by non-Indians.

The **TRIBAL HEADQUARTERS** and the two small communities of Suquamish and Indianola, where most of the tribal members reside, are strung along Miller Bay, with about 10 miles between them. By water, you could leave tribal headquarters on Agate Pass; go under the Agate Pass Bridge; past the site where Ole Man House once stood on the beach; around a wide point to the old ferry landing at

Suquamish, where Chief Seattle is buried on the hill behind the church; and cross the mouth of shallow Miller Bay to the old "Mosquito Fleet" passenger boat wharf at Indianola. **INDIANOLA** is a charming little place in the woods, with a single grocery store near the wharf, churches tucked into groves of madrona and fir, and cottage-sized houses—reminiscent of Puget Sound towns in the 1930s. One of the Suquamish's best-known basket weavers, Ed Carriere, lives in Indianola. (To find Indianola from Suquamish, follow Miller Bay Road north, and take a right on S Kingston Road NE.)

In the past decade or so the Suquamish Tribe of fewer than 800 members, which includes Chief Seattle's descendants, has become an enthusiastic participant in the resurgence of the "canoe culture." Joining with other shoreline tribes from British Columbia and Washington, they've formed a "**CANOE NATION**." Members are not only paddling some of the arduous routes of their seafaring ancestors but have hand-carved, from single-trunks of old-growth cedar, their own 6- to 11-person canoes.

Suquamish and the Port Madison Indian Reservation are off Hwy 305 on the Kitsap Peninsula, north of Bremerton and just west of the Agate Pass Bridge from Bainbridge Island. The Suquamish Tribal Center and Museum is on Sandy Hook Rd; watch for signs on Hwy 305. Suquamish is on Miller Bay Rd (Suquamish Wy), which heads north from 305 just west of Agate Pass. Check the tribe's Web site at www.sequamish.nsn.us/.

Chief Seattle's Grave Site

Chief Seattle is buried in the **SMALL TRIBAL CEMETERY** behind St. Peter's Catholic Church in Suquamish. In 1902 his body was moved to St. Peter's churchyard after the tribe was forced off their valuable waterfront property and their church was torn down. A Suquamish Native donated 5 acres of his own land allotment for a new church and cemetery. Chief Seattle was reburied there, with a marker bearing his baptismal name, Noah Sealth, a name adapted from the Salish language.

The doors and windows of the white-steepled St. Peter's Catholic Church are from the tribe's original church. **TWO CANOES** suspended over the grave were erected in 1976 to commemorate the Suquamish's traditional burial. A graveside memorial service is held in the cemetery each August during the Suquamish's Chief Seattle Days.

St. Peter's Catholic Church and cemetery are on South St, about a block from downtown Suquamish. From Hwy 305, take Miller Bay Rd (Suquamish Wy) to Augusta Ave and turn left uphill to the church parking lot on the right.

Ole Man House at Chief Sealth Park

Squeezed in between two waterfront homes in a housing development, a 1½-acre park and sandy beach commemorate the site where Ole Man House once stood. Ole Man House was actually a **SERIES OF LONGHOUSES** attached to one another, which housed multiple families. The site has been occupied for at least 2,000 years of the tribe's estimated 10,000-year occupation of the area. Ole Man House, burned by the military in 1870, is the most well known of 17 known Suquamish longhouses of similar dimension, occupied only during severe winter weather. **A FULL-SIZE REPLICA** of a portion of the longhouse is in the Suquamish Museum.

To reach Chief Sealth Park, turn right from Hwy 305 on Suquamish Wy to Division Ave, turn right on Division, then left on McKinstry St. The park is at the end of McKinstry, open dawn to dusk, daily.

Ed Carriere: *Suquamish-Style Baskets*

As a child, Ed Carriere learned to make Suquamish-style baskets by watching his great-grandmother, Julia Jacob, the adopted daughter of Wa'hal'chu (Chief Jacob), the last traditional chief of the Suquamish people. As an infant Julia was orphaned when her mother died enroute from Asia to Seattle on a three-masted sailing ship. She was raised by the Suquamish couple and their extended family in Ole Man House, the huge longhouse that once stood on the shore of Agate Pass.

Carriere grew up in his great-grandmother's house (a typical 1900-era American-style house) at nearby Indianola, and he lives today on the same property. He learned to find the right kind of cedar limbs and roots for basket weaving by delivering them to his grandmother and by examining those she rejected when she pitched them out the door without comment. Carriere made his first openwork clam-gathering basket at age 14. He later served in the U.S. Marines and worked at Boeing until he realized in 1969 that **SUQUAMISH WEAVING** would be lost if he himself didn't practice and teach the craft.

Wa'hal'chu, Ed Carriere's great-great-grandfather and the last traditional chief of the Suquamish, died at 112 years of age. His death certificate reads "incompetent Indian." "Wa'hal'chu's memory," says Carriere, "is dishonored in this way simply because he could not read or write English, and had to sign papers with his thumbprint."

Today Carriere lectures and demonstrates to groups, weaves almost daily and repairs baskets made in the 1800s (some of which originally took several years to make). Carriere also prepares cedar bark fibers to weave **TRADITIONAL CLOTHING**, and he has carved two **CEDAR CANOES**. In 1998 he was honored with the Governor's Heritage Award.

Ed Carriere, (360)297-2567. By appointment only.

Suquamish Tribal Center and Museum

Two nicely presented permanent exhibits are on display at the Suquamish Museum: **THE PEOPLE AND WAY OF LIFE AT D'SUQ'WUB** and **THE EYES OF CHIEF SEATTLE**. The museum is set up for a self-guided tour, with well-written interpretive captions. There are also guided tours through the museum that elaborate on food gathering, summer dwellings, fishing, and the boarding schools that many tribal members attended in Puyallup, on the Tulalip Reservation, and in Seattle. International visitors inquire about these topics most frequently. Look also for the Pacific Northwest Land Company's 1920 advertisements of their "Chief Seattle Park" housing development on the Suquamish's Port Madison land. The museum gift shop sells an Eyes of Chief Seattle exhibit catalog, and two videos are shown in the museum daily: *Comes Forth Laughing: Voices of the Suquamish People*, tribal elders' accounts of the past, and *Waterborne: The Gift of the Indian Canoe*. Visitors might observe a cedar canoe being carved outside of the museum, depending on the availability of materials and carvers.

A small foldout book of hand-tinted archival photographs and excerpts from Chief Seattle's memorable speech delivered in 1854 during treaty negotiations and first published by the *Seattle Sun Star* in 1887 (published in cooperation with the Suquamish Tribe by Sasquatch Books) is available from the museum's gift store. The tribe also sells a full-length version of the speech.

Suquamish Tribal Center and Museum, 15383 Sandy Hook Rd, PO Box 498, Suquamish, WA 98392; (360)598-3311, ext. 422. Turn left about a quarter mile past the Agate Pass Bridge (Hwy 305) onto Sandy Hook Rd and watch for signs. The museum is next to the tribal center. Admission fee includes a self-guided map to major sites on the reservation. Museum tours are $15 per person and must be arranged in advance. Open 10am–5pm, daily, May 1–Sept 30; 11am–4pm, Fri–Sun, Oct 1–Apr 30, or by appointment.

OLYMPIC PENINSULA

Kamilche: *Squaxin Island Tribe*

When the tide goes out, the saltwater marshes of the lower end of Puget Sound are revealed in all their glory: lush nurseries for shellfish, feeding grounds for shorebirds, and eelgrass meadows for spawning herring and other fish species. On a beautiful spot with views of the Olympics and Mount Rainier, between the towns of Olympia and Shelton, live the **PEOPLE OF THE WATER**, a group of Salish bands who occupied seven inlets on the southern end of Puget Sound for centuries. All **LUSHOOTSEED SPEAKERS**, these bands coexisted and intermarried, forming a coalition of traders with extended family ties throughout the Puget Sound, British Columbia, and the interior region. They consisted of the Noo'Seh'Chatl (Henderson Inlet), Sa'Heh'Wa'Mish (Hammersley Inlet or Big Skookum), Sa'Wa'Mish (Oyster Bay), S'Hotl'Ma'Mish (Carr Inlet), Squaks'Na'Mish (Case Inlet), Squi'Aitl (Eld Inlet), Steh'Chas (Budd Inlet), and T'Peeksin (Totten Inlet).

Donations to the Squaxin Island museum project are accepted in the form of cash, securities, real estate, bequests, fine art, and in-kind contributions. Contact the Squaxin Island Tribe, SE 70 Squaxin Ln, Shelton, WA 98584; (360)426-9781.

In the mid-1850s the bands were removed from their villages by the hotly contested Medicine Creek Treaty to a 1,500-acre island—Squaxin Island—near the entrance to the inlets. The island had no drinking water, however, and disease and the lack of food took an enormous toll on the people. During the Puget Sound Indian Wars of 1855–56, the Squaxin Islanders were imprisoned by the U.S. military on their island reservation; when the war ended, families moved to nearby communities on the mainland, where their children could attend school and remain with extended family.

The Squaxin Islanders began holding meetings in 1928 to discuss re-establishment of the tribe as a sovereign entity. One of the first tribes in the region to establish an autonomous relationship with the federal government (finally gained in 1965), the Squaxin Island Tribe purchased land in the 1970s and began the painstaking work of **ESTABLISHING THEIR NEW COMMUNITY** at Kamilche (a Chinook jargon word that means peaceful valley), in Mason County. In 1981 the first homes were built at Kamilche, and many tribal members returned after years of separation.

Today the tribe provides health and social services as well as housing and jobs for tribal members. They've retained the private use of Squaxin Island for fishing, hunting, shellfish gathering, camping and summer youth workshops. The tribe has built a casino, trading post, convenience store, and gas station complex on Highway 101, just east of Kamilche. The Little Creek Casino employs more than 300 people, making the tribe the third largest employer in Mason County.

At press time the tribe was embarking on a $2-million capital campaign to build the Squaxin Island museum library and research center on the waterfront: the **TU HA'BUTS CULTURAL CENTER**, to be created with assistance from the Burke Museum of Natural History and Culture at the University of Washington, will be built in traditional Northwest Coast architectural style, with a building that houses seven structural bays, representing the seven inlets of the tribe's original territory. There will be current and historical maps of Puget Sound (with Lushootseed place names) and historic and contemporary photographs of Squaxin Island families. Designed by museum design specialist Walter Schacht, the entry will be via a boardwalk that will go past a canoe-making shed on one side, the museum on the other, with a pond and view of Mount Rainier. The main gallery will contain reminders of the tribe's heritage: masks, carvings, photographs, historical documents, and other artifacts. Most importantly, it will illustrate the symbiotic relationship between nature and culture. The museum will also collaborate with the Washington State Historical Museum, the National Museum of the American Indian, and the Smithsonian Institution, receiving loans of artifacts held in various archives that originated from the Squaxin Island area.

Tribes of the Olympic Peninsula Region, written by the Olympic Peninsula Intertribal Cultural Advisory Committee (University of Washington Press), includes photos and maps and is available at visitor facilities on the Olympic Peninsula.

INDIAN SHAKER CHURCH

According to records and eye-witness accounts, John Slocum, the founder and spiritual leader of the Indian Shaker Church, died and was resurrected from death in 1882. These events occurred in a longhouse on the shore of Skookum Bay on Hammersley Inlet, near the present-day town of Shelton. Slocum's near-death experience is remarkably similar to accounts collected over the past 30 years from others who have experienced similar phenomena.

In Slocum's case, he recalled entering a fenced yard and an empty house. A voice told him to proceed to another room, where he was greeted by a well-dressed man who asked him if he believed in God. In another room Slocum's photograph revealed all his bad deeds in life. He begged to return to the living, and the angels there agreed if Slocum promised to preach the word of God. Before he returned to his body, Slocum was led to the roof, where he looked over a beautiful land of comfort and felt a sense of deep tranquillity. And then he awoke.

The church Slocum founded a year after this event was a hybrid of Catholic and Protestant liturgy and beliefs of the Coast Salish people. Though not associated with the Shaker religion practiced in the eastern United States, the Indian Shaker religion is Christian-based and incorporates the sign of the cross, bells, candles, flags, alms, holy pictures, chanting, and song to evoke spirit. Bodily experience in the form of "shaking" is believed to be proof of being seized by spirit.

The Squaxin Island Tribe has purchased the land where Slocum experienced this resurrection and where the first church services were held. One of the oldest Indian Shaker Churches buildings in Washington, the building stands on a forested hill near Mud Bay, east of Olympia. Other Indian Shaker churches were erected on reservations throughout the Northwest and into Northern California, representing last hopes to tribes who were undergoing world-shattering changes after white contact. Indian Shaker religion is still practiced on many reservations today.

Shelton: *Skokomish Tribe*

The **TWANA PEOPLE** once occupied nearly all of the land between the Olympic Mountains and the western shore of Hood Canal, along today's scenic Highway 101. It must have been even more beautiful generations ago, with trees to the water's edge and peaceful fishing villages at the mouths of most streams and along the upper reaches of the Skokomish River. Today the Twana's reservation is located at the delta of the Skokomish River. The name Skokomish, which the U.S. government used to refer to the Twana in its 1855 treaty with the people, was actually the name of only one community that occupied at least six sites along the Skokomish Rriver and its north fork. The site of today's reservation was a region shared by the Twana, who spoke *tuwaduqucid*, and the many bands of the Puget Salish, who spoke *dxwlesucid*.

The Skokomish Reservation was created in 1855 at the signing of the **TREATY OF POINT NO POINT**. Bands living along the rivers reluctantly ceded their lands and relocated to what they considered their territory's most important river delta, in terms of the richness of its estuary and its legendary salmon runs. Before the twentieth century's logging, which has silted and ruined many spawning grounds, the Skokomish River supported a thriving wild salmon run. The river's estuary supported native shrimp, crab, and in the late 1800s, oyster beds (before they died off from overharvesting).

Individual tribal members were allotted between 40 and 160 acres to establish family farms near the river mouth. Most of these farms are now under water in what actually is a huge swamp. You can tell this swamp is a fairly recent ecological event from the white trunks of old trees standing in water, the result of overlogging, siltation, diking, and a rising water table. Dozens of tribal members' homes have been lost to the encroaching swamp over the past 100 years.

Like many reservations, this one has minority Indian ownership: Simpson Timber Company is the major landholder on the reservation, followed by the City of Tacoma. In 1926 and 1930 Tacoma built dams on the Skokomish River, despite the tribe's protests that dams with no fish ladders would block spawning habitat and ruin one of the most important salmon- and steelhead-producing streams on Puget Sound.

The tribe itself owns only 250 acres of its former reservation lands, most of it acquired since 1972, when they owned only 16 acres, which supported a school and two tribal cemeteries. There's more heart and soul on this reservation than is readily visible from the highway, evident at the **SKOKOMISH TRIBAL CENTER**, located off the highway in a grassy clearing. The Skokomish Tribe's cultural committee is dedicated, teaching the smokehouse religion to young tribal members and reaching out to other Coast Salish communities.

Skokomish Tribal Center: *Native Art and Exhibits*

There's always something going on at the Skokomish Tribal Center, from elders' luncheons to tribal council meetings. The reception desk sits in a large room that contains two monumental **CARVED WELCOME**

FIGURES by artist Andy Wilbur. Between them is a Salish canoe carved in the 1930s by Henry Allen. Displays showcase wood **CARVINGS** by such Skokomish artists as Pete Peterson and Richard Cultie, and **BASKETS** by such weavers as Emily Miller and Louisa Pulsifer (who wove baskets long after she lost her sight). Be sure to read the interpretive text that accompanies the displays and describes basket weaving. Also look for the images denoting dogs that are woven into the baskets using sawgrass gathered from the swampy areas. The Coast Salish raised dogs for their hair, which they then wove, along with goat wool, into warm blankets.

The center also has a well-written narration of **TWANA AND PUGET SALISH HISTORY** and culture. A model of a smokehouse, where religious ceremonies and teaching take place, is flanked by two full-sized house posts, carved by Bruce Miller, which support the roof and represent the spirit guides of the people. (There are similar posts at the Swinomish Smokehouse near La Conner.) Edward S. Curtis portraits of tribal members taken in the early 1900s, donated to the center by local families, hang on the center's walls.

Skokomish Tribal Center, N 80 Tribal Center Rd, Hoodsport, WA 98548; (360)426-4232.

Pete Peterson Studio: *Traditional Bentwood Boxes*

Soft-spoken Pete Peterson, a Skokomish commercial fisherman and an artist for 20 years, is a **SELF-TAUGHT WOOD CARVER** whose specialty is bending cedar planks into large, lidded bentwood boxes. Traditional bentwood boxes were used as storage chests. Carved with formline designs and carefully painted in striking red and black, Peterson's artwork has been supported through endowments, including grants from the National Endowment for the Arts, and he has worked as an artist-in-residence at the Evergreen State College longhouse. In 1998, Peterson was named by his tribe as a "Cultural Treasure" and honored at a dinner held in Portland, Oregon, during Indian Art Northwest's four-day celebration of Indian culture. Peterson does not exhibit in galleries; rather he prefers to meet patrons and buyers in his modest home and studio, which are filled with his artwork, including stacks of **BENTWOOD BOXES, MASKS, CRADLES, CARVED BOWLS,** and other implements.

Pete Peterson Studio, PO Box 487, Hoodsport, WA 98548; (360)877-9158. By appointment only; please call in advance.

Andy Wilbur Gallery: *Coast Salish Art*

Andy Wilbur, born in 1955 on the Skokomish Reservation, began gathering basket materials and weaving baskets with Skokomish basket makers Emily Miller and Louisa Pulsifer when he was a young boy. After seeing Northwest Coast art in a museum at age 18, Wilbur was **INSPIRED TO CARVE**. While attending Evergreen State College for his degree in Native American studies, he carved his first "Welcoming Woman" with Makah carver Greg Colfax. In 1995 he helped Colfax carve the **MONUMENTAL THUNDERBIRD** installed over the entrance to the Evergreen State College longhouse. Wilbur also carved a monumental welcoming figure with Steve Brown, curator of Northwest Coast art at the Seattle Art Museum, commissioned by the King County Arts Commission and installed in Seattle's Richmond Beach Park. Wilbur has been represented by galleries throughout the Northwest, including The Legacy in Seattle. He has recently built his own gallery and studio next to his home on the Skokomish Reservation. Carvings by his wife, Ruth, and his three daughters, especially that by his daughter, Andrea, are also exhibited. Their work includes **BENT-WOOD BOXES AND CHESTS, PANELS, DRUMS, SPEAKERS' STAFFS, BOWLS, TOTEM POLES, PRINTS, AND BUTTON BLANKETS.**

Andy Wilbur Gallery, N 60 Hurley Hill Rd, Shelton, WA 98584; (360)877-0334. By appointment only.

COAST SALISH WOOD CARVER

Andrea Wilbur, daughter of Skokomish carver Andy Wilbur, learned to make button blankets and to weave baskets as a young girl. Under her father's tutelage, she learned Coast Salish wood carving. First exhibiting her spindle whorls and carved panels on the Skokomish Reservation, Wilbur was juried in 1998 into Indian Art Northwest's fine art exhibit and sale. Eagle Spirit Gallery owner Robert Scott saw her exquisite work there and bought everything she had created. Wilbur now exhibits her work in Scott's galleries in Vancouver, British Columbia; New York City; and Arizona. Within one year, the prices on her work have skyrocketed. One of the few women wood carvers in the Pacific Northwest, her work now commands at least $250 an inch; larger pieces sell for more than $3,000. For appointment, call the artist at (888)801-5277 or fax (360)426-2269.

Fruit, Homemade Bread, Smoked Fish, and Art

In a cluster of buildings on Highway 101 at Skokomish are several tribally owned enterprises. One is a spotless quick-stop grocery store, **TWIN TOTEMS GROCERY & DELI**. Racing canoes are stored up in the rafters; be sure to look up to see them. Nearby **MCDONALD'S FRUIT STAND** sells produce from both the Yakima Valley and the tribe's organic garden, including wild watercress, smoked and kippered salmon, homemade bread and pies, and if you get there early enough, freshly picked wild blackberries. The **TWANA TRADE CENTER**, (360)877-6748, is an art gallery and espresso cafe that sells work made by Skokomish artists. The **TWANA TRADE CENTER GALLERY** showcases artwork by Skokomish artists and craftspeople on consignment, along with Pendleton blankets, books, and Quinault Pride smoked salmon. Represented at the Trade Center Gallery, artists Marcle Tinaza (Skokomish) and Bobbie Bush (Chehalis) weave miniature baskets and combine them with beads for necklaces. Carol Summers makes small pins, and Stan James paints canoe paddles. Also look for Dale Clark's painted drums, and Gary Mean's carving. Andrea Wilbur also sells her work here: often striking, unpainted **SPINDLE WHORLS**, shaped like disks with a hole in the center, with Coast Salish designs.

Joan Pell's Smoked Salmon

Sunset Magazine rated Joan and Les Pell's smoked salmon the **BEST IN THE WEST**. Joan Pell drives to the Quinault Reservation on the Pacific Ocean to pick up fresh kings, silvers, sockeye (what Natives call "blue-back"), and steelhead for her smoker or has it shipped overnight from the Copper River Delta in Alaska. In the traditional Skokomish way, as taught to her by her grandmother Mary Adams, Joan has the fish fillets salted, refrigerated overnight, rinsed, and then smoked slowly over alderwood fires. The fish is then canned and vacuum-packed. The Pells also sell the Quinault's "Seafood Pride" label of smoked and cannned salmon.

Joan Pell Smoked Salmon, 20031 N Hwy 101, Shelton, WA 98584; (360) 877-6737.

The Sounder: Tribal Newsletter

The Skokomish tribal newsletter, called *The Sounder* and edited by Bonnie J. James, is published six times a year. Like many tribal news-papers, it's a great source of information about the Twana people in general, discussing both **CURRENT AND HISTORICAL EVENTS** and what's happening on the reservation.

For a subscription to The Sounder, *call (360)426-4232.*

Port Gamble, Blyn, Port Angeles:
S'Klallam Tribes

The S'Klallam tribes, whose roots may stem from the Fraser River area of southern British Columbia, once held much of Washington's coastal strip along the Strait of Juan de Fuca and the northern end of the Kitsap Peninsula. Although S'Klallam villages were near every fresh-water source in this area, and seasonal camps were revisited along most of the beaches, today there are few visible reminders of their presence. Clallam County, along the northern shoreline of the Olympic Penin-sula, is named after the S'Klallam tribes, small recompense indeed for the Point No Point Treaty, signed in 1855, that forced the tribes to give up rights to their land and disband as a unified culture.

THREE SMALL RESERVATIONS are occupied today by S'Klallam descendants. The Port Gamble S'Klallam are on the northwest end of the Kitsap Peninsula at "Little Boston." The Jamestown S'Klallam Tribe owns land on the Olympic Peninsula on Highway 101 at Blyn on Sequim Bay. The Elwha S'Klallam Tribe is located at the mouth of the Elwha River west of Port Angeles.

At Port Townsend, walk north on the public beach from Point Hudson toward the Point Wilson lighthouse and you'll find a ramp to **CHETZEMOKA PARK**, named after a S'Klallam chief. Few people know that Chief Chetzemoka's descendants live just 30 minutes away, in a small residential community called Jamestown, near Dungeness, north of Sequim.

Historic early-nineteenth-century **PORTRAITS OF S'KLALLAMS** (and Makahs and Quileutes) are at the Port Angeles Library. Ask the reference desk librarian for a file of reprints from the Burt Kellogg Collection. Accompanying text is sketchy but identifies gatherings of S'Klallams with their canoes, basket makers, seal harpooning and skin-ning, whale butchering, and fish drying on racks.

In recent years, the S'Klallam Tribes have been making their pres-ence more visible. The Port Gamble Tribe recently erected a long-house, totems, and carved housescreens, with the help of Tsimshian carver David Boxley at Little Boston. The Jamestown S'Klallams have hired carvers to erect huge totems in front of their casino and long-house at Blyn, and to decorate their parking lot, bus stop, and kiosk overlooking Sequim Bay with traditional art, making it a visible reminder that S'Klallams remain in the region.

Blyn: *Jamestown S'Klallam Tribe*

A campsite excavated in the Sequim area and thought to be a Native American quarry and workshop is one of the largest of its time period to be studied in all of Western Washington. The **ANCIENT CAMPSITE** yielded dacite cobbles that were once used to make tools to hunt large game animals and to process hides (dated to 5,000–8,000 years old). The site was in continuous use as a food-processing camp until about 1827, evidenced by the remnants of a small house structure and remains of elk, deer, bear, snowshoe hares, beaver, raccoon, coyote, and lynx, found with evidence of gathered acorns, hazelnuts, elder berries, and other foods. This discovery came as no surprise to the S'Klallams, who know their people have lived in this region for centuries.

For more information about the Jamestown S'Klallam, visit their Web site at www.olympus.net/personal/s'klallam/index.htm.

In 1874 troubles with white pioneers settling in S'Klallam territory, which resulted in epidemics and genocide, prompted several remaining S'Klallam families to pool $500 to buy from a logging company a 210-acre cleared meadow with a sandy beach. Today this land is a beautiful, low bank site that overlooks the Strait of Juan de Fuca and snowcapped Mount Baker. They called it **JAMESTOWN**. Some of the acreage of the original Jamestown, north of Sequim, has been sold over the years, but a core of individually owned S'Klallam land remains in the small community. Although in the mid 1850s, they signed the Point No Point Treaty, the Jamestown S'Klallam struggled along on their own for more than a century until they were finally recognized by the federal government in 1981. In their settlement; however, they received only 5 acres of trust land at Blyn, on Sequim Bay, where the tribal headquarters are now located.

Working together as a community since the 1960s for federal recognition, then under the direction of Tribal Council Chair W. Ron Allen (today he is the president of the National Congress of American Indians), the Jamestown S'Klallam have gradually become more visible to the public. They purchased land on Highway 101 on Sequim Bay, at Blyn (halfway between Port Townsend and Port Angeles), and built a striking **TRIBAL CENTER COMPLEX** overlooking Sequim Bay. They stocked **THREE ART GALLERIES**; one is the centerpiece of their large casino, the second is at the tribal center, and the third is in Port Townsend. The tribe has also helped develop Railroad Bridge Park, a historic railroad bridge over the Dungeness River, where the tribe is planning to build a small outdoor amphitheater for storytelling, Audubon wildlife talks, and other events. The tribe's natural resources department has raised millions of dollars to conduct scientific studies of the Dungeness River drainage and Sequim irrigation ditches for federal and state fish biologists to **REVITALIZE SALMON HABITAT**. They also own a shellfish-processing plant, which markets primarily to Asia. The tribe rents its community building, overlooking Sequim Bay, to small groups for meetings.

Visitors are welcome at the **JAMESTOWN S'KLALLAM TRIBAL CENTER** and its small playground right on the Blyn waterfront. The road to the tribal center is well marked from Highway 101. Watch for the tribe's information kiosk and free parking lot along the highway.

Northwest Native Expressions Galleries

Northwest Native Expressions is the name given to the three Jamestown S'Klallam art galleries. This trio of galleries, two in Blyn and one in Port Townsend, houses a small but carefully selected collection of **NORTHWEST COAST ART**. For sale are Northwest Coast and Coast Salish baskets, masks, clothing, limited-edition prints, and gold and silver jewelry. Serious browsers and buyers might cruise all three galleries, which feature many one-of-a-kind works of art and craft, much of it made on the Olympic Peninsula. There are lovely Coast Salish masks, rattles, and other pieces made by S'Klallam carvers Jeff Monson and Terry Johnson; **CANOE MODELS** by George Adams; and baskets by Ann Adams. Basket-weaving classes are taught to tribal members every Friday at the community center at Blyn; visitors are welcome to observe. The tribe's traditional and contemporary art program, which began in 1998, supports emerging artists. The galleries also sell Northwest Coast–style art made by non-Natives. Most pieces are carefully labeled as to Native or non-Native origin. If you don't see a label, ask. The galleries also sell books, tapes, and Southwest jewelry.

Northwest Native Expressions Galleries: one gallery is located in a historic waterfront building at 637 Water St, Port Townsend, WA 98368; (360)385-4770. A second showcase gallery, built in the traditional longhouse style, is inside the Seven Cedars Casino, 5 miles east of Sequim at 270756 Hwy 101 E, Sequim, WA 98382; (360)681-6757. The third gallery is across the highway from the casino at 1033 Old Blyn Hwy, Sequim, WA 98382; (360)681-4640; gallery@nw-nativeart.com; www.nw-nativeart.com. Call for hours.

Railroad Bridge Park: *Natural History Lectures*

This beautiful park on the banks of the Dungeness River includes an old railroad trestle that has been converted into a passenger bridge across the river. Tribal, state, and federal naturalists bring visitors here to explain renewed use of **TRADITIONAL WATERSHED RESOURCES** of the Dungeness River and restored salmon habitat, for which the S'Klallam Tribe has written more than $1 million in grants. In 1999 more than 2,000 people attended the annual two-day **RIVER FESTIVAL** (mid-September), held in conjunction with the Rainshadow Natural Science Foundation, the Olympic Peninsula Audubon Society, and the U.S. Forest Service. The festival includes a huge **STORYTELLING TENT** shaped like a fish, a walk-through salmon sculpture, a touch tank of sea creatures, and a "salmon run/walk" that follows the path of the returning salmon upriver from the Dungeness School House to the park. The tribe's **NORTHWEST NATIVE EXPRESSIONS GALLERY** sets up a booth to sell fine art and T-shirts (kids can decorate their own shirts with "fish prints"), and there's music and food both days.

Railroad Bridge Park, Sequim, WA. Take Hwy 101 to the 5th Ave stoplight in Sequim, turn north on Hendrickson Rd, and follow until it dead-ends at the park. The park is open to the public dawn to dusk. For information on the River Festival, call (360)683-1109.

Olympic Park Institute: *Native-Led Field Seminars*

Olympic National Park and the Olympic Park Institute have combined forces with naturalists, artists, and writers to offer field seminars in Olympic National Park April through October. The 1998 catalog of seminars included such programs as **"CELEBRATING S'KLALLAM TRADITIONS,"** led by tribal members Elaine Grinnell (Jamestown S'Klallam) and Jamie Valadez (Lower Elwha S'Klallam), who have devoted their time to reviving the S'Klallam culture and language. In a two-day workshop on one of the most beautiful glacier-morane lakes in the region, you can, for example, stay at the Rosemary Inn in Olympic National Park and learn about the history, religion, language, food, transportation, lifestyle, and medicines of the first people of the Olympic Peninsula; try your hand at making a walking stick and weaving a basket; or hike to Marymere Falls **TO HEAR THE LEGENDS** of the area surrounding what is now called Lake Crescent. Seminars might also include a backpack trip out to Cape Alava (the site of traditional Ozette Village) with a Makah tribal member or making cedar-bark baskets with weaver Anna Jefferson, a S'Klallam descendant who also teaches on the Lummi Reservation near Bellingham.

Olympic Park Institute, 111 Barnes Point Rd, Port Angeles, WA 98363; 360)928-3720; opi@olympus.net; www.olympus.net/opi. Most workshops last several days, include lodging and meals, and cost less than $200.

Jamestown Seafood

Dungeness Bay is protected by three natural sand spits, fed by Pacific Ocean seawater, and washed by cold mountain water from the Dungeness River. The cold water in the pristine bay makes for prime oyster-growing conditions, and fresh Pacific oysters and geoducks are harvested by the tribe mostly for discerning Asian markets. You can no longer buy live oysters in the shell from the S'Klallam Tribe, but you can get the **TRIBE'S FRESH SEAFOOD** at an all-you-can-eat seafood buffet on Friday nights at Seven Cedars Casino at Blyn. Ask there for directions to Dungeness Spit, a narrow band of sand, rock, and driftwood that extends more than two miles into the Strait of Juan de

Fuca. At low tide, the spit is one of the best bird-watching spots in the region; if you get caught out on the spit at high tide, expect to crawl back over driftwood.

Neah Bay: *Makah Tribe*

> In 1998, the Makah Tribe, legendary for their feats of hunting large marine mammals and whales from traditional canoes, caught and butchered their first whale in more than 70 years, amid great controversy. For information about Makah whaling from the Makah's point of view, see their Web site at www.makah.com.

The Makah Reservation is literally at the end of the road. Highway 112, which stretches from Port Angeles to the Makah Reservation at Neah Bay, has been patched many times; winter mudslides may shut it down for as long as two weeks at a time. The road ribbons in and out of clearcut slopes and dips down to narrow, rocky beaches and pockets of sandy beach along the Strait of Juan de Fuca. It leaves the last town behind at Clallam Bay and enters the **MAKAH RESERVATION** 23 miles later.

These last 23 miles of Highway 112 are the only path into Washington's rugged northwest corner, the westernmost point in the Lower 48, smack in the middle of the flyway for migratory birds and the path of migrating gray whales. The Makah Reservation includes Neah Bay, a well-known fishing port, once the first of five villages at the mouth of the Strait of Juan de Fuca.

The Makah, relatives of the **NUU-CHAH-NULTH BANDS** of western Vancouver Island, have inhabited this region of mountains, dense forests, and open seas for thousands of years. They were

> Years after the last Makah longhouse was destroyed in the late 1800s, an elder kept one of the remaining longhouse boards nailed to the wall above his sickbed, saying that it made him feel good to sleep under it as he had as a child. The weathered, hand-adzed board, silvery with age, now hangs on his grandson's wall.

once **EXCEPTIONAL SEAFARERS**, harvesting every kind of fish and marine mammal, including migrating gray whales. The surrounding rain forest's massive 1,000-year-old cedar trees provided pliable fiber that the Makah pulled off in strips and wove into waterproof clothing and hats, floor coverings, and even sails. The Makah used the roots in baskets, steamed the wood into storage boxes, or adzed it into planks for houses. Whole tree trunks were carefully carved and steamed into efficient, seaworthy canoes.

Today the Makah Reservation encompasses 47 square miles. Four of the **ORIGINAL FIVE MAKAH VILLAGE SITES**, which once were occupied year-round, are within the present-day reservation: Ba'dah, Dia'ht, Tso-yess, and Wa'atch. The site of the fifth village, Osett (pronounced "Ho-set"), is about 15 miles south of Cape Flattery. The multiple-family longhouses that once existed at these village sites faced the water. Made of planked cedar, they had shed roofs that could be opened to fresh air and sunlight, and rain gutters made of whalebone. Average houses were 60 by 30 feet, with 15-foot-high ceilings.

Before the early 1900s missionaries and Indian agents forced the Makah to pull down most of their longhouses and abandon their villages in favor of single-family dwellings. Most of these were built on streets facing Neah Bay. During World War I the U.S. military, occupying Cape Flattery for the sake of national defense, bulldozed and burned the last remaining Makah village of longhouses.

The new Makah Marina, (360) 645-3015, offers 200 slips behind a break-water for boats from 30 to 70 feet long; it can accommodate vessels up to 100 feet, and has water, power, pump-out services, new restrooms, and showers nearby.

The fifth Makah village, Osett or **OZETTE**, was buried some 500 years ago in a massive mudslide. The modern tribal members knew about it but did not disturb the ruins or reveal their existence until artifacts began washing onto the beach after a series of pounding storms in the late 1960s. Excavated by a team of anthropologists and their students in the 1970s, Ozette yielded more than 55,000 mostly intact artifacts, proving the existence of the **INCREDIBLE CULTURAL HERITAGE** the Makah had always claimed.

One square mile surrounding the original Ozette Village site, outside the reservation boundary, was returned to the Makah in 1970; Tatoosh and Waadah Islands, off Cape Flattery, were returned to the tribe in 1984. Today about 800 of the 2,200 enrolled tribal members live on the reservation, many of them commercial fishers. Neah Bay, the only town on the Makah Reservation, is thus the original Deah village site. Motels, owned and built mostly by non-Indians on land leased to them by the Makah Tribe, and the tribe's new marina have replaced the longhouses that 100 years ago lined the beach. There are no plans to rebuild longhouses for living quarters,

To keep cedar-bark clothing from scratching sensitive skin, the Makah intertwined the weave with hummingbird feathers, the soft fibers surrounding cattail seeds, and dog wool.

although one longhouse has been erected next to the cultural center for special events. Most visitors to the Makah Reservation come to see the **MAKAH CULTURAL AND RESEARCH CENTER**, the only museum in North America displaying artifacts found in Ozette Village. Visitors to Neah Bay can kayak in the bay and on the river, camp overnight, photograph Tatoosh Island from the Cape Flattery Trail, walk designated beaches, or tour the area with a tribal member.

Makah Cultural and Research Center

The discovery of the Ozette Village site is considered by many anthropologists to have revealed the **MOST SIGNIFICANT ARCHEOLOGICAL RECORD** in North America. Like the volcanic ashfall that buried

Pompeii, the mud sealed Ozette households intact in the seventeenth century. The site revealed the Makah's rich heritage, yielding perfectly preserved household, whaling, fishing, and hunting items. Among the items recovered was a fishing tackle pouch. Inside were weights, tackle, stone fishhook shanks, and codfish, bonefish, and halibut hooks. The most prized finds were a cedar carving of a female killer whale's dorsal fin, studded with more than 700 otter teeth, and metal tools predating European contact by about 300 years.

The pinecone-shaped "Ozette potato," believed to have come to the Washington coast from Peru with Spanish explorers, has been cultivated in the Cape Flattery region since the late 1700s and is still grown in some gardens on the Olympic Peninsula. Baked and skinned, the little potato was a welcome addition of carbohydrate food in the Makah's diet.

Also recovered from Ozette was a **CENTURIES-OLD FISHING NET** made of twined and woven nettle fibers. Modern-day Makah fishers, who had fought for decades in federal courts for the right to fish with nets, could finally prove their claim that ancestors had fished with such nets. When they presented the net as evidence in court, their case was won with no further argument.

Today the entire collection, containing more than **60,000 ARTIFACTS AND STRUCTURAL REMAINS**, is housed in the $3 million Makah Cultural and Research Center and state-of-the-art archival storage facility in Neah Bay. The center's board of trustees consists of 12 family representatives. The center's director is Makah tribal member and Dartmouth College graduate Janine Bowechop.

Lights in the cultural center are dimmed to protect fragile wood and fiber, lending a mystical air to the objects. The museum includes a life-size replica of the interior of a longhouse that visitors can walk into, and four full-size canoes equipped with touchable whaling and sealing gear. The **GIFT SHOP** offers a good selection of books, videotapes of the Ozette excavation, carved masks, bentwood boxes, and woven baskets. An ethnobotanical garden is in the works.

In the Makah Cultural Center is a miniature model of Ozette Village, built by tribal members Greg Arnold and Alex McCarty. Details include a woman with her dog in the forest, whale bones alongside the houses, petroglyphs on the rocks, and a baby cradled in a bentwood box.

Makah Cultural and Research Center, PO Box 160, Neah Bay, WA 98357; (360)645-2711. The center is on the left, just inside the gateway to the Makah Reservation, on Hwy 112 at Neah Bay. Open late May–mid-Sept, call for hours; Sept 16–May 31; closed Mon and Tues. Admission fee for adults; children under 5 free. Tours are led by museum staff for a small fee; please make tour arrangements two weeks in advance.

Makah Artists: *Carvers, Weavers, and Jewelers*

The Makah Tribe boasts many talented artists, among them fine basket weavers and canoe and mask carvers. Some carve feathers from cedar, so thin and etched with lines that they almost seem real. Black stems of maidenhair fern decorate woven baskets; jewelry is made of olive-shaped shells from shellfish indigenous to Neah Bay. Ceremonial drums may be painted with clan symbols. One **FAMILY OF ACCOMPLISHED BASKET WEAVERS** makes woven baseball hats, dolls, and earrings and weaves grasses around glass balls, lamps, and bottles, a tradition that stems back to the 1900 souvenir market. The names known best by collectors are wood carvers Greg Colfax, Michah Vogel, and Micah McCarty; totem carver Frank Smith; canoe carver and longhouse builder Lance Wilkie; the Parker family of basket weavers; and silkscreen artist John Goodwin (**DEE-AH SCREENPRINTS**), whose jackets and rainwear are adorned with totem crest signs. **WEST COAST CHARM**, owned by Fran Parker, silkscreens T-shirts, jackets, and aprons with designs inspired by the Ozette archeological site. Local artists are listed with the Makah Tribal Planning Department, which publishes a brochure of names, addresses, and phone numbers. Visit the Makah Cultural and Research Center's gift shop for art, inexpensive mugs, and T-shirts; also peek into **WASHBURN'S GENERAL STORE**, (360)645-2211, in Neah Bay (the only supermarket, it's just about the largest building in town).

Group art tours or meetings with individual artists can be arranged in advance through the Makah Tribal Planning Department at the Makah Cultural and Research Center, PO Box 160, Neah Bay, WA 98357; (360)645-2711.

Native American Adventures: *Tours of the Makah Reservation*

MAKAH TRIBAL MEMBER Donna Wilkie drives her van up a steep, graveled road west of Neah Bay to a spot near the top of Cape Flattery. As she drives, she discusses the clearcuts visible on surrounding reservation hills. The logging has helped finance the Makah Tribe when no other money was forthcoming, but it's caused rifts between those tribal members wanting to preserve the reservation as a wilderness and those favoring logging—a common conflict in the Pacific Northwest.

Near the top of Cape Flattery, a half-mile trail along the cliffs overlooks Tatoosh Island, the westernmost spot in the Lower 48. Rather than hike the trail, Wilkie drives past a No Trespassing sign (one of the advantages of **TRAVELING WITH A NATIVE TOUR GUIDE**) and pulls into a clearing overlooking the Pacific Ocean. Far below, the ocean swells crashing on the rocks of Tatoosh Island form a white meringue around the barren, rocky shoreline. It is a marvel that generations ago, Makahs beached their canoes on such dangerous ground.

Other trips with Wilkie may include a stop at her house at Sooes Beach, where she tells about her **GREAT-GRANDMOTHER'S WEDDING** in the mid 1800s. The bride came by canoe from Ozette to Sooes, dressed in veils of dentilium shell; the bridegroom had to split a cedar panel with the throw of a harpoon before the marriage could be consummated.

Tour guide Rich Sones, Wilkie's son, is a commercial fisherman who grew up on the reservation. His tours include hiking on the **CAPE FLATTERY TRAIL** to a viewpoint overlooking Tatoosh Island, to talk about the National Marine Sanctuary, which the Makahs helped establish. He speaks about potlatch celebrations, outlawed by the government in the early to mid-1800s, that were held secretly on Tatoosh Island until the laws were changed to make potlatches legal and to grant U.S. citizenship to the Native people.

Both Wilkie's and Sones's tours vary in length from one to three hours and may include the Makah Cultural and Research Center, the town and four nearby historic village sites, ocean beaches, and several archaeological sites.

Native American Adventures, PO Box 57, Neah Bay, WA 98357; (360)645-2554 or (360)645-2201. By appointment only, year-round.

Cape Flattery is a famous bird-watching spot in spring, during the annual bird migration. Dozens of raptors ride the thermals here, waiting for a south wind that will assist them across the 22 miles at the mouth of the Strait of Juan de Fuca to the next resting spot on Vancouver Island. For a free bird list naming 239 species on or near the cape, contact the Makah Tribal Planning Office, PO Box 115, Neah Bay, WA 98357; (360)645-2201.

Sandy Beaches on the Makah Reservation

Several sandy Pacific Ocean crescent beaches on the Makah Reservation are available to the public. Waatch Beach is just west of the Cape Flattery Tribal Center. A gentle stream, also accessible to the public, runs through a meadow near the beach and is deep enough for kids to kayak or innertube in. **HOBUCK BEACH**, (360)645-2422, has a grassy berm with campsites and a few rental cabins and is open for picnics (no fires), horseback riding, and surfing in certain areas from June 15 to August 30. **TSOO-YAS BEACH** (called Sooes on maps) is accessed by paying private landowners a parking fee.

The trail to **SHI SHI BEACH**, one of the best beaches on the Washington coast for tide pools, is accessible by driving through Neah Bay to the trailhead on the south end of the reservation. Check with the Makah Tribe for a list of public beaches, as well as for maps, rules and regulations, and fishing permits. The breakwater and the beach on the Neah Bay waterfront are also open to the public.

Makah Tribal Planning Office, PO Box 115, Neah Bay, WA 98357; (360)645-2201. The tribal office is in Bldg 12, at the old U.S. Air Force station near Cape Flattery, 6.7 miles southwest of Neah Bay. Follow Hwy 112 along the Neah Bay waterfront to the west end of the bay, turn left, and watch for signs.

Hiking and Camping Around Ozette Village Site

The trail through a roadless wilderness corridor to the site of the **MAKAH VILLAGE OF OZETTE** at Cape Alava is one of the premier hikes on the Olympic Peninsula. A **CEDAR-PLANK BOARDWALK**, which resonates like a drum under your shoes, winds through dark cedar groves, wetlands filled with broad-leafed skunk cabbage, and prairie resplendent with blue camas (a type of edible lily) in the spring. The trail ends at the cape, where haystack rocks rise dramatically offshore from a sea of kelp-covered stones and tidepools filled with sea stars, sea urchins, anemones, limpets, barnacles, and other sea creatures. Campers pitch their tents in well-worn but unusually clean primitive campsites among the exposed roots of the cedar trees that overhang the eroded bank. Deer are tame here, and often bring their newborn fawns within a few feet of visitors.

The **OZETTE VILLAGE SITE**, excavated in the 1970s, is about 500 yards north of the trail's end and marked with a small sign. The crows like to perch on top of the small cedar longhouse built by the Makah to memorialize their ancestors, who perished when the village was buried by a mudslide 500–700 years ago. Park ranger and Makah tribal member David Corpuz stands by the longhouse and answers questions asked by some of the thousands of travelers who have hiked the 3-mile trail to Ozette. From Ozette, hike 1 mile south on the beach to **WEDDING ROCK'S PETROGLYPHS** (ask for an interpretive handout at the ranger station). From Wedding Rock the trail continues another 2 miles south to Sand Point, where a second boardwalk loops back through the woods and skirts the north shore of Ozette Lake. At Sand Point adventurous hikers can continue hiking down the wilderness coastline to **RIALTO BEACH AND THE QUILEUTE RESERVATION**, a distance of about 25 miles, or all the way north to Neah Bay (be sure to check the tide tables and talk to rangers before doing this). Because it rains about 146 inches annually here,

Private timber companies have clear-cut lands adjacent to the road to the Ozette Trail, right up to Ozette Lake and the edges of streambeds—a stark contrast to the old-growth forest preserved in Olympic National Park. Scheduled for 2002, the Makah Tribe plans a new boardwalk from the marina to the museum and a hotel with a seafood restaurant. An RV park is scheduled for Hobuck Beach in 2001.

even day hikers should wear sturdy shoes (on the boardwalk, which is often slick, soft-soled sneakers to keep your footing are best) and bring along poncho-style rain slickers with hoods, a change of pants, dry socks and shoes, and food and water. Water from the creeks is full of natural tannin and therefore not potable.

The road to Lake Ozette is paved, but there are no services for 21 miles from the turnoff (between Hoko and Seiku) on Highway 112 to Ozette. The ranger station at the trailhead has modern restrooms, potable water, and kiosks with tide charts, and wildlife and trail information.

From Port Angeles, follow Hwy 112 past Clallam Bay to Seiku and watch for well-placed signs to Lake Ozette. From Forks, take Hwy 101 north to Sappho and continue north on Hwy 112 (Burnt Mountain Rd) to the town of Clallam Bay. Continue west 4 miles to the turnoff at Seiku. There are no stores or restaurants at Ozette. Food and supplies (even rain gear) may be purchased at supermarkets in Forks, Clallam Bay, or Neah Bay. There are 15 free camping sites on Lake Ozette: first come, first served. Backcountry camping permits are required for coastal sites. To make a reservation and get a confirmation number, call Olympic National Park headquarters, (360)452-0300. Pick up your permit from the ranger station at Ozette, (360)963-2725, upon arrival. Tide charts for hiking the beaches are essential. No pets.

Cape Flattery Trail: *Tatoosh Island Overlook*

The view at the Tatoosh Island Overlook at the mouth of the Strait of Juan de Fuca is truly spectacular, and the meandering boardwalk trail from the trailhead parking lot to the end of Cape Flattery has made the hike along the cliffs much easier and safer than in the past. The mile-long **MAKAH-BUILT TRAIL THROUGH OLD-GROWTH HEMLOCK AND CEDAR** ends at four observation decks on sheer cliffs overlooking haystack rocks and the northwesternmost point in the Lower 48: Tatoosh Island. The island has a rough shore, where **PACIFIC OCEAN BREAKERS** crash with full force. Several interpretive signs along the way discuss the cultural significance of area plants and wildlife and the history of the trail. A glorious place from which to watch the sunset for the spouts of migrating whales, the overlook is also a great place to sprawl on the wood deck on sunny days. The tribe built the trail with the help of other agencies.

For directions to Cape Flattery Trail, ask at the Forks Visitor Center, the Makah Cultural and Research Center, or Washburn's General Store on the reservation (also a good place to pick up a picnic lunch). Trail access is open to the public year-round. Free.

La Push: *Quileute Tribe*

Few people live in a more **BEAUTIFUL SETTING** than the Quileute Tribe. Surrounded by the rain forests of the Olympic National Park, their 1-mile-square reservation at the mouth of the Quillayute River faces a sandy crescent beach, haystack rocks, and the open ocean. Isolated on the undeveloped Washington coastline that is protected by the park, the Quileute live midway between the Makah and Quinault Reservations. The village of La Push (derived from La Bouche, named by French fur traders who bartered with the Quileute for seal and other skins) is off Highway 101, northwest of Forks, at the end of a 14-mile paved road.

From the 1950s to the early 1970s, when salmon were plentiful, La Push was a thriving salmon charterboat port. Local fishers still supply the fish processing plant, now leased to a non-Native, with crab, salmon, and bottom fish. But the little village is best known for the unpretentious **OCEAN PARK RESORT** and for the tribe's private beach, a driftwood-covered, sandy crescent with sloughing cliffs at one end and the Quillayute River jetty at the other. One of the **OLDEST CONTINUALLY OCCUPIED SETTLEMENTS** on the continent, La Push overlooks James Island, a tree-covered sea-stack at the river mouth, where many former chiefs are buried.

The resort is the first thing you see when entering La Push. Beyond it is the village, less than eight square blocks facing the river. The village looks poor and it is. Almost a third of the households earn less than $7,000 a year. The **QUILEUTE TRIBAL SCHOOL**, once housed in the picturesque 1920s-era Coast Guard station, is now located in a lovely new building overlooking the ocean, with a playground in the sand. The school has won national awards for its outstanding cultural education program, in which elders teach the Quileute language as well as carving and basket-making skills.

The tribe's dreams for the future include building an interpretive center and museum on an 11-acre island east of the village, accessible by footbridge, that will contain studio and workshop space for tribal

JAMES ISLAND: A QUILEUTE LANDMARK

James Island, a prominent haystack rock covered with tall firs, sits just offshore on the north side of the Quillayute River. Named after a settler who once perched his house up top, James wasn't an actual island until the U.S. Army Corps of Engineers changed the course of the river, which isolated the haystack from the village. Shaped like a horseshoe, with access to the top on the ocean side, James Island had many uses. It was a temporary home to the Quileute, who once moved their entire village of longhouses to the top to defend themselves during sieges by the neighboring Makah. It was also a traditional burial ground for chiefs. Bodies were wrapped in blankets woven from dog's hair and laid in a cedar canoe. The tribe also grew nettles 10 feet tall in a tended patch on the island's top, later harvesting them and twisting them into fine twine to use in weaving fishing nets.

members..The island is currently a well-trampled pasture favored by a herd of Roosevelt elk, which swim across the Quillayute River to reach it.

Most visitors to La Push come to the park resort to relax, walk on the beaches, surf, fish, and watch the sunsets. Whales linger just outside the surf during their spring and fall migrations. Some visitors leave the beach and stray into town. Walk along the marina with its weathered fishing boats (you may see one of the tribe's traditional canoes tied up at the dock), and see the tribe's displays of a few baskets in the tribal center. Walk further upriver to the lovely bronze monument erected by the tribe in tribute to several Coast Guard workers who lost their lives in a heroic ocean rescue in 1997.

Quileute Basket Weaving

One of the best things about meeting **QUILEUTE BASKET WEAVERS** is talking with them about how they collect materials. Bear grass, cattails, and cedar bark must be gathered and prepared, no matter what other events might be on the calendar. In 1997, Quileute weavers were put to the test when the U.S. Forest Service gave them permission to strip 300 pounds of thin cedar bark from trees marked for immediate clear cutting.

Green alder was once preferred for making ceremonial masks. The carver entered a grove of the white-barked trees, selected one tree, and carved the mask directly on its trunk. He then left it for a period of time so that spirits could enter the mask. Only then did he cut it out of the living tree, and finished the mask at his leisure.
—Chris Morganroth

TRIBAL ELDER Leila Morganroth remembers bedding down for the night in the canoe with her grandmother when out gathering cattails and other materials near Lake Ozette. Elder Lillian Pullen, a fluent speaker of the Quileute language and a master weaver, learned to weave beside her grandmother, who was considered one of the most skilled basket weavers in the Quileute tribe. Mrs. Pullen has taught tribal members how to gather and prepare the inner bark of cedar for baskets and such **TRADITIONAL WOVEN CLOTHING** as rainproof hats, vests, and cedar-bark skirts. Her daughter-in-law, Eileen Penn, and great-granddaughter, Ann, are weavers as well. They also incorporate Mrs. Pullen's weaving designs into knit sweaters, vests, hats, and mittens.

Other Quileute weavers include Arlene, Beverly, and Deanna Jackson, Margaret Black, Marian Schumack, Mary Leitka and her daughter, and Viola Riebe and her daughters.

Some Quileute basket weavers' work can be found in the cases at Ocean Park Resort, PO Box 67, La Push, WA 98350; (800)487-1267 or (360)374-5267. To meet local weavers, contact Leila Morganroth, (360)374-9708 or (360)374-2061. To make an appointment with Lillian Pullen or a member of her family, call (360)374-5842 or (360)374-9896.

THE QUILEUTES OF THE PAST

For thousands of years, before the "White Drifting-House People" arrived in their ships, the Quileute Indians lived, fished, and hunted sea mammals along the mouths of five rivers that flow from the glaciers of the Olympic Mountains to the seastack-strewn Pacific beaches. Legends indicate that the Quileute may be among the oldest inhabitants of the Pacific Northwest, their lineage stretching back to a time when ice covered most of the land and the people nearly starved to extinction. According to the Quileute origin myth, the people were created from wolves by a wandering supernatural Transformer. The Quileute speak English today, but their native tongue is a unique language, unrelated to any root language in the world.

The Quileute's stories say that their only kin, the Chimakum, were carried away in their canoes by a great flood through a passageway in the Olympic Mountains and deposited on the other side of the Olympic Peninsula. The present-day Chimacum, a crossroads town south of Port Townsend, is named after the Chimakum who lived there until the 1860s, when the Suquamish Indians, under Chief Seattle, wiped them out, leaving the Quileute with no known relatives.

From cradleboard to burial canoe, the Quileute depended on the help and inspiration of supernatural powers. Youths sought their own taxilit (personal guardian power) on solitary spirit quests. Such rituals as the first salmon ceremony guaranteed the goodwill of the salmon spirits, assuring the great fish would continue to fill the river each year and allow themselves to be caught. There were also thought to be a terrifying array of monsters, such as Daskya, the kelp-haired child snatcher, lurking in the area.

The Quileute signed a treaty with the U.S. government in 1856, agreeing to move south to the Quinault Reservation, the home of their traditional enemy. They didn't actually relocate, however, either because they could not translate the documents they had agreed to sign or because they decided to hold their ground. In 1889, President Grover Cleveland agreed that the Quileute could stay at La Push, at the mouth of the Quillayute River. Of all their traditional lands, however, they were allowed only 1 square mile of land surrounding the village. Shortly after they had secured their reservation, the village was burned to the ground by several white men who wanted the Quileute land. The elders (who had been left behind while the rest of the tribe was picking hops in the Puyallup Valley) were unable to save the houses or any of their ceremonial items when the village was engulfed by flames.

FOUR SPARKLING BEACHES TO EXPLORE:
QUILEUTE LANDS ACQUIRED BY THE NATIONAL PARK SERVICE

Deer have been observed leaping in the surf on Olympic National Park's mist-shrouded beaches, but most two-legged visitors rarely immerse themselves in the icy sea: hypothermia is a real threat to anyone staying in the water more than 10 minutes. Except for the surfers and ocean kayakers, who dress in insulated wet or dry suits, most visitors come to Olympic National Park ocean beaches for their unspoiled beauty. The beaches near La Push are some of the best on the coast. Two of them are easily accessible by road; two others are accessible only by trail.

First Beach, in front of Ocean Park Resort at La Push, is open year-round, with paths through the driftwood to the sand. Permits for beach fires are available from Ocean Park Resort for $2. Second Beach is less than a mile south of La Push, separated from First Beach at La Push by an impassable headland. Park in the well-marked lot next to the road and hike through deep, quiet forest on reservation land for less than a mile to the beach. Steep portions of the trail have broad stairs with handrails to make the descent easier, and benches to rest on during the tiring ascent back to the parking lot. Second Beach faces the Quillayute Needles, impressive spikes of rock that are part of the offshore national marine sanctuary, accessible at low tide for tide-pool exploring.

Third Beach is even farther south, separated from Second Beach by Teahwhit Head. Park in the lot next to the road and hike about 1 1/2 miles down an easy trail to the mile-long strand that ends at a plunging waterfall at Taylor Point. The trail continues from Taylor Point to the mouth of the untamed Hoh River, a distance of about 20 miles over the rugged headlands; consult National Park headquarters (360)452-4501, before hiking this portion of the trail.

The mouth of the Hoh River is more easily reached by continuing on Highway 101 past Forks to the turnoff to Oil City, and then taking the 15-mile-long gravel road to the Hoh's north shore. We've seen cougar tracks on the trail and herds of elk swimming the river here, as well as hundreds of brown pelicans and arctic terns fishing at the river's mouth. The narrow trail winds along the riverbank and ends at an impressively deep, and wide, pile of driftwood. Across the Hoh River is a small band of Quileute families, living on a few acres of land reserved for them by presidential decree in 1893.

North of La Push is Rialto Beach, also part of Olympic National Park. You can see Rialto Beach across the Quileute River from La Push, but to get there you must backtrack toward Highway 101. Take the Mora/Rialto turnoff and continue past the Mora campground, in deep woods, to the large, paved parking lot, with information kiosk and restrooms. The hike on Rialto Beach is richly rewarding. The surf pounds the steep shore with a satisfying roar. Huge red cedar logs, remnants of the logging era when the big cedars were being cut upriver, are strewn across the rocky beach. Most visitors walk a few feet from their cars, find a spot to sit against the big logs, and watch the surf. You can hike north on Rialto Beach about 2 miles to Hole in the Wall, a natural arch in the rock and a great place to poke about in tide pools.

From Hole in the Wall, you can continue to hike the wilderness beach all the way north to Ozette Village (see the Ozette listing in the Makah section) and on to Neah Bay, a distance of about 45 miles, best traveled at low tide. Creeks along the way are tea-colored by natural tannin and unsafe to drink; water must be portaged.

La Push Ocean Park Resort: *Quileute-Owned Lodging*

The glorious beach, relaxed atmosphere, and spectacular views are what bring travelers year-round to the Quileute's Ocean Park Resort and adjoining Shoreline Resort, despite the relentless winter rain. Ocean Park also offers the only OCEANFRONT ACCOMMODATIONS between Neah Bay and Kalaloch, about 100 miles apart, on the northern Washington coast. Accommodations range from A-frame cabins under the trees, where guests cook on a hot plate, heat water for dishwashing, and sack out in their own sleeping bags, to new three-bedroom townhouses with fireplaces, fully equipped kitchens, and barbecues on the deck. Newer cabins are equally spiffed up; most have fireplaces or glass-fronted woodstoves. Split, dry firewood and kindling are provided free in a box at the doorstep. The two-story Thunderbird and Whale motel units are nothing fancy, but each has a deck and fully equipped kitchen. The resort's water system pipes in clear, fresh spring water. Tent camping and RV hookups are also available. Pets are allowed in some units.

WHALE WATCHERS take over the place in March, April, May, and the first part of June, when the gray whales linger just beyond the breakers; July and August are equally popular months. November through March the storms hit with full force, sometimes knocking out the electric power. Candlelight and driftwood fires add to the charm of the place. Weekends are always busy. There are no restaurants at the resort or in La Push. A small grocery store is next door to the village; it offers mostly fast food. Full-service grocery stores are in Forks, about 16 miles away. From December through June you can buy freshly caught, iced Dungeness crab in the shell at **QUILEUTE SEAFOOD** (see listing in this section), a short walk from the resort. Espresso, videotapes of the Quileute tribe's first canoe project, printed information about the tribe, and gifts are available in the resort office.

Ocean Park Resort, PO Box 67, La Push, WA 98350; (800)487-1267 or (360)374-5267. Take the La Push/Quileute exit from Hwy 101 and stay on the road until the beach is visible. The resort office is on the left. Rates range from $10 a night for campsites to $36 for cabins; $50 for motel units to $125 for a fireplace cabins. Reservations are strongly advised. Weekends are usually booked three months ahead; holidays, a year in advance.

Quileute Seafood: *Buy from Indian Fishers*

Early in the day you can climb up on the La Push jetty, find a flat rock to sit on, and watch fishing boats chugging out to sea and fishers standing in skiffs checking their nets in the river. The boom time for such fisheries was in the 1950s to 1970s, when more than 300 fishing boats moored in La Push. Now there are 20. At Quileute Seafood's cold storage plant (next to the dock), you can buy freshly caught, **ICED DUNGENESS CRAB** in the shell (when in season), tasty with cocktail sauce. Whole coho and pink salmon, black and red sea bass, and other fish can be bought either singly or in quantity. The processing plant is leased to a non-Native who buys seafood from tribal fishers.

Quileute Seafood, 100 Main St, La Push, WA 98350; look for crab pots stacked in front of the blue building and the old firetruck parked in the lot. Open daily, hours vary according to the catch.

Although Quinault seafarers hunted seals through the early 1900s using sail-powered canoes, the art of canoe building was suspended in the 1930s when the U.S. government declared a moratorium on seal hunting (still in effect today). Decades passed before tribal members once again carved a canoe. That canoe, launched April 10, 1994, bears the Quinault name Mayee ("the Beginning"). Two more canoes have since been built.

Queets and Taholah:
Quinault Indian Nation

The Quinault Reservation is neighbor to Olympic National Park, a sanctuary of huge, ancient, moss-covered cedars and firs, crystal clear streams and mountain peaks; the Olympic National Forest; and the federally protected Olympic Coast National Marine Sanctuary off-shore. The largest reserve in Western Washington, the **QUINAULT INDIAN RESERVATION** is an enormous triangle of more than 200,000 acres facing the Pacific Ocean. At its southwestern end is the reservation's major village, Taholah, a beautiful and long-inhabited site at the mouth of the Quinault River. Where longhouses once stood facing the ocean, **TAHOLAH** has, in this century, been reworked into a grid of streets serving single-family houses, with two sports fields, a seafood processing plant, a new housing development, and a handsome tribal administrative complex.

Scenic coastal Highway 101 does not go through the reservation; rather it wraps around it, touching its eastern boundary on the shoreline of Lake Quinault. Just south of the lake, from Highway 101, you can take a direct route to the ocean, visiting a **FISH HATCHERY AND AN EXPERIMENTAL FOREST** (established in 1910) along the way. This 30-mile trip from the mountains to the ocean goes to Ocean Crest Resort at Moclips and, intersecting with Highway 109, leads to lodging and public beaches (and perhaps a future casino and hotel at Oyehut) south of Taholah. If you are driving to the Quinault Reservation from the south, there is a shortcut on State Route 109, from Aberdeen. The road parallels 23 scenic miles of oceanfront until it ends at Taholah.

The Quinault Indians signed a treaty with the U.S. government in 1855, in which they relinquished their claim to the majority of the Olympic Peninsula, retaining only the heart of their ancestral land. Eventually, other tribes—also forced by the U.S. government to give up their traditional lands—moved to the Quinault Reservation. The Quinault and these other tribes—Chehalis, Chinook, Cowlitz, Hoh, Queets, Quileute, and Quinault—make up the Quinault Indian Nation, a federally recognized government territory that predates Washington's statehood.

Some of the people living on the Quinault Reservation are of Chinook heritage. When treaties were signed in the 1850s, the Chinooks and other Western Washington tribes were displaced from their homelands to the Quinault Reservation. For more about the Chinooks and their descendants living in Bay Center, South Bend, and other towns on Washington's southern coast, see the Columbia River Gorge and Basin chapter.

Many visitors come to Taholah to buy fresh and smoked seafood. Fewer know of the reservation's fabulous **QUINAULT RIVER TOURS**—bird-watching, fishing, kayaking, or dugout canoe tours. Knowledgeable and courteous tribal members escort these tours. Tour guide Michael Cardwell, a planner for the tribe, calls his hilarious commentary the reservation's "rant and rave" tour.

Northwest Pride Gallery: *Quinault Art*

Throughout the town of Taholah you will find **CARVINGS AND TOTEMS** on schools and other community buildings, perhaps because the Quinault Nation's sign ordinance prescribes carved wooden signs for all public buildings. Art clearly has a place here. The tribe has opened the Northwest Pride Gallery at the Southshore Mall in Aberdeen (the direct, freeway route from Olympia to the Pacific Ocean). The gallery's centerpiece is a replica of the tribe's **33-FOOT OCEAN-GOING CANOE**, carved by Taholah high school students and filled with **GIFT BASKETS** for sale (based on the notion that when other tribes came to visit along the coast, their canoes were loaded with gifts for their hosts). **RANDY CAPOEMAN**, a printmaker and painter, sells his screened prints, drums, cards, and T-shirts at the gallery and demonstrates his work on site. You'll also find John Boyer's limited-edition prints, paintings, and carvings. Other artists represented are Michael Cardwell-Snqhepi'wes (a Salish word meaning "spirit") and occasionally Guy Capoeman, who carved the Quinault's Mayee canoe and performs with the Quinault Indian Nation Dancers, is sometimes represented; Guy's work is rare in this gallery, however; he shows mostly in major metropolitan art galleries, such as Quintana in Portland, Oregon.

Also look here for **QUINAULT PRIDE SEAFOOD** products, plus jams and jellies, sauces, vinaigrettes, and other Northwest gourmet foods. The gallery also carries Southwest Indian arts and crafts and Native American music and books.

Northwest Pride Gallery, Southshore Mall, 1017 S Boone, Ste 106, Aberdeen, WA 98520; (360)533-4585. Open daily.

The Queets Mercantile: *Tribal Arts and Crafts*

Just off Highway 101, north of Lake Quinault, stop at the Quinault Nation's mercantile to see the traditional art and crafts that are on display. You might see work by artisans Eunice Williams (crocheted dolls), Charlotte Kalama (baskets), or Rick Obi (miniature and life-size racing canoes). The mercantile has a gas station, RV spots, and hot showers (it's a great stop for bicyclists), and here you can get information about guided fishing trips, hiking, and general tourism.

The Queets Mercantile, 402 Jackson Heights Dr, Queets, WA 98331; (360)962-2003. Open daily.

Forestry Tour: *Led by Tribal Foresters*

Most of the Quinault Nation's old-growth trees have been logged. The Bureau of Indian Affairs, which managed the land, gave out large, long-term contracts to a few logging companies. The companies made enormous profits while their logging practices destroyed whole water-sheds, filling salmon-spawning streams with wood debris. In 1971 the Quinault Tribe risked arrest to protest these practices by blocking roads into logging units. Their effort to bring the destruction to public attention worked; the tribe gained local support and eventually took over the management of their remaining forests.

To reverse more than 100 years of ecological damage, the Quinault rehabilitate streambeds and plant more than a million trees annually. These **YOUNG FORESTS**, planted with diverse species, are healthy, with ferns, mushrooms, blackberries, beargrass, and multitudes of shrubs and wildflowers. Tribal foresters offer guided tours of these forests, which are a haven for herds of **ROOSEVELT ELK, BLACK BEAR, BLACKTAIL DEER, BALD EAGLES, COUGARS**, and many other animals.

For tour information, contact the Quinault Natural Resources Department, PO Box 189, Taholah, WA 98587; (360)276-8211.

Fishing Through the Quinault Reservation:
Native-Guided Tours

Quinault tribal member Clayton Butler, who works for the Olympic National Park, offers **GUIDED FISHING TOURS** year-round on the Quinault, Queets, Salmon, and Raft Rivers and on Cook Creek, all of which flow through the Quinault Reservation. Two streams, the Salmon and the Cook, are tributaries of the 37-mile-long Quinault River and are enhanced with fish spawned and raised in tribal hatcheries. The Raft River hosts one of the few robust runs of **WILD SALMON** left in the Pacific Northwest. In winter Butler takes fishers on the rivers in a jet-boat so they can reach selected fishing holes; the salmon season for coho and chinook is September through November, followed by winter steelhead fishing through April. All streams have healthy runs of rainbow, cutthroat, and pink-fleshed Dolly Varden trout. In summer Butler guides fly-fishing for steelhead and king salmon. While fishing on these wild rivers, look for bear and other wildlife along the riverbank. Butler also leads sightseeing tours.

Clayton Butler, (360)962-2191 or (360)962-2283; fax (360)962-2066. Prices start at $100 per day, per person. Fishers provide their own gear, lunches, and snacks.

Hiking, Fishing, and Bird-Watching: *Quinault-Guided Trips*

The western Olympic Peninsula is home to a wide variety of birds, from **BALD EAGLES AND OSPREY** to rufous-sided hummingbirds, cormorants, and little sandpipers skittering through the surf. **BROWN PELICANS** are annual visitors to the Quinault River, sometimes traveling in flocks of up to 200. Lake Quinault boasts more than 20 pairs of

TRUMPETER SWANS, which nest along its shoreline. Teaming up with local Audubon chapters and WINGS, an international bird-watching organization, QUINAULT TRIBAL MEMBER Mike Mail offers several unusual bird-watching tours. Ride with Mail in a traditional Quinault River cedar canoe (outfitted with a small motor) from Lake Quinault downriver to Point Grenville, south of the river's mouth. Kayak groups may also contact him for a two-day tour that includes an overnight campout on the riverbank.

Winter or summer, Quinault guides offer STEELHEAD AND TROUT FISHING TOURS on the Humptulips, Queets, Quinault, and Salmon Rivers or on Lake Quinault. Guides must accompany hikers on the reservation, or visitors can pick up a daily pass at the tribe's administration complex, 1214 Aalis, Taholah, to use the Quinault coastal beaches that are open to the public.

For a list of tribal tour guides, contact the Quinault Department of Community Development, PO Box 189, Taholah, WA 98587; (360)276-8211.

Quinault Pride Seafood: *Canned and Smoked Fish*

The Quinault Tribe established Quinault Pride Seafood, a seafood processing plant in Taholah, to market local fishers' catches. During the peak season, more than 80 people are employed here. Fishers deliver daily, and within hours the catch is cleaned and processed. Begun in a wooden shack in the 1950s, Quinault Pride is now housed in a spacious building overlooking the Quinault River, with state-of-the-art equipment to fast-freeze, can, and smoke seafood. Their products sell throughout the Northwest.

The plant's shop sells ALDERWOOD-SMOKED FISH in handsome paper boxes or handcrafted wooden gift boxes with braided rope handles, with labels designed by Quinault artist Randy Capoeman. Also available are variety GIFT PACKS of smoked razor clams, sturgeon, albacore tuna, and three kinds of salmon (including rare Quinault blueback salmon) as well as cards, gift baskets, baseball caps, T-shirts, and fishing gear. The shop ships orders anywhere in the world. Factory tours are free (no canned speeches).

Quinault Pride Seafood, 100 Quinault St, Taholah, WA 98587; (800)821-8650 or (360)962-2180. Call or visit the plant for order forms and price list. Open 8am–5pm, Mon–Fri, year-round

Quinault National Fish Hatchery

In 1976 the Quinault Tribe opened their hatchery on Cook Creek, a small stream that flows under the Moclips Highway. Each year the hatchery produces more than 8 million **CHINOOK, CHUM, COHO, AND STEELHEAD SALMON.** Visitors are welcome to tour the facility during working hours. The information center at the hatchery displays mounted specimens of adult fish and explains the fish life cycle. You'll also see some **HISTORIC PHOTOGRAPHS** of the Quinault Reservation here.

Quinault National Fish Hatchery, PO Box 80, Neilton, WA 98566; (360)288-2508.

Oakville: *Chehalis Tribe*

The Chehalis are known for their **SKILL AS FISHERS** and for their **FINE BASKETRY**. Located on the Chehalis River at Oakville, their reservation occupies the former site of one of their largest ancestral villages. They were called the *Chehalis*, derived from their name for Hanson Point, *tshels*, on the south side of Grays Harbor. Others say the name means "people of the sand," because all of their villages were situated on the sandy banks of the Chehalis River, including two very large villages near present-day Elma and Grand Mound. The Lower Chehalis occupied land at the mouth of the Chehalis River to the mouth of the Satsop; the Upper Chehalis lived in the region from the Satsop to the present-day town of Chehalis. The two groups spoke different dialects of the same Coast Salish language.

The Chehalis did not sign a treaty. During the 1850s they banded together, refusing to move to the Quinault Reservation (the first of many Puget Sound area tribes who refused to relocate), where they had been assigned. With the help of an Oakville teacher, adults over age 18 homesteaded the land that is today incorporated into the **CHEHALIS RESERVATION,** 4,224 acres that were officially set aside by executive order on July 8, 1864, at the confluence of the Black and Chehalis Rivers. Today about 575 people are enrolled as tribal members; around 250 live on the reservation at Oakville. Available at the **CHEHALIS TRIBAL CENTER,** the book *The Last Canoe* documents the carving of the last Chehalis canoe; the publication *The Chehalis People* tells the tribe's history. Smoked salmon, caught from the Chehalis River, can also be ordered here.

Chehalis Tribal Center, 420 Howanut Rd, Oakville, WA 98568; (360)273-5911. From I-5, take the Oakville/Rochester exit. Travel 8 miles west on Hwy 12, turn left on Anderson Rd, and go to the top of the hill. At the stop sign, take a right, go past a church, and watch for signs. Open 8am–4:30pm, weekdays, year-around.

Hazel Pete Institute: *Chehalis Basketry*

Hazel Pete teaches **CHEHALIS-STYLE BASKETRY** year-round at her home, on a portion of the original 90-acre parcel that was homesteaded by her great-great-grandmother Jane Moxley (Guma). Pete learned basketry from her grandmothers, who shared the homestead, and then taught materials gathering and basket-making to her family. Today her nine children, who live across the United States, come home each year to participate in the family's **THANKSGIVING WEEKEND BASKET SALE**. During this sale they gather such materials as cattail from the marshes and sweetgrass from the mouth of the Chehalis River, and weave baskets under their mother's direction. The great-grandchildren weave angels, cattail dolls, and bookmarks; the grandchildren and adult children weave the more complicated baskets. **COLLECTORS FROM ALL OVER THE WORLD** come to buy Pete family baskets. Members of the extended family have put themselves through college by making baskets and telling stories. Pete herself returned to school in her 60s, ultimately receiving her bachelor of science degree from Evergreen State College and master's degree in Indian education from the University of Washington.

Pete's basketry can be seen at the American Indian Community House Museum in New York City, the Institute of American Indian Art in Santa Fe, the University of Washington's Burke Museum of Natural History in Seattle, and the Washington State Capitol Museum in Olympia. She also teaches basketry in the spring and fall, to anyone interested, at her Oakville home.

Hazel Pete Institute of Chehalis Basketry, 137 Anderson Rd, Oakville, WA 98568; (360)273-7274 (after 4pm). From I-5, take the Oakville/Rochester exit and on Hwy 12, travel 8 miles west. Turn left on Anderson Rd, and travel 1 mile to the top of the hill. The house is on the lefthand side of the road, past the stop sign.

WESTERN OREGON & NORTHERN CALIFORNIA

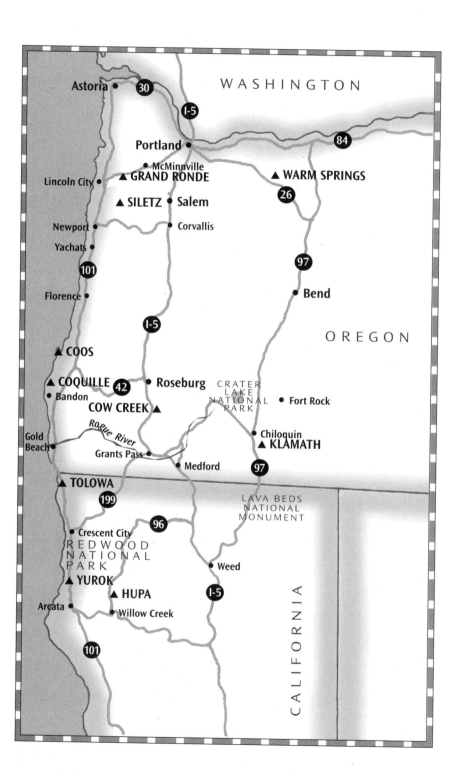

WESTERN OREGON & NORTHERN CALIFORNIA

Before European contact, more than 100 tribes and bands of Native peoples lived along the coast and interior valleys of what is today is Western Oregon and Northern California.

Recently uncovered archaeological and geological evidence indicates that at least 12 major earthquakes and tsunamis have struck the coastline over the past 6,500 years, or about every 300 years. The most recent was a huge quake that struck in 1700. House remains discovered on the sand spit at Netarts Bay, in Oregon, have enabled experts to reconstruct what may have happened that night, yielding more and more information about the coast's geological history and the peoples who inhabited it for thousands of years.

The people on this coast were struck again in the late 1700s and early 1800s, this time by a series of epidemics that swept south from the Columbia River basin into Western Oregon, often decimating entire villages of people. By 1860, Native populations in Western Oregon and Northern California were reduced further by forced removal of all remaining Indians from their homelands to the Coast

Reservation, an area that stretched from Tillamook Bay to Florence on the Oregon coast. Hunters tracked down Indians who did not move to the reservation and killed them.

When land developers from the Portland area became interested in properties along the Oregon coast, the reservation was cut in half by decree of the Oregon state legislature. As early as 1865, the land was divided and sold to make way for a railroad route. Indian homes and farms were confiscated by white speculators, who auctioned off the Indians' land. The reservation was open to white settlement, except for a 30-mile strip between Lincoln City and Newport, which came to be known as the Siletz Reservation. In all more than 1 million acres of premium land were taken, despite treaties the tribes had signed with the Federal government. That there are descendants of the people who first occupied this land still living today is a miracle indeed. Yet amazingly, even a century later, there is no museum or interpretive center in Oregon or California that tells this epic story.

In Western Oregon visit the Confederated Tribes of the Grand Ronde, with tribal members descended from many Willamette and Rogue River Valley tribes, who have regained a small amount of land between McMinnville's wine country and Lincoln City. The Confederated Tribes of Siletz Indians owns a small pocket of land east of Newport, Oregon, and several parcels in Lincoln City—all that is left of the original Coast Reservation. About 100 miles south of Siletz, in Coos Bay, are the Confederated Tribes of the Coos, Siletz, and Lower Umpqua, and the Coquille

Indian Tribe. Inland is the Cow Creek Band of Lower Umpquas, located in Roseburg.

Today the many bands that once settled every river drainage in Northern California own very small *rancherias* along the coast, most of them about 160 acres, reduced from a 25,000-acre reservation set aside for them in the original treaty. Only the Hupa Tribe has a reservation, occupying 12 square miles of their aboriginal territory along the beautiful Trinity River where they practice traditional brush dances and white deer skin dances.

In Redwood National Park, the aboriginal territory of the Yurok, people continue to quietly practice their traditional religions and fish for salmon on the Smith and Klamath Rivers and tributaries. The Hupa Tribe, on the east side of Redwood National Park, offer tours through their museum and raft trips down the Trinity River to look at village sites.

WESTERN OREGON

Portland: *Chinook*

Portland, Oregon, is situated on land once inhabited by Native peoples, yet like other metropolitan cities in the Pacific Northwest, it focuses very little on the heritage of those tribes. Within the city limits, **16 MAJOR CHINOOK VILLAGES** once stood. Both Multnomah County and the region's most spectacular waterfall, Multnomah Falls, are named after the Multnomah Band of Chinooks who lived on the shores of the Columbia and Willamette Rivers, where Portland is now located. Multnomah Channel, a narrow waterway 14 miles north of

Portland that flows along the west bank of **SAUVIE ISLAND**, is also named after the band. Although five archaeological digs have been completed on Sauvie Island—a marshland once rich with starchy wapato, fish, and waterfowl—few people know that Multnomah Chinooks once occupied the island. **STONE FIGURES** carved of basalt, unearthed from the island, are part of the Oregon History Center's collection. The few Multnomahs who survived the epidemics that swept through the lower Columbia and all of Western Oregon in the 1830s intermarried or were moved to reservations in the 1850s—some of them to Grand Ronde near the Central Oregon coast, some north to the Quinault Reservation on the Washington coast.

Like its sister cities of Vancouver, British Columbia, and Seattle, Washington, Portland offers a broad taste of **PAN-NATIVE AMERICAN ART**, literature, and culture through its galleries, bookstores, museums, and annual art showcase **INDIAN ART NORTHWEST**, a three-day festival held each Memorial Day in the city's Cultural District.

The Bureau of Indian Affairs regional headquarters are located in Portland, as are the offices of the Affiliated Tribes of Northwest Indians, which represents 54 tribes from six states. The Columbia River Inter-Tribal Fish Commission, a consortium of four tribes with fishing rights on the Columbia River, also has an office in Portland. More than 11,000 "**URBAN INDIANS**," who have moved to Oregon from all over the United States, live within the city limits and cosponsor an **ANNUAL POWWOW** each summer at Delta Park, near the airport.

The historical **FORT VANCOUVER**, the Northwest headquarters of the Hudson's Bay Company, founded in 1830, is just across the Columbia River, about a 10 minute drive from downtown Portland.

Indian Art Northwest: *Native Arts Festival*

This **ANNUAL CELEBRATION OF NATIVE ART** showcases the work of Native artists each Memorial Day weekend in an outdoor marketplace in Portland's beautiful Park Blocks. Covering about three square blocks, the tented event takes place under gigantic elm trees among rose gardens, bronze statues, and brick-paved courtyards, sandwiched between the Portland Art Museum, the Performing Arts Center, and the Oregon History Museum. The festival is modeled after the Santa Fe Indian Art Market, which was established in the 1920s.

The event begins with a sunrise prayer ceremony overlooking the city and includes a gallery walk, the **LIVING CULTURAL TREASURES** dinner honoring elders who have maintained traditional lifeways, breakfast with the Portland Art Museum's curator of Native American art, an Indian art seminar, the gala awards ceremony, and art demonstrations. Traditional dancers and storytellers demonstrate on stage.

The fine art shown here includes works by some of the **BEST NATIVE ARTISTS** in the country—people who exhibit and sell their work to museums and collectors worldwide. Northwesterners not familiar with fine Indian art may suffer sticker shock, but be assured that the money is well spent. This artwork is often one of a kind and rapidly increases in value. It is best to circle the booths several times, to become familiar not only with the art but the artists. Bonds established between buyers and sellers can go on for years when nourished by these annual reunions.

The festival produces *Northwest Indian Magazine* several times a year and a children's activity guide, illustrated by Native artists. Artists will ship your purchases home for you.

Indian Art Northwest, (503)224-8650; IANcouncil@aol.com; www.northwestindian.com; or call the Portland Oregon Visitors Association, (503)222-2223.

Froelick Adelhart Gallery: *Contemporary Native Art*

Represented by the Froelick Adelhart Gallery, Rick Bartow (Yurok) is one of the best-known **CONTEMPORARY NATIVE PAINTERS** in the Northwest. He draws and paints images inspired by spiritual and psychological transformation; his **ANIMAL SPIRITS** represent guides in the journey of life. A resident of Newport, Oregon, Bartow also shows his work on walls enclosing the escalators at Saks Fifth Avenue in Portland. The gallery also hosts a show of contemporary **BASKET MAKERS' WORK** each May.

Froelick Adelhart Gallery, 817 SW Second Ave., Portland, OR 204-3005; (503)222-1142.

Quintana's Galleries: *Northwest Native Art*

Quintana's sells the Native arts of the Pacific Northwest, British Columbia and Alaska. Among their artists are such contemporary Alaskan artists as David Boxley (Tsimshian) and John Hoover (Aleut). Also shown are many **NORTHWEST COAST-STYLE DANCE MASKS, RATTLES, AND POTLATCH BOWLS** carved from cedar and alder. The gallery also carries the distinctive artwork of ceramic artist Lilliam Pitt (Yakama, Warm Springs), whose jewelry, masks, and installations depict the legends of the Columbia Gorge peoples. Inuit and Eskimo stone and ivory carvings are also displayed. New shows often open with **NATIVE DRUMMING, SINGING, AND DANCING**.

The gallery sells original photographs, photogravures, and gold-tones produced by Edward S. Curtis, who photographed Indians throughout the west from 1898 to 1928.

Quintana Galleries, 501 SW Broadway, Portland, OR 97205; (800)321-1729 or (503)223-1729; www.quintanagalleries.com. Open Tues–Sat.

OREGON COAST QUAKE WIPES OUT NATIVE VILLAGES

On January 26, 1700, at 9pm, catastrophe struck Indian villages along Oregon's coast, when a major earthquake shook houses to the ground and a tsunami, which also struck the coastline of Japan, swept inland for almost a mile. According to the record of quakes shown in the stratigraphic layers of soil at Netarts and Nehalem Bays, where remains of houses have been excavated, at least 12 severe quakes have shaken Oregon's coast in the last 6,500 years.

Estimated to be a 9.0 on the Richter scale, the 1700 quake caused the floors of houses in Netarts and Nehalem Bays to drop as much as 2 feet, collapsing supporting house posts and dropping heavy cedar beams and ceiling and wall planks on the occupants. Entire forests dropped and collapsed into the bays. About ten minutes after the ground stopped heaving (according to evidence encoded in layers of cliff side sediments), a huge tsunami crashed inland, sweeping everything aside and burying it all with a layer of sand.

University of Oregon doctoral candidate Robert Losey speculates that the devastating quake struck after dark during the height of the winter ceremonial season. Families would have been visiting one another from all along the coast and from far inland, staying for extended periods of time, enjoying reunions with relatives who had married into other tribes. Game,

Fort Vancouver: Restored Hudson's Bay Trading Site

Fort Vancouver National Historical Site is just 15 minutes from downtown Portland, across the Columbia River in Vancouver, Washington. A stockade and seven buildings have been reconstructed at the original site of Hudson's Bay Company's Fort Vancouver; the fort's lively interpretation is set historically in 1845. For a complete description of the fort, see The Lower Columbia section of the Columbia River Gorge and Basin chapter.

Fort Vancouver National Historic Site, 1501 E Evergreen Blvd, Vancouver, WA 98661; (360)696-7655. Located across the Columbia River from Portland. From I-5, take the Mill Plain Blvd exit and follow the signs. From I-205, take the Vancouver exit, go west on Hwy 14 for 5 miles, and then turn right on Grand Blvd. Open daily; tours and cultural demonstrations are offered throughout the day. Admission.

Portland Art Museum: Native Artifacts and Art

The Portland Art Museum was one of the first art museums in North America to recognize the "art" in Indian artifacts and to purchase a major collection. The **AXEL RASMUSSEN COLLECTION**, purchased in *fish, sea vegetables, tubers, and nuts that had been laboriously gathered through the summer for the long winter's daily meals and for elaborate feasts—prepared and stored in hand-woven baskets and stone-lined pits under the floorboards of houses—were swept away. Hung from the rafters perhaps were basket-making materials—bear grass, sea grasses, cattail, and maidenhair fern—gathered and dried for weavers to work on during the long winter days.*

Also swept away were house planks, hand-hewn with stone adzes and assembled to be easily dismantled and quickly moved during high water and floods. Firewood, gathered inside the longhouses and piled for the ceremonial fire pit, was taken too. The Indians' laboriously made tools, points, and fish hooks were lost.

When the quake struck, houses collapsed and fires were extinguished. In the confusing darkness, the sea receded with a sucking roar before the horrifying tsunami crashed ashore.

Those who survived, if there were survivors, would probably have gone to live inland with extended families. There are few tales about this natural disaster because passage of oral history has diminished over the generations. In particular, many tribal oral historians were lost to the epidemics of the 1830s and the forced relocation of the Coastal tribes that brought illness and starvation to Indians on a mass scale.

1948, brought to Portland **500 OBJECTS** collected in the 1920s and 1930s in Southeast Alaska and British Columbia. A school superintendent from the midwestern United States, Rasmussen was in British Columbia at the time that Native winter ceremonies and potlatches were outlawed. Tribal members were forced to give up ceremonial items to Indian agents to obtain the release of family members incarcerated for practicing their traditional religious ceremonies. Unfortunately, although some items were boxed and sent to Ottawa for safekeeping, many were sold to collectors. These items are the source of many Northwest Coast collections of art and artifacts throughout North America. Much of Rasmussen's collection came from Alert Bay (see the British Columbia chapter). It includes **CHILKAT BLANKETS, AN 8-FOOT-LONG CEREMONIAL POTLATCH SERVING BOWL, BENTWOOD BOXES, MASKS**, frontlets, and household items. Many of these items, which have been in storage for years, are newly installed in the museum.

The museum's Elizabeth Cole Butler Collection of Native American Art contains traditional artwork such as **BASKETRY AND PLAINS**

There's a great deal of personal satisfaction (and large tax benefits) to be had in returning authentic traditional stone tools, baskets, beadwork, masks, and other items to the tribes and their museums, who often can't afford to buy back these items. If you have an item you'd like to return but don't know which tribe made it, contact the Affiliated Tribes of Northwest Indians, 222 NW Davis, Ste 403, Portland, OR 97209; (503)241-0070.

INDIAN BEADWORK. Butler, of Choctaw ancestry, began collecting in 1970, purchasing items from dealers and at auctions. The museum has also purchased **CONTEMPORARY ARTWORK** by Northwest Indian painters James Lavadour (Umatilla), Rick Bartow (Yurok), and others.

Traveling exhibitions of Indian art, such as a collection of children's clothing and toys from the 1800s, as well as major shows of North American contemporary work, are periodically displayed. Traditional Indian artists also demonstrate their skills in (sometimes weeklong) workshops.

Portland Art Museum, 1219 SW Park Ave, Portland, OR 97205; (503)226-2811. In downtown Portland. Call the museum for current hours, exhibits, and admission charges.

Oregon Historical Society: Northwest Indian Collection

Across from the Portland Art Museum, on a pleasant pedestrian avenue of trees and rose gardens called the Park Blocks, is the Oregon Historical Society's museum, library, and photograph collection.

Native American collections include **BASKETRY, BEADWORK, LEATHERWORK, AND STONEWORK** representing many Northwest tribal groups, including Oregon's Paiute, Tillamook, and Wasco and Idaho's Nez Perce. Artifacts from the collection are exhibited on a regular basis. Researching the Native American collections can be arranged by contacting the director of Museum Collections. Access to records is currently through a manual card catalog system. Computerized access to the collections is being developed. Collections are shared with other museums, including all Native American museums in Oregon and Southwestern Washington.

The **PHOTOGRAPH COLLECTION**, housed in the center's library, includes more than 1,000 images relating to Northwest Indians. The earliest images are sketches, including one of a Native fisherman with a dip net at Willamette Falls, made during the 1840s. Photographs are arranged by subject, and detailed cross-references include tribal identity when known.

The manuscripts collection, also housed in the center's library, covers the missionary/pioneer era through the reservation era, mostly through firsthand accounts. Most letters, drawings, interviews, and diaries are from missionaries, pioneers, military men, and Indian agents. A few manuscripts were penned by Indians.

The Oregon Historical Society is also home to the Oregon Folk Arts Program, which awards teaching fellowships to traditional artists. Their work is often on display in the museum. The museum's gift shop has a large selection of **NATIVE-RELATED BOOKS, MAPS, ART PRINTS, CARDS, AND GIFTS**, including a line of products, based on a Wasco basket elk design, that helps support the center and Indian education programs.

Oregon Historical Society, 1200 SW Park Ave, Portland, OR 97205; (503)222-1741. In downtown Portland. Call for museum, library, and gift shop hours. Admission fee.

Affiliated Tribes of Northwest Indians: *Visit the Offices*

The Affiliated Tribes of Northwest Indians was formed in 1953, when tribal leaders in the Northwest grew concerned about the federal policies (termination acts) that attempted to abolish tribal governments. After successful efforts to stop such policies, the tribal leaders maintained the coalition, believing it could help ensure a better life for their people today and for generations to come. Today the organization represents **54 NORTHWEST TRIBAL GOVERNMENTS** from Oregon, Idaho, Washington, Southeast Alaska, Northern California, and Western Montana. Visitors are welcome.

Affiliated Tribes of Northwest Indians, 1827 NE 44th, Ste. 130, Portland, OR 97213-1443; (503)249-5770; fax (503)249-5773.

Contemporary Northwest painter Rick Bartow (Yurok) draws and paints images inspired by spiritual and psychological transformation. His animal spirits represent guides in the journey of life. His work illustrates walls enclosing the escalators at Saks Fifth Avenue in Portland, Oregon. A resident of Newport, Oregon, he is represented by Froelick Adelhart Gallery, 817 SW Second Ave, Portland, OR; (503)222-1142.

Powell's City of Books:
Used and New Indian Books

With more than half a million titles, Powell's City of Books includes 5,000 new and used books both by and about Native Americans. Most are grouped in the Native American section, though some are interspersed in the rare book, literature, poetry, or language sections of the store. Such **NORTHWEST NATIVE WRITERS** as Coeur d' Alene/Spokane writer Sherman Alexie, Spokane poet Gloria Bird, and Warm Springs poet Elizabeth Woody are well represented. Old books, a rich source of information about the bias that contributes to an understanding of past federal policies, are among the collection. Available titles along those lines include *Our Wild Indians*, written in 1885 by Colonel Richard Irving Dodge (aide-de-camp to "Indian fighter" General William Sherman). What you won't find in the Native American section are "new age" authors who often misrepresent and exploit Native spirituality.

Powell's City of Books, 1005 W Burnside, Portland, OR 97209; (800)878-7323 or (503)228-4651; www.powells.com. At the corner of 10th and Burnside in downtown Portland. For a schedule of readings at Powell's, ask to be put on the mailing list. Open daily.

AN 1857 VIEW OF THE INDIAN TREATIES

"My own observation in relation to the treaties which have been made in Oregon leads me to the conclusion that in most instances the Indians have not received a fair compensation for the rights which they have relinquished to the government. It is too often the case that in such negotiations that the agents of the government are over anxious to drive a close bargain. . . . The Indians, in the sale and surrender of their country, are surrendering all their means of obtaining a living; and when the small annuities come to be divided throughout the tribe, it exhibits but a pitiful and meager sum for the supply of their individual wants. The Indians, receiving so little for the great surrender they have made, begin to conclude that they have been defrauded; they become dissatisfied, and finally resort to arms, in vain hope of regaining their lost rights, and the government expends millions in the prosecution of a war which might have been entirely avoided by a little more liberality. . . . A notable instance of this kind is exhibited in the treaty of September 10, 1853, with the Rogue River Indians. The country which they ceded embraces nearly the whole of the valuable portion of the Rogue River Valley, embracing a country unsurpassed in the fertility of its soil and value of its gold mines; and the compensation which those nine hundred and nine people, now living, receive for this valuable cession is forty thousand dollars, in sixteen equal installments of two thousand five hundred dollars each, a fraction over two dollars and fifty cents per annum to the person, which is the entire means provided for their clothing and sustenance. . . . It is true that the government can congratulate itself upon the excellence of its bargains, while the millions of dollars subsequently spent in subduing those people has failed to convince them that they have been fairly dealt with."
—Commissioner of Indian Affairs, Annual Report, 1857

Willamette Valley

Perched on cliffs above Willamette Falls at the northern end of the fertile Willamette Valley, what is today Oregon City was once one of the **VILLAGE SITES OF THE CLACKAMAS**, who were part of the Chinook-speaking tribes that lived along the Willamette and Columbia Rivers. They shared fishery and trading sites in the area near

Willamette Falls with the Kalapuya. The Molallans lived southeast in the foothills of the Cascade Mountains. All the tribes in this area increased food production in the thick forests of the Willamette Valley by burning the trees to create swaths of berry patches, camas meadows, and grassland. When the first pioneers arrived in the region, an estimated 45,000 Indians were living in northwestern Oregon. Surviving Kalapuya, Mollallans, and Clackamas Indians were forced off their lands in the mid-1800s and relocated to the Grand Ronde Reservation, west of Salem. The 2,000-mile long **OREGON TRAIL** ended at the pioneer settlement of Oregon City.

End of the Oregon Trail Interpretive Center

At the end of the Oregon Trail was the pioneer settlement of Oregon City, a bustling pioneer town and staging area for farmers settling the fertile Willamette Valley. The **ORIGINAL INHABITANTS**, the Clackamas, were displaced by the white settlers. Today the End of the Oregon Trail Interpretive Center, made up of three buildings shaped like huge covered wagons, describes the **WHITE MIGRATION AND SETTLEMENT** of the Willamette Valley. It is also working with the Grand Ronde Tribe to expand its interpretation of the Native Americans who lived in the area when pioneers first arrived. Currently, both a slide and live presentation tell the story of the Chinook, Clackamas, Kalapuya, and Molalla Tribes.

End of the Oregon Trail Interpretive Center, 1726 Washington St, Oregon City, OR 97045; (503)657-9336. South of Portland, take exit 10, off I-205. Open daily. Call for hours. Admission fee. Gift shop. Group tours (503)557-8542.

Jensen Arctic Museum: *Inupiat and Yup'ik Artifacts*

About an hour south of Portland, in Monmouth, the Jensen Arctic Museum houses one of the largest collections of **NATIVE OBJECTS FROM ARCTIC ALASKA** in the United States. Like most museums, it exists thanks to a generous donor, even though the materials exhibited here are a long way from home.

University professor Robert Jensen, from Western Oregon College (now Western Oregon University), worked in **INUPIAT AND YUP'IK ESKIMO** villages in Alaska during the 1950s and 1960s, teaching bilingual education and collecting more than 3,000 objects. These form the basis of the Jensen Arctic Museum. In addition, more than seventy donors, many of them educators who have worked in Native villages, have also donated items that range from children's parkas to exquisite **IVORY CARVINGS** from the early 1900s. A permanent exhibit answers the question of transportation in the Arctic with displays of skin boats, snowshoes, and dog sleds, and even an old ice crampon carved from walrus ivory. The museum includes a **27-FOOT UMIAK** (skin boat), covered with walrus hide and filled with everything needed for whale hunting, and a 12-foot wooden-framed kayak from Kotzebue used by a missionary family in the 1950s. Unique articles of clothing include a 97-year-old seal intestine parka and woven grass socks worn on a trip around Kodiak Island in spring 1900, and a **CORMORANT SKIN PARKA** and **SALMON SKIN MUKLUKS** from St. Lawrence Island. There is also a large ethnographic collection of tools, toys, cooking utensils, dolls, baskets, and large animal mounts: a polar bear, musk ox, caribou, and wolves. They're all housed in a 1930 bungalow that's been cobbled together with a large exhibit gallery and smaller outbuildings.

Throughout the year the museum hosts exhibits of **CONTEMPORARY AND TRADITIONAL TRIBAL ART** made by Alaska Natives, many of them living in the Northwest, with an annual six-week-long art exhibit of master work from mid-June through August. In the museum's permanent art collection are ink drawings on seal skin by Florence Nupak and Ahgupuk from the 1930s, as well as contemporary prints, drawings, and carvings. Artists Oomittuk (Inupiat) and Larry Ahvakana (Inupiat), both Oregon residents, are museum board members.

Jensen Arctic Museum, 590 W Church St, Monmouth, OR 97361; (503)838-8468; macem@wou.edu; www.wou.edu/offices/advancement/jensen/jensen.html. Open Wed–Sat. Free. Tours available on request. Monmouth is about an hour south of Portland, off I-5.

THE WILLAMETTE VALLEY BEFORE WHITE CONTACT

The northern end of the Willamette Valley, including the present-day Portland area, was once a paradise of abundant fish, game, and plants capable of sustaining an enormous population. More than 45,000 Indians lived in this region in 1800, with more than 16 villages in the Portland area alone, some with as many as 1,500 inhabitants.

The elk, cougar, and deer were larger than they are today, which indicates either a genetic strain that has since disappeared or the fact that animals were selectively harvested and fattened in abundant meadows made possible by controlled burning. Great numbers of fish migrated up the Columbia and Willamette Rivers. When white settlers entered the Willamette Valley at the end of the Oregon Trail, the land had been so well tended by the Indians that to the settlers it resembled a park.

University of Oregon Museum of Natural History: *Native Artifacts*

Luther Cressman founded the Department of Anthropology and the Museum of Natural History at the University of Oregon. Since then the museum has been the principal repository for archaeological materials and artifacts found in Oregon and elsewhere, such as Alaska (more than 500,000 objects). The museum also houses 90 pairs of **PREHISTORIC SANDALS** Cressman discovered in Central Oregon's Fort Rock Cave. Radiocarbon dating proved the sandals, woven from sagebrush fibers, to be 9,053 years old, the oldest preserved footwear ever found.

The museum's archives hold 500 examples of **ETHNOGRAPHIC BASKETRY** made before 1900, nearly as many items of prehistoric basketry, and some 500 examples of **SOUTHWESTERN INDIGENOUS POTTERY**. The permanent exhibit Archaeology of Oregon examines about 10,000 years of indigenous human history and tells the stories of the Wasco and Wyam trade fairs at Celilo Falls on the Columbia River and the ancient trade of obsidian toolstone quarried from Oregon's volcanoes. Traveling exhibits have included *The Kalapuya: Native Peoples of the Willamette Valley* and *The Dalles: 10,000 Years of Fish and Trading.*

University of Oregon Museum of Natural History, 1680 E 15th Ave, Eugene, OR 97403-1224; (503)346-3024. Open Wed.–Sat. Call to find out about tours of the collection, field trips, lecture, workshops, the annual mock archaeological dig and identification day, when visitors are invited to bring in their artifacts or specimens for examination by experts.

Grand Ronde: *Grand Ronde*

Most tourists didn't give Grand Ronde, a little whistle-stop town on Highway 18 between Portland and the beaches of Lincoln City, a single thought—until the **SPIRIT MOUNTAIN CASINO RESORT COMPLEX** was built in 1996 right next to the road, announcing an Indian presence. Even fewer knew that Grand Ronde was the northern end of the **CONFEDERATED TRIBES' TRAIL OF TEARS**, the 69,000-acre Coastal Reservation where almost all the Indians living in Western Oregon were forced to move. Among those who were marched to Grand Ronde through the inland valleys were the Chinook, who lived along the lower Columbia River; the Tillamook, who came from the northern Oregon coast; the Santiam, Tualatin, and Yamhill; the Calapooia, Chelamela, Chepanefo, Hanchuyuk, Luckiamute, Mohawk, Tekopa, Winnefilly, and southern Yoncalla, from the rivers in the mid-Willamette Valley; and the Molalla bands, who were driven from the western slopes of the Cascade Range. A few Indians also came from the Umpqua and Rogue River valley of southern Oregon. All of the tribes had been ravaged by smallpox, measles, and influenza epidemics and attacked by white vigilantes who called themselves "exterminators." As the tribes moved onto the reservation, each group settled in its own area, each speaking its own language. Eventually, all spoke Chinook jargon, the language used between fur trappers and Indian traders. Today, however, everyone on the **GRAND RONDE RESERVATION** speaks English, and Chinook is the only Native language remaining.

Over time the 69,000-acre reservation shrank to a fraction of its former size. As white settlers took more of the land, boundaries established between the tribes also dissolved, and the Indian groups were united by a common reservation government, intermarriage, and participation in the **GHOST DANCE AND INDIAN SHAKER RELIGION.** They also worked together in the Willamette Valley's hop fields. By the late 1800s most of the reservation's inhabitants had been converted to Catholicism, due to the efforts of Father Adrien Croquet. A kind and well-loved missionary, Croquet came to Grand Ronde in 1860 and built a church and mission boarding school that was run by nuns for 35 years.

The **DAWES SEVERALTY ACT OF 1887** reduced the tribes' land holdings drastically. After each head of household received 160 acres of land within the reservation, about 25,971 acres of "surplus" land was returned to the U.S. government. By the time the government terminated all of its treaty agreements with the Grand Ronde tribes in the 1950s, only 597 acres were left in the reservation. The land was controlled by a government-appointed trustee who was given the dictate to dispose of it. He sold the land to private interests for $1.10 an acre. Each tribal member received $35.

Some of the tribes that had given up their land in the 1850s and moved to the Grand Ronde Reservation, such as the Tualatin, never received any compensation for their losses, however. When the federal government terminated its services to the reservation, there were few jobs. As a result, many tribal members moved away. In 1970 tribally owned land and buildings consisted of 2.5 acres and a toolshed.

Grand Ronde Tribal Center: *Basket-Weaving Exhibit*

Basketry and quilt making were primary industries for the Grand Ronde Tribe in the late 1800s to early 1900s. A few examples of **TRADITIONAL BASKETS** are on view in glass cases at the Grand Ronde Tribal Center. Visitors can also see the trade beads Martha Jane Sands, a survivor of the Indian Wars, was wearing when she walked barefoot to the reservation in 1860; a mortar and pestle for grinding camas lily bulbs; and photographs of St. Michael's Church and its school.

Grand Ronde Tribal Center, 9615 Grand Ronde Rd, Grand Ronde, OR 97347; (503)879-5211. Call for permission to visit and for directions.

**THE TOOLSHED: WHERE THE FIGHT
TO RESTORE TREATY RIGHTS BEGAN**

If there were a shrine to perseverance, the toolshed on the Grand Ronde Reservation would be it. In 1974 the toolshed became the headquarters from which an elected tribal council began to work for restoration of treaty rights. On November 22, 1983, the federal Restoration Act gave the tribe recognition once again. Five years later the Grand Ronde Reservation Act gave the tribe 9,811 acres of public timberland in Yamhill County, managed by the Bureau of land Management. Income from the timber was the seed money for the tribe. There was a price to pay, however. The tribes had to agree not to export timber or compete in the local timber market for 20 years, to set aside 30 percent of the money for economic development, and to give Yamhill and Tillamook Counties 20 years' worth of payments for tax and timber revenues lost from the land taken for the new reservation. Ironically, the land the tribe received from Congress was some of the very land they had been forced to give up, without compensation, in the 1800s. Today the toolshed, where all of this started, still stands next to the tribal cemetery on Grand Ronde Road. Tribal headquarters are at 9615 Grand Ronde Rd, Grand Ronde, OR 97347; (503)879-5211.

Spirit Mountain Lodge: *Native-Owned Hotel*

The Grand Ronde Tribe's Spirit Mountain gets its name from a hill, visible northeast of the intersection of Grand Ronde and Hebo Roads. Owned by a timber company, it is recognizable by the treeless area near the summit. The hillside was used by tribal members who had relocated to the Grande Ronde Reservation in the 1850s and subsequent generations for **TRADITIONAL VISION QUESTS**, which followed fasts and meditation. The hotel adjoining their casino, built in a meadow near the river, has 100 rooms decorated with **INDIAN THEMES**, including Pendleton blankets woven especially for the lodge. The lobby and other public spaces are decorated with bronze sculpture with wildlife themes.

Spirit Mountain Lodge, Hwy 18 at Grand Ronde; (800)760-7977. Open year-round. Room rates, $83–$93, double occupancy. Meals and convention center in adjoining Spirit Mountain Casino.

MARTHA JANE SANDS, SURVIVOR OF INDIAN WARS

As a child, Martha Jane Sands survived a massacre of her village in the Rogue River valley by hiding in a beaver dam. She was captured and forced to walk barefoot with other prisoners to the Grand Ronde Reservation. Sands married a white gold miner, raised a family, and carried on the tradition of the Rogue River basket weavers. She traded her handmade baskets throughout the Willamette Valley for food and clothing for her family, and became a revered elder, teacher, and guardian of tribal culture. She died in the early 1900s.

Great-grandson Lon Mercier sketched Sands's picture from a photograph taken shortly before her death, and this portrait served as the basis for a bronze statue that now sits in the Grand Ronde's Spirit Mountain Casino foyer. True to Mercier's sketch, Sands sits on the ground, barefoot, as she always liked to be. Her strong hands hold a nearly completed basket, made of hazelnut switches. Her granddaughter, Gertrude, sits at her feet, switches clutched in her small hand, learning to weave. Hand-tinted prints of Mercier's rendering of Sands are available at the Spirit Mountain Casino in Grand Ronde on Highway 18.

Shortly after the statue of Mary Jane Sands was installed in the Spirit Mountain Casino foyer, people began to lay flowers at her feet and to tuck money around her skirt. The tribes decided to donate the money to local Head Start programs.

Siletz: *Coast Reservation*

For many the Oregon coast is a 350-mile-long public playground. Tillamook Bay, the sand dunes of Pacific City and Florence, the cliffs of Depoe Bay, and the big aquarium and historic bay front of Newport are well known to most Oregonians. But for 10 years in the mid-1800s, the entire Central Oregon coast—including those playground towns of Florence, Yachats, Newport, Depot Bay, Lincoln City, Neskowin, Pacific City, and Netarts—was all Indian reservation, known as the **COAST RESERVATION**, and as bleak a place as any internment camp.

The reservation's northern boundaries were at rugged Cape Lookout in present-day Tillamook County; its southern boundaries below present-day Florence—a stretch of more than 100 miles of scenic coastline. Beginning in 1856, Indians from Western Oregon, including the villages along the rivers of the Coast Range—the Alsea,

Coos, Coquille, Rogue, Sixes, and Umpqua—were marched at gunpoint by the federal government to the Coast Reservation. This **TRAIL OF TEARS** is a tragic counterpoint to the famous Oregon and Applegate Trail stories of white immigration and settlement that permeate Oregon lore. Although it is rarely mentioned today, thousands of archived documents detail the **REMOVAL OF MORE THAN 40 TRIBES** from Native homelands. There are a few reminders. Along the north shore of Yaquina Bay, for example, a spot on the map, Coquille Point, was named for the members of the Coquille Tribe, who were relocated from their homes on what today is the historical commercial district of Bandon. Underneath Newport's popular historical district lies a village **WHERE YAQUINA INDIANS LIVED FOR THOUSANDS OF YEARS**. When the U.S. military arrived in the 1850s, they erected their blockhouse on the Yaquina's burial grounds, pushing more than 50 burial canoes out to sea on the outgoing tide.

Few of the Indians arriving at the Coast Reservation spoke the same language. Many came from isolated river villages, where they had lived in small bands of 30 to 150 people. Those speaking the same language clustered together on the reservation and began the labor of **TRYING TO SURVIVE**. Eventually, they learned where to fish (the D River in Lincoln City was a favorite salmon-harvesting spot), where to gather shellfish, and where to find plants for food, medicines, and basket materials. They cleared land and built houses. In exchange for ceding their aboriginal homelands, the government provided tools and building materials as well as limited provisions in the form of sugar, lard, coffee, and flour that arrived by ship in Yaquina Bay. The tribes learned to speak to each other in sign language and **CHINOOK JARGON** (the trader's language, composed of Northwest Indian languages, French, and English).

A journal kept by a corporal during the forced marches to the Coast Reservation chronicles the experience. Among 32 Indians captured in southern Oregon was a blind woman the corporal calls Amanda. As the group worked its way along the trail that traversed the sheer rock cliffs of Heceta Head, he recorded that "Amanda, who is blind, tore her feet horribly over these ragged rock, leaving blood sufficient to track her by. One of the Boys led her around the dangerous places. I cursed Ind[ian] Agents generally."

As early as 1865, however, just a few years after treaties had been signed, the Coast Reservation was cut in half by decree of the Oregon State legislature to make way for a railroad route and the "development" of the coast. The middle of the Coast Reservation, which included 200,000 acres surrounding Yaquina Bay (present-day Newport), was the first target. Land that had been settled by Indians who had built houses and were now farming was opened to white settlement and speculation. With the consent of Oregon's state legislature, Indian homes and farms were confiscated by white speculators who forced them to leave their property, then stood on their porches and auctioned their farms off to the highest bidder.

Ten years later the remaining reservation land was again opened to white settlement, except for one 30-mile strip between Lincoln City and Newport, which came to be known as the SILETZ RESERVATION. In the 1890s even this small region was "allotted" among the Indian families, as part of the Dawes Severalty Act of 1887. After all the allotments were handed out, the remaining land was declared "surplus" and labeled as the public domain. In all over these 40 years more than 1 million acres of premium land was taken from the reservation, despite the treaties the Coast tribes had signed and the federal government had ratified.

> In the 1850s Oregon's coastal Indians had an estimated 10,000 traditional tales—all committed to memory. Etiquette dictated that when a person spoke, the listener tried to repeat verbatim what was said. Working alongside their elders, children learned to repeat every tale they were told.

In the 1950s the Confederated Tribes of Siletz Indians were struck another blow when their treaty rights were officially terminated by the federal government. The Siletz tribal government was formally disbanded but continued to meet anyway, without federal recognition or support. Finally, the tide turned in 1977. After years of lobbying and legal battles, the U.S. Congress once again recognized the Siletz. In 1980 legislation was passed that returned some scattered parcels of land, about 3,600 acres. However, to get the reservation bill passed, the Siletz had to agree to give up all hunting, fishing, and gathering rights guaranteed by their first treaty with the U.S. government.

The Siletz Reservation today consists of 3,900 acres of mountainous forestland, 230 acres surrounding the Rock Creek Fish Hatchery, and 36 acres in the town of Siletz. Siletz is inland, between the coastal towns of Lincoln City and Newport, 24 miles up the Siletz River, on Highway 229. The area of town called Government Hill, now a lovely wooded park where the TRIBE'S CULTURAL CENTER stands, was the site of the original Indian agency, boarding school, and cannery. Another historical landmark in the area is DEPOT SLOUGH, where government-issued provisions were dropped off for the Siletz Tribe from the ships docking in Yaquina Bay.

In 1990 the Siletz Tribe's economic development group borrowed money and bought property at Lincoln City to build a convention center and a casino and to raise money for tribal housing, health programs, and environmental rehabilitation of the Siletz River and watershed. Ironically, the price the tribe paid for just 10 acres of beachfront property was more than twice what they received for the loss of more than a million acres of the Coast Reservation.

DEPOT SLOUGH HISTORICAL SITE

Much of Depot Slough has been filled, but you can see what's left of it at the junction of Highway 20 and Highway 229. Follow the cattail marsh about a mile north along Highway 229 to the Lincoln County interpretive sign that marks the slough landing site. Provisions for the Coast Reservation were unloaded from ships at Yaquina Bay and portaged through Depot Slough, then taken by horse and wagon to the raft that crossed the Siletz River. Although most of the slough has been filled for road bed, Highway 229 generally follows the original supply route.

Ceremonial Dance House: *Restoration of Siletz Culture*

A **CULTURAL REVIVAL** is under way for the Siletz, who are maintaining the language, dances, and ceremonial regalia of their Chetco, Tolowa, and Tututni ancestors. In honor of their past, the tribe has completed a traditional dance house in a grove of trees, the first structure of its kind on the reservation since the 1870s. Structured after semisubterranean dance houses, once common on the southern Oregon coast, a pitched roof is supported by the round trunks of large fir and cedar trees and shelters the earthen dance floor and central fire pit. **CEREMONIAL FEATHER DANCES** are held here on the solstice.

Ceremonial Dance House, open to the public only by prearranged tour. Contact the Siletz Tribal Cultural Center, (541)444-4294.

Nesika Illahee Powwow: *Expanding the Circle of Friendship*

Be part of the "Circle of Friendship" at the Siletz's **ANNUAL POW-WOW**, held the second weekend in August on Government Hill in Siletz. Activities include crowning Native royalty, competition dancing all three days, and a salmon feast on Sunday afternoon. There are also **NATIVE ARTS AND CRAFTS** and food booths. More than 300,000 people attend this pan–Indian event.

Shuttle buses run to the Nesika Illahee Powwow from the bottom of Government Hill in Siletz every 15 minutes. For information, contact the Siletz Tribal Cultural Center, (800)922-1399. Free.

Siletz Tribal Cultural Center: *Interpreting Native History*

It's difficult to interpret Native history from what you see in busy Lincoln County, Newport, and along the Siletz River, but it's possible to cobble together some bits and pieces. Take Highway 101, 4 miles south of Lincoln City, to Highway 229 and drive the winding road along the river. Between clearcuts are long stretches of alder and maple, and turnouts overlooking the river.

At the little town of Siletz, visit the **SILETZ TRIBAL CULTURAL CENTER** on Government Hill. Before shelter was built for the hundreds of Indians arriving at the Siletz Reservation, the U.S. military built themselves administration buildings, a school, and a blockhouse on Government Hill. Now a deeply shaded park with carefully tended lawns, this lovely 36-acre site contains a handsome cultural and community center and **POWWOW GROUNDS**.

Although physical exhibits here are limited to a few stone tools, baskets, and other artifacts, the tribe is working on compiling an exhibit that tells the **STORY OF THE COAST RESERVATION** and the history of Yaquina Bay. Their exhibit will address both the Yocina Indians, who lived at present-day Newport and around the Bay, as well as the reservation period, when tribal bands, such as the Coquille Indians, staked out a part of the bay to settle (hence the name Coquille Point). Working with doctoral candidate Scott Byram, the tribe dates fish weir stakes from Yaquina Bay to 2,100 years old. The tribe's cultural resources department also works with the Southwestern Oregon Research Project to retrieve documents about the Oregon coast that have been archived in Washington, D.C., since the 1850s.

Seeing Yaquina Head, Yaquina Bay, Lincoln City, Newport, Yachats, and other familiar landmarks on the Oregon coast through the eyes of **TRIBAL HISTORIANS** makes this region far more interesting than an ordinary trip to the beach.

Every year, descendants of the Rogue River Tututni Tribes retrace the steps of their exiled great-grandparents. Carrying an eagle staff and stopping to pray at sites where relatives died during the exodus, the descendants run more than 239 miles of coastal highway, from Siletz to their tribes' former homelands along the Rogue River.

Siletz Tribal Cultural Center; (541)444-4294. From Hwy 229 at Siletz, take Logsden Rd to the marked road and follow that to the top of Government Hill. Free. Call in advance to schedule tours and group lectures.

Oregon Coast History Center: *Siletz Exhibit*

There's a historic Victorian house library and a log cabin museum side by side off Highway 101 in Newport, with one room of the museum dedicated to the Siletz Reservation. However, you won't find much here about the Yacona Indians, who first lived around Yaquina Bay, or about the formation of the Coast Reservation. Like many museums, the Oregon Coast History Center's exhibits are limited to donated collections, and in this case, the Siletz exhibit is built primarily on the **300-OBJECT COLLECTION** of Clarinda Copeland, the first woman in the United States licensed to trade on an Indian reservation. She owned the mercantile on Government Hill in Siletz between about 1880 and

1910, and worked as a dentist and undertaker as well. In return for her services, and probably given as gifts, were ceremonial items, such as dance aprons, baskets, and other items. The city of Newport purchased the majority of Copeland's collection from the auction block after her death in the 1930s and gave it to the center in the 1960s.

There are some puzzling items here, such as dance regalia that seems to have been made with turkey feathers and dime-store materials. When people from the Rogue River were marched to the Coast Reservation, many of their villages were burned to the ground and all items—ceremonial or functional—had to be left behind. During the early 1900s headdresses and other items were therefore made of materials at hand, because of difficulty in obtaining traditional materials, such as the feathers of pilated woodpeckers and doeskin. **DANCE REGALIA** from the Copeland collection is taken out of the museum and used, or "danced," during the summer and winter solstices.

Look for a few pictures of Fourth of July parades through Newport and a feather dance held on Nye Beach, as well as fascinating early pictures of the Siletz school and the interior of Copeland's store. The library, in the Victorian house next door, contains early photographs and newspaper clippings, and the gift shop sells a book by Leone Kasner, *Survival of an Artifact*, which describes how basket weavers "carried the culture" from ancestral lands to Siletz during the forced relocation.

Oregon Coast History Center, 579 SW 9th, Newport, OR 97365; (541)265-7509. Call for hours. Free.

Depoe Bay: *Siletz Tribal Smokehouse*

The Siletz Tribal Smokehouse store sits on the south side of the famous arched Depoe Bay bridge on Highway 101, on a plot of land allotted to "Depot Charlie," a worker at the army depot at Yaquina Bay. His family eventually changed their last name to DePoe. In 1927, Sunset Investment Company bought the land, platted a town site, and named it Depoe Bay after Charlie. The "t" was changed to an "e" by the U.S. Post Office.

The smokehouse is both a gift shop and an outlet for the **TRIBE'S SMOKED SALMON, ALBACORE TUNA, AND STURGEON**. First soaked in brine then alder-smoked, the fish has a firm texture and a rich smoky taste. Buy it fresh from the cold case (smoked oysters and fresh-cooked Dungeness crab are on ice too, when in season), along with cold-smoked lox and smoked beef jerky. The smokehouse will vacuum-pack and freeze selections on the premises and ship them to your home.

You can buy smoked salmon in attractive red boxes, as well as salmon pâté (made of smoked salmon, cream cheese, and herbs) in tins—neither product requires refrigeration until after opened. The smokehouse will also create and ship custom gift packages that may contain the tribe's blackberry preserves, Tillamook cheese, and their own smoked products in fragrant pine boxes. No preservatives or artificial color are added.

Also look here for **NATIVE AMERICAN GIFTS**, Ken Hatch's Northwest Coast–style hand-carved seals and whales, T-shirts—and pick up a free tide table.

Siletz Tribal Smokehouse, 272 SE Coast Hwy, PO Box 1004, Depoe Bay, OR 97341; (800)828-4269 or (541)765-2286. www.traditionalgatherings.com. Depoe Bay is between Lincoln City and Newport on Hwy 101. Open daily, year-round.

KAYAKING THE SILETZ RIVER

The Siletz Valley is almost completely surrounded by the river. Inner-tubers, kayakers, and canoers can put in at the Siletz Tribe's Hehe Illahee Park (which means "happy place" in Chinook jargon), and float the oxbow loop to the boat ramp at the old mill site. Boaters can pull out and walk only four or five blocks back to the parking lot at Hehe Illahee, but the river is slow—it's a daylong float on an inner tube, a bit faster with a paddle. (Be prepared for a fast ride in early spring or to portage over exposed riverbed during summer's low water.) Farther downriver, some of the best canoeing and non-white water kayaking on the coast is found between Morgan Park (milepost 18) and Strom Park (between mileposts 13 and 14) on Highway 229, between the mouth of the Siletz River and the town of Siletz.

If you need clearer directions for the Siletz River loop, contact the Siletz Tribe's Department of Natural Resources, in the tribal administration building behind Hehe Illahee Park: 201 SE Swan St, PO Box 549, Siletz, OR 97380; (800)922-1399. Hehe Illahee Park, Morgan, and Strom Parks, all on Hwy 229, have parking lots and paved boat ramps. Free.

Florence, Reedsport:
Coos, Lower Umpqua, & Siuslaw

Oregon Coast Interpretive Centers:
Glimpses of the Coastal Tribes' Story

The epic story of the removal of the Oregon coast tribes from their homelands deserves a museum of its own, but for now the story is only mentioned in several small exhibits on Oregon's south coast. At the **OREGON DUNES NATIONAL RECREATION AREA** interpretive center in Reedsport, you can find a mural depicting the people of the Umpqua River in their village before white contact. There are also drawings of Fort Umpqua, where Indian families were held during the forced march north along the coastline to the Coast Reservation; and of the reservation period on the coast. An audio portion of the exhibit introduces the Native language of the region. (Oregon Dunes National Recreation Area, Reedsport, OR 97467; (541)271-3611.)

At the **UMPQUA DISCOVERY CENTER** in Reedsport, the region's Indian history is woven through a timeline in an exhibit that includes displays of precontact villages dating to 6,000 B.C. There are also representations of early white explorers looking for untapped resources. The center explores the forced removal of Indians from their villages to the Coast Reservation as well as pioneer life. Maritime connections, tidewater towns, and the experience of Chinese laborers in the canneries along the Umpqua River are also examined. (Umpqua Discovery Center, 409 Riverfront Wy, Reedsport, OR 97467; (541)271-4816; www.coos.or.uis/~discover.)

A Hitsi: *Replica of Native Hunting Shelter*

A *hitsi*, or hunting shelter, stands near its original site on Heceta Head, the Siuslaw people's former hunting grounds. It was reconstructed a few years ago by Florence Boy Scout Troop 777, with the guidance of the Confederation of the Tribes of Coos Bay, Lower Umpqua, and Siuslaw. Surrounded by a split-rail fence, the **PIT-STYLE SHELTER**, built into the side of a bank and barely large enough for two people, was one of many in the coast range providing shelter for hunters.

The hunting lodge is 8 miles north of Florence on Hwy 101. To reach the trailhead, follow Herman Peak Rd up the hill on the north side of C&M Stables, about a mile from the south side of Heceta Head to the Coast Horse Trail. Ride your horse or hike to the site, between mileposts 11 and 12 on the 18-mile trail along the ridge. There's a hitching post for horses at the site.

Westward Ho: *Siuslaw Indian History Aboard a Riverboat*

A bit of Siuslaw Indian history is narrated on board a sternwheeler that travels up the Siuslaw River from the "old town" dock at Florence, about 30 miles north of Coos Bay. The bands of the Siuslaw were one of the few in Oregon allowed to remain on their **ORIGINAL VILLAGE SITES** along the Siuslaw River. Descendants of the tribe are the source of some of the information shared with passengers during the 6-mile journey upstream. The boat, a 65-foot, double-deck replica of the sternwheelers plying the Columbia River at the turn of the century, goes through the estuary, past old homesteads, cannery sites, railroad bridges, and other points of interest, including an old **SIUSLAW FISH WEIR** on the North Fork. Narration is by boat owner Dawn Eden, a non-Native former professor at Lewis & Clark State College in Lewiston, Oregon.

Westward Ho! PO Box 2831, Florence, OR 97439; (541)997-9691. Located at Florence's "old town" dock. Historical tours (1.5 hours) begin at 11am, Tues–Sat, May–Oct. Off-season schedule tours are weekends only. Call first.

Coos County: *Coos Coquille*

Coos Bay is the **TRADITIONAL HOME** to two closely related tribes. Each had its own language. The Hanis lived around most of the bay and along the Coos River. The Miluk lived around the edge of the bay city limits, at what is today Empire, Charleston, South Slough, and Cape Arago, and down the Oregon coast almost as far as the Coquille River.

The bay, with sand dunes on its north shore, is carved with sloughs that are rich with shellfish, fish, and nutritious sea plants. It is protected from the Pacific Ocean swells by the high cliffs of Cape Arago. Today the entire cape is state parkland: Cape Arago, Shore Acres, and Sunset Bay State Parks form a network of trails along the cliffs.

The **CONFEDERATION OF THE TRIBES** of Coos Bay, Lower Umpqua, and Siuslaw has more or less been together since 1860, when the Coos and Lower Umpqua were removed from their homelands north of the Siuslaw River near Florence. Even before that time, however, although the tribes spoke different languages, their cultures were similar, and travel and trade among the tribes was fairly easy.

Like other southern Oregon tribes, they had the misfortune of living in an **AREA COVETED BY MINING COMPANIES**. In 1853 the Coos Bay Commercial Company, a joint stock company, was formed in the Rogue River valley expressly to explore, stake mining claims, and settle Coos Bay. In just two years miners had extracted more than $1.9 million in coal and gold from the area. Three years after the miners arrived, peaceful Coos Indians were forced from their villages at Coos Bay. Under armed guard, nearly **700 PEOPLE WERE MARCHED TO FORT UMPQUA**, on the sand spit on the north side of the mouth of the Umpqua River. In November, as the weather turned from Indian summer to winter squalls, the new superintendent of Indian affairs cut off the refugees' food rations. He claimed that no treaties had been signed; if they had, he didn't know about them. Nearly half of the Indians starved to death.

In 1859 about **400 REMAINING COOS AND LOWER UMPQUA** Indians were again moved; this time from Fort Umpqua to Yachats Prairie on the north side of Cape Perpetua. Today the area is a popular coastal town with soaring property values, but in 1859 the Indian refugees subsisted on shellfish torn from the rocks at low tide. Most of the land they were supposed to farm was sand or timber-covered slopes. In their first five years at Yachats, more than half of the Coos Indians died from exposure and starvation. Conditions were so terrible that Indians periodically fled to their old homes in Coos Bay, only to be rounded up by the U.S. Army and returned.

The Coquille Cultural Preservation Conference hosts lively historical and anthropological discussions about both pre-historic and modern environments and the cultures of southern Oregon and the Oregon coast. Held in May, the conferences are open to the general public. For registration, call the Coquille Tribe at (541)756-0904.

Over the next 16 years, the land at Yachats was laboriously cleared and fenced. Indians erected barns and homes. But in 1875, Congress closed the entire southern part of the reservation, including Yachats and Siuslaw (present-day Florence), and threw all the land, including Indian farms, open for settlement. At this time, the Indians came home to Coos Bay. Many intermarried with whites. Some worked as wood cutters or domestic laborers for room and board; others found seasonal work during the cranberry harvest.

It wasn't until 1984 that the Confederated Tribes of Coos Bay, Lower Umpqua, and Siuslaw were **FINALLY RECOGNIZED BY THE U.S. CONGRESS**. This recognition was based on a treaty they had signed at Empire in 1855, which the government had first denied, then ignored. Today the tribe owns less than 6.12 acres in the former city of Empire, between the towns of Coos Bay and Cape Arago.

Coos County Historical Society Museum: *Basket Exhibit*

With the help of the neighboring Coquille Tribe, the Coos County Historical Society has put together the Legacy Basketry exhibit, a traveling, interpretive display of **TRADITIONAL COOS/COQUILLE WOVEN BASKETS** and other cultural information from historic and prehistoric times. In winter the exhibit is on the road or at Coquille Tribal headquarters; in summer you can see it at the Coos County Historical Society Museum. The museum has also recently worked with Denise Mitchell, a Coquille tribal member who is finishing her master's degree in cultural anthropology, to catalog, interpret, and design a new installation for its 228-piece basket collection. On display in the Coquille Tribe's office is a basket far older than any in the museum, unearthed from the Coquille estuary's mud banks.

Coos County Historical Society Museum, 1220 Sherman Ave, North Bend, OR 97459; (541)756-6320; museum@harborside.com.

BRINGING HISTORICAL DOCUMENTS HOME

The Southwest Oregon Research Project (SWORP), a partnership between the Coquille Indian Tribe, UO Knight Library, Smithsonian Institute and other Western Oregon tribes, was formed in 1995 to bring copies of historic documents back to Oregon from the National Archives housed in Washington D.C.

Coquille tribal member George Wasson, heading up a panel of researchers, says that more than 70,000 documents—ethnographic notes, diaries, military accounts, surveyor's notebooks, letters from Indian agents to the Dept. of War and other materials—have been copied or brought back on microfilm and are now being catalogued for public use. In a new millennium kind of potlatching, a ceremony where families once demonstrated their ability to attract abundance by giving away their wealth, SWORP will give away information to anyone who wants to use it.

Coos Tribal Hall: *Historic Building*

Although it is small, the Coos Tribal Hall, built in 1938, is more significant than many buildings three times its size. Not much larger than a cottage, it was built for the tribe's use by the Bureau of Indian Affairs on 6 acres of land donated to the Coos in 1937 by the Empire Development Company. When the Bureau of Indian affairs ended the tribe's relationship with the federal government in 1956, title to the building was given to the city of Empire. Although the city had promised to maintain the building for the use of Indians living in the Coos Bay area, they leased it instead to non-Indians and refused to make repairs. In the 1970s, with the help of attorneys, the tribe got back their sole asset, were reimbursed for damages, and filed for incorporation. The tribe has added a few acres of land to the property, restored the shingled, cottage-style building, and built another small structure next door to house health care services for tribal members. The tribal hall has a small **EXHIBIT OF COOS HISTORY**. Visitors are welcome, but call first. The tribal government offices are located in the former Elks Lodge, which the tribe purchased and remodeled in Empire. Visitors are also welcome there.

Coos Tribal Hall, 338 Wallace, Coos Bay, OR 97420; (541)888-3536. Tribal offices are at 1245 Fulton St. For directions and current telephone number, call the Coos Tribal Hall.

Baldya'ka on Cape Arago: *Former Village Site*

A U.S. Coast Guard station and lighthouse stand today on an **OLD COOS VILLAGE SITE**, Baldya'ka (pronounced "bald-yakka"). In his

1828 journals explorer Jedediah Smith reported seeing Baldya'ka. The area has been considered for an interpretive center for the Coos Tribe, but rapid erosion may overtake even the lighthouse that sits there now.

The site, high on a bluff, overlooks the cliff-sheltered **SUNSET BEACH STATE PARK** and the Pacific Ocean, west of Coos Bay. Baldya'ka, like many Coos villages, was built high above the sea as protection from canoe raids for slaves, perhaps by the Chinookean people from the north. Legend says that this village site was destroyed by the Tututni from the south.

The beach was probably used for fish drying, food preparation, and as a put-in for canoes. Offshore is Chief's Island, where a lookout watched for raiders, and Squaw Island, with 40-foot-high sheer rock walls. With a steep trail to the top, Squaw Island is accessible at low tide from Sunset Beach State Park.

Follow the signs to ocean beaches and Charleston from Hwy 101 to the three state parks on Cape Arago (campgrounds, hiking, beaches, overlooks). Sunset Beach State Park is the first park you'll come to. The tribe hopes to raise $15 million for an interpretive center and reconstructed village site at Baldya'ka, in cooperation with state agencies and the Coast Guard. Tax-deductible donations are gratefully accepted. Contact the Coos Tribe at 455 S 4th, Coos Bay, OR 97420; (541)267-5454.

Arrow Chain: *A Video about Coos History*

Stashed in museums and archives across the United States are recordings of traditional Coos songs, oral literature, and language; original basketry and clothing; and hundreds of pages of manuscript notes collected by anthropologists, linguists, Indian agents, and diarists. Since 1990 the "**CAPTURED HERITAGE**" project, officially the Southwestern Oregon Research Project, has worked with the Smithsonian Institution, the University of Oregon's Knight Library, the Coquille Tribe, and graduate students to find and copy data onto microfilm and tape. From these recordings, an excellent 28-minute video of Coos, Lower Umpqua, and Siuslaw history, *Arrow Chain*, was produced in 1995 as a result of cultural resource coordinator Don Whereat's search for **NATIVE HISTORICAL DOCUMENTS**. His daughter, Patty, now the tribe's cultural resources director, is working with her father to put the tribe's complex language on CD-ROM.

Order the videotape from the Coos Tribe, 455 S 4th, Coos Bay, OR 97420; (541)267-5454. $25, including handling and shipping.

Coquille Tribal Enterprises

The Coquille Tribal headquarters are located in North Bend, where the tribe also operate their casino, resort, and Plankhouse Cafe overlooking the scenic waterfront—one of the few places along Coos Bay's industrial waterfront with a view of ships coming and going from nearby docks. Near the city are the tribe's health clinic, housing, and a **CRANBERRY FARM** located on 1,000 acres of tribal property. The tribe began commercial production in 1998 of organic cranberries from 10 acres of bogs. The tribe also manages 5,400 acres of their **ANCESTRAL TERRITORY** within more than 300,000 acres of Bureau of Land Management (BLM) land in Coos County. Timber cuts support tribal education and governmental programs and the preservation of significant cultural resource areas for future generations. Year-round, the public may access the Coquille Forest, BLM land, and the National Forest for recreation.

Information about bicycling roads, campgrounds, historical sites, scenic areas, and old-growth forests in the county can be found at the Bay Area Chamber of Commerce in Coos Bay, the BLM district office in North Bend, and the Siskiyou National Forest Powers Ranger Station. Bay Area Chamber of Commerce, 50 E Central, PO Box 210, Coos Bay, OR 97420; (541)269-0215. For more information about tribal businesses, contact the Coquille Indian Tribe, 3050 Tremont St, North Bend, OR 97459; (541)756-0904.

South Slough: *Miluk Territory*

The people who lived around South Slough were related by language to the Lower Coquille, who lived at present-day Bandon. The reason that the Miluks and the Coquille are not part of the same tribe today is because they were separated during the reservation period. The South Slough Miluks were marched to Yachats with the Hanis and Lower Umpqua. The lower Coquilles were relocated to the Siletz River, near present-day Siletz. These kinds of divisions and regroupings of people were common.

South Slough is the heart of **MILUK COOS ABORIGINAL TERRITORY**, and an area where families of mixed South Slough Miluk and Upper Coquille descent settled in the late 1800s after they returned from the Siletz Reservation. It is one of the few estuaries in the Northwest still in its **WILD AND NATURAL STATE** (although you can't say that about the surrounding clearcut hills). Follow a 3-mile trail along Hidden Creek to the salt marsh and tide flats, take a short hike along Wasson Creek, or launch kayaks and canoes into the long fingers of the slough on the rising tide. The reserve's **INTERPRETIVE CENTER** contains exhibits about estuarine ecology and the flora and fauna of South Slough. Summer workshops include explorations on the mud flats, wild edibles, and bird-watching. Many of the creeks flowing into the slough carry the names of families, such as the Wassons, who lived there in the 1800s and whose descendants live and work in the Coos Bay area today.

South Slough National Estuarine Research Reserve, PO Box 5417, Charleston, OR 97420; (541)888-5558. South Slough is located 4 miles south of Charleston (west of the town of Coos Bay) on Seven Devils Rd. Open summers, daily; weekdays only, Sept–May. Free admission. Call for a summer schedule of classes.

Coquille Tribe's Mill Hotel

In the spring of 2000, the Coquille Tribe opened its new 115-room hotel, adjacent to its casino on the pier overlooking Coos Bay. The rooms have **NORTHWEST-NATIVE STYLING** and lodge-type furniture, with custom-designed Pendleton blankets on the beds reflecting Coquille culture. The hotel lobby has the look and feel of a plankhouse with a cedar log canopy surrounding the circular stone fireplace, and a cultural display area telling the story of the tribe and life on the bay with baskets, tools, and pre-contact fishing gear. Sunrise rooms overlook the bay and estuary and the navigational turning point where tugs nose freighters heading back to sea. Two waterfront corner suites have jacuzzi tubs overlooking the bay. Standard rooms have queen beds with custom-designed **PENDLETON BLANKETS**, overstuffed chairs, and writing desks. All rooms are equipped with cable tv, coffee pots, hair dryers, and two phone lines with internet access. The big deck along the waterfront has an outdoor seating area. Waterfront dining is available in the adjoining casino.

The stone enclosing the circular fireplace in the lobby of the Coquille Tribe's hotel comes from the upper Coquille River, near a former village site. Floors in the lobby replicate the blue-green color of blue schist from Bandon, from which tools were made. With no funding for a museum, the tribe put display cases inside the hotel that are designed to provide museum-quality archival storage for such artifacts as baskets and stone tools, donated to the tribe or repatriated from other museums.

The Mill Casino Hotel, 3201 Fremont Ave, North Bend (Hwy 101 between North Bend and Coos Bay), OR 97459; (800)953-4800; www.themill@ucinet.com.

THE GRANDMOTHER, OR TUPPER, ROCK

Many people have taken a seat on one of the big rocks on the Coquille River jetty to fish or just watch the ocean waves crash on the beach. But few know that the rocks, colored an unusual serpentine green laced with white crystal and flakes of gold, are fairly uncommon. The rocks are actually the fractured remains of a huge monolith, known as Tupper Rock, or before that, the Grandmother, that was dynamited in 1903 to build the Coquille River jetties. According to geologists, the Tupper, or Grandmother, Rock was created by extremely high compression far below the earth's surface. The rock then rose and broke through the earth's crust before it could be further transformed by the heat, forming a huge haystack monolith. The fractured remains of the rock are among the largest collections of blue schist anywhere in the world. According to one version of a local story, after the monolith was blasted apart, an Indian man came down out of the forest and warned the mayor that Bandon would burn three times for what it had done. To date, the city has burned twice—once in 1916 and again in 1936, when more than 480 buildings went up in flames.

Bandon: *Coquille*

Anthropologist Roberta Hall (Oregon State University) has investigated the lower Coquille River village sites for 26 years, including undertaking some of the first excavations of Coquille village sites under Bandon's Old Town. Her book, People of the Coquille Estuary, includes ethnographic material collected by the first explorers of the region and discusses the health and biology of the earlier Coquille people. Her work details the stone and bone tools they used as well as the plant and animal resources employed. Her archaeological studies of the ancient Indian village explore the region's geologic history and how weather, earthquakes, and white contact affected the environment. The book is available from Words & Pictures Unlimited, 620 NW Witham Dr, Corvallis, OR 97330-6535; osu.orst.edu/dept/anthropology/coquille.htm.

The small coastal town of Bandon, Oregon, boasts gorgeous beaches, gigantic haystack rocks offshore, and a picturesque white lighthouse perched on the north jetty at the mouth of the Coquille River, making it a favorite destination for tourists. Bandon and the shoreline on both sides of the lower river were once home to the No-so-ma bands of Coquille Indians, inhabitants of the lower tidewater reaches of the Coquille River, and ancestors to many of the family groups of the modern Coquille Indian Tribe. **ARCHEOLOGICAL EXCAVATIONS** in the Old Town part of Bandon date prehistoric human occupation there to at least 3,500 years ago. During the summer, tribal members collaborate with University of Oregon and Oregon State University scholars in ongoing projects to investigate, interpret, and preserve local archeological sites. Today's tribal members also descend from groups living farther upriver.

Permanent villages were located at the modern-day towns of Coquille and Myrtle Point, and eastward into the Camas Valley near Roseburg. Coquille tribal members also descend from the South Slough region of lower Coos Bay, where shared resources and intermarriage between ancestral Coos and Coquille families gave rise to the many Coquille tribal members who today claim Coos/Coquille as their heritage. The Coos County Historical Society Museum, located in North Bend, has a **COLLECTION OF AT LEAST 200 BASKETS** and many artifacts that are attributed to this shared ancestry and culture.

More than **200 PREHISTORIC ARCHEOLOGICAL SITES** have been found within the Coquille ancestral territory that is now Coos County; many are village sites, shell middens, and fish weirs that remain along the rocky headlands and estuary shorelines of the Southern Oregon coast. Farther south, at Cape Blanco in Curry County, the archeological **RECORD OF HUMAN OCCUPATION IS 8,000 YEARS OLD**, near the site of the historic Cape Blanco lighthouse.

Near the mouth of the Coquille River was the village called No-so-mah. About half a mile away, on the shore stood a massive haystack monolith of an unusual blue-green. One name for it was Grand-mother; in recent times the monolith was called **TUPPER ROCK**. The rock towered above the bluffs, the largest vantage point for miles. In 1903 the U.S. Army Corps of Engineers dynamited the rock to build the two jetties that today channel the river into the Pacific Ocean.

In 1851 the No-so-ma village was shelled by the U.S. Army in retaliation for a guerrilla attack on white surveyors. The villagers rebuilt their cedar plank houses and moved back in. But on the night of January 28, 1854, in an **UNPROVOKED AMBUSH**, 40 gold miners surrounded the village and fired into the villagers' houses, gunning down those who resisted or tried to escape. The village was again attacked in 1855, when whites took 40 Native women and children prisoners.

The adjoining bands of Coquilles were eventually forced from their homes and removed to a temporary reservation at Port Orford, south of Bandon, along with Indians from the Chetco, Pistol, Rogue, and Sixes Rivers in southern Oregon, whose villages had also been burned to the ground. In 1856 the remaining Natives in the area were forced to abandon their villages and move to the Coast Reservation.

In 1990 the Port of Bandon returned a few acres where the Grandmother rock once protected the river. In 1993 the tribe built **HERITAGE PLACE** on top of the site, a three-story, assisted-living residential facility, with views of Bullard State Park, the ocean, the lighthouse, and the river. Today, the tribe is involved in organic cranberry farming, timber farming, and owns the Mill Resort and Casino on the Coos Bay waterfront.

The Coquille River Museum: *A Few Native Artifacts*

This small museum displays Native artifacts gained from several decades of archeological research conducted in the Bandon area. Look here for **BASKETRY** native to the region. Unfortunately, as in most small museums, donated artifacts from other regions (such as models of Alaska Native kayaks) are displayed with local Indian artifacts.

Coquille River Museum, Filmore St, Bandon, OR 97411; (541)347-2164. Operated by the Bandon Historic Society. Open Mon–Sat.

EXCAVATING COQUILLE VILLAGE SITES:
PIECING TOGETHER THE PAST

Encouraged by the coastal tribes, anthropologists and scholars have worked for the past 30 years in the estuaries and along the banks of Oregon's coastal rivers to compile oral history and gain new insights into Native life as it was lived in the centuries before white contact.

Archaeological evidence uncovered from the mudflats along tidal rivers has revealed dozens of details of daily life from the past 6,500 years. For example, fine stone tools were carved from difficult-to-work blue schist from the mouth of the Coquille River, once an extensive, rich salt marsh. Stone arrow points and spear points were made on the spot, as evidenced by hundreds of flakes found in the soft mud.

Scott Byram, University of Oregon doctoral candidate whose research has focused on fish weir technology, has added to this emerging picture of the past his mapping of a sophisticated system thousands of years old for trapping quantities of fish in the outgoing tide. Stakes uncovered in Yaquina Bay and the Coquille River date to at least 1500 years old. Buried in silt so fine that objects have been perfectly preserved, wooden stakes look new. They still have bark clinging to them, and visible chop marks from the adze that shaped them. Stakes were made of hemlock and spruce, woods that waterlog easily and so would not bob to the surface after they were pounded into the soft bay silt.

Port Orford: Chetco, Tututni, Tolowa

This pretty little town, 20 miles south of Bandon, was the site of one of the **OREGON COAST'S LARGEST CONCENTRATION CAMPS**, where Tututni, Chetco, and Tolowa people were held before being loaded onboard ships destined for the Coast Reservation.

By the early 1850s, trappers, miners, and farmers had infiltrated the entire length of the Rogue River, the traditional lands of the Tututni, Chetco, and Tolowa peoples. Their plows and livestock destroyed the grass seeds, acorns, and camas—all important food sources for the Native people. Mining depleted trout and salmon runs.

In 1855, the **COAST RESERVATION** was created in preparation to receive what would soon be displaced Natives. U.S. troops were put into place to begin the removal of the Native dwellers from the aboriginal lands. Tension mounted, and there were attacks all up and down the Rogue River by both whites and Natives, culminating in the 1855–1856 Rogue River Wars. In the end, about 1,200 Natives were marched to the coast and held at Port Orford in open pens until the steamship *Columbia* deported them north to the Coast Reservation. The last resisters, **CHIEF "JOHN"** and his band, were marched 125 miles up the coast.

For years a state historical sign stood at Port Orford, explaining a military victory over the Indians. Like many of the state's historical signs erected in the 1950s and 1960s, this one promoted the white military version of victory, and gave no context for the Indian "uprising." Up until the early 1960s, the town even staged an annual event commemorating the Rogue Indian Wars by throwing an effigy of an Indian man off Battle Rock, a promontory overlooking the boat harbor. Today, however, the old sign and a new interpretive sign stand together on Battle Rock. The new sign reads in part:

"This site was once part of the **DWELLING AREA OF THE TUTUTNI** people. They inhabited what is now the Southern Oregon coast and lower Rogue River thousands of years prior to the first contact with white men."

In 1858 Chief John was accused by the Federal Government of inciting unrest on the Coast Reservation. He and his son were arrested at Siletz, taken to Fort Vancouver, and tried and convicted to serve time at Alcatraz prison. John's daughters, living on the Grande Ronde Reservation, appealed, and he was released after several years of imprisonment. He died in 1864 at Fort Yamhill. In 1996 artist Peggy O'Neal illustrated the march of Chief John (Tecumtum) and his people with a poster commissioned by the Confederated Tribes of Siletz Indians. Posters and fine art prints are available from the artist at (541)444-1347.

Canyonville: *Cow Creek Tribe*

The North and South Umpqua Rivers, which flow toward the ocean from the foothills of Mount Mazama, are two of the most beautiful rivers in Oregon. In the upper reaches they pool around big boulders and rush through narrow canyons. In the spring the wildflowers in the meadows and along the banks of the Umpqua are so plentiful that nearby Glide, Oregon, has held a wildflower festival every April for the past 25 years to show off nature's bounty.

FIVE INDIAN GROUPS made their homes along both the North and South Umpqua. One of those, the Cow Creek Band of Umpqua Tribe of Indians, owns tribal facilities at Canyonville, which is located just off Interstate 5 south of Roseburg, where two creeks enter the South Umpqua River.

The Cow Creek people once built **PERMANENT WINTER VILLAGES** along rivers and creeks, to make use of the abundant resources. From along the Rogue River and the Umpqua Divide, they gathered huckleberries; at South Umpqua Falls (where the tribe still holds its annual powwow), they fished for salmon and hunted in the surrounding forests. Trees in the Jackson Creek watershed were prized for both their utilitarian and medicinal value. In the spring, camas carpeted the fields with blue flowers. The people dug the bulbs from the ground and also harvested tarweed seeds, hazelnuts, wild onions, acorns, mushrooms, and vitamin-rich lambs-quarters. Yerba buena leaves were used fresh or dried to make tea, still a favorite today. Fish weirs were made from hazelnut sticks, and small flutes were made from the dry stalks of wild parsnip.

During the early 1800s, the Cow Creek's territory became an important **RENDEZVOUS SITE FOR FUR TRADERS**. Many French traders married into the tribe, and tribal names such as DuMont, LaChance, Rainville, Pariseau, Rondeau, and Thomason clearly stem from that time. In the 1840s an influx of white settlers swept into southern Oregon via the Applegate Trail. Beginning near the Shoshone-Bannock's land in eastern Idaho, the trail crossed the mountains between Crater Lake and Mount Shasta, turned north toward the Willamette Valley, and finally ended at Jason Lee's mission near present-day Salem. Following Indian trails that parallel today's Interstate 5, the Applegate Trail passed right through the heart of Cow Creek territory.

When gold was discovered in southern Oregon, **HUNDREDS OF MINERS** moved up from the goldfields of California and filed claims on streams and riverbanks. Hydraulic mining muddied the rivers with mining debris, destroying salmon runs. Farmers homesteaded camas meadows, blocking the Cow Creek from their most important source of food. Epidemics ravaged the tribe. When the Cow Creek signed their treaty with the federal government, they were reimbursed 2.3 cents an acre for their 800 square miles of land at a time when Donation Land Claim buyers were paying the government $1.25 an acre for the same land.

But all this changed in 1982, when a settlement was negotiated with the government to springboard economic development. The tribe today is the **SECOND LARGEST EMPLOYER** in Douglas County, purchasing land for development, employing nearly 1,000 people in their various endeavors, and providing housing and health care for tribal members. Like many other tribes in the Pacific Northwest who promote self-reliance for the tribe as a whole and for individual members, the Cow Creeks have invested a good portion of their earnings in the well-being of tribal members through education, social, health, and charitable programs for the tribe and the local community.

Pioneer-Indian Museum: *Exploring Cow Creek Legends*

In 1969 a group of Cow Creek tribal members joined pioneer descendants and founded the South Umpqua Historical Society to establish a Pioneer-Indian museum in Canyonville. The little museum is on the original Applegate Trail, an alternative trail to the Oregon Trail that avoided the Columbia River. It entered the lush Willamette Valley (Salem area) from the south. Today's Interstate 5 follows much of the original Applegate Trail. Cow Creek legends and **RECOVERED ARTIFACTS** shown in the museum establish the tribe's existence before the eruption of Mount Mazama, which formed Crater Lake.

Pioneer-Indian Museum, 421 W 5th St, Canyonville, OR 97417; (541)839-4845. Open Thur–Sun, year-round. Free.

Seven Feathers Resort: Native-Owned Lodging

At the gateway to Crater Lake National Park and 19 miles from Wildlife Safari (a huge park preserve of primarily African animals), the Seven Feathers Resort of the Cow Creek Tribe hotel is the **LARGEST IN THE AREA**, with 150 guest rooms. Located in Canyonville, south of Roseberg, the hotel has luxurious rooms, a pool, two saunas, a fitness center, an arcade for the kids, and a 22,000-square-foot convention and performing arts center (the Umpqua Ballroom). The Camas Room offers fine dining, the Cow Creek Restaurant is more casual, and the ice cream parlor offers the Cow Creek's own flavor of ice cream: huckleberry. An adjoining RV park, with full amenities, has space for 33.

Seven Feathers Resort, 146 Chief Miwaleta Ln, Canyonville, OR 97417; (800)548-8461. Open year -round. Room rates, $69–$129.

> "It's helpful to remember that the Oregon/California border is an artificial line that cuts through the center of traditional Tolowa territory. Tolowa culture, with a number of bands that occupied village sites all along the coast and that spoke different dialects, extended from the Sixes River in Oregon, south into Humboldt County in Northern California."
> —Loren Bommelyn, Tolowa linguist

NORTHERN CALIFORNIA COAST

The **CALIFORNIA GOLD RUSH** of 1849, which began with the discovery of gold in the mountains of Northern California near San Francisco, ultimately determined federal Indian policy. Fearful that any large Indian reservation might place tribes on top of a potential gold strike, **INDIAN LAND OWNERSHIP** was confined to *rancherias*. Native peoples were forced to determine a single area of most importance—for example, the clam beds in a bay or a fishing hole on a river—and then the entire tribe was confined to that one spot. **RANCHERIAS** were often less than 100 acres for an entire tribe.

Pick up free detailed maps showing the trails, campgrounds, and picnic areas of Redwood National and State Parks from park headquarters (1111 2nd St, Crescent City, CA 95531; (707)464-6101). An informative 16-page pamphlet, Living in a Well-Ordered World: Indian People of Northwestern California, is also available. Rancherias are private, but you're welcome to stop by tribal offices, such as the Tolowa's Rancheria office at the mouth of the Smith River on Hwy 101.

On the Northern California coast, near the Oregon border, the first rancheria is Tolowa Rancheria, which today looks like a small subdivision, at the mouth of the Smith River. Another small rancheria is next to the Smith River, several miles to the east. Nearby farmers grow fields of white Easter lilies on land that gently slopes to the beach.

The next 40 miles of coastline, from Crescent City to Eureka, is **REDWOOD NATIONAL PARK**. Highway 101, which winds through nearly 40 miles of the park, is one of the state's most scenic drives, with access to sandy beaches, rocky headlands, and shady groves of towering redwoods, many of them more than 2,000 years old and 300 feet tall.

It may come as a surprise to people who have driven Highway 101 for years that what is today called Redwoods National Park is **HOME TO THREE NATIVE TRIBES**: the Tolowa, the Yurok, and the Chilula. These tribes continue to perform traditional sacred dances and ceremonies within the park boundaries, as they have on this coastline for centuries. There is a little coverage of Indian culture and history in the Redwood National Park headquarters in Crescent City and in Orick. For that, visitors can walk through a replica of a traditional Yurok village site in Patrick's Point State Park, near the town of Trinidad. Two museums in the area display extensive private collections of Northern California basketry.

Visitors can also drive to the mouth of the Klamath River near Requa to **WATCH NATIVES CATCHING SALMON**, then drive up to the brow of the cliff, 600 feet above the river, to the Klamath Overlook and the trailhead of the 25-mile-long coastal trail. The Avenue of the Giants, a 33-mile byway through the oldest redwood groves on the coast, gives you an idea of how the forest looked before white contact and logging.

Smith River Rancheria: *Tolowa Tribal Lands*

Although the tribes in this area were assured in a treaty of a 25,000-acre reservation, the discovery of gold extinguished that promise.

Many Tolowas in the California side of the tribe's territory were shipped to the Hupa Reservation, where it was illegal to move away until 1902. The Tolowa Tribe today has **TWO RANCHERIAS**, one up the Smith River and one at its mouth, both about 160 acres, where the tribe have struggled to survive for more than a century. Drive into the Smith River Rancheria, off Highway 101 on North Indian Road, and follow the road past the **INDIAN SHAKER CHURCH**, built in 1928, and past the cemetery overlooking the Pacific Ocean, to a small park overlooking the mouth of the Smith River. The Tolowa chose this **FORMER VILLAGE SITE**, which they call Nelechundun, because it gave them access to the river, so they could continue to fish for salmon and dig clams on the beaches.

Smith River Rancheria Tribal Center, 501 N Indian Rd, PO Box 239, Smith River, CA 95567; (707)487-9255. Visitors are welcome at the tribal center (just off Hwy 101), but call first for an appointment and directions to the office.

*Thumbs up for **News from Native California: An Inside View of the California Indian World**. This quarterly magazine, available from Heyday Press, is devoted to California Indian history and culture, contermporary issues, and myth, with contributions from Native American scholars and others. Heyday Press, PO Box 9145, Berkeley, CA 94709; (510)849-0177. Cost is $19 a year for four issues. Also available are Heyday's free catalog of Native American titles and California Indian art notecards.*

Klamath Overlook: *Traditional Salmon Runs*

"In the beginning there were only spirits. One day the Creator called them together to ask what they wanted to be—trees, rocks, or animals. Oregos, the helpful one, chose to be the Guardian Rock at the mouth of the Klamath River. She tells the salmon when the rains have swollen the rivers and it's time to come back." That's the brief message on the **INTERPRETIVE SIGN** at the edge of the Klamath Overlook, 600 feet above the Klamath River; no doubt the story is longer in a face-to-face telling.

Salmon used to run all the way through the coastal range of Northern California to the marshes of Klamath Lake in Eastern Oregon, and from there up the Sprague, Wood, and Williamson Rivers to spawn. **TRADITIONAL INDIAN FISHERS** at the river's mouth knew which fish were theirs by the density of the eggs packed inside the females; those more densely packed were destined for spawning in tributaries far upstream. Traditionally, fish were caught in weirs, but enough salmon were always let through to feed the tribes upstream. Today Native fishers fish from boats at the river's mouth.

You can see the Guardian Rrock from the impressive Klamath Overlook by turning west on Requa Rd from Hwy 101 and continuing uphill to a clearly marked parking lot at the head of the 2.5-mile coastal trail.

Patrick's Point State Park: *Sumeg Yurok Village*

In a quiet, grassy field speckled with white daisies and purple lupine, tucked away from the campgrounds, playgrounds, beaches, and tide pools of Patrick's Point State Park, is a replica of a traditional Yurok village. In an unusual arrangement between State Parks and the Yurok people, seven buildings have been erected in the park that are used both as exhibits for the general public and for annual ceremonies. Three **TRADITIONAL FAMILY HOUSES** made of split redwood lashed together with hazelnut and spruce roots look almost Japanese in design. Each house is surrounded by paving stones. The doorways are small and perfectly round; to enter, you must crawl in on your knees onto a ground-level platform that was used to store items such as food, firewood, and cedar boxes that held ceremonial regalia. Living space was about 3 feet below ground, insulated by the earth and centered around a square fire pit. Four other buildings are tribal dressing and preparation areas, a dance arena and sweat house. The **ANNUAL BRUSH DANCE** is conducted here, usually the last weekend in June. The public may observe, but because this is a religious ceremony, no cameras, food, or pets are allowed. Pick up a self-guided village tour brochure at the park gate. **YUROK DOCENTS** conduct tours of the village by appointment.

Dollmaker Nadine Van Mechelen, a descendant of the Yurok-Karok and Tolowa Tribes of Northern California, handcrafts one-of-a-kind dolls inspired from various Native cultures of North America. Some dolls are simple cloth-bodied dolls; others are large dolls with sculpted faces and dressed in elaborate regalia. For information, contact Van Mechelen at her Pendleton, Oregon, home, (541)276-2566.

Patrick's Point State Park, 4150 Patrick's Point Dr, Trinidad, CA 95570; (707)677-3570. Take Patrick's Point Dr off Hwy 101 between Big Lagoon and Trinidad. Open daily, year-round; tour the site from 8am until dusk. Park entrance fee.

Clarke Memorial Museum: *Native Basket Collection*

Founded by Cecile Clarke in 1960, this is one of the most extensive collections of **YUROK, KARUK, AND HUPA BASKETS** in the world. Clarke befriended many Indian families when she taught their children in school. She purchased most of the baskets in this collection. Oral-history audio tapes of interviews with 17 northwestern California basket makers are available (by appointment), and photographs of the tribes are exhibited in the museum's hall. Contact the museum for information about basket-weaving classes with Vera Ryerson (Yurok).

Clarke Memorial Museum, 3rd and E Sts, Eureka, CA 95501; (707)443-1947 for recorded message. Open Tues–Sat, year-round. Donations appreciated.

Del Norte County Historical Society Museum: *Native Collection*

Two rooms in this large museum, housed in Crescent City's historical hall of records and jail, are dedicated to the Native American collection, which includes more than 80 **TOLOWA AND YUROK BASKETS AND WOVEN CAPS, REGALIA, AND A DUGOUT CANOE.** The second room is dedicated to Native items donated to the museum over the years, such as gut raingear from Alaska (these treasures are rare), Navajo woven blankets, and an American Indian photography exhibit.

Del Norte County Historical Society Museum, 577 H St, Crescent City, CA 95531; (707)464-3922. Open Mon–Sat, May–Sept. Admission fee.

If you'd like to read more about the Indian cultures of Northern California, visit the Humboldt County Library's special collections section (1313 3rd St, 95501; (707)269-1900) and Humboldt State University's Library, special collections (1 Harps St, Arcata, CA 95521; (707)826-3011).

"End of the Trail" Museum: *Hupa and Yurok Baskets and Clothing*

A gigantic statue of Paul Bunyan still shoulders his ax outside the "Trees of Mystery" (Redwood) tourist attraction in Klamath, as he has since the place was built in the 1940s. In a wing next to one of the biggest souvenir stores north of San Francisco is the owner's private collection of **INDIAN ARTIFACTS**, including a large number of extraordinary woven hats made by local Yurok and Hupa women. Most were purchased by the museum owner, Marylee Thompson Smith, in the 1940s and 1950s; others were gifts. Unfortunately, this collection displays Indian burial items that may offend Indian people and others sensitive to grave robbing. About these items, however, other Natives have said that they have a long, amicable history with the owner and are grateful that she allows them to borrow the items, such as **SHELL-ADORNED DRESSES** for ceremonial use.

"End of the Trail" Museum and Trees of Mystery, PO Box 96, 1550 Hwy 101 N, Klamath, CA 95548; (707)482-2251. Open daily, year-round. Gift shop and museum are free.

Redwood National Park Information Center: *Exploring Chilula, Tolowa, and Yurok Cultures*

The natural and cultural history of Redwood National Park's ecosystem is explained at this information center right on the beach. The center addresses the culture of the Yurok, Chilula, and Tolowa, both in prehistory and contemporary times. A rough-hulled, 18-foot **REDWOOD DUGOUT CANOE**, shaped like an ocean-going cargo canoe, is also on display; a brochure explains the lumps of wood inside, which give the canoe life, symbolizing the boat's nose, heart, lungs, and kidneys.

During summer, check the park schedule for **CULTURAL DEMON-STRATIONS** by Yurok artists and lectures by park rangers, curators, and archeologists.

Redwood National Park Information Center, PO Box 7, Orick, CA 95555; (707)464-6101, ext 4265. On Hwy 101, 1 mile south of Orick, on the beach. Open daily, year-round.

Hoopa Valley: *Hupa*

The emerald-green Trinity River rushes through boulder-filled canyons covered with oak, madrona, pine, and fir, but slows as the gorge widens into the Hoopa Valley in Northern Cal-ifornia. The flat valley, 7 miles long and about a mile wide, is one of several **ORIGINAL VILLAGE SITES** of the Hupa Tribe. The valley is east of Redwood National Park, 60 miles inland from the California coast.

"All history is seen from Hoopa Valley, the center of the Hupa world, the place where according to legend 'people came into being.' It is family history. the story of a culture still remembered, still cherished, and—one rejoices at the miracle— still very much alive."
—Malcolm Margolin

Every two years, determined by a lunar phase, the Hupa Tribe's traditional people shed their T-shirts and jeans, or suits and ties, and don ceremonial kilts, head-gear resplendent with the feathers of red-headed woodpeckers, and deerhide dresses adorned with seashells to dedicate a week to a **RITUAL CALLED "WORLD RENEWAL PRAYER."** Their prayer asks for abundance for everyone in the world. Some say that the reason the world is now so imbalanced is that the rest of us have forgotten how to dance. The **WHITE DEERSKIN DANCE** begins at one end of the valley, with dancers moving each day to the next prayer site. The dance continues aboard dugout canoes, becom-ing The **BOAT DANCE**, and crosses the Trinity River. Reaching the opposite shore, the dancers drag trunks packed with traditional regalia and camp gear up a steep trail. They finish the dance near the sum-mit of Bald Hill, overlooking the Hoopa Valley.

In the Hoopa Valley, near the center of commercial development, there are reconstructed houses built of Port Orford cedar on the very stone foundations of the original houses that stood here. One of the foundations is known to have been that of a **MEDICINE PERSON'S HOUSE** because it contains a smooth stone engraved with calendar marks and the lunar phases.

Yet, in every other way, the Hoopa Valley is a modern place. The shopping center, teen center, and high school look like any other. The local cafe and service station do a booming business. Kids swim in the river and ride their bikes through town. Forestry and logging are central to the valley's economy, but now that the Bureau of Indian Affairs no longer makes decisions for the tribe, these industries are conducted by the tribe in a more thoughtful manner. With only 12 square miles of property, taking meticulous care of the land for future generations is the essential work of the tribal council and its nationally respected leadership. Tours of the valley and explanations of Hupa culture are available through the **HUPA TRIBAL MUSEUM**. Raft trips down the Trinity River take you through one of the most scenic river valleys in California, showing you original village sites along the way. Take home a momento of your visit to the Hoopa Valley with a seedling from the tribe's Tsemeta Forest Nursery.

HUPA TRIBAL ARCHIVES

In 1991 the Hupa Tribe built a public library based on the ancient Hupa house design. Because the tribe has worked hard to bring back archival documents from museums in Washington, D.C., storage space was needed. The library has been dedicated as the tribe's official archives. The building is now closed to the general public, but the exterior is a prime example of designing a modern building based on the aesthetic of Hupa architecture. Hand-hewn cedar planks cover the exterior, and the moon-shaped doorway and sloped roof echo the lines of the Hupa's first, subterranean dwellings. From the street its landscaping makes the building appear to be barely above ground. The building is a memorial to Kim Yerton, a young Hupa woman who in the 1970s compiled archival documents and photographs of Hupa history, culture, and art from the Smithsonian Institution and Chicago's Newberry Library. The library is across from the Hoopa Valley High School.

Tish Tang Campground: *Hupa Village Site*

This is a gorgeous campground, built on one of the Hupa's largest **VILLAGE SITES**. It's easy to imagine why people would pick this spot to live. More than 40 primitive campsites are nestled into 1,641 acres along the Trinity River.

Tish Tang Campground, on the Hupa Reservation's southern boundary. A former U.S. Forest Service campground, hosted full time and checked regularly by both tribal police and the Humboldt county police. Rest rooms with showers. First come, first served.

Hupa Tribal Museum: *Private Artifacts, Ceremonial Clothing, and Basket Collections*

Every other August all of the Hupa Tribal Museum's **CEREMONIAL CLOTHING**, including deerskin dresses and aprons, disappears from its glass cases, checked out to dancers to wear during traditional ceremonies. Missing too are a few of the women's bowl-shaped caps with stunning geometric designs woven of hazel sticks, willow roots, porcupine quills, bear grass, and the black stems of maidenhair fern. This museum is different from any other in the United States; it's a repository for individuals' private artifact and basket collections. Owners can remove items for their use at any time.

That's not to say the museum is ever empty. Hundreds of **NATIVE BASKETS** are exhibited, including those that hold tobacco, an integral part of medicine ceremonies, as well as **HEADDRESSES** made of the bright-red-feathered crowns of woodpeckers. Look here too for carved elkhorn purses, canoes, baby baskets and rattles, and **DENTALIUM-SHELL CURRENCY** wrapped with the colorful skin of the "money snake" and strung on threads made from iris stems.

During an hourlong tour, you can visit a village site, learn about the ceremonial dances, and discover the meanings of basket designs and other items in the museum. Two-hour tours include a trip to the top of Bald Mountain for a scenic overlook of the Hoopa Valley.

A gift shop sells contemporary Native American art and crafts, and books.

Hupa Tribal Museum, PO Box 1348, Hoopa, CA 95546; (530)625-4110. On the left hand side of the Hoopa Valley shopping center complex, behind the Tsewenaldin Inn. Open weekdays, year-round; Saturdays only during the summer. Free. Call for hours and tour information; discounted tour prices for groups.

> *The hundreds of seashell beads, acorns, and dried juniper berries that adorn Hupa ceremonial dresses make a soft, tinkling sound when a dancer makes the slightest move. Each dress has its own sound. Imagine the world being so quiet that you could hear the difference between the dresses.*

Guided River Trips: *Hupa-Led Tours*

The Hupa Tribe, who in the mid-1800s had fought a guerrilla war against the U.S. Cavalry to stay on their land, also stood up to federal marshals in the 1970s who tried to stop the Hupas from fishing. Tribal members shouted "Hupa—Fish On!" during the standoff; hence the name of Raymond Carpenter's guide service, Hupa Fish-On. Carpenter is both a teacher of traditional culture and a licensed, insured white water guide. One-day trips down the Trinity River include cultural information—whether you go with him to fish for salmon, steelhead, and trout; to run white water and swim; or for the **NATIVE AMERICAN CULTURAL TOUR**. One trip begins at Tish Tang, the site of a large village on the reservation's southern boundary (now a public campground) and stops at old village sites along the river. The village site Medilding ("The Place of Many Boats") is so named because in the 1850s up to 28 houses were located here, with many redwood canoes all along the river bank. Carpenter points out the differences in houses, and shows you how cool these structures were in summer and warm in winter. He talks about brush dances, basketry, and native foods, and if there's time will take you to Tak-imilding, where today the white-deer ceremonial dances begin. An educator, Carpenter is **WELL VERSED IN INDIAN ISSUES.** The isolated Trinity River valley is a rare beauty, forested with many species of trees and home to bald eagles, herons, otters, bears, and cougars. The river that serpentines through the 12-square-mile reservation is swift and clear, with lots of good swimming holes. Carpenter's guides are trained in swiftwater rescue, CPR, and lifeguarding and his company is licensed and insured. Daylong or multiple-day trips are available.

Hupa Fish-On with Raymond "Chuckie" Carpenter, PO Box 894, Hoopa, CA 95546; (503)625-0049. Multiple-day tours booked on request.

> *"We are blessed in ways you don't see. It's not the money that matters. When we fish, we give part of the catch to the elders without them asking for it, offering money for it, or even saying 'thank you.' I teach the kids that this fishing and giving it away is one of the most satisfying things they can experience."*
>
> *—Raymond Carpenter*

Assist Tribal Biologists with Conservation Projects

Gain valuable insights and experience assisting tribal wildlife biologists and foresters with **CONSERVATION PROJECTS** as a research assistant on the reservation—from clearing trails and replanting to helping record wildlife observations (a marbled murrelet survey, for example). You bring the gear and camp in a reserved site along the Trinity River; the tribe will feed you three square meals a day; and you are treated to a raft trip downriver at the end of a challenging 10 days of work.

For scheduling and costs, contact the Hupa Tribal Wildlife Department, (530)625-4267.

Tsemeta Forest Nursery: *Tribally Owned*

The Hupa Tribe **RAISES MORE THAN 300,000 TREES ANNUALLY** in their silvaculture greenhouses. Coastal redwood, giant sequoia, ponderosa pine, incense cedar, Japanese black pine Mexican junipers, Italian cypress, and other conifers are grown here from seed. Foresters collect seed from the biggest trees, such as coastal redwood and giant sequoia. Seedlings are sold all over the world to large growers—from Christmas tree farmers to the U.S. Forest Service and timber companies. Brush species that put nitrogen back into eroded, barren clear cuts, such as deerbrush, buckbrush, elderberry, and

> *People living and fishing along the Trinity River have seen a steady decrease in salmon runs since construction of the Lewiston Dam, about 100 miles upriver. The dam, built in 1964 without fish ladders, blocked off more than 100 miles of spawning habitat. The Hupa Tribe's Fisheries Department is currently working with the U.S. Bureau of Reclamation to increase habitat and salmon populations.*

western redbud, are grown for both erosion control and soil restoration. The tribe also maintains a private tree seed bank for their own use in cold storage. In the process of becoming certified organic so that they can offer medicinal herbs, the nursery also plants and harvests seed of native grasses, such as blue wild rye, for restoration projects. Visitors are welcome. Take home a seedling as a memento: seedlings are sold in 6-inch and 10-inch containers for as little as 65 cents each.

Tsemeta Forest Nursery, 123 Marshall Ln, PO Box 368, Hoopa, CA 95546; (530)625-4206. Off Hwy 96 in the Hoopa Valley's north end, 1 mile past the Hoopa Valley shopping center. The nursery also offers ecotours through Port Orford cedar groves.

TRADITIONAL CURRENCY PURSES

Hupa artist George Blake's traditional dentalium currency purses, carved from hollow elk antler and inscribed with geometric figures, are for sale at galleries and shops throughout the Northwest. Dentalium is about an inch-long snow-white shell raked from deep water off the shores of British Columbia and was used by Native Americans until white contact as currency and to keep track of gift exchanges. Up until the early 1900s, dentalium shell was still used as currency in some reservation stores. Often worn on strands, similar to wampum beads and money belts made out of a specific kind of drilled clam shell used to keep covenants on the Eastern seaboard, dentalium shell in the Hupa region was kept in lidded containers made from elk horn.

Tsewenaldin Inn: *Tribally Owned Lodging*

From the motel's balcony you can see the morning sun sparkling on the Trinity River, a lovely place to drink your morning coffee—either on the balcony or taking it down the trail to the river. Tsewenaldin Inn and an adjoining shopping center are built on the **SITE OF AN ANCIENT HUPA VILLAGE**, near a wide bend in the river. Except for the modern buildings and parking lot off Highway 96, the area probably looks about the same as it always has. Pronounced "say-when-ALL-din," the motel's name means "the place of happy meetings." All 19 rooms and two suites of the two-story inn have river views, as does the small conference room. An enclosed, shaded patio surrounds a swimming pool and spa. Wade into the cold river stream or just sit on the riverbank. The tribal members working here are nice folks; if you want to fish or river raft, they'll hunt up a for-hire **HUPA GUIDE** to go with you to point out old village sites and teach you about native plants used for food, medicine, and basket making.

Tsewenaldin Inn, Hwy 96, Hoopa, CA 95546; (530)625-4294. Open daily, year-round.

COLUMBIA
RIVER
GORGE &
BASIN

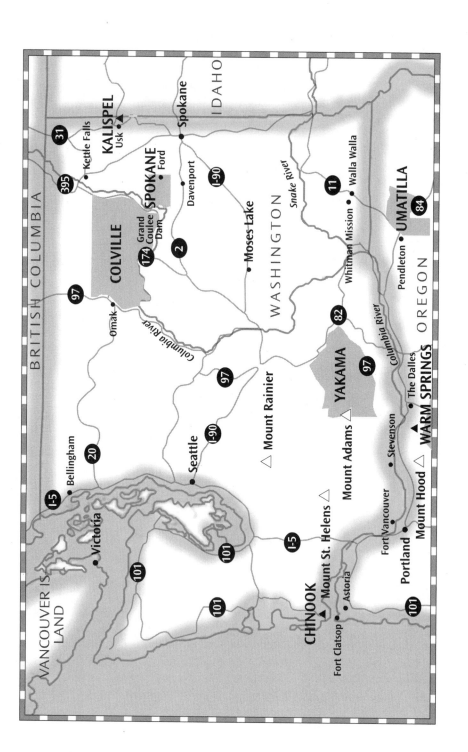

COLUMBIA RIVER GORGE & BASIN

The snub-nosed prow of an 800-year-old dugout canoe, unearthed from a Chinook village site on Washington's southern coast and donated to the Ilwaco Heritage Museum, is a treasure to today's Chinook tribal members. It's a reminder of the days when their ancestors controlled the Washington and Oregon coastlines north and south of the mouth of the Columbia River. The Columbia served as a superhighway for tribes living along it and along the extensive network of tributaries. Canoes could travel nearly 400 miles eastward from the Columbia's mouth, squeezing through a narrow gorge and portaging over a wall of water at Celilo Falls, before the river turned north for another 500 miles to present-day Canada. Along the way, tributaries such as the Deschutes, Umatilla, Walla Walla, Snake, Yakima, Okanogan, and Spokane Rivers greatly expanded the reach of the network, connecting the Columbia to the mountains and high plateaus of present-day Eastern Oregon and Washington, Idaho and Montana, and farther. The Snake River, a major river system itself, extends as far east as Wyoming.

For centuries, hundreds of Indian villages, encampments, and fishing sites lined the riverbanks of the Columbia Gorge and Basin. In their journals American explorers

Meriwether Lewis and William Clark reported that along the Columbia River they were rarely out of sight of an Indian village. More than 50 Chinook villages lined the lower Columbia, a stretch of about 150 miles, and extended north along the Washington coastline, including Willapa Bay and Grays Harbor.

By the early 1800s, however, epidemics had killed nearly 90 percent of the Native populations on the lower Columbia River. Today none of the original villages remain, except in the hearts of tribal members who fight to protect ancient burial sites from development. Near the mouth of the Columbia, visitors can see Fort Clatsop, where Chinook Chief Comcomly, who had exchanged gifts with ship captain Robert John Gray in 1792, greeted Lewis and Clark in 1805. The Chinook's small tribal office is in the town of Chinook, on the river's north side. Across the Columbia River from the Portland International Airport is Fort Vancouver, a reconstructed Hudson's Bay trading post that in the 1830s was the center of the fur trade as well as the provisioner for white immigrants arriving via the Oregon Trail.

East of Portland, and moving upriver alongside the dramatic cliffs and rock formations of the Columbia River Gorge, visitors can see petroglyphs and pictographs left on the rocks by the river's earliest human inhabitants, or learn the story of the Bridge of the Gods from guide Ed Edmo. The Columbia Gorge is the traditional home of the Cascade Indians; territories on both sides of the river were the original sites of various Sahaptin-speaking people— removed from the river by treaty in the 1850s to the Warm Springs, Yakama, and Umatilla Reservations. Indians are not

confined to reservations; many have returned to the area
to buy property along the river banks and maintain scaffolding platforms along the river, catching
salmon in the traditional way with long-handled dip nets, as well as with modern methods—by boat with lines and nets. Within a few
hours of Portland are three Indian reservations
that welcome visitors: Warm Springs and
Umatilla in Oregon, and Yakama in Washington. Up north, in Eastern Washington, the
Columbia River divides the Colville and
Spokane Reservations. The most northern point is the small
reservation of the Kalispel Tribe, on the banks of the Pend
Oreille, a Columbia River tributary.

*Sahaptin is a root
language, like Latin or
Chinese, with many
dialects. A complex
language that is difficult
to learn, it was spoken
by tribes in the mid-
Columbia River region.
A number of elders
and traditional tribal
members in the area still
speak Sahaptin dialects.*

THE LOWER COLUMBIA

Lower Columbia River: *Chinook*

The **GATEKEEPERS OF THE MOUTH OF THE COLUMBIA RIVER** were the
Chinook Indians. Their villages were the first point of contact for the
canoe seafaring tribes and European traders entering the river from
the Pacific Ocean. Villages were numerous and larger than some present-day towns along the river, when explorers Lewis and Clark
recorded them in their journals. The village of Cathlapotel, for example, recently excavated by Portland State University archeologist Ken
Ames, originally housed 900 to 1,500 inhabitants, living in at least four
huge longhouses near present-day Ridgefield, Washington.

Chinook chiefs, in a manner similar to European kings, married
off their daughters to trading partners, often to newly arrived Europeans, successfully forming strong trade alliances. With the consent
of the Clatsop Band of Chinooks, American John Jacob Astor built

To communicate with one another, the European traders and Native tribes developed a language called Chinook jargon—a combination of Pacific Northwest Indian languages, primarily Nooksack and Chinook, and English and French. Many place names in the Northwest, such as Seattle's Alki Beach and the Washington coast village of La Push, as well as words such as tyee (chief) and illahee (the earth), stem from Chinook jargon. For more information, refer to Chinook: A History and Dictionary of Chinook Jargon, by Edward H. Thomas (Binford & Mort, 1970), available from Fort Clatsop National Memorial, PO Box 604-FC, Astoria, OR 97103; (503)861-2471.

the **FIRST FUR-TRADING FORT IN THE REGION** in 1811 at present-day Astoria. The British fur traders with the Hudson's Bay Company followed a decade later, building their trading post first near the river's mouth, then moving 60 miles upriver to Fort Vancouver.

Trade with Europeans had its down side, however. **SMALLPOX, MEASLES, AND MALARIA** decimated the Chinook and other tribes of Western Oregon. A four-year-round of "fever and ague," which broke out during the summer of 1830 at Fort Vancouver, emptied most of the villages along the Columbia. Losses were devastating, as more than 90 percent of the Chinooks died. In the 1850s, Chinook survivors of these epidemics who hadn't married into pioneer families were moved to various reservations.

Today people of Chinook ancestry live throughout the Northwest. About 1,600 are tribal members, many of whom live in the little town of Bay Center on Willapa Bay and in South Bend, near the mouth of the Willapa River. Both are **VERY OLD VILLAGE SITES**. Others own land allotments or live at the Quinault Reservation on the Olympic Peninsula. Chinook descendants living in this area, representing five bands of Chinooks who once lived along the Columbia, are actively seeking federal recognition. The Chinooks rent a 1920s schoolhouse for their **TRIBAL OFFICE IN THE TOWN OF CHINOOK**, Washington, on the north side of the Columbia, across the river's mouth from Astoria, Oregon. Visitors are welcome.

Chinook Indian Tribe, PO Box 228, Chinook, WA 98614; (360)777-8303.

Bay Center: Ancient Village Sites

The picturesque village of Bay Center, located at the end of a spit on the southeast side of Willapa Bay, is the site of the ancient Chinook village of **NUTSKWETHLSO'K**; and today many of the town's population are Chinook descendants. A kiosk, located across the road from the only general store and two blocks from the county park, explains some of the Chinook history and the geography of the Willapa Bay area, including Chinook names of villages that once stood around the bay and the lower Columbia River. For example, present-day Oysterville, in sight of Bay City, near the end of the Long

Beach Peninsula, was the village of **TSE'YUK**, Nahcotta was **NU'PAT-STCTHL**, and Ilwaco was **NOKSKA'ITMITHLS**.

Bay Center is on the southeast side of Willapa Bay, at the end of a spit, accessible from Hwy 101.

REALLY BIG OLD HOUSES

Although Lewis and Clark's journals descibe Chinook villages situated along the Columbia River, none are visible on the landscape today. However, over the last decade, Portland State University professor Kenneth M. Ames has excavated and studied the remains of several huge Chinook houses near Ridgefield, Washington, which have been unearthed from sites long overtaken by vegetation. These huge multi-family dwellings, divided into living units much like a modern apartment building, were made entirely of planks handhewn with stone adzes. Ames estimates they stood through 400 years of continual use, their timbers being replaced as they deteriorated. The amount of lumber used in one of these traditional Chinook houses over the centuries would be enough to build a small housing development today, says Ames—about a million board feet of clear-grained cedar (a standard American house today uses about 11,000 board feet). Houses were often built in the flood plain, but when water rose during annual floods, they could be disassembled and moved to higher ground. "If the coastal tribes had built lasting basalt foundations for their houses," says Ames, "the Northwest Coast would today have more ruins than the Southwestern United States."

—*Peoples of the Northwest Coast, Their Archaeology and Prehistory, by Kenneth M. Ames and Herbert D. G. Maschner (Thames and Hudson, 1999).*

Chief Comcomly Memorial: *Revered Chinook Leader*

Chief Comcomly, then a young man, was **HEREDITARY CHIEF** of the Chinook when Captain Robert Gray sailed into the mouth of the Columbia River in 1792. Comcomly also welcomed Lewis and Clark at the end of their journey in 1805, and helped the Astor fur traders survive their first few winters near present-day Astoria. He died at age 66 of the fever that swept the lower Columbia in 1830. He was **INTERRED IN A RAISED WAR CANOE** near his village, **QUATS-A-MTS**, on the north shore of the Columbia, where the Astoria bridge touches the Washington shore.

To avoid grave robbing by white traders seeking souvenirs, Comcomly's family moved his body to a burial site in a nearby forest. Soon after internment, a young Hudson's Bay Company naturalist and physician, Meredith Gairdner, **SECRETLY EXHUMED** the body, decapitated it, and took Comcomly's head with him to Hawaii. He eventually sent the head, packed in a box, to his friend, Dr. Richardson, in England. The skull, along with a grisly letter from Gairdner describing the difficulty of severing **COMCOMLY'S HEAD** from his body, lay in the Royal Naval Hospital Museum in Gosport, England, for 117 years before it was returned to the Astoria Historical Society in the early 1950s. Despite the Chinook's pleas for its return to them for burial, the skull was displayed as a curiosity in the society's Flavell House Museum for more than 20 years. Instead of returning the remains, the town of Astoria, Oregon, in 1961 raised a memorial, a black **BURIAL CANOE** cast in concrete, to Comcomly on its highest hill.

Comcomly's skull and the accompanying letter were finally returned to the Chinook in 1972, but only after the tribe had threatened legal action, notified the press, and proved they had purchased a headstone and burial plot. Comcomly's remains were interred by his family in an Ilwaco graveyard north of his old village site. The tribe retains the letter.

To see Comcomly's memorial in Astoria, take 16th St to the top of the hill and follow signs to the Astoria Column. To read a copy of Gairdner's letter, contact the Chinook Indian Tribe, PO Box 228, Chinook, WA 98614; (360)777-8303.

Fort Clatsop: *Interpreting an Historic Meeting*

Explorers Lewis and Clark spent four months in the winter rain with the Clatsop Band of Chinooks at Fort Clatsop, near present-day Astoria, Oregon. The Clatsop taught the explorers methods of tanning hides, hunting, and gathering food. The Clatsop also contributed to the party's botanical research and shared their knowledge of local waterways. Lewis and Clark's journals documenting the Clatsop culture provide important historical records of the tribe, essential because so much was lost when epidemics raged through this region. Five miles southwest of Astoria, Oregon, near the mouth of the Columbia River is a restoration of Fort Clatsop, a unit of the National Park Service. Fort Clatsop National Memorial exists where it does (next to a freshwater spring) because the Clatsop band of Chinooks invited Lewis and Clark to their side of the Columbia River telling them they'd find more elk, better shelter, good water and an area to make salt. A number of Clatsop villages stretched along this northern coast of Oregon as far south as Tillamook. At Fort Clatsop is a reconstructed fort, a canoe landing and recently carved traditional Chinook canoe, exhibits of Clatsop culture, and historic interpretations presented by costumed narrators. In the entryway, notice the adze marks on the traditional Chinook canoe on display. Canoeing and kayaking up the Lewis and Clark River is encouraged so that you can experience the lush forest and waterways in which the Clatsops lived for thousands of years—and that Lewis and Clark "discovered" nearly 200 years ago.

Fort Clatsop National Memorial, Box 604-FC, Astoria, OR 97103; (503)861-2471. Near Warrenton, west of Astoria. From Hwy 101 or Hwys 26 and 30, follow signs to Fort Clatsop. Open daily in summer; call for calendar of events; small admission charge. In winter, grounds and the small center are open daily; free.

Ilwaco Heritage Museum: *Chinook History*

The prow of an **800-YEAR-OLD DUGOUT CANOE** is displayed, along with stone tools, baskets, cedar handwork, and turn-of-the-century photographs, in one room of this tiny museum in Ilwaco, a fishing town north of Chinook on the Washington coast. The canoe was unearthed in an archaeological dig and given to the museum. Everything else on display was donated by local people, many of Chinook ancestry.

Ilwaco Heritage Museum, 115 SE Lake St, Ilwaco, WA 98624; (360)642-3346. Admission fee.

The story of the Chinooks is told in the video series "Indians of North America." You can purchase the 30-minute tape at the Ilwaco Heritage Museum gift shop (115 SE Lake St, Ilwaco, WA 98624; (360)642-3446), or order it directly from Schlessinger Video, (800)843-3620.

TRADE ITEMS AT FORT VANCOUVER

Many of the items offered for trade with the Indians at Fort Vancouver were novelties, such as mirrors, clay pipes, rum-soaked tobacco, bells, Jew's harps, and popular Venetian-cut glass beads. More practical trade items included small iron axes and knives, flint, lusterware jugs, copper kettles, cloth, and heavy wool blankets. Most in demand as trade items were the beautiful faceted glass beads, which Indian artists used to replace their naturally dyed porcupine quills, bone, and beads to adorn garments and personal possessions. As coveted as cut diamonds are today, these beads were easily transported, taking the place of dentilium shells that had been used when the Hudson's Bay Company arrived. The official currency for buying goods at the trading posts (determined by Hudson's Bay) was beaver pelts, which were plentiful and easily caught with the metal traps made in the fort's blacksmith shop and available at the company store. In turn, the pelts were used in England for hats, a fashion that abruptly ended when Chinese silk became more popular.

Fort Vancouver: *Restored Hudson's Bay Trading Site*

Fort Vancouver National Historical Site, maintained by the National Park Service, is in Vancouver, Washington, on the north bank of the Columbia River, 15 minutes from downtown Portland.

A **STOCKADE AND SEVEN MAJOR BUILDINGS**, including a shop furnished with goods that in 1845 would have been traded with Chinook, Cascade, and Cowlitz bands, and other Indians in exchange for beaver pelts and other furs, have been reconstructed on their original footings at the site of Hudson's Bay Company's Fort Vancouver.

The original British trading fort and farm were constructed on the flood plain of the Columbia in 1829 and expanded until 1840. The fort's lively interpretation is set historically in 1845, the last year that the British and Americans jointly occupied what they called the Oregon Territory. The fort was located near the center of a network of **LONG-ESTABLISHED INDIAN TRADE ROUTES** along the Columbia and its tributaries, and west of the site of huge Indian trade gatherings and exchanges in the Columbia Gorge. The fort was actually a warehouse complex that supplied 20 to 30 smaller trading posts throughout the Northwest. It also shipped furs from the Northwest to Great Britain.

Felted top hats from Hudson's Bay Company made from beaver pelts fueled the 1820s British fashion. But when the king of England appeared in public wearing a hat made of real silk, everyone had to have one. Trade shifted from the Pacific Northwest's beaver to China's silkworm cocoons.

Reconstructed on the fort grounds are the **INDIAN TRADE SHOP**; the chief factor's residence and kitchen, furnished with period pieces and reproductions; a fully stocked blacksmith shop; a bake house; a fur warehouse; and a period flower, ornamental plant, and vegetable garden—a fraction of the original 7 to 9 acres that provided food for those who lived inside the fort. The fort's stockade and bastion are also reconstructed; they were originally built to defend the British against Americans disputing the national boundary, not against Indian attacks.

Since the fort was first excavated in 1947, approximately 1.5 million **NATIVE AND HISTORICAL ARTIFACTS** have been uncovered, including thousands of trade beads that had fallen through the cracks in the floor of the Indian trade shop. One shortcoming in the fort's interpretation: It does not tell the story of the Indian and native Hawaiian laborers who were employed at the fort.

Fort Vancouver National Historic Site, 1501 E Evergreen Blvd, Vancouver, WA 98661; (360)696-7655. Located across the Columbia River from Portland. From I-5, take the Mill Plain Blvd exit and follow the signs. From I-205, take the Vancouver exit, go west on Hwy 14 for 5 miles, and then turn right on Grand Blvd. Open daily; tours and cultural demonstrations are offered throughout the day. Admission.

Clockwise from top: "Soul Catcher," by Marvin Oliver (Quinault/Isleta Pueblo). COURTESY OF MARVIN OLIVER GALLERY. "Sun Mask," by Wilson "Buddy" George (Nuu–chah–nulth). COURTESY OF THE LEGACY LTD. "Sea Monster Mask," by Richard Hunt (Kwakwa̱ka̱'wakw). COURTESY OF THE LEGACY LTD.

Clockwise from top: Historic photograph by Edward S. Curtis. COURTESY OF FLURY & COMPANY.
"Thunderbird and Sisiutl Headdress," by Mervin Child, pictured (Kwakwaka'wakw). COURTESY OF THE
LEGACY LTD. Jacket by Betty David (Spokane). COURTESY OF THE ARTIST.

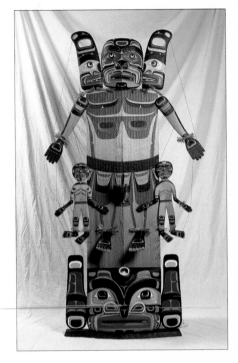

Clockwise from top: Chief Kyan Totem, by Israel Shotridge (Tlingit). COURTESY OF SHOTRIDGE STUDIOS. Tokwit Screen, by Tom Hunt (Kwakwaka'wakw). COURTESY OF THE LEGACY. Lee Wallace (Tlingit/Haida) carving a totem at Saxman Native Village. PHOTOGRAPH BY JAN HALLIDAY.

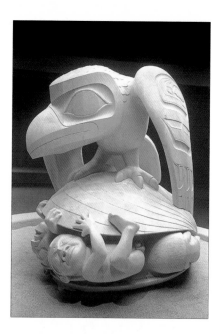

Clockwise from top: "Tetons" (detail), by Marvin Oliver (Quinault/Isleta Pueblo). COURTESY OF
MARVIN OLIVER GALLERY. "Raven and the First Men," by Bill Reid (Haida). COURTESY OF
UNIVERSITY OF BRITISH COLUMBIA MUSEUM OF ANTHROPOLOGY. Ceremonial Raven mask, by Israel
Shotridge (Tlingit). COURTESY OF SHOTRIDGE STUDIOS.

Clockwise from top: "Skauk," by Ed Archie NoiseCat (Salish). COURTESY OF THE ARTIST. Bentwood bulge bowl, by Israel Shotridge (Tlingit). COURTESY OF SHOTRIDGE STUDIOS. "Kolus," by Ed Archie NoiseCat (Salish). COURTESY OF THE ARTIST.

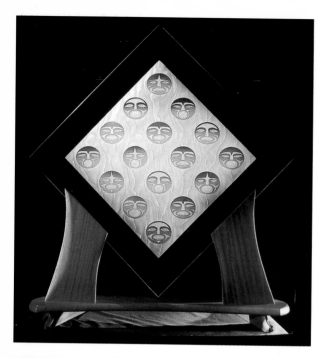

"Four Corners," by Susan
Point (Musqueam).
COURTESY OF COAST
SALISH ARTS.

"In the Beginning,"
by Ed Archie NoiseCat
(Salish). COURTESY OF
THE ARTIST.

"Androgeny," by Joe David (Nuu-chah-nuulth). COURTESY OF THE LEGACY.

Etched glass bowl, by Preston Singletary (Tlingit). COURTESY OF VETRI, WILLIAM TRAVER GALLERY.

Top: Chilkat blanket, by Anna Brown Ehlers (Tlingit). PHOTO BY KEN WAGNER. COURTESY OF SACRED CIRCLE GALLERY. *Bottom:* "Spirit of Haida Gwaii," by Bill Reid (Haida). COURTESY OF UNIVERSITY OF BRITISH COLUMBIA MUSEUM OF ANTHROPOLOGY.

Clockwise from top: Bear mask, by Tom Hunt (Kwakwaka'wakw). "Moon," by Calvin Hunt (Kwakwaka'wakw). Rattle, by Art Thompson (Nuu-Chah-Nulth). Bentwood box, by Andy Wilbur (Skokomish). ALL COURTESY OF THE LEGACY.

"Helldiver, Sawbill, and Crane," by Andy Wilbur (Skokomish). COURTESY OF THE LEGACY.

Traditional dancer, Tamara Arlene James (Yakama/Colville). Copyright 1996 by Ben Marra, Photographer.

Parfleche bag,
Plateau Collection,
The Museum at
Warm Springs.
COURTESY OF THE
MUSEUM AT WARM
SPRINGS.

Cornhusk bag,
Plateau Collection,
Burke Museum of
Natural History and
Culture. COURTESY
OF BURKE MUSEUM.

Klickitat huckleberry basket. COURTESY OF MARYHILL MUSEUM OF ART.

Wasco-Wishram–style twined bag. COURTESY OF MARYHILL MUSEUM OF ART.

Clockwise from top: Beaded floral handbag (detail), by Maynard White Owl (Cayuse/Nez Perce). COPYRIGHT MARLENE WHITE OWL-LAVADOUR. Beaded floral handbag (detail), by Maynard White Owl (Cayuse/Nez Perce). COPYRIGHT MARLENE WHITE OWL-LAVADOUR. Necklace, by Jo Motanic-Lewis (Umatilla). COURTESY OF CROW'S SHADOW INSTITUTE. Necklace, by Jo Motanic-Lewis (Umatilla). COURTESY OF CROW'S SHADOW INSTITUTE.

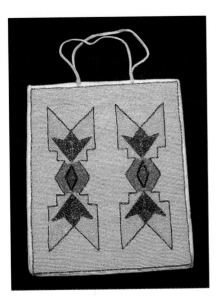

Clockwise from top: Flat beaded bag, Plateau Region. COURTESY OF HIGH DESERT MUSEUM. Beaded bag, Plateau Region. COURTESY OF HIGH DESERT MUSEUM. Beaded deerskin vest, Plateau Region. COURTESY OF THE MUSEUM AT WARM SPRINGS. Beaded vest, by Maynard White Owl (Cayuse/Nez Perce). COURTESY OF THE ARTIST.

Clockwise from top: Mixed media, by Peter Bryan (Choctaw). COURTESY OF CROW'S SHADOW INSTITUTE. Etching, by Anne McCormack (Nez Perce). COURTESY OF CROW'S SHADOW INSTITUTE. "Nest of Suns" (oil on board), by James Lavadour (Walla Walla). COURTESY OF PDX GALLERY, PORTLAND.

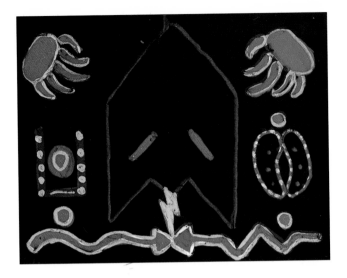

Top: Monotype, by Andrew Wildbill (Cayuse). COURTESY OF CROW'S SHADOW INSTITUTE.
Bottom: "Rabbit Boys" (acrylic), by Richard M. Gendron (Colville). COURTESY OF THE ARTIST.

Top: "Omak Encampment, 1988," by Caroline Orr (Colville). Courtesy of Burke Museum.
Bottom: The Museum at Warm Springs, by Stastny & Burke Architecture. Courtesy of The Museum at Warm Springs.

Four black-and-white photographs by Loretta Alexander. ALL COURTESY OF THE ARTIST AND CROW'S SHADOW INSTITUTE. *Clockwise from top:* "Nettie." "Red Elk." "Sky." "Dancer with Baby."

Clockwise from top: Untitled monotype print, by Ellen Taylor. COURTESY OF THE ARTIST AND CROW'S SHADOW INSTITUTE. Jewelry necklace by Jo-Motanic Lewis. COURTESY OF THE ARTIST AND CROW'S SHADOW INSTITUTE. "Horse Play," by Claudette Enos. COURTESY OF THE ARTIST AND CROW'S SHADOW INSTITUTE.

COLUMBIA RIVER GORGE

Columbia River Gorge: *Native-Led Tours*

Poet and professional storyteller Ed Edmo, of Shoshone and Yakama descent, offers tours of the Columbia River Gorge from a Native perspective. Based in Portland, he begins his tours at the Cascade Locks, where Edmo tells the **INDIAN LEGEND OF THE BRIDGE OF THE GODS**. The tour then travels upriver to Celilo Falls and the Memaloose Island overlook, east of The Dalles. Edmo grew up in The Dalles during the 1950s; he remembers when Celilo Falls was submerged by The Dalles Dam. When he was young, only one local restaurant—Johnny's Cafe—served Indians. Today Edmo's tours usually include a stop at Johnny's, for coffee and a snack. The cafe was opened by Polish immigrant John Wantalak, who ran it with his wife, Nancy, for 24 years. Their daughter, Barb Tumilson, now owns the cafe.

To arrange tours, contact Ed Edmo, (503)256-2257; ededmo@juno.com. Johnny's Cafe, 408 E 2nd, The Dalles, OR 97058; (541)296-4565.

Salmon, Scaffolding, and Dams: *Traditional Fishing Methods*

To catch the salmon migrating upstream to spawn, Natives once used such tools and devices as stone weights, seine nets, harpoons, leisters, willow and stone weirs, gill nets, dip nets, and baited bone chokers on hemp lines. Just 150 years ago, nets were still made of silky Indian hemp, laboriously gathered, prepared, and twined by Native women before it was woven into nets.

During the past 85 years or so, 81 dams have been built on the Columbia River and its tributaries. Thousands of rapids, eddies, and falls have disappeared beneath slackwater pools. Villages, fishing camps, and trails along riverbanks, **USED BY INDIANS FOR AT LEAST 10,000 YEARS**, are now underwater. Today most Indians have turned to modern fishing methods and gear.

In the Columbia River Gorge, however, some Natives still employ **TRADITIONAL FISHING METHODS**. Standing on wooden scaffolding attached to the river's basalt outcroppings, they scoop salmon out of the water with long-handled dip nets. You can see Indians fishing from scaffolding at Cascade Locks Port Marina Park in Oregon and at the mouth of the Klickitat River in Lyle, Washington. One of the most exciting places to **WATCH NATIVE FISHERS WORK** is at the falls at Sherar Bridge, on the Deschutes River, southeast of The Dalles.

Fish scaffolding is left up year-round. For more information on the salmon fishery or to purchase a video explaining Indian positions on salmon issues, contact the Columbia River Inter-Tribal Fish Commission, 729 NE Oregon, Portland, OR 97232; (503)238-0667.

Columbia Gorge Interpretive Center:
Controversial Artifacts

Located in Stevenson, Washington, the Columbia Gorge Interpretive Center was built primarily to house eclectic collections donated to the Skamania County Historical Museum from former residents of the Columbia Gorge. There are donations from Baron Eugene Fersen, a Russian refugee who believed his land near Prindle, Washington, was a spiritual vortex; from Donald Brown, who owned the largest collection of Catholic rosaries in the world; and amateur archaeologist Emory Strong, who spent 40 years **RECORDING PETROGLYPHS, PICTOGRAPHS, AND ANCIENT VILLAGE SITES** in the gorge—information the tribes generally do not share with non-Indians.

Strong also "salvaged" countless Native artifacts, digging up **HUNDREDS OF STONE TOOLS, TRADE BEADS, MORTARS, AND PESTLES**, taking them for his private collection (a practice that is against federal law today). Stone's family donated the entire collection and library to the interpretive center, which houses both in a room intended to resemble Strong's den. A founder of the Oregon Archaeological Society and author of two books, *Stone Age on the Columbia* and *Stone Age in the Great Basin*, Strong probably encouraged thousands to appreciate the region's first inhabitants. His methods, however, inspired a rash of plundering of sites that the Indians regard as sacred ground.

Also on display at the interpretive center is a full-size model of **TRADITIONAL INDIAN FISHING SCAFFOLDING**, and a replica of the McCord Creek Fishwheel, a device placed at the mouth of streams and used to scoop spawning salmon out of the rivers for canneries—a practice that virtually destroyed breeding stocks and salmon runs in the early 1900s.

Columbia Gorge Interpretive Center, Hwy 14, Stevenson, WA 98648; (509)427-8211. From Oregon, cross the Bridge of the Gods at Cascade Locks and travel 1.5 miles east toward Stevenson. Open daily, year-round. Admission.

Columbia Gorge Gallery: *Native Photographs*

Located in historic downtown The Dalles, the Columbia Gorge Gallery specializes in fine-art photography by owner and writer Chuck Williams, a Cascade Indian. His father's great-grandfather signed the treaty that created the Confederated Tribes of Grand Ronde (see the Western Oregon and Northern California chapter), of which Williams is a tribal member. Williams's photography has been featured in many publications and at numerous Northwest museums, including the Yakama Indian National Museum and the Discovery Center in The Dalles. His numbered color **PORTRAITS OF REGIONAL TRIBAL MEMBERS** are printed on archival paper and signed by both the artist and the subjects, with whom Williams shares the proceeds. The gallery has a large collection of images of contemporary Columbia River Indians, Northwest festivals, musicians and other artists, wildlife, and scenic landscapes. The gallery is also home of Elephant Mountain Arts, an **INDIAN-OWNED PUBLISHING COMPANY** that produces calendars, cards, and books, including Williams's beautifully written *Bridge of the Gods, Mountains of Fire: A Return to the Columbia Gorge.*

Columbia Gorge Gallery, 318 E 4th St, The Dalles, OR 97058; (541)296-5555 or (541)298-FISH; gorgegallery@gorge.net.

Lone Pine Village: *Native Historical Site*

The lone pine tree is gone, and a few buildings do not a village make. But the humble, weather-burnished shacks create a startling contrast to the nearby spillways of Bonneville Dam. The little **NINETEENTH-CENTURY INDIAN SHAKER CHURCH** that was moved here from its original site on the highway has collapsed and lies in a heap among several unpainted buildings, which were constructed in about 1896 by settler Henry Gulick for his Indian wife, Harriet. If you look carefully, you'll see fishing scaffolding hanging on the cliffside—signs of a **TRADITIONAL FISHING SITE** still in use.

Lone Pine Village is visible on the edge of the cliff behind the Shilo Inn, exit 87 off I-84 at The Dalles. The village is accessible on foot through the breezeway from the inn's parking lot.

Celilo Falls: *Traditional Fishing Site Silenced*

Dams provide cheap hydroelectric power, water for irrigating the rich plains east of the Cascades, and stair steps of pools for barging wheat from the irrigated fields to the international port of Portland. These were the reasons given for constructing The Dalles Dam and others like it along the Columbia River during the 1940s.

Little heard in the rush to create these technological "miracles," however, were the Indian voices along the Columbia, whose cultures were built around the annual migrations of plentiful salmon. Celilo Falls, in the lower Columbia, and Kettle Falls, in present-day Eastern Washington, were **TWO OF THE GREAT NATIVE FISHING SITES ON THE COLUMBIA**, where salmon were easily caught with nets as they fought their way over the falls. Before the dams were built, water cascaded over these basalt cliffs with a roar that could be heard for miles.

In the 1940s, however, Celilo Falls was silenced by The Dalles Dam, and Kettle Falls by the Grand Coulee. Dam builders included fish passages at The Dalles, but Grand Coulee, with no fish passages, blocked salmon from the upper river with its wall of concrete. With 81 dams on the main river and its tributaries, the Columbia today is a series of large lakes; the **ONCE-ABUNDANT NATIVE STOCKS** of salmon are near extinction.

CELILO PARK is just off Interstate 84, at the edge of Celilo Lake (the lake created by The Dalles Dam). The little park looks as if it is stepping right into the lake. If the dam were to break, the park would find itself perched on a rock shelf above the reborn roaring falls. Under the placid lake lie rock cliffs that drop more than 100 feet and extend all the way across the river. This is the site of the former Celilo Falls, which was one of the most important and famous Native fishing sites on the Columbia.

One of the most **WELL-KNOWN PHOTOGRAPHS** of the Columbia region is of Indian fishers netting salmon at Celilo Falls. See this and other photographs, and hear the story of Celilo Falls, at the Yakama Nation Cultural Heritage Center in Washington or the Museum at Warm Springs in Oregon. Warm Springs tribal member and poet Elizabeth Woody writes of the silencing of the falls and its effect on the psyche of the region's Indian people. Her books are available from booksellers throughout the Northwest.

In the longhouse at Celilo Village, Indians of the Columbia River, many of them from the Yakama and Warm Springs Reservations, hold an annual **FIRST SALMON CEREMONY**, welcoming the first spawning salmon each spring. Separated from the river by the freeway, Celilo Village consists of a few trailers and houses—all that remains of the original village.

At the Columbia Gorge Discovery Center in The Dalles (500 Discovery Drive, (541)296-8600), you can learn about 40 million years of geology and natural history and the last 10,000 years of human occupation of the Columbia River Gorge. There's a 33-foot-long working model of the Columbia River. It shows how the river would be with the dams removed, exposing Celilo Falls, a chasm of roaring waterfalls and a former primary Indian fishery on the river, silenced in the 1950s by The Dalles Dam. Call the museum for Indian-related events throughout the year.

Celilo Park (a highway rest stop with a boat ramp) is about 10 miles east of The Dalles, off I-84. The longhouse at Celilo Village is rarely open to guests, except during the annual First Salmon ceremony (date is announced in local newspapers each spring).

Memaloose Island Burial Ground

Memaloose Island was the **LARGEST OF THE INDIAN FUNERAL ISLANDS** in the Columbia River Gorge, and one of the few not completely submerged by the dams. The deceased were taken to the island by canoe and interred in **SMALL WOODEN GRAVE HOUSES**.

Native fishing artifacts—including nets, weights, and evidence of weirs—have been found at sites near The Dalles, Oregon. Some of the artifacts have been dated to 9,000 years old.

The Bonneville Dam, completed in 1937, submerged all but a small portion of the island's original 4 acres. Families removed the remains to higher burial grounds before the dam was completed. What is left of the island today is visible from Interstate 84. The gravestone that can be seen from the riverbank is that of Victor Trevitt, a white man from The Dalles who before his death in 1883 said he'd rather **FACE ETERNITY WITH THE INDIANS** than with the whites.

To view Memaloose Island, follow I-84 east of Hood River for 10 miles to a rest stop overlooking the river.

Horsethief Lake State Park: *Ancient Petroglyphs*

The **MOST FAMOUS PETROGLYPH** in the Columbia Gorge is the large-eyed Tsagaglalal (She Who Watches) chipped into stone high on a cliff overlooking an ancient village and trading site across the Columbia River from The Dalles. She Who Watches and other **PETROGLYPHS AND PICTOGRAPHS** are visible today in Horsethief Lake State Park. The area is protected and closed to the public except for tours led by park staff.

Carbon-dated to between 1700 and 1840, She Who Watches is thought by some to represent a guardian spirit or to be a warning sign to stay away from an area associated with death and epidemics such as smallpox. For centuries the locale near the petroglyph was a major gathering spot for trade fairs of Indians from up and down the Columbia River. During such gatherings, contagious diseases could have spread rapidly. In addition, numerous **TRACES OF CREMATION BURIALS** (a rare practice in the Columbia Gorge region) have been found, as well as images—carved in bone, stone, and antler—associated with burial offerings. Interpretations of the meaning of the petroglyphs and other remains are highly controversial, however.

Horsethief Lake State Park is on Hwy 14, east of Murdock, WA; (509)767-1159. From The Dalles, cross the Columbia River on the Hwy 97 bridge. To view the petroglyphs, arrange a narrated tour with a park ranger. There is usually one tour a day, Apr–Oct, Fri–Sat. Reservations required; admission.

JAMES SELAM AND NCH'I-WANA, THE GREAT RIVER

Born in 1919 at Rock Creek, Washington, and raised along the Columbia River, between Celilo Falls and the John Day River, John Selam lived in a tule mat longhouse at Blalock, Oregon. He would travel with his parents to fish at Celilo Falls and to pick berries and hunt at what is now called Indian Heaven Wilderness near Trout Lake, Washington. Selam is bilingual, a fluent speaker of both Sahaptin and English.

For 14 years Selam and his family have shared their encyclopedic knowledge of their traditional environment with University of Washington ethnobiologist Eugene S. Hunn. Hunn and Selam wrote Nch'i-Wana: The Big River (University of Washington Press, 1990), which since its publication has overturned many misconceptions about Native Americans. Selam and Hunn explain the term "hunting and gathering" as it applies to Columbia River tribes. Their "root gathering" was actually a carefully timed harvest of bulbs and tubers; one person would collect an average of 50 pounds a day. The Indians' taxonomy defines plant species to an even finer degree than does the scientific Latin categorization

Selam sometimes lectures through the North Cascades Institute, as do other tribal members in Washington State. For a free catalog of classes, contact the North Cascades Institute, 2105 SR 20, Sedro Woolley, WA 98284; (360)856-5700.

Maryhill Museum of Art: *Native Basket Collection*

The Maryhill Museum of Art is housed in a two-story mansion that stands alone, high on a grass-covered hill above the Columbia River Gorge. The museum houses the Queen of Romania's furniture and personal items, sculptures by Rodin, and a large collection of **KLICKITAT AND WASCO BASKETS** from the Columbia River Gorge.

The baskets were collected by Reverend W. C. Curtis, pastor of the First Congregational Church at The Dalles, and his son, Winterton Curtis. Responding to the public's interest in American Indian baskets, and inspired by the Arts and Crafts Movement of the early 1900s, the two men bought dozens of Columbia River Gorge baskets directly from Klickitat and Wasco basket weavers. In the 1940s, Winterton Curtis donated the collection to the Maryhill Museum.

To appreciate the arduous labor of basket making, enroll in one of the **MUSEUM WORKSHOPS** taught by some of the best basket weavers in the world, including Nettie Jackson, whose work has been included in the Smithsonian Institution's collection.

At the museum's gift shop, look for curator Mary Dodds Schlick's *Columbia River Basketry: Gift of the Ancestors, Gift of the Earth* (University of Washington Press, 1994). The gift shop also sells a video on basket making featuring Northwest weavers, titled *Baskets of the Northwest People: Gifts from the Grandmothers.*

Maryhill Museum of Art, 35 Maryhill Museum Dr, Goldendale, WA 98620; (509)773-3733. Cross the Columbia River from Oregon at Biggs Junction on Hwy 97. Open daily, Mar 15–Nov 15. Admission.

CENTRAL COLUMBIA RIVER BASIN

Toppenish: *Yakama*

For more than a century the Yakima Valley, in south-central Washington, has drawn down water from nearby rivers to irrigate its 350,000 acres of fruit orchards, hop farms, and wineries. Once dry grassland, the irrigated valley today is Washington's breadbasket. Although the valley floor receives only 8 inches of rain a year, perfectly adapted native plants once grew here in abundance. These desert plants provided the bulk of the Native diet. Roots and berries were carefully harvested so they would reseed themselves and never had to be planted, cultivated, or watered. In this way **NATIVE PEOPLES LIVED WITHOUT DAMS OR IRRIGATION**.

The 14 Confederated Tribes and bands of the **YAKAMA INDIAN NATION** are the Palouse, Pisquouse, Yakama, Wenatchapam, Klinquit, Oche Chotes, Kow was say ee, Sk'in-pah, Kah-miltpah, Klickitat, Wish ham, See ap Cat, Li ay was, and Shyiks.

The Yakama Nation's travel agency provides airline reservations with on-site ticketing, Amtrak and hotel reservations, and car rentals. For visitor information packets, including a calendar of events, contact the Tourism Program, Yakama Nation, PO Box 151, Toppenish, WA 98948; (509)865-2030 or (509)865-5121. Offices are open Mon-Fri.

Nipo Tach Num Strongheart was born on the Yakama Reservation in the town of White Swan, west of Toppenish. At age 11, he joined Buffalo Bill's Wild West Show. Later he was an actor and technical advisor on Indians in Hollywood.

The word *Yakama*—meaning, "a growing family" or "tribal expansion"—comes from their Salish-speaking neighbors. They spelled it *Yakima*, like the nearby town of Yakima, until 1994, when the Confederated Tribes passed a resolution to revert to the original spelling of Yakama, as written in the Treaty of 1855.

The Confederated Tribes today live on 1.3 million acres of forest, range, and agricultural land. ONE OF THE LARGEST RESERVATIONS IN THE UNITED STATES, the Yakama Reservation is one and a half times larger than Rhode Island. The predominant physical and spiritual landmark of the Yakama territory is the snowcapped peak of 12,276-foot Mount Adams, south of the Yakima Valley. The Yakama name for the mountain, Pahto, means "standing high," a name used for all of the area's volcanic peaks— Mount Hood, Mount Rainier, and Mount St. Helens.

Yakama elders are revered today as the historians and teachers of the confederation's spiritual heritage and traditional culture. Most of the 8,560 tribal members own land near the towns of Brownstown, Harrah, Toppenish, Union Gap, Wapato, and White Swan. Visitors are welcome to STOP BY THE TRIBAL HEADQUARTERS, located in a large complex of buildings in Toppenish. The one-stop complex also includes a restaurant, gift shop, theater, library, cultural heritage center, and RV park. Visitors can see HISTORIC FORT SIMCOE on the reservation and view murals in Toppenish depicting various aspects of Native heritage. On the reservation, walk along trails in a protected wildlife refuge or drive over Satus Pass to the section of the spectacular Mount Adams Wilderness run by the tribe, for alpine camping and hiking.

Tule is a bulrush that can grow up to 10 feet tall. Collected from marshes, dried stems can be woven into large mats. Tule mats, laid like shingles against a sturdy framework, are excellent insulators from the cold because their interior structure is similar to Styrofoam.

Yakama Arts and Crafts: Workshops, Fairs, and Gift Shops

"When you walk into our house it looks like the place exploded," says Norma Jack, who works at the YAKAMA'S SUMMER CAMP in the mountains, teaching Native kids how to tan hides and how to make dance bustles, drums, cedar-bark baskets, and featherwork for powwow fancy dancing regalia. "It's just one big workshop," says Jack. She suggests that learning how to make things is a form of watchfulness. "You learn from elders by watching and trying to imitate them, until you get it right." Numerous Indian artists raised by their grandparents remember playing with cast-off materials, such as small scraps of cat-tail and spruce root or beads, at the feet of a grandmother or grand-father, and then imitating the crafts until they became skilled themselves.

Arts and crafts created by Yakama tribal members are sold dur-ing special events held on the reservation as well as through some shops and galleries. Following are some recommended sources of Yakama art.

The largest art event of the year is the **SPEELYI-MI ARTS AND CRAFTS TRADE FAIR**, held annually in mid-March for more than 30 years. It usually takes place in the **YAKAMA NATION CULTURAL HERITAGE CENTER**'s winter lodge room, next to the museum; (509)865-2800, admission fee charged.

The center's gift shop offers clothing, including traditional wing dresses and jingle dresses (dresses adorned with dozens of cone-shaped bells that jingle when the wearer dances), vests, skirts, and embroi-dered or printed jackets and caps from all over the Northwest. There's a large selection of jewelry on dis-play, much of it from the Southwest. You'll also find locally made beaded wallets, key chains, and other souvenirs. Ask clerks to point out gifts made by Yakama craftspeople.

You can buy art directly from the artisans them-selves on tribal paydays in the main hallway of the **YAKAMA'S ADMINISTRATION OFFICES**. There are some real gems here—a tiny handwoven basket hanging from a beaded necklace, for example. Beadwork, deerskin moccasins, and other crafts are for sale at lower prices than in stores, and some artisans will chat about how they create their crafts. From Highway 97, at the Toppenish intersection, go west on Fort Road. The administration building is the first large building on the right. Park in the lot out front and walk in; (509)865-5121.

At the Real Yakama Fruit and Produce stand, you can buy fresh apples, melons, apricots, and other seasonal fruit and vegetables grown by Yakama tribal members. Collectible Yakama Nation apple labels are for sale as well. The stand is 20 miles west of Toppenish, on the out-skirts of Yakima, on Hwy 97; (509)877-7256 or (509)865-5121. Open seasonally when crops are being harvested.

At **INTER TRIBAL SALES**, Tom Estimo Sr. designs handsome wool coats for men, women, and children using Indian-motif fabric milled in nearby Pendleton, Oregon. The coats are hand-sewn at his store (2 Buena Wy, Toppenish; (509)865-7775; www.intertribal.com).

Delores George and her children often make the crafts sold in the **WAPENISH AMERICAN INDIAN TRADING POST**. She also sells Native American arts and crafts and beadworking supplies. (Open daily, except Sun. 702 W 9th St, Wapato; (509)877-4554). Wapato is between Toppenish and Yakima, on Highway 97.

Toppenish Murals: *Local Indian History*

A few years ago the Toppenish Mural Society started painting the town with **HISTORICAL MURALS**. Now nearly 80,000 visitors a year come to view the town's past, illustrated by murals on more than 40 buildings. Some murals depict local Indian history; most portray the settlement and farming of the Yakima Valley since 1830. Those illustrating Indian history include The Indian Stick Game, Signing of the Treaty of 1855, The Blanket Traders, Indians' Winter Encampment, Cow Camp, and Haller's Defeat. The Rhythms of Celilo, which shows Indians fishing from scaffolding thrust over the Columbia River at Celilo Falls, is painted on Pacific Power and Light's building at the corner of Third and Elm Streets.

Pamphlets with self-guided tours are available from the Toppenish Mural Society, 11A S Toppenish Ave, Toppenish, WA 98948; (509)865-6516.

Cliffside Ancient Rock Art

On the outskirts of Yakima near the Yakima Sportsmen State Park campground, **PICTOGRAPHS** are painted on a 70-foot-high cliff of columnar basalt.

The area was undeveloped when the cliffside was made part of the state park in the 1950s. Now megastores and houses surround it, but that doesn't diminish the awe people feel about the **NATIVE ROCK ART,** which extends across the basalt wall for about 400 feet. Anthropologists surmise that the Indians painted the cliffs from canoes at a time when the valley floor was submerged by a prehistoric lake. The area's cultural significance was recognized as early as 1924, when the Northern Pacific Railroad Company gave Yakima County the title to 17.6 acres around the cliffs to protect the pictographs. Nonetheless, the paintings have suffered plenty of abuse. Water leaking from a wooden irrigation flume kept them continuously wet, and construction blasts for a second flume buried some of them in talus. In the early 1900s Yakima merchants even painted ads over the pictographs. Most of these have faded away by now, leaving the ancient paintings intact, a remarkable testament to the original paint formula of pure minerals mixed with fish oil and other organic substances.

In traditional Yakama culture, a large ball of woven Indian hemp twine, about the size of a softball, was worth a horse in trade. The twine was strong enough to hold a 900-pound sturgeon.

Follow signs on Powerhouse Rd south of Hwy 12 between Gleed and Fruitvale (the old Chinook Hwy). Park on the shoulder of the road and follow the trail to the cliffside.

Yakama Nation Cultural Heritage Center Complex:
Museum, Library, and Movies

The Yakama Nation Cultural Heritage Center Complex was designed by internationally known architect Pietro Belluchi and tribal consultants, based on the Yakama's **TRADITIONAL TULE MAT-COVERED LONGHOUSE**. It was built on Yakama ancestral lands. Inside the large building are a gift shop, library, and theater, as well as the first tribally owned museum built in the Northwest.

It's best to tour the museum exhibits with a guide who can explain how objects on display were made. Permanent exhibits include an **EARTHEN LODGE** made of willow branches, reeds, grasses, and mud, similar to the kinds that were used as permanent dwellings thousands of years ago in the valley and along the Columbia River. There is also a dwelling made of tule mats as well as a re-creation of the fishing grounds at Celilo Falls and fishing gear, tools, and baskets. Don't miss the **"INDIAN TIME BALL,"** a string diary made from hemp twine. Over the years the string is knotted and rolled into a perfectly round ball to record the significant events in a woman's life. Six rotating exhibitions are mounted throughout the year.

Yakama culture is alive and well today. Many traditions are still practiced with reverence by some tribal members, who live by gathering food in the same way as their ancestors did, practice their Native religion, and speak both English and Sahaptin.

In the same building housing the museum is a user-friendly one-room library with an emphasis on Native American culture. More than 12,000 volumes in the Native American section were donated by Nipo Tach Num Strongheart, a Yakama descendant. Included in the collection are 30 **BOOKS OF NATIVE LEGENDS** written for chidren. Strongheart's books can be used only in the library.

First-run movies are shown at the center Thursday through Sunday for about half the price of other theaters. The 400-seat auditorium with stage lighting is also used for lectures, presentations, and other entertainment. One recent event was a fashion show of traditional women's buckskin dresses, most made before the twentieth century, adorned with Native beadwork and porcupine-quill embroidery.

Yakama Nation Cultural Heritage Center Complex, 280 Buster Rd, PO Box 151, Toppenish, WA 98948; (509)865-2800. From Hwy 97, take the Buster Rd exit. The complex is next to the highway. The museum is open daily; admission. The library is open Mon–Sat. The theater is open for films and events. Call for museum, library, and theater hours and special events.

The American Hop Museum:
Commemorating Yakama History

The Yakima Valley is one of the world's largest suppliers of hops, producing more than 25 percent of the world's crop. Before modern
machinery, Yakama tribal members played a vital part in the harvest.
Many Yakama elders remember the tepee encampments to which they
returned, with bruise-swollen hands, after picking hops all day under
the scorching sun. At the end of the season, Native women gathered
twine on which the hop vines had grown, to reuse in weaving projects. A **MURAL AND BRONZE STATUE OF A YAKAMA WOMAN** with a
basket of hops commemorate the hard work. Both artworks are in
the Old Timers Plaza in the center of town. The American Hop
Museum, which houses hop memorabilia from all over the world,
contains several photographs of Native laborers.

*American Hop Museum, B St (near E Toppenish Ave), Toppenish, WA 98948; (509)865-
4677. Admission fee.*

Toppenish National Wildlife Refuge:
Preserving the Ecosystem

A small portion of the Yakima Valley's natural ecosystem is preserved
as Toppenish National Wildlife Refuge, in the **HEART OF THE YAKAMA
RESERVATION**. It is actually three refuges connected by a stream. Natural grasslands and nesting grounds cover more than 1,000 acres, with
another 580 acres flooded to create wetlands. Corn, barley, wheat, and
alfalfa are sown to keep wintering birds from consuming nearby commercial crops. The refuge is a **GREAT PLACE TO BIRD-WATCH**, except
during hunting season, mid-October through mid-January. In the
spring mallards, shovelers, and wood ducks trail ducklings; by summer's end the shorebirds drop in during their southern migrations.
Fall and wintering birds include pintails and Canada geese. You can
see some of the birds from Highway 97, but it's best to take the less-
traveled Old Goldendale Road to view eagles, hawks, herons, gulls,
egrets, and terns. Thousands of songbirds nest in brush along Toppenish Creek, which connects the three refuges. Expect to hear the
hoots of great horned owls; watch for deer and muskrats (and signs
of badgers' burrows). For hiking trails, take Highway 97 south from
Toppenish to parking sites on Robbins Road and Pumphouse Road.
No camping or overnight parking.

*For maps of Toppenish National Wildlife Refuge, contact 21 Pumphouse Rd, Hwy 97 S, Top-
penish, WA 98948; (509)865-5121.*

Hunting, Fishing, and Camping on the Yakama Reservation

Canada geese, game birds, and rabbits can be hunted on the Yakama Reservation with a valid permit. You'll also need a current map of areas open to hunters. No big-game hunting, or hunting of any other animals, is allowed. Fishing is allowed in certain reservation streams, pursuant to tribal regulations. Permits and maps are available at sporting goods stores, motels, and other outlets in Toppenish and Yakima, but not directly from the tribe. Permit prices change seasonally. The tribe also has a fish pond, where children under 12 can fish without a permit.

Ask for the "Feel Free to Hunt Map," available from Toppenish National Wildlife Resource Management; (509)865-6262.

Camping at Mount Adams: *Yakama Sacred Mountain*

In 1972, President Richard Nixon helped the Confederated Tribes and Bands of the Yakama Indian Nation **REGAIN THEIR SACRED MOUNTAIN**, Pahto, lost in treaty negotiations in 1855. Millions of acres of pristine wilderness are now managed by the Yakama, with the 21,000 acres of the Mount Adams Wilderness open to the public July 1–September 30. The tribal wilderness area (known as "Tract D") almost entirely encompasses the mountain's broad east slope and includes **FOUR GOR-GEOUS CAMPGROUNDS** on three high mountain lakes (Bench, Mirror, and Bird). The lakes are stocked with foot-long cutthroat trout raised in **YAKAMA HATCHERIES**. At elevations above 4,700 feet, the lakes are accessible via primitive roads (a Honda Civic can make it; a loaded RV can't). Bird Creek Meadows, just below Mazama Glacier, where small streams trickle through fragile subalpine glades, is filled with thousands of wildflowers in early summer. Hikers can take an easy 5-mile loop from Bird Lake Trail up to Bluff Lake's viewpoint, and then to the Trail of the Flowers (stay on trails through the meadows). Continue on to the Hellroaring Overlook, and then head back down via the Crooked Creek Falls Trail. Campsites are first come, first served; weekends are busiest. Bench Lake has 41 campsites; Bird Lake, 21; Mirror Lake, 6; and Sunrise Camp, 12. Drinking water and rest rooms are available at all except Sunrise Camp. Trailer hookups are not available.

The best way to reach Mount Adams Wilderness Area (Tract D) from the Yakama Reservation, about a 90-minute drive, is south on Hwy 97 over scenic Satus Pass to Goldendale, then west on 142 to the Glenwood cutoff. Continue to Trout Lake. The Mount Adams Ranger Station, in Trout Lake, has detailed maps of the area; 2455 Hwy 141, Trout Lake, WA 98650; (509)395-3400. Open daily. For information about hiking and camping in Tract D, contact the Forestry Development Program, Yakama Nation, PO Box 151, Toppenish, WA 98948; (509)865-5121, ext 657.

Yakama Nation Review: *Weekly Indian News*

The journalists' office in the little cinder-block building next to the tribal center on Fort Road looks like any other small-town weekly newspaper office: Stacks of paper bury the desks, and bookcases spill over onto the floor. The 12-page weekly paper, subsidized by the tribe, is packed with **YAKAMA INDIAN NEWS**, thought-provoking editorials, impassioned letters to the editor, a calendar of events, and Native American news from all over the country. The paper keeps the tribe informed and is an eye-opener for non-Indians.

Subscriptions are $26 a year from Yakama Nation Review, PO Box 310, Toppenish, WA 98948; (509)865-5121.

PAH TY-MUU THLA-MA DANCE COMPANY

More than 100 young people perform traditional music and dance in the Pah Ty-Muu Thla-Ma (Messengers of the Healing Generation) Dance Company under the direction of founder Sue Rigdon and cultural director Willie Selam, and with the guidance of tribal elders through the Wapato Indian Club. "The inexplicable truth of the performance is gathered from a spiritual pool that has been replenished over generations, back to the time of Creation," says Rigdon, who founded the program in the Wapato schools 23 years ago. "The mystical training from the elders of our people enables us to teach the children a way to draw from this pool of collective knowledge and energy."

Audiences are often deeply moved during the Pah Ty-Muu Thla-Ma's hourlong performances. This is work from the heart, taking years of preparation. Whole families are involved in handcrafting the traditional dance regalia—from beaded deerskin moccasins and clothing to feather bustles. "When the children dance for you, they are conveying a message of reverence toward the past, environmental care, brotherhood, and peace that transcends time and race," says Rigdon. The group includes non-Indian students as well. Dances and songs are drawn from Indian cultures all over North America, including those originating in the Columbia River basin. The group is accompanied by the Selam Family Drum, men trained in the centuries-old spiritual discipline of "Na-Ti-Tayt" singing.

Pah Ty-Muu Thla-Ma dances for state, national, and international multicultural conferences, and for special events, such as Treaty Days, held in June.

Fort Simcoe State Park: *Steeped in Yakama History*

Fort Simcoe State Park, about 30 miles west of Toppenish on Fort Road, is a beautiful grassy area at the foot of the Simcoe Mountains. Next to a bubbling creek and surrounded by a shady grove of oaks, the site was once the location of a large encampment where a number of important trails converged. It was also the beginning of the trail from the Yakima Valley, through a gap in the mountains, to the YAKAMA'S FISHING SITES on the Columbia River. Known as Mool Mool ("Many Springs"), it was the home of Yakama leader Skloom, one of the signers of the Treaty of 1855; it was also used as a TEPEE ENCAMPMENT in the summer and early fall, when food was gathered.

A bugle regiment from the U.S. Ninth Infantry Division was stationed at the site in 1856 under Robert Selden Garnett. The infantry was supposedly there to keep the Indians safe from aggressive settlers. The real reason, however, was that Nisqually Chief Leschi, from the Puget Sound area, had ridden over the Cascade Range to warn the inland tribes that the treaties offered by Territorial governor Issac Stevens were not in their best interest (see the Western Washington chapter).

The troops renamed Mool Mool Simcoe Valley after the Yakama phrase *sim quwe*, which means "a dip between two hills like a saddleback." It later was the site of both the headquarters for the Bureau of INDIAN AFFAIRS' YAKAMA AGENCY AND A BOARDING SCHOOL for Indian children.

The area was named a historic site in 1956, but the sparkling white buildings and barracks there now are reconstructions. All four homes, including one representing the turn-of-the-century boarding school, are appointed with period furnishings. It's a beautiful place for a picnic on the lawn, but the history of Fort Simcoe is not so pleasant. After the Indian Wars of 1855–1856, won by the U.S. cavalry, soldiers randomly lynched young Indian men and left their bodies hanging in the trees all across the Yakima Valley to discourage any further resistance.

Fort Simcoe State Park, 5150 Fort Simcoe Rd, White Swan, WA 98952; (509)874-2372. 30 miles west of Toppenish; follow Fort Rd from Toppenish west to the end of the pavement. The park is open daily Apr–Oct. Buildings are open Wed–Sun, or by appointment. Free.

Yakama Nation Resort RV Park

The Yakamas, recognizing that roaming RVers were in need of an encampment in the Yakima Valley, have installed a first-class (AAA-approved) RV park with 95 full-hookup spaces (50 amps), a tent camping area, swimming pool, showers, hot tub, laundry, basketball court, jogging track, and other amenities. The most popular lodgings are 14 **COLORFULLY DECORATED TEPEES**, raised and ready for groups of up to 10 people per tepee; each tepee has an outdoor fire pit.

Yakama Nation Resort RV Park, 280 Buster Rd, Toppenish, WA 98948; (800)874-3087 or (509)865-2000. Next to the Yakama Nation Cultural Heritage Center complex, accessible by footbridge over the canal. Reasonable prices.

Heritage Inn Restaurant: *Yakama-Owned Fine Dining*

A common meal for Yakamas is *luk-a-meen*, a traditional **YAKAMA INDIAN DISH** of button-sized dumplings with flakes of fresh or smoked salmon, served with Indian fry bread. In other western regions luk-a-meen can be flavored with buffalo, venison, or elk, but Yakamas always use fresh salmon. The inn's menu includes other items from Native American food traditions, mostly from the Southwest (for example, Papago cactus salad, corn salsa, buffalo stew, and Pueblo barbecued pork). Most traditional Yakama foods, except for fresh salmon, are too labor-intensive to serve in a commercial restaurant. Don't leave without ordering a piece of pie made with tart huckleberries from the slopes of Mount Adams.

Large groups can book the restaurant to experience unique Yakama heritage dinners. The meal includes *sshaxu chuush* (saltwater clams); *waykaanish* (salmon), *ayay* (trout); or *pay'umsh* (stuffed game hen); wild rice; luk-a-meen and fry bread; dessert and coffee. The meal is enhanced by **TRADITIONAL DANCING AND STORYTELLING**. Guests leave with a small souvenir.

Heritage Inn Restaurant, 280 Buster Rd, PO Box 151, Toppenish, WA 98948; (509)865-2551 or (509)865-2800, ext 740. From Hwy 97, take the Buster Rd exit. The complex is next to the highway. Open daily for breakfast, lunch, and dinner. Espresso cart. Excellent Sunday brunch (with huckleberry crêpes). Reasonable prices. Reservations recommended.

Warm Springs: *Warm Springs*

The **WARM SPRINGS RESERVATION** begins on the southeastern flanks of Mount Hood, where tribal people still pick their year's supply of wild huckleberries, and descends through cinnamon-barked ponderosa pines to the sagebrush-covered high desert of Central Oregon, where the sun shines almost year-round. In the spring the desert floor blooms with hot pink phlox, blue camas, and chartreuse wild buckwheat. Wild iris clings to the river banks; its bright yellow flags resplendent against the rimrock. The 600,000-acre reservation, 1 to 1.5 hours from Portland, Oregon, is **HOME TO THREE TRIBES** who arrived here after signing the Treaty of 1855. The first two tribes to arrive were from the Columbia River Gorge area, today about an hour's drive north of the reservation. One of these tribes spoke a dialect of Chinook. The other spoke Sahaptin. Both tribes traditionally used the interior, where today's Warm Springs Reservation lies, to gather food. Included in the treaty they signed with the U.S. government was the agreement to leave their traditional villages along the Columbia River but to retain the right to fish, hunt, and gather food in usual and customary places, including the Columbia and some of its tributaries.

The Northern Paiutes, who arrived on the reservation 20 years later, were hunters from northern Nevada and southeastern Oregon; they spoke Shoshone. Today they are together called the Confederated Tribes of Warm Springs. The tribes' administration offices are housed in the town of Warm Springs, right off Highway 26, in a collection of historic and modern brick and wood-frame buildings. Nearby is the **SPLENDID MUSEUM AT WARM SPRINGS**, with the largest tribally owned collection of artifacts in the United States. The **TRIBE'S KAH-NEE-TA RESORT AND VILLAGE** is about 14 miles over the top of a ridge and down into the beautiful and isolated Warm Springs River canyon. Just south of the reservation, the Deschutes, Crooked, and icy Metolius Rivers converge behind Round Butte Dam, creating Lake Billy Chinook, one of the largest recreational lakes in Oregon.

Each spring a traditional Root Feast ceremony is held in the Warm Springs tribal longhouse. Elders select those who will dress in traditional clothing and basket hats and dig roots for the ceremony with original tools. During the day of the feast, there are worship dances, prayers, and blessings over fish, deer, pyaxi, lu'ks, xa'us, celery, mosses, and fruit. For a thorough explanation of the Root Feast, see the exhibit at the Museum at Warm Springs.

The Museum at Warm Springs:
Monument to Land and Ancestors

The Museum at Warm Springs is an inspired work of art. Even the building is a **MONUMENT TO THE LAND AND THE ANCESTORS** of the Warm Springs people. A creek flows around volcanic boulders at the entrance; thick fir columns support the ceiling. The rooflines echo the form of a tule mat dwelling, a plank house, and a travois; the exterior brick walls are set in a traditional basket-weave design.

When the museum was conceived in the 1960s, tribal leaders knew that their traditions were fading. Not only were the languages and old ways disappearing but speculators in Native American art were paying cash for **FAMILY HEIRLOOMS**. These heirlooms were then resold to private collectors and museums, disappearing from the reservation forever. Concerned that their children were losing their heritage to strangers, the Confederated Tribes decided to establish their

A poet and professor of creative writing at the Institute of American Indian Arts in Santa Fe, New Mexico, Elizabeth Woody has written three books of acclaimed poetry and prose. In 1988 her **Hand into Stone** won an American Book Award. **Luminaries of the Humble** and **Seven Hands, Seven Hearts** were published in 1995. Her books are available from the Museum at Warm Springs gift shop and from booksellers throughout the Northwest.

own museum. They allocated $50,000 a year to buy heirlooms for the museum and spent more than $900,000 for artifacts and historical photographs. They appropriated another $2.5 million in 1988 to underwrite construction of the award-winning $7.5 million museum.

The most stunning display in the self-guided museum tour is a **REPLICA OF A WEDDING** among the Wasco, one of the tribes in the Confederation. The gift-giving aspect of the ceremony is narrated as a spotlight shines on each member of the wedding party and the exquisitely beaded and woven gifts they are exchanging. One gift is a horse dressed in vivid beaded trappings. The faces were cast from those of Wasco tribal members living on the reservation today and thus seem very real.

There are also **MODELS OF NATIVE DWELLINGS**: a Paiute wickiup, a Warm Springs tepee, and a Wasco plank house. In an intimate circular room, sit and listen to **SONGS OF OUR PEOPLE**, a 20-minute videotape of drumming and singing. The program includes a fragment of a ceremonial Washat and Feather religious song, a powwow round dance, energetic stick game songs, and one song sung when gathering roots. In another alcove is a gallery of **HISTORICAL PHOTOGRAPHS** showing the early days on the reservation, accompanied by recordings of elders discussing their childhoods.

None of the items in the museum's collection is anonymous, as is typical of Native items in museum collections. Each of the 200 **CORNHUSK BAGS** made by master weavers, 150 **KLICKITAT BASKETS**, and **RARE PAIUTE WILLOW BASKETS** has a known history. Identifying some of the objects was a challenge to the tribe. For example, a hollow piece of sheep's horn, carved and lidded, was a mystery until one elder remembered its purpose: Women once kept sunburn salve in it and used the salve when going into the desert hills to dig the year's supply of roots and bulbs.

Elders and artists give daylong **"LIVING TRADITION" PRESENTA-TIONS** at the museum on weekends, from Memorial Day through Labor Day. Lectures cover such topics as traditional knot tying, sally bags (a basket style unique to the Columbia River area), cedar-root basketry, Paiute artifacts, and tribal landmark history. The presentation might include powwow fancy dancing by the Spotted Eagle Dancers, performances by the Dry Creek singers and dancers, and poetry readings by author Elizabeth Woody, of Warm Springs descent.

The museum complex includes a gift shop (look for Lillian Pitt's raku ceramic masks and Pat Courtney Gold's baskets) and the Changing Exhibits Gallery, featuring **INDIAN ART**.

The Museum at Warm Springs, PO Box C, Warm Springs, OR 97761; (541)553-3331; www.tmaws.org. On Hwy 26 at the town of Warm Springs, 1.5 hours from Portland. Open daily. Admission. Museum members receive a gift shop discount, unlimited admission, invitations to events, a subscription to the museum's quarterly newsletter, and other benefits.

Dry Creek Ranch: *Traditional Wanapam Sweats*

This isolated horse and cattle ranch, on the banks of the crystal-clear Deschutes River, is available to individual travelers and groups for a salmon or Indian taco lunch, tours of the reservation, overnight stays in tepees or tents, private retreats, and healing traditional Wanapam sweats at dawn. Owner Lucinda Green teaches guests about **TRADITIONAL AND CONTEMPORARY WANAPAM CULTURE**; her own Wanapam ancestors were fishers living in villages along the Columbia River, from Celilo Falls to The Dalles, until they were forced to move inland when the Warm Springs Treaty was signed. Green's cousins are poet and writer Elizabeth Woody and well-known ceramist Lillian Pitt.

Artist Pat Courtney Gold gathers the natural materials she uses in basket making from marshes along the eastern Oregon-Idaho border. She uses Indian hemp (which is spun into cordage), the red bark of Indian dogbane, tule reed, the entire leaf of cattails, sedges, and wild grasses. Basket-making materials are threatened today by the use of herbicides on federal and privately owned lands. Gold lectures on traditional and contemporary Columbia Basin art, basketry, and Wasco Indian culture; (541)553-3331.

Sweats begin long before dawn with a dip in the icy cold river prior to entering the **SWEAT LODGE**, which is heated by rocks fired in a bonfire, carried inside, and placed in a center circle. After three rounds (a round consists of piling a new set of fired rocks in the circle), bathers enter the river. "It's up to people to release or receive," says Green. "Some pray, some sing, some sit in silence," she says. "Usually everyone feels some sort of healing release when they enter the river." Traditionally, sweats are women or men only, and the sweat lodge is constructed to accommodate the size of the group. While at Dry Creek Ranch, take a look at Green's pin-dotted world map and guestbook with names from every corner of the globe. The ranch is a popular place for women's retreats, including a large group of traditional African women healers.

Dry Creek Ranch, 6130 Lower Dry Creek Rd, PO Box 452, Warm Springs, OR 97761; (541)553-5040. Open year-round. Prices vary. There is no charge for sweats; bathers may give a donation or offerings. Eco-Tours of Oregon (541)382-4754, also picks up visitors in

Portland for personalized tours of the Warm Springs Reservation, the Museum at Warm Springs, and Green's interpretation of Warm Springs traditional and contemporary cultures during lunch at Dry Creek Ranch.

River Bend Guide Service:
Native-Led Fishing and Bird-watching

Guide Al Bagley is a **WASCO MEMBER OF THE WARM SPRINGS TRIBE**, so he has the tribe's permission to escort fishers and wildlife watchers into a 13-mile stretch of the Deschutes River that is typically off limits to non-Indian sports anglers. Bagley guides fly fishing for trout and steelhead 10 months a year, but he'll also take you out in his drift boat to bird-watch or just relax in the river. The Deschutes forms the eastern boundary of the Warm Springs Reservation for more than 30 miles, much of it fenced to keep cattle and horses from trampling streamside habitat.

River Bend Guide Service, PO Box 976, Warm Springs, OR 97761; (541)553-1051; riverbend@madras.net. Anglers need a state fishing license and a tribal permit. Call for details.

Kah-Nee-Ta Resort and Village

Kah-Nee-Ta was the Indian name of the woman who once inhabited the canyon floor along the Warm Springs River. Her name means Root Digger, perhaps a name given to her by tribal elders because she was an especially gifted food provider. The resort was built in the early 1970s, in the Warm Springs River canyon.

Local and regional news is published biweekly in Spilyay Tymoo (Coyote News) by the Confederated Tribes of Warm Springs. Its offices are in the basement of the girls' dorm of the historic tribal school at 1115 Wasco Street. For a subscription, write PO Box 870, Warm Springs, OR 97761; (541)553-1644. The cost is $9 a year, or $15 outside the United States.

The spring water bubbling from the ground near the Warm Springs River is hot, but unlike other natural springs, it doesn't smell like sulfur. From the air, the **139-ROOM LODGE**, perched on a hillside overlooking the Warm Springs canyon, resembles an arrowhead with a handsome swimming pool recessed in the center. Down along the river is the pool fed by **HOT SPRINGS YEAR-ROUND**—an Olympic-size pool three times larger than a typical swimming pool, which features decks, diving boards, and fountains shaped like bears clutching salmon. The new bath house contains a health and beauty spa (facials, massage, the works) and soaking pools. There's also a **TEPEE ENCAMPMENT** consisting of 20 canvas tepees raised on real lodgepoles over concrete floors with wood-burning fires inside. Kid heaven. The resort complex also includes 50 RV parking spaces, a 30-room motel building (the best place for family stays), a gift shop, tennis courts, and an 18-hole golf course along the Warm Springs River.

RENT HORSES from Warm Springs chief Delvis Heath (a former rodeo competitor) for trail rides, or take an easy kayak trip down the Warm Springs River. A full-time recreation counselor is on hand at the swimming pool office.

Ask at the resort's main desk for "Gary the Gard'ner's" 25-cent maps of the resort grounds, which explain the area's geology and plants. Hand-printed and reproduced on a copy machine, the map's pages look like those torn out of Gary's journal. "Well, I hope I haven't confused anyone beyond recovery," he has scribbled in the middle of the page containing his "geo-hike" map. This hike is a good way to shift your kids' attention to the canyon's rocks and wildflowers. Easy-to-read **HIKING AND BIKE TRAIL MAPS** are free. A caution, however: Hiking is limited. Most of the 600,000-acre Warm Springs Reservation is private and off limits to visitors.

Fry bread and huckleberry preserves are served with dinners in the lodge's Juniper Room, overlooking the canyon. Lunch is served in the Pinto Grill. Salmon is a specialty here, as well as "bird in clay" (Cornish game hen stuffed with wild rice and baked and served in its own clay pot). Popular outdoor **SALMON BAKES** are featured Saturdays from Memorial Day through Labor Day. Fillets are skewered on alder sticks, a traditional method, and baked around an alderwood fire.

Kah-Nee-Ta Resort and Village, PO Box K, Warm Springs, OR 97761; (800)554-4786 or (541)553-1112. Follow the signs from the Simnasho exit on Hwy 26 or from the town of Warm Springs on Hwy 26. Charter airlines land at the Madras airport, 25 miles from the resort. Commercial airlines land at the Redmond airport, 52 miles from the resort. Resort room and suite (all with views) rates, $120–$295, double or single occupancy; no tax. Open daily, year-round. Gift shop on premises. The village pool is open to the public year-round, free to guests.

Warm Springs Fish Hatchery: *Salmon Restoration*

Spring Chinook salmon and steelhead come up the Warm Springs River from April through July—some of them wild stock that have been coming back to the river for thousands of generations. Sorted from hatchery fish at a small dam, the wild fish continue their spawning migration upstream. The crystal-clear, narrow Warm Springs River runs through a mostly untouched canyon; the fish hatchery is one of the few places on reservation property **OPEN TO VISITORS**. During winter, ponds are frozen over and snow covers the ground, but from April through September you can watch the huge salmon swimming in the tanks and the young fish churning as they wait to be released.

Warm Springs Fish Hatchery, PO Box 790, Warm Springs, OR 97761; (541)553-1692. From Hwy 26, take the Simnasho exit to Junction 3, and follow the signs to Kah-Nee-Ta. Watch for fish hatchery signs on your right. Open daily.

EASTERN COLUMBIA RIVER BASIN

Pendleton: *Umatilla*

The sagebrush is a soft dusky green and shadows are lavender against the rolling fields of ripe yellow wheat along the Umatilla River canyon. In the distance are the Blue Mountains, a ribbon of hills stretching from north to south as far as the eye can see, like an indigo wave on the horizon.

The **UMATILLA INDIAN RESERVATION**, about 4 hours east of Portland, adjoins the town of Pendleton at the foot of the Blue Mountains in northeastern Oregon. Descendants of the Umatilla, Walla Walla, and Cayuse Tribes share the small reservation. All three tribes were speakers of the Sahaptin language and once shared the Columbia River basin at its eastern end, from the John Day River to the river's big bend near Walla Walla. The Cayuse also shared territory with the neighboring Nez Perce. Both the Cayuse and Nez Perce acquired horses in the early 1700s and became **EXTRAORDINARY HORSE BREEDERS**.

When white fur traders made their way into the area in the early 1800s, the dominant Cayuse seized the opportunity to increase trade, encouraging the establishment of a fur-trading fort at the confluence of the Columbia and Walla Walla Rivers. White accounts of the Cayuse describe them as reserved and imperial; their own language describes them as "the superior people." By the mid-1800s the Cayuse's herds of horses numbered in the thousands, grazing bunchgrass growing in the meadows and valleys from the John Day River to the Wallowa Mountains.

At the time of white contact, the Cayuse, Umatilla, and Walla Walla Tribes lived in semipermanent, narrow, tule mat-covered lodges, up to 60 feet long. It was not uncommon to have 10 related families living together within a lodge, each family with its own health. Mud baths and sweat houses were close to home.

A virulent attack of measles hit the tribes after the last wagon train of the season pulled into Presbyterian minister Marcus Whitman's mission near Walla Walla, shortly after Whitman returned from the East Coast, where he had arranged to help more whites enter the area. On November 29, 1847, after burying their deceased children, a group of enraged Cayuse men, suspicious of Whitman's true motives, killed the missionaries and took 50 people hostage. This incident came to be called the **WHITMAN MASSACRE**.

Consequently, the Umatilla, Cayuse, and Walla Walla Tribes were forced to sign a treaty with the U.S. government in 1855, **CEDING MORE THAN 6 MILLION ACRES OF LAND**, leaving the tribes with only 245,699 acres.

The Umatilla River flows through the reservation to the Columbia River from artesian springs. The word *Umatilla* means "water rippling over sand."

The Slater Act of March 3, 1885, and the later Dawes Act divided the reservation into parcels, assigned land allotments to Native families, and gave the rest to white homesteaders, further eroding the tribe's lands.

The land is still called the Umatilla Reservation, but its 120,000 acres is today a **CHECKERBOARD OF INDIAN AND NON-INDIAN OWNERSHIP**. The reservation adjoins the Umatilla National Forest, forming a wildlife corridor with Ochoco, Wallowa-Whitman, and Malheur National Forests—all of which is the tribe's former territory, now all public land that dominates Oregon's northeast corner. Additional thousands of acres of public land taken from the reservation are today owned by the Bureau of Land Management and are leased to ranchers.

The Umatilla have accomplished astounding feats in the past decade—from **RESTORATION OF FISH HABITAT** in the Umatilla River to building **TAMASTS-LIKT CULTURAL INSTITUTE**, a huge interpretive center and museum showcasing their Native culture and art, as well as telling the story of the **OREGON TRAIL FROM AN INDIAN PERSPECTIVE**. They've restored an old mission school into a first-rate **NATIVE ART INSTITUTE**, constructed award-winning tribal housing, and transformed an old farm into a wild plant nursery. There are also a casino, golf course, and RV park for travelers.

One of the best newspapers in Indian country, the Confederated Umatilla Journal, is published monthly. One issue covered this story of about 31,000 artifacts that had been recovered from an Irrigon couple by state authorities and returned to the tribe. The collection included "400 arrowheads, 1,000 sinker weights, 50 pestles, 2,000 grinding and hammer stones and thousands of flakes—rock debris left after stone tools were made." To subscribe, call (541)278-7602.

Tamastslikt Cultural Institute:
Plateau Indian Interpretive Center

The building housing this treasure of an interpretive center and repository of Plateau Indian culture is an enormous, handsome, wood, stone, and glass structure on 640 acres, surrounded by wheat fields and golf course greens. Tamastslikt (pronounced "Ta-MUST-slicked"), an $18-million complex at the foot of the Blue Mountains, is an important stop for anyone interested in an **INDIAN PERSPECTIVE OF THE WHITE MIGRATION** of the Oregon Trail. It's the **ONLY INDIAN-OWNED INTERPRETIVE CENTER** on the National Historic Oregon Trail Route, which stretches across seven states from St. Louis, Missouri to Western Oregon. Everything in this museum is told through the eyes of, and in the words of, the Cayuse, Umatilla, and Walla Walla people. More than **10,000 SQUARE FEET OF EXHIBITS** showcase life on the Columbia Plateau before the nineteenth century, the impact of white settlement on the tribes, and what life is like today for Columbia Plateau Indians.

Groundbreaking for the Tamastslikt Cultural Institute was on the 140-year anniversary of the signing of the Treaty of 1855. The museum includes an absorbing **TIMEWALK** through history detailing pre- and postcontact periods, a gallery devoted to **CAYUSE HORSES** and the role they played in the Plateau economy, a huge **NATIVE ART GALLERY,** a gift shop, and fire-safe and burglar-proof storage for tribal members' traditional regalia and heirlooms. **RAPHAEL'S CATERING** (an Indian-owned business that won the 1997 Oregon Restaurateur of the Year Award) provides excellent lunches at the institute's cafe, including smoked quail, cajun salmon salad, and fettucine to go.

Tamastslikt Cultural Institute, PO Box 638, Pendleton, OR 97801; (541)275-3165; www.ncinet.com/~umatribe/nr.html.

Crow's Shadow Institute: *Native Arts Center*

Crow's Shadow Institute, a nonprofit arts facility, is housed in the historic St. Andrew's Mission school. It includes a **PRINTMAKING WORKSHOP AND STUDIO SPACE** in which guest artists teach. Nationally known artist James Lavadour, a tribal member and landscape painter whose work is in the Louvre and other major museums, grew up on the Umatilla Reservation and co-founded the **NONPROFIT ARTS INSTITUTE** with his wife, JoAnn, and other Umatilla tribal members. The goal is to assist artists in rural Eastern Washington and Oregon with everything to build a successful art career: a place to work, access to equipment and technology, quality instruction, and interaction with the mainstream art community. The renovated facility includes a print studio, gallery and meeting room, computer graphics lab, and photography darkroom. Workshops are made possible by generous grants from the Confederated Tribes of the Umatilla Indian Reservation, the Collins Foundation, the Lamb Foundation, the Bess Spiva Timmons Foundation, and Pendleton businesses and individuals. The facilities are open to the public by reservation only. College credit for art students is available through Blue Mountain Community College. Camping, RV spaces, and motel accommodations are available on the reservation for visiting art students.

Artists teaching at the institute have included such LOCAL NATIVE ARTISTS as Calvin Shillal (beadworking, traditional leggings), Lonnie Alexander (traditional baby boards), Stephen Thomas Noyes (cedar-root basketry), Ramon Murillo (porcupine-quill work), Pat Courtney Gold (Plateau basketry), Joey Lavadour (miniature corn husk baskets), and Terry Toedtemeier (photography).

Visitors are welcome. Look for young artists' work (see the photographs in this book for examples of work from Crow's Shadow artists).

Crow's Shadow Institute (in the schoolhouse adjoining St. Andrew's Church), Rt 1, Box 517, Pendleton, OR 97801; (541)276-3954; crow@oregontrail.net. Take Hwy 30 east to St. Andrew's Rd and watch for signs. Ask for a printed schedule of workshops. Look for postings of art events as well as tribal members' studio hours and phone numbers.

Marilyn Whirlwind, the doctor's receptionist on CBS's Emmy Award-winning television series Northern Exposure, *was played by actress Elaine Miles, whose parents are Cayuse and Nez Perce. She also played the character who drives backward in Sherman Alexie's 1998 film* Smoke Signals. *Miles is also skilled in traditional arts (she's beader Maynard White Owl's cousin), and is a prize-winning traditional dancer.*

Cayuse Gallery: *Traditional Beadwork*

Gallery owner and artist Maynard White Owl (Cayuse/Nez Perce) grew up at the knees of his grandmothers, traditional beadworkers specializing in glass tapestry. In his early 40s, White Owl is one of this country's premier beadworkers, working in the PLATEAU FLORAL AND GEOMETRIC STYLE. Museum consultant and winner of the 1997 Oregon Governor's Award, his work is in permanent collections of the Smithsonian Institution, the Heard Museum in Phoenix, and the Institute of American Indian Arts Museum in Santa Fe. White Owl's pieces are also installed in the permanent collections of the Tamastslikt Cultural Institute in Pendleton and the Oregon History Center in Portland. His early work, which includes ornate horse regalia, is shown at the Whitman Mission National Historic Site in Walla Walla, Washington. He also attends regional and national Indian conferences, such as the quarterly meetings of the Affiliated Tribes of Northwest Indians, where he sells smaller, more affordable items. His distinctive BEADED EYEGLASS CHAINS sell like hotcakes, and now he's selling images from his tapestries transferred onto computer mousepads. The beautiful spirals and flow of beads in the background of these images are stunning. White Owl's wife, Marlene, is Navajo and also a beadworker, specializing in smaller pieces. You can commission White Owl's work or find his existing work in Pendleton at the Cayuse Gallery.

New technology helps contemporary Native artists, such as Maynard White Owl, accurately recreate the dazzling color combinations that were designed by tribal artists working in the past century. A computer program has been developed to "read" the shades of gray in old black and white photographs and translate them into color—a technique developed when black and white films were colorized.

Cayuse Gallery, 151 SE 1st St, Pendleton, OR; 97801; (541)966-1191. Call for hours.

Doris Bounds Collection:
Plateau Bead Tapestry and Art

Throughout her life Hermiston resident Doris Swayze Bounds collected **DEER TAIL-ADORNED CEREMONIAL DRESSES**, beaded and cornhusk bags, cradleboards, and other items, including a cornhusk diaper bag and the first **MOCCASINS** given to her by her Nez Perce nanny. Bounds, a banker and friend of the Umatilla, was also adopted in a formal ceremony by the Montana Blackfeet in 1965. She accumulated more than 3,000 items over the years, many of them given to her by tribal members for safekeeping. Her collection, one of the largest of its kind in the United States, is housed at the **HIGH DESERT MUSEUM**, just south of Bend, Oregon, a drive of several hours from the Umatilla Reservation through John Day Fossil Beds National Monument (see the High Desert Museum listing in the Central Oregon chapter).

High Desert Museum, 59800 S Hwy 97, Bend, OR 97702; (541)382-4754. From the Umatilla Reservation, head south on Hwy 395 to Hwy 7, then drive through the John Day Fossil Beds National Monument (the original border of Cayuse territory) and Ochoco National Forest to Bend, about a 3-hour drive. After a stop at the museum, loop back to Portland north on Hwy 26 through the Warm Springs Reservation. The High Desert Museum is open year-round. Admission.

The Pendleton Round Up and Happy Canyon Pageant:
Rekindling Native Tradition

The Pendleton Round Up, held over a four-day period every September on the rodeo grounds in downtown Pendleton, would be just another rodeo if it weren't for the **200-TEPEE ENCAMPMENT**, top-name country-western performers, and the "Let 'er Buck Room" bar. The roundup is just as well known for the Happy Canyon Pageant held nightly during the rodeo. Visitors may walk through the roundup's Indian encampment, where **NATIVE CRAFTS, ART, SOUVENIRS**, and fry bread and other treats are for sale.

Today's roundup has its **ROOTS IN NATIVE TRADITION**. The tribes once raced their horses during their own roundup, held where the arena now sits. It was such a popular event that the tribes and the townspeople in 1909 brainstormed together to form a rodeo extravaganza. In addition to the Pendleton Round Up, they devised an energetic pageant about Pendleton's mixed heritage, the Happy Canyon Pageant. The first segment begins in an idyllic Indian world threatened by storm clouds and ends with the tribe sadly dismantling their tepees, accompanied by the sentimental "Indian Love Song." The stage goes dark and then bursts into life with the raucous arrival of the settlers and a slapstick parody of frontier Pendleton.

Indian bronc rider Jackson Sundown, taken when he was named Outstanding Rodeo Performer of the Year, is part of a series of sepia-tinted note cards, posters, and silk-screened T-shirts available throughout the Pendleton area.

Over the years, the pageant has generated some controversy, however. Defenders claim that the pageant memorializes a way of life that ended abruptly and sadly. But critics counter that Indians didn't disappear; that, in fact, they are still here. They also argue that although stereotypes may make a play more entertaining, there is nothing funny about the pageant's portrayal of Pendleton's Chinese laborers in coolie hats.

Regardless of how the pageant may change in the years to come, however, the Pendleton Round Up will continue to be a much anticipated event in the Indian community. The Indians hold private ceremonies on the reservation before entering the rodeo grounds. Then Indian families and friends set up their canvas tepees in the adjoining encampment and gather to enjoy **TRADITIONAL DANCING, DRUMMING, AND SINGING**—it is a treasured family and community event.

Pendleton Round Up, PO Box 609, Pendleton, OR 97801; (800)457-6336. The rodeo grounds are at 1205 SW Court on the west side of downtown Pendleton, which adjoins the Umatilla Reservation. The roundup is held each September. The Happy Canyon Pageant takes place Thur–Sat evenings during the roundup. Roundup tickets range from $7–$17.50; pageant tickets are $7–$12.

St. Andrew's Mission: *Cayuse and Catholic Cooperation*

In 1838, Cayuse chief Taawitoy asked missionaries visiting Fort Walla Walla to baptize his infant child. Nine years later, the chief gave the Catholics a log cabin on the banks of the Umatilla River for their **FIRST MISSION**. The priests set up housekeeping in 1847, just a few weeks before the Whitman family was murdered at their Walla Walla mission. Shortly after the massacre, the priests—who had been blamed by the Protestants for inciting hatred toward them—narrowly escaped from their cabin before it burned to the ground. The Cayuse gave the Catholic priests another cabin in 1864 and added a church and boarding school. Jesuits took charge in 1888.

The present-day mission, open to visitors, was built on higher ground in the 1930s, in California mission style, with stucco walls and a red-tiled roof. The modern church contains hand-carved wooden statuary from Romania and is decorated with **NATIVE BEADWORK, ALTAR CLOTHS, AND BLANKETS**. Wooden crosses on the oldest graves in the nearby cemetery were destroyed by wildfire in the 1950s, but many burial sites are marked with headstones. Do not walk in or photograph the cemetery, please.

St. Andrew's Mission. Take Hwy 30 east to St. Andrew's Rd. Call for a tour, (541)276-6155.

JACKSON SUNDOWN, ROUND UP HALL OF FAME COWBOY

A member of the Chief Joseph Band of Nez Perce, Jackson Sundown survived the Nez Perce War as a young boy and became one of the best bronc riders in the country. In Pendleton he was a roundup crowd favorite, earning his way to the bronc-riding semifinals four years in a row and winning third place in 1915. When he was named Outstanding Rodeo Performer of the Year, the roundup awarded him a golden belt buckle. That same year, at the age of 50, Sundown won the world champion bronc-riding title. In 1972 he was posthumously inducted into the Round Up Hall of Fame for his outstanding performance as a rodeo cowboy. When he wasn't on the rodeo circuit, Sundown lived on the Flathead Reservation in northwestern Montana. The Round Up Hall of Fame's selection of memorabilia includes photographs of the Happy Canyon Pageant court and some of their regalia. The photographs of Sundown show the intricate floral beadwork on his gauntlets. The Hall of Fame is located under the south grandstand on the rodeo grounds. Round Up Hall of Fame, PO Box 609, Pendleton, OR 97801; (541)276-2553. Open year-round, call for hours. Admission fee.

Whitman Mission National Historic Site: Documenting Cayuse-Missionary Conflict

This historic site near Walla Walla, 40 miles north of Pendleton, for years told only one side of the conflict between the Cayuse and the missionaries. Now it incorporates the **CAYUSE POINT OF VIEW** in its interpretation of the "Whitman Massacre." Marcus and Narcissa Whitman built their mission from adobe bricks, apparently unaware they were situating the mission in a food-gathering site the Indians called "Waiilatpu," an area resplendent with Great Basin wild rye and giant wild rye, which was palatable for the Cayuse's horses in the spring.

The Whitmans and most of their adopted family were murdered on this site in 1847, and the mission buildings burned at the hands of a few Cayuse men who had watched half of their tribe die from smallpox and measles after the missionaries' arrival. The Catholic-hating newspapers of the day blamed the Jesuits, however, who had arrived only four days before the massacre, for "inciting the Indians."

The men who had killed the Whitmans believed that the missionary was deliberately killing the tribe's children while his own lived, as well as encouraging a flood of pioneers to invade and ruin Indian lands. After the massacre several Cayuse men were rounded up at random, tried in a kangaroo court, and hanged in Oregon City (the end of the Oregon Trail), a part of the story most accounts of the event leave out. At the historical site, there's a loop through the grounds and **UMATILLA INDIAN INTERPRETERS** to tell the Cayuse perspective; Umatilla tribal member Maynard White Owl designed most of the beadwork shown in the interpretive center.

Whitman Mission National Historic Site, Rt 2, PO Box 247, Walla Walla, WA 99362; (509)529-2761; www.nps.gov/whmi. 7 miles west of Walla Walla on Hwy 12. The interpretive center is open daily, summers; shorter hours during the winter. Park grounds are open dawn until dusk. Admission; children under 17, free. A 10-minute orientation slide show is shown every half hour. Trails to the mission, graves, and monument are self-guided.

National Forests and Wilderness Areas:
Traditional Cayuse and Umatilla Territories

The 1½-million-acre **UMATILLA NATIONAL FOREST** was once Cayuse and Umatilla territory filled with grazing horses. Threaded with unimproved trails, the mostly pine forest now includes heavily timbered slopes, grassland ridges and benches, and bold granite outcroppings. Elevations range from 1,900 to 7,000 feet. Summers are warm and dry, with cool evenings. Expect snow in the winter. The primitive trails often cross small clear creeks without bridges. The forest supports more than 200 species of birds, including several kinds of woodpeckers. In April and May watch for wild turkeys, hummingbirds, and bighorn lambs (born in late May). Elk calves and fawns are dropped in June and July.

Follow Highway 395 south of Pendleton for 8 miles to **MCKAY CREEK NATIONAL WILDLIFE REFUGE** to see gulls, sandpipers, killdeer, pheasants, partridges, and golden and bald eagles during summer. In winter, waterfowl, mostly Canada geese and ducks, live on the refuge.

Another pretty spot is **NORTH FORK UMATILLA WILDERNESS**. Take time to look closely at the cliffs on the way, which are covered with wildflowers and fluorescent green moss in the spring. Bring binoculars to look for waterfowl, wild turkeys, chukars, and wood-peckers in the ponderosa pine groves along the river, as well as nest-ing birds in the willows. On either side of the Umatilla River are steep, wooded cliffs that rise to plateaus covered with native bunch-grass. The wilderness area offers 27 miles of trail, with climbs of 2,000 to 5,400 feet. Horses are allowed; motorized and mechanized vehi-cles, including mountain bikes, are not. Anglers may fish for wild native trout and steelhead with a state permit, available in local sport-ing goods stores. Watch for elk and deer, as well as blue and ruffed grouse. On the Umatilla Reservation follow the Umatilla River Road (all roads on the reservation are open to the public unless posted) to Gibbon and continue along the river on Forest Road 32 to North Fork Umatilla Wilderness.

Several trailheads begin near Umatilla Forks. A favorite short hike is the **BEAVER MARSH TRAIL** used by schools in outdoor education classes. Beavers have flooded the last section of the trail; if you tread quietly, you may see them at work.

For free road maps, call the Oregon Department of Tourism; (800)547-7842. For free maps and brochures about national forests in the area, stop at the Umatilla National Forest head-quarters, 2517 SW Hailey, Pendleton, OR 97801; (541)278-3716.

CAYUSE HORSES

The Cayuse horse was distinctive, with a large head, muscular little body, and long mane and tail—a descendant of the Spanish mustang brought to the Americas by the conquistadors. Bred for their intelligence, toughness, and endurance, the horses were adorned in elaborately beaded masks, martingales (breastplates that drape over the chest), and ribbons and feath-ers. The breed virtually disappeared when the animals were killed by the U.S. cavalry in an effort to extinguish the Cayuse's will to fight. Nearly all of the remaining wild horses, considered a nuisance by ranchers, were rounded up in the 1950s, loaded into boxcars, and shipped to slaughter. The neighboring Nez Perce lost their horses much the same way.

Fortunately, in the 1920s remnants from wild herds that had strayed into remote areas were gathered by a packer and mapmaker for the U.S. Geological Survey. He registered and bred the strays over the years to preserve the bloodlines. Antone Minthorn, chairman of the Umatilla Tribe's General Council, remembers Cayuse horses from his childhood and plans to bring them back to the reservation. An entire gallery in the Tamastslikt Cultural Institute is devoted to the Cayuse horses and annual roundups.

Indian Lake Recreation Area: *Tribally Owned Campground*

Indian Lake Recreation Area has a tribally owned campground open to the public next to a pristine 80-acre reservoir in the Blue Mountains. A full-time attendant is on duty during summer to monitor the 42-site campground. Amenities include running water, cooking grills, fire pits, picnic tables, and rest rooms. The lake is stocked annually with trout. Only nonmechanized boats and boats with electric outboards are allowed. An **ANNUAL FISH DERBY** is held on Father's Day, with cash prizes.

For Indian Lake Recreation Area campground reservations, call (541)443-3338 or (541)276-3873. The campground is 18 miles southeast of Pilot Rock, OR (on Hwy 395), at an elevation of 4,200 feet. Watch for signs.

Pendleton Woolen Mills: *Intertwined with Plateau Tribes' History*

The histories of the Pendleton Woolen Mills and the area's Indians are intertwined. The **PLATEAU TRIBES** of Eastern Oregon, Washington, Idaho, and Montana traditionally wove heavy blankets from mountain goat hair, with a warp of vegetable fibers. The mill, built on the Umatilla River in 1896 near the western border of the Umatilla Reservation, began mechanically weaving wool blankets but modified the complex Indian designs over the years, until they became the more simple patterns of the present day. The mill is operated by the non-Native Bishop family, descendants of the original owners.

Want to check out some gorgeous Indian designer blankets? These beautiful blankets are commissioned by fine artists and woven by Pendleton Woolen Mills. The sales of the blankets help support college scholarships. Visit the American Indian College Fund at www.collegefund.org.

Pendleton blankets are today a favorite gift among Indians. The blankets are exceptionally well loomed, and with their Legendary Blanket series, the company incorporates into their blanket patterns both **NATIVE-STYLE DESIGNS AND IDEALS**. The first Chief Eagle Robe was dedicated to Chief Seelatsee of the Yakama Tribe, and in 1985 the company honored Chief Clarence Burke of the Umatilla Tribe. The company has also recently issued the Hope Series, a limited edition series of blankets designed by Indian artists; sales benefit the American Indian College Fund.

Pendleton Woolen Mills, 1307 SE Court Pl, Pendleton, OR 97801; (541)276-6911. The mill sells clothing, handbags, yardage, and blankets, as well as seconds. Open daily; there are four free guided tours, Mon–Fri. For a free catalog of the Hope Series blankets, contact the American Indian College Fund, PO Box 367, Camden, NC 27921; (800)987-3863.

Raphael's Restaurant and Catering:
Food with a Native American Flair

Raphael Hoffman is a **MEMBER OF THE NEZ PERCE TRIBE**, and her namesake restaurant, located in Pendleton, offers one of the best dining experiences in the region. Located in a historic home, the restaurant contains three intimate dining rooms decorated with Indian art, and a small bar (try the wild huckleberry daiquiri). The food shows a distinctive Native American touch: wild greens in the dinner salads, huge portions of hickory-smoked prime rib, succulent salmon wrapped in spinach and smothered with wild huckleberries, and marinated quail finished with a sauce seasoned with juniper berries. **WILD GAME** such as rattlesnake and elk is featured during the fall hunting season. Wines include a good selection of moderately priced Northwest vintages.

Raphael's Restaurant and Catering, 233 SE 4th St, Pendleton, OR 97801; (541)276-8500. On the corner between Court and Dorion Sts in downtown Pendleton. Full bar. Moderate prices; credit cards and checks accepted. Call for dinner hours.

THE UPPER COLUMBIA RIVER BASIN

Nespelem: Colville

The Columbia River runs through the middle of Eastern Washington, a vast, mostly undeveloped area that ranges from wheat fields to pine forest and desert. The **COLVILLE RESERVATION**, near the U.S.–Canada border, occupies a spectacular landscape that resembles the setting of a Western movie—rimrock canyons, boulder-strewn sagebrush prairies, clear mountain streams, azure lakes in bowls of solid granite, and forested mountains. The Columbia River wraps the reservation's southern and eastern borders, and the rushing Okanogan River defines its western edge. Among the better-known attractions and events here are Grand Coulee Dam and the Omak Stampede. Among the lesser-known are the **COLVILLE CONFEDERATED TRIBES MUSEUM**, the **HISTORIC CATHOLIC MISSION**, and the **ANNUAL POWWOW**. The reservation is surrounded on three sides by national forest lands, including the Pasayten,

Glacier Peak, and Lake Chelan-Sawtooth Wilderness, which together make up the largest roadless area in the Northwest United States.

Before European settlement, Indians lived along the upper Columbia River and its tributaries, both in permanent villages and in fish camps, as they **FOLLOWED THE MIGRATION OF SALMON.** The premier fishing grounds on the Columbia were at Kettle Falls, near the present-day Canadian border, a cataract so large that its roar could be heard for miles. Numerous tribes annually converged at the falls to catch their year's supply of salmon. In 1826 the Hudson's Bay Company built a trading post near Kettle Falls, exchanging furs for wool blankets, beads, and ironware. From 1826 to 1871, Indians coming to the falls brought beaver, buffalo, deer, and other hides—as many as 20,000 pelts a year.

Kettle Falls, as well as the site of the old trading post and what later would become the U.S. Fort Colvile, is **NOW SUBMERGED UNDER LAKE ROOSEVELT,** created by the Grand Coulee Dam. The trading post and fort are memorialized by a small stone monument in a stand of thick pines; a one-room cabin nearby is a replica of the area's first mission, St. Paul's. The site is an important one in Northwest history; summer fishing camps in the area date to A.D. 600.

The **ORIGINAL RESERVATION,** so large it covered a third of Washington, was established by treaty in 1855; by 1872 the reservation had been reduced to about 5 million acres. Three months later settlers again forced the federal government to rewrite the treaty and push 12 tribes from Eastern Washington to an area between the Okanogan and the Columbia Rivers—creating today's Colville Reservation.

Of the 12 tribes that moved to the reservation, the Lake and Okanogan Tribes (who occupied the lands along the entire length of the Okanogan River valley to its source in Canada) were the largest. They were joined by the Entiat/Chelan, Methow, Moses Columbia, Nespelem, Palouse, Sanpoil, Senijextee, Skitswish, and Wenatchis—nearly all of the tribes of Eastern Washington. All spoke dialects of the Salish language except for one band of Nez Perce, who spoke Sahaptin. This group, **CHIEF JOSEPH'S SURVIVING BAND,** was moved to the reservation when they returned from their exile in Oklahoma (see the Nez Perce section in the Idaho and Western Montana chapter). Joseph, who died in 1904 while sitting outside his tepee on the Colville Reservation, is buried near the tribal headquarters in the town of Nespelem.

Both the Colville Reservation and Fort Colvile were named after Andrew Colvile, director of the Hudson's Bay Company. Federal government Indian agents often chose English or American names for reservations because they had difficulty in pronouncing and spelling Indian place names. Today tribal members prefer the spelling Colville to Colvile.

When the Lake and other tribes signed the 1855 treaty that created the reservation lands, they retained their traditional fishing rights. During the annual salmon migrations, the tribes continued to meet and fish at Kettle Falls. Then, in 1941, the Grand Coulee Dam was completed. This massive hydroelectric project drew an impenetrable concrete curtain across the Columbia River—creating 150-mile-long Lake Roosevelt, silencing Kettle Falls under 90 feet of water, and **BLOCKING SALMON MIGRATION** to the upper Columbia.

In 1906 "surplus" reservation land was put up for homesteading after 80 acres were allotted to each tribal member by the federal government. In 1916 the act that gave away the Indians' land was amended to reserve land for schools, mills, cemeteries, and missions. The rest of the unclaimed land was offered by the government for settlement: In a one-day land rush nearly the entire southwest side of the Colville Reservation was claimed by non-Indians for homesteading. In 1956 ownership of still-undisposed land was returned to the Confederated Tribes of the Colville Reservation. Today about half of the 8,231 enrolled tribal members live on the reservation.

Many people mistake the town of Colville for the Colville Reservation. The reservation is large—about the size of Massachusetts and Rhode Island combined. One end of Grand Coulee Dam, which is visited by more than a million people a year, adjoins the Colville Reservation. Roads feed into the reservation from all directions. Except where posted, paved roads on the reservation are open to the public. The best towns for tourist services are Omak and the town of Coulee Dam.

A **GREAT WAY TO SEE THE RESERVATION** is to take a driving tour. The trip from Inchelium to Nespelem (in Salish, "the place of the beautiful valley") takes about an hour, across a forested mountain pass. When we reached the Nespelem Valley, the sun was obscured by sheets of rain that drew a gray curtain across the light like the color of the sky during a solar eclipse. Trees bowed in the wind. Thunderbolts struck around us in all directions. The rain hit with the force of a firehose and continued until we drove across some imaginary line into the desert, where it abruptly stopped. Dry pavement. Blue sky. We liked the effect so much that we pulled off the road, turned around, and drove in and out of the curtain of rain again.

The most direct route to the Colville Reservation is to cross the Columbia River on Highway 155 on the steel-girder bridge in front of the Grand Coulee Dam, to the small town of Coulee Dam. Two free ferries cross the Columbia River to the reservation as well. On the southern border a ferry leaves the town of Wilbur and docks at Keller, on the reservation. On the east side of the reservation, a ferry runs between Gifford, on Highway 25, and Inchelium. Ferries leave Wilbur and Gifford daily, every half hour, 6:30am–10:30pm.

GRAND COULEE DAM

The dams were built on the Columbia River to make it easier to pump water out of the canyon to irrigate the desert; to produce the hydroelectric power needed to cheaply manufacture aluminum, build airplanes, and win World War II; to create inland shipping routes; and to create acres of lakes.

This upbeat message is delivered via loudspeakers and a laser light show projected on Grand Coulee Dam's blank concrete face every summer night after sundown, with a male narrator playing the part of the powerful but domesticated river. The U.S. Department of the Interior wrote this optimistic script for the laser light show. Missing from the script, however, is how Indians felt (and still feel) about losing their ancestral villages and sacred sites along the river's submerged banks, or the cultural effect of losing the salmon. More than 1,000 linear miles of wild salmon spawning habitat were blocked when the dam was erected and no fish ladders were installed.

(Grand Coulee Dam Visitor Arrival Center, Hwy 155, PO Box 620, Grand Coulee, WA 99133; (509)633-9265. Open daily, year-round. The laser light show, viewed from a small amphitheater facing the dam, is shown nightly after sundown, May 30–Sept 30.)

Colville Confederated Tribes Museum and Gift Shop

This small museum is rich in cedar baskets, fishing gear, and **ARCHIVAL NATIVE PHOTOGRAPHS**. Among the hundreds of photographs is one of Chief Moses (1829–99), of the Moses Columbia Tribe, who hunted buffalo on the Great Plains as a young boy and rode into battles against the Blackfeet with Salish allies. Many members of his family and tribe died in battles with the U.S. cavalry. Moses narrowly escaped his death at Hangman Valley with other leaders during the Indian Wars of 1855–60. Later, after negotiations with the U.S. government, he reluctantly moved to the Colville Reservation. Moses then provided refuge for many of the region's war chiefs, including Nez Perce chief Joseph and Yakama chief Kamiakin. Their pictures are in the museum as well. Kids will enjoy the stuffed buffalo and elk in this museum.

Colville Confederated Tribes Museum and Gift Shop, 512 Mead Wy, Coulee Dam, WA 99116; (509)633-0751. The town of Coulee Dam is on Hwy 155; the museum is in the former St. Benedict's Catholic Church. Open Mon–Sat. Admission by donation.

Colville Reservation Artists

More than 120 craftspeople and artisans are on the Colville Reservation's artists registry, 39 of them graduates of the Institute of American

Indian Arts in Santa Fe. It's difficult to find their work on or near the reservation, however. Some of the best artists sell their work at local church bazaars and other fund-raisers. Look for art at the **FOURTH OF JULY CELEBRATION POWWOW** grounds across from the tribal center in Nespelem; at the Omak Stampede and Suicide Run encampment the second weekend in August; or at the annual fall show of Colville art at the **CONFLUENCE GALLERY** in Twisp, in the Methow Valley on Highway 20, (509)997-2787.

If you've never seen the raw materials used for beading, stop at the **BEAR'S DEN**, a private home with hanks of tiny cut-glass beads hanging on the living room wall as well as beaded baseball caps and shirts for sale. (Milepost 47, Hwy 155, Nespelem, WA 99155; (509)634-4922.)

Skolaskin Church: *Honoring Chief Skolaskin*

The **HUMBLE WOODEN CHURCH** on Highway 55, next to Colville Confederated tribal headquarters near Nespelem, is named after Chief Skolaskin (1839–1922), a **RESPECTED PROPHET AND MEDICINE MAN** who predicted the 1872 earthquake that shook the area. The Skolaskin Church, built in 1874, was moved from a village called Whitestone before the dam flooded the valley. Now closed, the church is a great spot for a photograph. Behind the church is a monument to the tribe's veterans.

Outside the church is a weathered tree trunk. Look closely to see a human figure cut into the tree, distorted by 200 years of growth. Some of the figures and symbols blazed in many other trees in the Okanogan Valley may have served spiritual and directional purposes.

The Skolaskin Church is on Hwy 155 on a shaded lawn south of Nespelem at the tribal center.

St. Mary's Mission: *Today's Pascal Sherman Indian School*

The handsome St. Mary's Catholic Church, built in 1886 and restored 100 years later, is the **CENTERPIECE OF ST. MARY'S MISSION**, today the Pascal Sherman Indian School. The mission is in a spectacular **GRANITE CANYON**, near the town of Omak, about 50 miles north of Grand Coulee Dam.

In the late nineteenth century, Indians wanted nothing to do with Jesuit Father Etienne de Rouge until he saved a child from drowning in rain-swollen Omak Creek in 1886. That year Chief Smitkin gave de Rouge land to build the mission on a knoll above the creek.

The historic mission is **STILL USED AS A BOARDING SCHOOL**. Other buildings in the area include those built in the 1920s, with wide covered porches reminiscent of Santa Fe's early architecture.

Priests used a cave behind the school for private meditation and prayer. Find the school's bus garage and ask anyone to point the way to the cave. Near the cave is a pleasant waterfall over an irrigation dam, where rocks are carved with **PETROGLYPHS**. Watch for rattlesnakes.

Pascal Sherman Indian School, Omak Lake Rd, Hwy 155, Omak, WA 98841; (509)826-2097. Watch for signs on Hwy 155, east of Omak. Visitors must first register at the school's administration office. A student or staff member may be available to show you around. Donations appreciated.

Monument to Chief Joseph: *Nez Perce Warrior's Grave*

Probably one of the most epic stories in Western history is that of Chief Joseph's band of Nez Perce, who held off the U.S. cavalry during their 1,500-mile journey toward Canada. After they surrendered near the Canadian border, the band was exiled to Oklahoma (see Nez Perce section in the Idaho and Western Montana chapter). Some survivors, including Joseph (Heimont Toolyalaket), eventually returned and found a permanent home on the Colville Reservation, where he died in 1904.

A **HANDSOME MONUMENT** to Joseph, carved in white marble, stands in the **NEZ PERCE CEMETERY** at Nespelem. About a block away is another commemorative marker to him, in a turnout on Highway 155. (The second marker, built and maintained by the Washington State Highway Department, is less than you'd expect for a man of Joseph's stature, however.) To see the white marble monument, the Nez Perce request that you park next to the highway monument and walk to the cemetery, rather than kicking up dust or parking on the road that runs through a residential area. Please do not enter the cemetery, however.

Look for the turnout on Hwy 155, south of Nespelem. The Nez Perce monument to Chief Joseph is clearly visible from the cemetery gate, under a lone tree.

Omak Stampede and Suicide Run: *Traditional Overland Races*

Horses prance and riders tense in anticipation as they wait for the signal to gallop over the brink and charge down the steep sandy hillside, swim the Okanogan River, and thunder to the finish line during the annual Suicide Run, the highlight of the four-day Omak

Stampede. Held annually in the second weekend in August, the Suicide Run harks back to tribal gatherings and overland races, in which horses zigzagged through trees, struggled up rocky hillsides, and plunged into rivers or lakes at the bottoms of steep sandy hills. The Suicide Run, the last leg of the traditional race, was added to the rodeo competition 60 years ago. Today the races are the Omak Stampede's main event, with two runs during the day and two after dark, lighted with flares.

One of the most spectacular lake views in the Pacific Northwest is from graveled Omak Lake Road which overlooks the deep (300- to 400-foot), blue-green Omak Lake in a granite basin. What is visible here, except for a few small towns and roads, is almost exactly how this country looked when families lived along the banks of the Columbia River in pit houses 12,000 to 18,000 years ago.

More than 100 tepees fill the encampment near the rodeo grounds. **TRADITIONAL FANCY DANCING, DRUMMING AND SINGING** contests, and stick games go on during the four-day event. Booths featuring food and local **INDIAN ARTS AND CRAFTS** are open to the public.

For Omak Stampede and Suicide Run tickets and information, contact the Omak Chamber of Commerce and Visitor Information Center, 401 Omak Ave, Rt 2, PO Box 5200, Omak, WA 98841; (800)225-6625 or (509)826-1880. Also for purchase at the visitors center are videotapes of historic Suicide Runs and interviews with Indian participants.

Kettle Falls Historic Sites: *Traditional Native Lands*

Kettle Falls, once one of the most important fisheries on the Columbia River, is now submerged under 90 feet of water; the rock islands that channeled the river to the falls are visible only on the rare occasions when the water behind the Grand Coulee Dam is drawn down. A bridge on Highway 20 crosses the Columbia where the falls once roared.

The Kettle Falls Historical Center's **PEOPLE OF THE FALLS EXHIBIT**, located in a warehouse-style building near the river, attempts to explain the importance of the falls using dioramas and limited artifacts collected along the river. **BEADWORK AND EMBROIDERY** are also displayed. Unfortunately, the miniature sweat lodge, made of green cedar boughs, is about as effective in helping you understand what happens inside such a lodge as displaying an unplugged jukebox would be in explaining swing dancing. Each summer there is a **NATIVE AMERICAN ART SHOW**, showcasing work from the Northwest.

About a quarter-mile from the center, in a pine grove, is a 1939 **RECONSTRUCTION OF ST. PAUL'S MISSION CHURCH**. There is also a monument to the area's first trading post. The single-room, cabinlike church was built in 1840 of hand-hewn pine by Father Anthony Ravalli. It is very different from the Cataldo Mission church, which

Ravalli built with the Coeur d'Alene Indians in Idaho (see the Coeur d'Alene section of the Idaho and Western Montana chapter).

Kettle Falls Historical Center and St. Paul's Mission are located off Hwy 395, on the east side of the Kettle Falls bridge; watch for a red-roofed building in the trees; (509)738-6964. National Park Service brochures explaining the area's history are free. The center is open May–Sept. Call for hours. Admission.

COLVILLE PAINTER CHERYL A. GRUNLOSE

Every family band within a tribe had its own variation of adornment that distinguished them from other families. Most elders over 90 can look at a black and white photograph taken in the late 1800s and tell you to what family that person belonged based on the necklaces, earrings/beaded tapestry, and other symbols adorning their clothing. Cheryl A. Grunlose, a Colville painter (Rattle Snake Mountain Studio (509)633-2818), uses historic photographs of Colville and other tribal members dressed in their beautiful regalia, combining these images with styles of European painting by Matisse, Mary Cassatt, and other impressionists. Grunlose herself wears the same abalone earrings worn by her great-grandmother. She received them from her family in a give-away celebration.

Native Storyteller and Oral Historian

Professional storyteller and oral historian Ken Edwards (Rainbow Cougar) has a repertoire of more than 1,000 **NATIVE AMERICAN STORIES**—from animal-people stories (such as Raven and Coyote) to more recent true-life tales from Indian reservations across North America. He regales listeners at schools and colleges, as well as at Indian markets, fairs, powwows, museums, libraries, and bookstores. A versatile performer, Edwards can tell up to three or four hours of stories on any subject, including love stories on Valentine's Day and scary Native American stories on Halloween. He also has a fine arts degree from the Institute of American Indian Arts in Santa Fe, and his artwork illustrates numerous calendars, cards, and books sold nationally.

Ken Edwards, Rt 2, PO Box 72-S, Omak, WA 98841; (509)826-4744. Available for sale is an hourlong storytelling videotape from Edwards.

Canoe, Kayak, and Hike on the Colville Reservation

Elevations in the Colville Reservation range from 800 feet to more than 7,000 feet. The reservation's forests, and shrub and grassland steppes, provide ecological niches for more than **300 SPECIES OF FISH**

AND WILDLIFE—from black bears to pond turtles. Three of Washington's rare loon-nesting grounds are here. Drive slowly, or kayak or canoe, to see wildlife. A copy of tribal regulations comes with reservation fishing and hunting permits (sold at most convenience stores and marinas on the reservation, as well as at nearby stores off the reservation). Note: Campgrounds and public beaches are sometimes closed to nontribal members on short notice.

Before arrival at the reservation, direct all questions about camping, swimming, and fishing to the Confederated Tribes of the Colville Reservation, Parks and Recreation Department, PO Box 150, Nespelem, WA 99155; (509)634-8867.

MOURNING DOVE, A SALISHAN AUTOBIOGRAPHY

Christine Quintasket had little formal education and labored during the day in the orchards and fields. But by night she wrote and by her life's end, she had published a novel, one of the first by a Native American woman, as well as a volume of short stories. The original draft of the remarkable Mourning Dove: A Salishan Autobiography was published in 1990, more than 50 years after Quintasket's death. Scholar Jay Miller's preface discusses obstacles facing the tribes of the Colville Reservation and other individuals caught in the cross-cultural conflict well into this twentieth century. The book is available from the Colville Confederated Tribes Museum and Gift Shop, 512 6th St, Coulee Dam, WA 99116; (509)633-0751.

Rainbow Beach Resort: *Colville-Owned Lodging*

West of Inchelium, at Rainbow Beach Resort, rent a quaint log cabin with a comfortable sitting porch overlooking North Twin Lake. Cabin rentals include a small rowboat. Some cabins have a wood range or fireplace. The pristine Twin Lakes, covering 1,500 acres and surrounded by pine forest, are stocked with trout and bass. Tent and RV camping areas are also available. The resort has a small grocery store, laundry, gas and oil, and VCR rental; the store sells fishing tackle and licenses.

Rainbow Beach Resort, PO Box 146, Inchelium, WA 99138; (509)722-5901. Reservations essential. Open Apr–Oct.

Tribally Maintained Houseboats and Campgrounds: *Explore on Your Own*

The Confederated Tribes of the Colville Reservation maintain a **FLEET OF 40 HOUSEBOATS** at two marinas on the shores of Lake Roosevelt. The fully furnished boats are 46–52 feet long, sleep 10-13 people, and are equipped with front and rear decks, full galleys, hot water, bathrooms with showers and tubs, and extras such as water slides and barbecue grills. You can also rent skiffs, runabouts, jet-boats, or patio boats for waterskiing and exploring the lake's nooks and crannies. In addition, the National Park Service and the Confederated Tribes operate more than **32** **CAMPGROUNDS** in the area. Summer temperatures in the canyons range between 75 and 100 degrees Fahrenheit; water temperatures reach the 70s in August.

Recreational maps of the entire Lake Roosevelt area are available from the National Park Service Headquarters, 1008 Crest Dr, Coulee Dam, WA 99116; (509)633-9441.

Houseboats can be rented from Keller Ferry Marina or from Seven Bays Marina, both on the Washington side of Lake Roosevelt.

Roosevelt Recreational Enterprises Reservations Office, PO Box 5, Coulee Dam, WA 99116; (800)648-5253 or (509)633-0136. Lake Roosevelt is about 260 miles from Seattle and 70 miles from Spokane. Call for a brochure that explains houseboat rental, or reservations, rates, and campground maps. Houseboats are available Mar–Nov; reserve boats at least a year in advance for July and August. Cost is $1,045–$2,010 per week plus $300 deposit, sales tax, optional insurance, and gas and oil. Campground maps are provided with houseboat rentals. To reach Keller Ferry Marina, take Rte 2 to Wilbur, then travel north on Hwy 21 for 14 miles. Keller Ferry has a store; nearby are lakeside RV and tent campgrounds managed by the National Park Service. Seven Bays Marina is 25 miles north of Davenport. It offers RV campers full hookups with lake views, marina store, laundry facilities, showers, waste disposal, and fresh water. To reach Seven Bays, take Hwy 2 to the Hwy 25 exit, then turn left on the Miles/Creston Rd.

Wellpinit: *Spokane*

According to Spokane oral historians, much of present-day northeastern Washington was once a huge lake that took several days to cross. Salish villages dotted the lakeshore and perched on various islands. One morning a cataclysmic event overturned boats and created tidal waves that engulfed the villages. Some people fled to Mount Spokane, as the entire lake was sucked out of the valley. The earth reeked of dead fish and game. The few people who survived eked out a meager existence until spring. When the snow melted, a roaring river cut its way over the rocks, bringing new life to the country. A waterfall roared to life, and its spray held a rainbow. This is the place the people decided to call home. The legend chronicles geologic fact: The dramatic Columbia River basin was shaped by a cataclysmic breaking of a natural dam that backed up an enormous lake over the entire northeast corner of Washington and the Idaho panhandle about 10,000 years ago.

The Spokane ("children of the sun") shared their territory around the lake and the Salish language with the tribes that today make up the Coeur d'Alene, Colville, Flathead, and Kalispel Tribes. The Spokane consisted of three bands that lived along the Spokane River, a short tributary of the Columbia River with headwaters in Coeur d'Alene Lake. Spokane Falls, today a natural highlight in the city of Spokane, was the tribe's center of trade and fishing.

In 1808 the Hudson's Bay Company built "Spokane House" next to the river, a large trading post that included a ballroom and horse track. It closed in 1825. By 1887 settlers had taken most of the rich agricultural land around Spokane Falls. Fearful that they would lose all of their land, the three Spokane bands entered an agreement with the U.S. government to cede title and move to other reservations. Many moved to the Coeur d'Alene Reservation in Idaho and the Flathead Reservation in Montana before another agreement was reached to create the **SPOKANE RESERVATION** on the lower reaches of the Spokane River.

The Spokane Reservation encompasses a stunning landscape of conifer-covered slopes, basalt cliffs, and wheat and hay fields—most of which is undeveloped. It's bounded by the Spokane River on the southern border and the Columbia River (Lake Roosevelt) on the west. The most scenic route to the reservation is from Spokane on Highway 291, which follows the Spokane River to the reservation, then turns about a mile inland. A **HISTORIC CATHOLIC CHURCH** is just off the road to the Spokane tribal headquarters at Wellpinit, followed by the **TRIBE'S HATCHERY**. Open to the public on the reservation's west side are Two Rivers, a recreation development at the conjunction of the Spokane River and Lake Roosevelt, as well as 32 small parks.

Father Pierre-John De Smet, one of the first Catholic missionaries in the region, recorded his journey through the Spokane plain in the early 1800s as "dry, stony, undulating, covered with bunch and nutritious grass, with prickly pear and wormwood. The basaltic and volcanic formations which extend through the whole of this region are really wonderful. We frequently passed ponds and small lakes imbedded between walls of basaltic rocks—immense ranges of dark shining pillars, as if forced from the bosom of the plain, extend for some miles, resembling, not infrequently, forts and ancient ruined cities and castles. . . The Indian frequent these regions in search of the bitter and camash roots, very abundant here."

Alex Sherwood Memorial Tribal Center Museum

The small collection in this temporary one-room museum in the Spokane Tribal Center (the Spokane are planning a new cultural learning center and museum) reflects both **TRADITIONAL AND CONTEMPORARY NATIVE LIFE** on the Spokane Reservation. Displays include arrowheads, ceremonial items made of beadwork, buckskin, and other natural materials. For sale at the museum is *Children of the Sun,* a booklet of history, culture, language, stories, and contemporary issues of the Spokane Tribe, written by tribal member David C. Wynecoop.

Alex Sherwood Memorial Tribal Center Museum in the Spokane Tribal Center, PO Box 100, Wellpinit, WA 99040; (509)258-4581. At Ford, cross the bridge onto Wellpinit Rd and travel for 12 miles. The tribal center is in a stone building just past the four-way stop in Wellpinit. Open Mon–Fri. Free.

Cheney Cowles Museum: *Plateau Collection*

Located in Spokane's historic Browne's Addition neighborhood, the Cheney Cowles Museum houses one of the most **SIGNIFICANT AMERICAN INDIAN COLLECTIONS** in the United States, now on display in a huge new wing overlooking the Spokane River. The museum's holdings include more than **35,000 NATIVE ITEMS,** mostly from the Plateau region of the Pacific Northwest, which encompasses the Coeur d'Alene, Colville, Flathead, Kalispel, Kootenai, Nez Perce, Spokane, Umatilla, Warm Springs, and Yakama Reservations. Because of size limitations, only about 150 items are exhibited at a time. Reproductions of **HISTORIC PHOTOGRAPHS** are available for purchase from the museum's research library and archives, which also house manuscripts, maps, oral history tapes, and ephemera (researchers must make an appointment). Special events include art shows and lectures by members of the Colville, Spokane, Coeur d'Alene, and Kalispel Tribes.

The museum sponsors an **ANNUAL FRIENDSHIP DANCE** the first Saturday in January that honors the traditions of the Plateau tribes (those of Eastern Washington, Idaho, and Oregon), as well as a 10-day introductory course on Salish culture and language taught by a Spokane tribal member.

Cheney Cowles Museum, 2316 W 1st Ave, Spokane, WA 99204; (509)456-3931. Located in the Browne's Addition National Historic District, 5 minutes west of downtown. From I-90, take exit 280A; turn north on Walnut, then west on 2nd Ave. Follow signs. Open Tues–Sun. Admission.

St. Joseph's Catholic Church: *Spokane Easter Pilgrimage*

Around the time that St. Joseph's Catholic Church was built in 1912, tribal members from all over the region brought **TEPEES AND WAGONS** to camp on the site. Those Spokane tribal members who are members of the Catholic church still make a pilgrimage to St. Joseph's each Easter. The church is a symbolic classic, with a bell tower and stained-glass windows.

Spokane tribal member Gloria Bird's first collection of poetry, Full Moon on the Reservation (Greenfield Review, 1993), has received accolades. She teaches Native American literature and writing courses at the Institute of American Indian Arts in Santa Fe, New Mexico. Her book is available at the Alex Sherwood Museum.

St. Joseph's Catholic Church. At Ford, take the Wellpinit Rd and continue to the second road to the right (unnamed). The church, marked as a historic site by the Spokane Tribe, is about a half mile down that road. Usually open daily.

Turnbull National Wildlife Refuge:
Traditional Plateau Indians Hunting and Gathering Area

This public wildlife refuge, 6 miles south of Cheney, is part of a larger prairie. About 27 square miles, it is filled with lakes and ponds pooled in bedrock, a **HAVEN FOR NESTING WATERFOWL**. The refuge, originally part of a huge Plateau hunting and gathering area, was obtained in 1937 by the U.S. Department of the Interior and restored from farming to wetlands specifically to protect waterfowl nesting grounds. Once abundant with camas fields and other edible plants, such as biscuitroot and bitterroot, this area was also used by Spokane and Coeur d'Alene to seasonally harvest plants, waterfowl, deer, and antelope. Other tribes from the south and north, even into Canada, traveled here to gather the Cheney camas. Temporary camps were erected on the prairie during harvesting months, with conical mat lodges used at campsites. On the refuge itself, rock ovens, used to roast camas bulbs and other plants, have been found along with rock cairns and **ARCHE-OLOGICAL EVIDENCE OF CAMPSITES**.

The prairie was taken by whites after the Indian Wars of the 1850s, the lakes drained and the lakebeds farmed. The refuge today has 20 small lakes and more than 100 ponds, sparsely wooded with Ponderosa pines and groves of quaking aspen scattered among the grasslands. More than 100 species of birds nest here. A 5-mile tour route (by car) and hiking trails originate at the refuge headquarters. Tribal people **RETURN ANNUALLY TO GATHER ROOTS**; the Spokane Tribe's natural resource department provides training to staff at Turnbull about fire management of natural meadow regeneration. Turnbull's environment education program also uses **TRIBAL TEACHING METHODS** to teach elementary school kids about native plants.

Turnbull National Wildlife Refuge, S 26010 Smith Rd, Cheney, WA 99004; (509)235-4723. 6 miles south of Cheney. Call for interpretive programs offered throughout the summer. Open daily year-round.

Public Campgrounds on Spokane Reservation Lands

Tucked into the trees along the Spokane River and on the shores of Lake Roosevelt are 32 gorgeous small parks; 16 are open to the public for camping and picnicking. All are marked with signs naming the parks (even No-Name Park) and are cared for by rangers from the **SPOKANE TRIBAL PARKS DEPARTMENT**, who issue permits for camping and fishing. Campgrounds range from one to seven sites. All have shelters and fire pits or barbecues; most do not have potable water. Fresh water can be obtained at the Two Rivers Resort.

Spokane Tribal Parks Department, 6828 B, Hwy 25 S, Davenport, WA 99122; (509)722-5500. The parks department at Two Rivers Resort is well marked. Stop for maps of campgrounds, permits, and directions from the helpful staff. Overnight tent camping is $10; RV parking is $16. Some of the parks are closed periodically.

Two Rivers Resort: *Tribally Owned Marina*

At the entrance to Two Rivers Resort, on the reservation's west side, is a large sculpture cast by Spokane tribal member George Hill, depicting an Indian fisherman holding a spear and a salmon. Several **HORSE SCULPTURES** cast in iron by Spokane tribal member George Flett are perched on the slope above Two Rivers, memorializing the Spokane's herds of horses that were killed by the U.S. cavalry in the mid-1800s.

Two Rivers offers a large marina, an RV park, and a campground at the junction of the Spokane and Columbia Rivers (Lake Roosevelt). With the only floating store on Lake Roosevelt, the full-service marina also has 200 boat slips (many of which are covered) in a sheltered spot in the mouth of the Spokane River. Overnight moorage is available. The gas dock, with gas card service, is open 24 hours a day, as are rest room facilities with showers. Permits are available for fishing.

The adjoining RV park has hookups with water, power, and pump-out stations. The tent campground is on a promontory that juts into the confluence of the two rivers. Once a hay field, the campground is perfectly flat and newly landscaped with young pines. With 100 sites, a pavilion for large gatherings, rest rooms with showers and laundry, it's a perfect place for group campouts.

Two Rivers Resort, 6828 C, Hwy 25 S, Davenport, WA 99122; (509)722-5500. For RV or campground reservations, call the on-site Spokane Tribal Parks Department; (509)722-4029. From Davenport, south of the reservation on Hwy 2, take Hwy 25 and travel north for 25 miles until you cross the Spokane River. The marina, RV park, and campground are open year-round.

Spokane Tribal Hatchery

The Spokane Tribal Hatchery is at Metamootels ("upwelling springs" in Salish), ice-cold springs that flow into Chamokane Creek, the Spokane River, and eventually the Columbia River. Here the Spokane Tribe annually raises 1.4 million kokanee salmon (a landlocked sockeye salmon that grows to about 3 pounds) and 530,000 rainbow trout, from both wild and hatchery stock.

The hatchery is a fascinating place to visit not only because of its pretty setting but also because of its displays, which include **TRADITIONAL STONE PESTLES AND PROJECTILE POINTS** found on the site, and artists' renditions of pit house dwellings and camas ovens (subterranean ovens used for roasting camas bulbs). Ask manager Tim Peone, who was raised on the reservation, about building camas ovens and eating the roasted lily bulbs when he was a child or about annual root-digging ceremonies on the reservation.

Spokane Tribal Hatchery, PO Box 100, Wellpinit, WA 99040; (509)258-7297. At the Ford/Wellpinit junction, go west toward Wellpinit for 2.5 miles to Martha Boardman Rd, and watch for signs. Open daily year-round. Call first for tours.

Usk: *Kalispel*

In the late 1700s, 1,500 Kalispel Indians lived on the banks of the Pend Oreille River, a lovely, meandering stream that flows out of Lake Pend Oreille in present-day Idaho and runs north to Canada, by way of a narrow valley in Washington's Selkirk Mountains. The Kalispel lived in villages all along the valley, fishing for salmon on the river and killing deer by driving herds into deep snow. By 1911 the tribe was down to only 100 members, however. They had lost most of their land to settlers, who claimed it as if it were unoccupied. Today the tribe owns just 10 miles along the Pend Oreille River, but a stunning 10 miles they are. In the spring fragrant mock-orange blossoms litter the roadside and yellow lilies cover the forest floor. Hundreds of birds, including osprey, nest in the trees along the river or in the tall grasses along the riverbank. On the hillside is a path through the underbrush to a large cave, the New Manresa Grotto, where in 1844 missionary Pierre-John De Smet celebrated Christmas Mass with the Kalispel.

In a grassy meadow next to the river is the **SITE OF THE KALISPEL'S LARGEST VILLAGE**, photographed by Edward S. Curtis in 1910. There the tribe has built a **CEREMONIAL PARK**. The buildings, which include a powwow dance arbor, are circular, designed of poles and cedar in the original lodge and longhouse style. In the spring, before the **SALISH FAIR, POWWOW, AND RODEO**, the only sound in the park is the chattering of hundreds of swallows that swoop in and out of their mud nests under the roof of the open-air dance arena.

Enclosed by a sturdy fence in a lush pasture is the **KALISPEL TRIBE'S BUFFALO HERD**, which has grown to nearly 100 head since 1978, when the tribe received 12 buffalo from the U.S. Fish and Wildlife Service. The tribe is now able to provide free buffalo meat to their elders. Heads and hides are also sold. And when the powwow comes around every year, guests are treated to a buffalo barbecue.

Kalispel Reservation Tours

On the Kalispel Reservation, there's always someone who can show you around; point out the many nests along the river, the buffalo, and the ceremonial park grounds; and take you up to the **NEW MANRESA GROTTO** (a short walk up a rocky hill, so wear sturdy shoes). Church services are held each fall in the grotto, which has a gorgeous view of the river from both of its entrances. Ask for the tribe's free 37-page book, **THE KALISPELS: PEOPLE OF THE PEND OREILLE**, explaining their fascinating history. Please call in advance to schedule a tour.

Kalispel Tribe, PO Box 39, Usk, WA 99187; (509)445-1147. Usk is located on Hwy 20, between the Canadian border and Spokane. Take the bridge across the Pend Oreille River at Usk. Just after crossing the bridge, turn left down a narrow road to the Kalispel Reservation. Tribal headquarters are well marked.

CENTRAL
OREGON

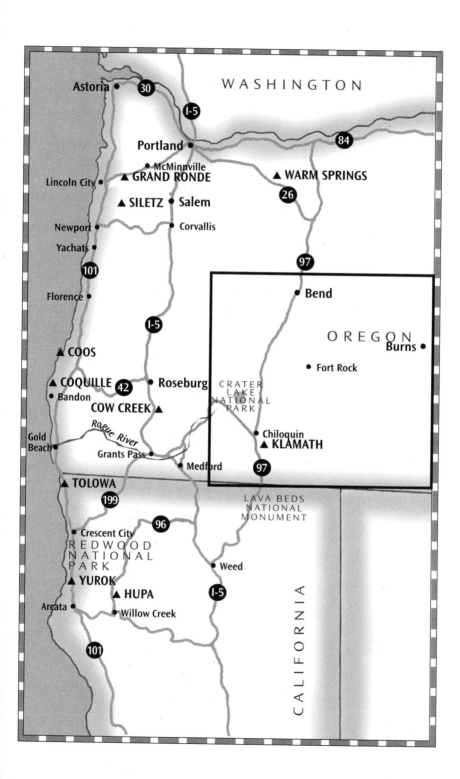

CENTRAL OREGON

Central Oregon's high desert, a vast area of juniper and sagebrush-covered prehistoric lake beds and dry rivers, is one of the most lovely outposts in the United States. Tucked into the desert are places of wonder, such as the John Day Fossil Beds, rugged red and green mineral-stained canyon lands embedded with the fossilized remains of prehistoric animals and tropical vegetation. Once a place of lush rain forests where mammoths, saber-toothed tigers, and prehistoric horses roamed, the landscape of Central Oregon was permanently altered by volcanoes and climatic change. The most recent explosion of volcanic activity was nearly 7,000 years ago, when Mount Mazama erupted, forming what we now call Crater Lake in its scooped-out summit.

Evidence of human habitation (firepits, house remains, and thousands of obsidian chips and projectile points) dates to about 10,000 years ago when the region was covered with hundreds of shallow lakes and marshes. Obsidian from this region's volcanoes, an opaque, black, glasslike material that forms laser-sharp cutting edges, was traded throughout North America. Several very old artifacts have been found in natural lava caves scattered throughout Central Oregon, including a beautiful, soft blanket woven from rabbit fur, and dozens of sandals made from sagebrush fibers. The typical art form of this region, called the Plateau style, uses leather, woven plant fibers, and bead and porcupine quill embroidery—very different from the Northwest Coast styles of artwork. The best examples of Plateau bead tapestry are in the Doris Bounds Collection, displayed in a new wing of The High Desert Museum in Bend. You can meet people of the Plateau at the Warm Springs, Umatilla, Yakama, and Colville Reservations (see the Columbia River Gorge and Basin chapter) and the Coeur d'Alene, Nez Perce, and Fort Hall Reservations (see the Idaho and Western Montana chapter). In Central Oregon, you are welcome to visit the Burns-Paiute tribal office in Burns, and learn about the Klamath, Modoc, and Yahooskan people at the southern end of the state near Klamath Falls.

AN OVERVIEW OF NORTHWEST PREHISTORY

Anthropologists discuss the Northwest's past at the annual Northwest Anthropological Conference each spring. In 1999 more than 193 papers on a variety of topics were delivered in three days at four concurrent sessions. The conference is a painless and provocative way to get an overview of Northwest history and prehistory. Presenters may include Native anthropologists, who bring insight and passion to their work. A field trip is often included: One year it was to the shores of Yaquina Bay and Government Hill, with Siletz cultural director Robert Kentta and doctoral candidate Scott Byram (University of Oregon), who had studied fish weir technology at the mouths of the bay's numerous sloughs. Conference registration is less than $50 for three days and includes a 75-page book with synopses of papers being presented. For more information, contact Oregon State University, Department of Anthropology, (541)737-0123; www.osu.orst.edu.

Burns: *Burns-Paiute*

The Burns-Paiute Tribe descends from the Waditika band of Paiutes who moved their camps throughout this area as game migrated and plants ripened for harvest—a land base that covered about 5,250 square miles bounded by Oregon's Cascade Mountains and Idaho's Payette Valley, just north of present-day Boise. Their territory included parts of the Ochoco Mountains, the present-day John Day Fossil Beds, the Steens Mountains, and the Alvord Desert. The region provided the Paiutes with plenty of food and materials for subsistence. Clothing was made from bird and deer skins, and other animal hides, and inventive use was made of plant fibers. Small game was caught with duck decoys and traps, and fish were caught in nets, also knotted from plant fiber.

As the lakes dried up, the people began seasonal migrations to hunt and collect seeds and roots that could be stored for winter use. In fact, the Waditika band's name comes from the nutritious wada seeds they gathered from pond lilies collected on Malheur Lake, now a national wildlife refuge.

As in other regions, migrations of whites along the Oregon Trail through Paiute territory brought epidemics of smallpox and cholera. In the 1860s settlers began to stray into what is now Harney County, taking huge tracts of land to run livestock and leaving in their wake trampled food sources and stream beds.

To stem protests by the Paiutes, the U.S. military set up Camp Alvord and Fort Harney. In 1868, prevented by the army from undertaking their seasonal migrations for food, the Paiutes lost half their people to starvation. The Paiute chiefs signed a treaty in 1869 that guaranteed them a reservation, protection from encroaching settlers, and food. It was not ratified by the federal government.

Harney County is a fascinating region, with hundreds of acres of public land that used to belong to the Paiutes, including the Ochoco National Forest, the John Day Fossil Beds, the Malheur National Wildlife Refuge, Steens Mountain Recreation Lands, the Malheur National Forest, Diamond Craters, and Steens Mountain National Back Country Byway. Rugged mountains, rolling grassy hills, and high desert are resplendent with antelope, wild horses, huge herds of deer and groves of quaking aspen. For brochures and listings of restaurants and lodgings, contact the Harney County Chamber of Commerce, 18 W D St, Burns, OR 97720; (541)573-2636.

Because they continued to resist plans to move off their lands to other reservations, the Paiutes were granted the Malheur Reservation in Oregon's southeastern corner. Almost 2 million acres in size, it included all of Malheur Lake, and the north and south forks of the Malheur River. Cattlemen ran their huge herds of cattle and sheep on the new reservation anyway, fencing off important camas-root gathering meadows and other food sources. In 1876 settlers took all the lands surrounding Malheur Lake, one of the Paiutes most important gathering sites.

The Indians' revolt against illegal settlement, which began with a Bannock attack near the Fort Hall Reservation in Eastern Idaho and spread throughout most of Central Oregon, became known as the Bannock Indian War. Subsequently, all Paiute bands were rounded up and held at Fort Harney; then in the dead of winter, 500 Paiutes were shackled and ordered to walk to Fort Simcoe on the Yakama Reservation and Fort Vancouver in Washington State. Some Paiute families found refuge on the Warm Springs and Yakama Reservations. Some swam the Columbia River and found their way back to the desert, living on what they could find and, ironically, working for local ranchers. In 1883 the Malheur Reservation became public domain, legally open to settlers under the Homestead Act.

The Waditika people camped in Burns. In 1928 the Egan Land Company gave them 10 acres on top of the old city dump outside the city limits. In 1935, 760 acres of homestead land was purchased by what was now called the Burns-Paiute Tribe. In 1968, the tribe's constitution and bylaws were written and approved; in 1972 the tribe established its sovereignty with the federal government. Today there are 281 members of the tribe; about a third live on the small reservation, living a modern life but continuing to hunt and gather traditional foods such as bitterroot, biscuit root and camas, chokecherries and berries, and willow and tule for basketmaking.

Visitors are welcome to drop in at the Burns-Paiute Tribal Center at 100 Pa Si Go Street, Burns, OR 97720; (541)573-2088. A booklet, containing historical photographs and a list of reading materials (such as The Paiute Wadatika Ma-Ni-Pu-Neen: A History and Culture of the Burns Paiute Tribe) *is available to visitors.*

Oards Store and Museum: *Paiute Cradleboard Collection*

One of the largest collections of Paiute cradleboards in the world (80 or more) is in Mavis Oard's museum, attached to her store, 23 miles east of Burns at the foot of the Stinking Water Mountains. A longtime friend of the Paiutes, Oard, whose grandparents settled in Buchanan, Oregon, in 1872, has 32 showcases containing old baskets, clothing, and pioneer-era items collected over a lifetime, most of them from Eastern Oregon. In her large store, she carries 45 to 50 pairs of **BEADED MOCCASINS**, made with traditional brain-tanned leather by tribal members, as well as other beadwork and leatherwork items by Native artisans Rena Beers, Justine Brown, Betty Lou FirstRaised, and Earl Louie. Oard also personally buys works from **PAIUTE ARTISTS** living on the McDermitt Reservation on the

Oregon/Nevada border, and from Indians living all over the West. All work is guaranteed to be authentic.

Oards, HC74, 1604 Buchanan, Burns, OR 97720; (541)493-2535; fax (541)493-2534. 23 miles east of Burns on Hwy 20.

Bend

High Desert Museum: *Collection of Plateau Tribes' Art and Culture*

The dazzling 7,000-piece **DORIS SWAYZE BOUNDS COLLECTION**—including jewelry, ceremonial regalia tools, weapons, clothing, and spectacular bead tapestry—showcases the vibrant Plateau culture in "By Hand Through Memory," a permanent exhibit about the Plateau Native cultures of Oregon, Washington, and Idaho.

Scripted by **WARM SPRINGS POET** Elizabeth Woody, the exhibit is housed in its own wing of the High Desert Museum: the Henry J. Casey Hall of Plateau Indians.

CONTEMPORARY WORK BY PLATEAU ARTISTS addresses themes such as Sacred Star Woman, spiritual power in Plateau life, resistance and reality, trade and social exchanges, family and reservation communities, politics and empowerment, prevailing traditions in art, and "computer age Indians." Paintings by Smoker Marchand (Colville) link the Plateau world view, spirituality, and art. Ledger painting by George Flett (Spokane) interpret treaty negotiations and the creation of reservations. Beaded bags by artists Sophie George (Yakama) and Maynard White Owl (Cayuse/Nez Perce) show evolving artistry that combines tradition with popular culture.

High Desert Museum, 59800 S Hwy 97, Bend, OR 97702; (541)382-4754; www.high-desert.org. Open 9am–5pm daily, year-round. Admission fee. Check the Web site or write for a schedule of interpretive talks.

Klamath Falls: *Klamath*

From the broken rim of southern Oregon's Mount Mazama, 7,100 feet above sea level, there are two views. One is of the ultramarine blue surface of Crater Lake, 1,000 feet below the rim of the mountain's crater, created by a series of violent volcanic explosions about 7,000 years ago. The other is of the valley floor—the Klamath basin, a lovely mosaic of soft greens, yellows, and blues. The basin, once part of a huge

The Klamath tribal archives include 225 legends recorded on computer disks, a plant-gathering manual, and a Klamath-Modoc and Yahooskin phrase book with accompanying audiotape.

Pleistocene lake that covered most of southeastern Oregon, is now reduced to marshes and shallow lakes spreading across the arid land for nearly 100 miles.

Though it seems at first glance devoid of history, the basin holds many surprises for travelers: Not only were **9,000-YEAR-OLD SANDALS** discovered at Fort Rock and fragments of baskets similar to those made by the Klamaths found in the lake that once surrounded Fort Rock, but the saga of the 1870 Modoc War is well documented at **LAVA BEDS NATIONAL MONUMENT**, and the Klamath Tribe is planning to open a museum explaining their history and culture sometime in the next decade. Members of the Klamath Tribe specializing in cultural resources can also take you into the marsh and explain how their people lived so well for so long in the harsh climate and unstable geology of southeastern Oregon.

Highway 97 weaves through the ancient lava flows that cover most of Central Oregon. In the north, the highway skims John Day Fossil Beds National Monument. In Central Oregon it slices through a section of Newberry National Volcanic Monument, the major source of obsidian used for arrowheads and knife blades by Indians all over North America. In the south, in the shadow of Mount Mazama, it threads its way between extensive marshes and lakes, the **ANCESTRAL HOME OF THE KLAMATH AND MODOC INDIANS**.

Just over the California border, Highway 97 enters Lava Beds National Monument, home of the Modoc and **SITE OF THE MODOC WAR** with the U.S. cavalry in 1870. Both the Modoc and Klamath were witnesses to Mount Mazama's explosive volcanic eruption 6,800 years ago. Both the explosion and the gradual renewal of the basin after the cataclysmic event are chronicled in their legends.

From the Klamaths' aboriginal lands flow three rivers—the Williamson, the Wood, and the Sprague—which eventually reach the Pacific Ocean—and an abundance of sweet, freshwater springs that feed the marshes, making this oasis in the high desert lava beds an ideal place to live. These waters were once the source of all food and shelter for the Klamaths on the north end, the Yahooskans in the east, and the Modocs in the south. Today the Klamaths, Modocs, and Yahooskins, who were moved together onto the huge **KLAMATH RESERVATION** near the northern marsh and Klamath Lake, are mostly landless. The tribe's relationship with the federal government was terminated in the 1950s as part of a disastrous federal attempt to negate treaties; subsequently many tribal members lost their land and moved to the cities. A core of people remain on their aboriginal lands, with a tribal office just south of Chiloquin.

KLAMATH-MODOC BASKET COLLECTION

The McLeod-Rutenic collection of Klamath-Modoc baskets, the largest in the world, was purchased in 1998 by the Klamath Tribe. Sellers gave the tribe 10 months to raise money before the collection would be sold to another purchaser. Three days before the deadline, the tribe met the seller's $500,000 purchase price. The collection is stored in an Oregon State University repository and unavailable for public viewing until the tribe can raise money to build a museum. Included in the collection are baskets 120 to 150 years old, which were used as barter with the pioneer McLeod and Rutenic families, as well as pothunted items that may be well over 1,000 years old.

(By federal law, it is illegal to possess Indian artifacts without permission. The Klamath Tribe, working with the Oregon State Police, pursues the conviction of anyone tampering with village or grave sites in their ancestral territory.)

Chiloquin: *Site of Mbusaksuwas Village*

The little town of Chiloquin, at the junction of the Sprague and Williamson Rivers, was until the 1850s, Mbusaksuwas (which means "good flint-making place") and ONE OF THE LARGEST PERMANENT KLAMATH VILLAGES in the area. People lived here in round lodges with insulating woven tule-mat flooring. Few household items from that time remain in the area. The largest collection of Klamath utensils, baskets, fishhooks, weirs, nets, bows, arrows, and other necessities taken from here is held in the archives of Chicago's Field Museum. Even though Chiloquin was in the center of the Klamath Indian Reservation, during the reservation era about half the town was occupied by white settlers.

Little dolls woven of tule reeds, a species of bulrush, were not toys, but were given to each girl child by her grandmother. The child kept the doll, which carried the wisdom of the household, throughout her life until she herself was a grandmother and passed "Grandma's wisdom doll" down to her own granddaughter.
—Gordon Bettles, Klamath consultant

Klamath Lands

Termination of the Klamath Tribe began during a 1945 Lake County Chamber of Commerce meeting with a motion made by Eugene Favell. But congressional legislation to liquidate the tribe's land holdings by condemning them was orchestrated by Secretary of the Interior Douglas McKay, a former car dealer and former governor of Oregon. He appointed three personal friends to oversee the legislation in 1955. Other "management specialists" appointed by McKay were Lake and Klamath County real estate developers. **KLA-MATH LAND HOLDINGS,** with large stocks of old-growth ponderosa pine forests, for the most part, became federal property in the form of national forest and Bureau of Land Management lands. Those lands have subsequently been logged for profit by private timber companies, such as Weyerhaeuser, as the federal agencies put sections up for bid. Lake County, one of the poorest counties in the state, was blocked in 1995 by federal court from acquiring yet another section of former reservation lands now in Fremont National Forest.

WOCUS

Wocus is the fruit of a water lily, a green seed pod about the size of a large fig. Inside the pod are hundreds of plump seeds, the same color as the lily's butter-yellow bloom. When the seeds ripen to a soft gray, they are ready to harvest. Sun-dried, roasted, and ground like wheat, the seeds make a highly nutritional cereal that can be stored through several winters before it spoils. Boiled, it's similar to bran; dried, it's crunchy like Grape Nuts cereal, delicious with dried or fresh wild plums.

Klamath Lake and Marsh

The Klamath Basin, comprising a network of more than 100 miles of springs, rivers, lakes, marshes, and wetlands, covers land from southeastern Oregon into Northern California, from the valley east of Crater Lake all the way to the lava beds northeast of California's Mount Shasta.

Birders come from all over the world to see the **SPECTACULAR WATERFOWL MIGRATIONS** in the spring and fall, when thousands of ducks and geese converge on the Tule Lake marsh, Klamath Lake, and Klamath Marsh. Twenty-four species of hawks, owls, and falcons live here year-round. The largest concentration of bald eagles in the Lower 48 also winters here.

To catch ducks at night, fires were built in stone basins on the stern of the canoe. The birds, attracted by the light, fluttered into the air, flew toward the fire, and got tangled in upraised nets made of nettle fibers.

Most of Tule Lake and Lower Klamath Lake, below the town of Klamath Falls, was drained in the early 1900s. Upper Klamath Lake, the big lake visible from Highway 97, which nearly fills the valley between the towns of Chiloquin and Klamath Falls, is only 4 to 12 feet deep.

North of Chiloquin, the Klamath Forest National Wildlife Refuge on the Klamath Marsh is bisected by a paved road. About half the marsh is diked for grazing land; the other half has been restored in the last four years. Listen for the throaty call of red- and yellow-winged blackbirds and look here for raptors (especially rough-legged hawks), great blue herons, and cinnamon teal. Great horned owls perch on roadside markers at night. On the east side of Klamath Marsh, in a stand of oak and ponderosa pine, is an **INTERPRETIVE "PLAT-FORM"** where you can learn about **VILLAGE SITES** that once perched on Wocus Bay. The area is visited regularly by Native people whose families once lived here.

Signs that herald the fish coming upriver to spawn: (1) Falling snow changes from hard powder to large, fluffy "fish blanket" flakes. (2) The fish constellation ("Orion's belt") appears on the southwestern horizon.

Hwy 97 follows the Klamath basin from one end to the other. To cross Klamath Marsh, take Silver Lake Road north of Chiloquin off Hwy 97 and head east. Three roads, including Hwy 97 and Hwy 140, loop around Klamath Lake. For detailed maps and an excellent guide to the basin's wildlife, look for A Birder's Guide to the Klamath Basin, published by the Klamath Basin Audubon Society, for sale in the tribe's Natural Resources Department, 116 E Chocktoot St, PO Box 436, Chiloquin, OR, 97624; (541)783-2095.

Fort Rock: *Site of Human Occupation*

According to their legends, the Klamath people found refuge in the caves of Fort Rock when **MOUNT MAZAMA** exploded 6,800 years ago. It's possible that they were able to travel to the rock shelter by canoe, since the marsh system, the vestiges of what was once a huge Pleistocene lake, probably extended all the way from Klamath Lake to Fort Rock, which is now surrounded by sagebrush covered high desert about 45 miles northeast of Chiloquin. Certainly the Klamaths used Fort Rock as shelter at one time; woven sandals found in a Fort Rock cave were carbon-dated as **MORE THAN 9,000 YEARS OLD.** Archaeologists have been excavating the caves since 1938, when **MORE THAN 40 SANDALS WERE DISCOVERED,** and have recently excavated the old marsh bottom, finding even more **EVIDENCE OF OCCUPATION** that dates back at least 13,000 years. The Klamaths' sacred mountain, 8,196-foot Yamsey, is between Mount Mazama and Fort Rock.

The Klamaths and Modocs designed a mudshoe for walking in the soft marshes. It was made of willow and round like a snowshoe. Their canoe poles were split at the bottom, to hook plant stems and pull the boats canoes through shallow waters.

Fort Rock is a good spot for a picnic on the long drive south; a mom-and-pop grocery store is nearby, as is a small pioneer museum.

To reach Fort Rock, travel south on Hwy 97 from Bend, and then take Hwy 31 east at La Pine. On Hwy 97, from Klamath Marsh, take the Silver Lake Hwy east through the middle of Klamath Marsh, past Yamsey Mountain.

Traditional Bows and Arrow Maker

Tribal member Ivan Jackson has researched Modoc culture for more than 14 years. Based on this knowledge, he uses juniper, yew, chokecherry, wild rose, and serviceberry woods collected near the marshes to make **TRADITIONAL MODOC ARROWS AND BOWS.** Such arrows are rated by collectors as some of the strongest and truest in the world. Arrow tips are made of carved mountain mahogany (also called ironwood), and both arrows and bows are painted with red ocher, yellow, and green pigments obtained from the lake bed.

For more information, contact Ivan Jackson at (541)356-2197.

Native Fish Hatchery

Since 1988, the Klamath Tribe has funded scientific research on the **LAST TWO SPECIES** of mullet left in Klamath Lake: the Lost River sucker and shortnose sucker, both endangered. For the first two years, fisheries biologists learned how to raise the delicate fish in a hatchery environment; now the focus is on genetics, larvae predation, vegetation, chemistry, and water-level studies as a baseline for **UNDERSTANDING THE ECOLOGY** of Klamath Lake. No fish are released from this hatchery. "There's no reason to," says one biologist, "until we find out what is killing them in the river and lake." The tribe has given staff biologists free rein to investigate the problem—all studies are subject to unbiased peer review by out-of-state scientists.

The fish hatchery is near the old Braymill lumber mill in Chiloquin, near the tribe's ceremonial site on the Sprague River.

Fort Klamath and Kintpuash: *Captain Jack*

In 1870, disenchanted Modoc chief Kintpuash, known as "Captain Jack," led the **MODOC TRIBE** back to their Tule Lake homelands across the California border and refused to return to the Klamath Reservation, where they had been forced to move. Pressured by the settlers, troops from Fort Klamath were dispatched to bring the Modocs back to the reservation by force. As the troops burned the Modocs' Tule Lake village, the tribe fled into the lava beds that came to be known as **"CAPTAIN JACK'S STRONGHOLD."** The incident was highly publicized on the East Coast, and sympathies were with the Indians until two negotiators were killed. Then the government increased its forces, bringing in more than 1,200 troops to fight 60 Indian men. The Indians held them off for nearly four months in the **ONLY MAJOR INDIAN WAR FOUGHT IN CALIFORNIA.**

In 1873, Captain Jack, Boston Charley, Schonchin John, and Black Jim (all nicknames) as well as several other Natives were executed by hanging, in an aspen grove adjoining Fort Klamath at the upper end of Klamath Lake. The remaining members of the Modoc Tribe were exiled to the Quapaw Reservation in Oklahoma, where many of them died. The present-day **MODOC TRIBE OF OKLAHOMA** are descendants of only seven prisoners of war, many of them women and children. About 140 Modocs were exiled to the Klamath Reservation.

The bodies of the men hung outside Fort Klamath were decapitated and their heads sent to the Army Medical Museum in Washington, D.C. There, a collection of at least 3,000 skulls of Indian men, women, and children was used in a **"CRANIAL STUDY"** to correlate intelligence with skull size. The project was abandoned when the skulls of some Native peoples proved to be larger than that of Daniel Webster, considered the standard of genius at the time. The Smithsonian Institution's department of anthropology inherited the collection.

The Fort Klamath site (a monument and small cabin) and the old grove of aspen where the execution took place (unmarked, south of the cemetery) are on Hwy 62, a few miles south of the town of Fort Klamath. Watch for Fort Klamath signs.

Lava Beds National Monument: *Site of the Modoc War*

Captain Jack and 60 male Modocs were able to defend themselves against 1,200 troops of the U.S. cavalry for more than four months, in the dead of winter, by withdrawing to the tortuous landscape of the lava beds at the edge of 94,000-acre Tule Lake. The natural clefts and gullies, caves, overhanging ledges, and jagged boulders were formed about 30,000 years ago after the eruption of a nearby volcano. The lava beds continued to form until the last volcano erupted 1,000 years ago. Lava tubes and dozens of caves, some filled with ice year-round, were well known by the Modocs, who lived on the shores of the nearby marsh. The lava beds provided an **ALMOST IMPENETRABLE CITADEL** that failed only when the army cut off the Modocs from their fresh water supply. Free **INTERPRETIVE HANDOUTS AND MAPS** are available at Lava Beds National Monument Visitor Center. Also look for a lengthy (but inexpensive) booklet that maps a **SELF-GUIDED WALK** through 23 sites, outposts, defense lines, firing positions, and fortifications with hand-built rock walls, including the cave where Captain Jack's family hid during the siege.

Lava Beds National Monument Visitor Center, PO Box 867, Tulelake, CA 96134; (916)667-2282. The visitors center is at the south end of the lava beds, off Hwy 139. Take Hwy 39 south from Klamath Falls to the town of Tulelake and drive about 15 miles through the lava beds to the campground, picnic area, and visitor center at Indian Well. $4 per car. Best times to visit are May–Oct. Wear sunblock and good boots, and watch for rattlesnakes on the trails.

IDAHO &
WESTERN
MONTANA

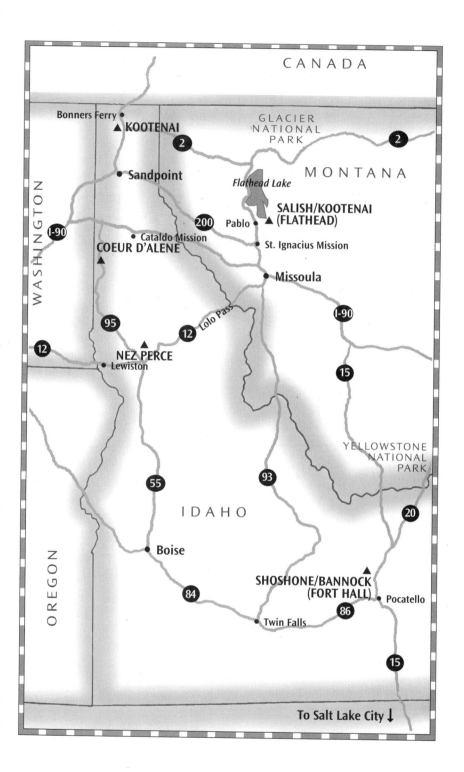

IDAHO & WESTERN MONTANA

The six tribes of Idaho and Western Montana described in this chapter live in some of the most beautiful stretches of scenic wonderland in the West.

In Idaho the Nez Perce Reservation adjoins the spectacular Hells Canyon, the deepest canyon in North America. In the heart of Idaho's Palouse country the Coeur d'Alene Reservation encompasses rolling wheat fields, deep pine forests, and nearly half of Lake Coeur d'Alene. The Kootenai Tribe, who have no reservation, live in the town of Bonners Ferry on the Kootenai River in the northern Idaho panhandle, minutes away from world-class downhill skiing and some of the best fishing in the West. In the southeastern corner of Idaho is the Shoshone-Bannock's Fort Hall Reservation, at the edge of American Falls Reservoir near the Snake River, just south of the Sawtooth Mountain range and Craters of the Moon National Monument.

In Montana, just south of Glacier National Park, the Flathead Reservation encompasses lovely Mission Valley and half of the 28-mile-long Flathead Lake. The 1.5-

Before you begin your Idaho and Western Montana adventure, write for free information packets, which include good state maps and accommodations lists, from the Idaho Travel Council, PO Box 83720, Boise, ID 83720; (800)635-7820; and from Travel Montana, 800 Conley Lake Rd, Deer Lodge, MT 59722; (800)847-4868.

million-acre Blackfoot Reservation is 13 miles east of Glacier National Park, just south of the U.S.–Canadian border.

Not only is the scenery of this region spectacular but
each tribe also offers the traveler a unique cultural experience. These tribes, whose territorial lands bordered those
of the Plains Indians, participated in both buffalo and
salmon harvests. Yet each has a fascinating history all its
own. The Coeur d'Alene and Interior Salish, for example,
were among the first western tribes to invite Catholic missionaries into their territories. Nez Perce National Historical Park includes portions of the original 1,500-mile route
of Chief Joseph's band of Nez Perce, who traveled by horseback and foot as they fled from the U.S. cavalry. The
Shoshone-Bannock's land was a pioneer hub: Nine emigrant trails, including the Oregon Trail, converged on their
wintering grounds at Fort Hall, and the wagon ruts are still
visible there.

This is also the region in which to buy intricate beadwork, tepees, buckskin clothing, or a chandelier made from
elk and deer antlers. The art created by tribes of this region
more closely resembles the art of the Plains Indians, and is
quite different from the art typical of Natives of British
Columbia and Southeast Alaska.

To visit all of the tribes and regions described in this
chapter, several weeks are necessary, especially if you want
to include stops at Yellowstone National Park, Glacier
National Park, and Hells Canyon. To save time, fly into
towns adjoining reservations and then rent a car. You can
fly from Portland and Seattle to Spokane, Washington (near

the Coeur d'Alene); to Lewiston (near the Nez Perce) and Pocatello, Idaho (near the Fort Hall Reservation); and to Kalispel and Missoula, Montana (at either end of the Flathead Reservation).

IDAHO

Lapwai: Nez Perce

The Nez Perce are famous for two things of almost mythical dimension in the American imagination: that of "**CHIEF JOSEPH'S CROSS-COUNTRY FLIGHT**" from the U.S. cavalry, and that of their **APPALOOSA WAR HORSES.** "Nez Perce" is what French fur traders named the Nimiipu (or Nee-Me'-Poo) who did not pierce their noses. They occupied three of the most rugged river canyons in the Northwest—the 1,000-foot-deep canyons of Idaho's Clearwater, Salmon, and Snake Rivers. More than 75 Nimiipu village sites have been identified along the Snake and its tributaries. Some have been carbon-dated to 11,000 years ago, or about 500 generations; there are also indications of far older settlements.

The Snake's famous **HELLS CANYON**, with its staircase rapids rushing through a chasm deeper than that of the Grand Canyon, contains **MORE THAN 112 PIC-TOGRAPHS** left by the Nimiipu's ancestors, in addition to well-worn trails down the canyon's steep walls. Hells Canyon today is the dividing line between Idaho and Oregon.

In 1997 more than 10,000 acres of privately owned ranchland were returned to the Nez Perce in an agreement orchestrated by the U.S. Trust for Public Land. The Nez Perce now manage the beautiful canyonland, which plunges nearly 1,000 feet to Joseph Creek, as home to bighorn sheep, antelope, deer, coyotes, river otters, and raptors.

The Nimiipu lived on the Oregon side of the canyon, in a verdant alpine valley in the shadow of the Wallowa Mountains, home of Chief Joseph.

The Treaty of 1855 ordered the Nez Perce to relinquish their ancestral territory and relocate to Oregon's Umatilla Reservation with the Walla Walla, Cayuse, and Umatilla Tribes. All the tribes so opposed this plan, however, that Territorial governor Isaac Stevens granted the

Nez Perce the right to remain in their own original territory, on the condition that they relinquish nearly 13 million acres to the U.S. government.

Today the **NEZ PERCE RESERVATION** is much like an island surrounded by rivers. Nearly 90 percent of former reservation land is owned by non-Indians, and most of the plateau that once sprouted blue-flowering camas and other native plants is now planted with wheat and other grain crops. Tribal enrollment is approximately 3,000. About two-thirds live on the reservation, primarily in Lapwai; however, tribal sovereignty extends from the reservation's current boundaries and continues to the much larger boundaries of the first reservation as it was originally drawn, before it was reduced in size. The tribe coordinates fish and wildlife management with sustained-yield forestry on about 47,640 acres, most of it beyond the reservation. Many locales in Nez Perce territory still carry Nez Perce names, such as Lapwai and Kamiah.

Every year thousands of visitors sign the register at **NEZ PERCE NATIONAL HISTORICAL PARK**, located on a wide, grassy clearing above the Clearwater River. The park includes a museum displaying artifacts of the Nimiipu that primarily date from the early 1800s, several restored mission buildings, and a self-guided interpretive tour that encircles the reservation and extends more than 100 miles. On this route, signs point out the creation site of the Nimiipu, the White Bird battlefield, and a spot where explorers Meriwether Lewis and William Clark camped on the Clearwater River on their way to the Pacific Ocean.

The tribal government center is a few miles down Highway 95 from the park, in Lapwai. (*Lapwai* is a Nimiipu word meaning "place of the butterflies.") A few of the old Indian agency buildings remain at Lapwai, but mostly you'll see new housing, a modern school, the tribal office complex, the **PI-NEE-WAUS COMMUNITY CENTER**, and pastures filled with grazing Appaloosa horses.

Nez Perce Tribe, Pi-Nee-Waus Community Center, PO Box 305, Lapwai, ID 83540; (208)843-2253.

Understanding Nimiipu Territory

To fully appreciate the land that shaped the Nimiipu, begin your visit near the site where Chief Joseph's band had their summer camp, on the shores of **WALLOWA LAKE** in northeastern Oregon. This teardrop of clear water cupped in the eye of the Wallowa Mountains, near the town of Joseph, was shaped by a glacier and became the final resting place of **TUEKAKAS (OLD CHIEF JOSEPH)**, the father of Chief Joseph.

Drive farther east, to the town of Imnaha, and follow the Imnaha River road south to Hat Point Overlook in Wallowa-Whitman National Forest. From the overlook you can see across the 7,900-foot chasm of **HELLS CANYON**. Retrace your route back to the town of **ENTERPRISE**, in the northeastern corner of Oregon, and travel over the hair-raising Rattlesnake Ridge (paved Highway 3) out of the Wallowa Valley and into the Snake River Canyon (caution: there are several drop-offs and few guardrails). When you arrive at the deepwater ports of **LEWISTON AND CLARKSTON**, named after the explorers Lewis and Clark, think about how many times the Nimiipu traveled this same route and what they called this place: Tsemiiniicum ("place where two waters meet"). This was **HOME TO NEZ PERCE CHIEFS** Weeptes Sumpq'in (Old Looking Glass), and Timothy before the treaties of the 1800s evicted them from the land.

Nez Perce National Historical Park: *Museum, Tour, Film*

The Nez Perce National Historical Park visitors center is located on the site of the old Spalding (also called Lapwai) Mission, about 11 miles east of Lewiston, Idaho, on Highway 95. This is one of 38 national park sites in Idaho, Montana, Oregon, and Washington that define the Nez Perce story. The mission was founded in 1836 by Presbyterian reverend Henry Harmon Spalding and his wife, Eliza, who traveled west with Marcus and Narcissa Whitman in 1836. The Whitmans went on to Walla Walla, Washington. Invited by both the Salish-Kootenai people and the Nez Perce, the missionaries were cared for by their respective hosts. This was the beginning of a long history of newcomers who would arrive in Nez Perce country.

The park offers **PROGRAMS ABOUT NEZ PERCE CULTURE**, including a tour through the museum's artifacts collection, presented by park rangers three times a day during summer and by request during winter. The museum includes a gallery housing stunning **NEZ PERCE HORSE REGALIA**, distinctive cornhusk bags, and beadwork, most of it on loan from other museums. Watch the half-hour documentary produced by Phil Lucas.

The park also offers a **SCENIC, SELF-GUIDED, 100-MILE-LONG TOUR** route that encircles the reservation, with stops at **HISTORIC LANDMARKS** such as the White Bird Battlefield, where the first battle between Chief Joseph's band and the U.S. cavalry occurred.

The park grounds are spacious. Spalding's original Presbyterian church, next to a creek, was built on the original Lapwai Indian village site, which had been occupied for thousands of years. The site today includes stones from the Spalding Mission's chimney, and interpretive signs point out the locations of the former gristmill and sawmill. Watson's store still stands, and you can walk past the mission cemetery, where the Spaldings and Nez Perce tribal members are buried. (Please keep in mind that the Nez Perce regard the old cemetery as a **SACRED BURIAL GROUND**. Even though it is surrounded by mowed lawns, it would be disrespectful to use it for picnics, Frisbee games, or any other recreational purpose.) Nearby landmarks include the 1874 **ST. JOSEPH'S MISSION** (the first Catholic mission among the Nez Perce); and **FORT LAPWAI**, built by the U.S. Army in 1883.

In 1971 the Nez Perce Tribe commissioned famed Nez Perce stone sculptor Doug Hyde to create a memorial tombstone for Josiah Redwolf, the last surviving veteran of the tribe's 1877 flight to Canada. The railroad tracks paralleling the river also have a history: Chief Joseph rode a train along these tracks back to Lapwai, when he returned to the West after his exile in Oklahoma.

The park's visitors center has a small gift shop stocked with **BOOKS ABOUT THE NEZ PERCE**. Kevin Peters, a Nez Perce painter and flute maker who works as a park ranger, illustrated the stunning cover of *Sapatqayn: Twentieth-Century Nez Perce Artists*, a full-color catalog presenting 20 contemporary Nez Perce artists. The catalog is available at the gift shop. Posters of the book's cover may also be available.

Nez Perce National Historical Park, National Park Service, Rt. 1, Box 100, Spalding, ID 83540; (208)843-2261. Take Hwy 12 about 11 miles east from Lewiston; at the bridge take the Hwy 95 south exit. Open daily. Free. Park rangers' programs are presented at 10am, 12pm, and 2pm throughout summer and on request during winter. Jun–Labor Day, Nez Perce artists demonstrate traditional and contemporary arts at the visitors center. Ask for free handouts on everything from edible plants to beadwork. Also ask for the Nez Perce National Historical Park Map and Guide containing the free loop tour, as well as a four-state map of the 38 national park sites connected with the 1877 War and Nez Perce culture.

Nez Perce Artists

WHITE EAGLE TRADING POST, (208)476-7753, in Orofino sells only **AUTHENTIC BEADWORK, LEATHERWORK, FEATHERWORK,** and Native crafts; many of its items are made by owners and tribal members Larry and Pam White Eagle. Their shop is in a clearing among the trees a couple miles east of Orfino on Highway 12.

From Highway 95, at Lapwai, you might be able to spot one of Connie and Steve Evans's **APPALOOSA-SPOTTED CANVAS TEPEES** set up in their backyard. These custom-made tepees are weatherproofed, and some are painted. Make an appointment to look at or custom-order a tepee at **OLD WEST ENTERPRISES**.

ARTHUR TAYLOR, (208)843-2967, weaves **TRADITIONAL FLAT CORNHUSK BAGS**, a skill he learned as a child from Rose Frank, one of the Nez Perce's most respected weavers. Taylor is currently on the Nez Perce Tribal Executive Committee. His work to help preserve Nez Perce culture and protect the pictographs in Hells Canyon leaves him little time for his art. As a result, his weavings are in high demand and are done mostly on commission.

Brochures with photos of the artists and their work, including painters Nakia Williamson and John Wasson, stone sculptor A. K. Scott, and beadworker Allen V. Pinkham Jr. are available from the **PI-NEE-WAUS COMMUNITY CENTER** off Highway 95, at Lapwai. (The center is on the corner of Main St and Beaver Grade, PO Box 305, Lapwai, ID 83540; (208)843-253.)

Nez Perce Sculpture Garden: *Commemorating Native Hosts*

In a circle of magnificent cottonwood trees on the Lewis and Clark State College campus is a pretty sculpture garden commemorating the Nez Perce's care and guidance to explorers Meriwether Lewis and William Clark. A fountain made of limestone blocks cut from the Nez Perce quarry signifies the confluence of the Snake and Clearwater Rivers, where the explorers turned to make their way to the Columbia River. In the sculpture garden **CHIEF TWISTED HAIR**, and his young son "Lawyer" meet with the two explorers. Beside them, a Nez Perce woman picks berries and drops them into woven baskets, and a grandmother shows her granddaughter how to dig camas roots. The **NEZ PERCE FIGURES**, created by internationally known **NEZ PERCE SCULPTOR DOUG HYDE**, are depicted in traditional clothing, wearing moccasins and carrying cornhusk bags. Nez Perce elders honored the 1993 installation of the sculptures with a **SACRED PIPE CEREMONY**.

In 1806, upon the request of explorers Lewis and Clark's young Shoshone guide, Sacagawea, a band of Nimiipu graciously received the travelers and allowed them to stay at the tribe's Clearwater River camp during the winter, an action that probably saved the explorers' lives.

Lewis and Clark State College, 500 8th Ave, Lewiston, ID 83501; (208)799-5272. From Hwy 12, turn at the 5th St stoplight, drive 6 blocks. The garden is in the center of the campus. Open daily, year-round.

St. Joseph's Mission: *The Nez Perce and Catholicism*

In 1831 two Nez Perce and two Salish men traveled to St. Louis to inquire about the "white man's book of heaven," which they had learned of from French fur traders. In Plateau culture, gaining spirituality meant having more ability to help others and thereby more status. In seeking the newcomers' religion, the Natives hoped to add to their spiritual wealth, not replace it. The Catholics answered the call of the Coeur d'Alene and the Salish; responding to the Nez Perce was the Reverend Henry Harmon Spalding, a Presbyterian missionary, who **ESTABLISHED A MISSION IN 1836** at Lapwai. The Catholic "black robes" were latecomers, arriving in 1872 with Father Joseph Cataldo at the helm.

The conflicts between the Presbyterians and the Catholics that had been going on for centuries in Europe continued in the missions of the western United States. The Protestants blamed the Catholics for supporting Indian resistance to white settlement. Spalding and others for a time also successfully fought Cataldo's desire to build mission boarding schools for the Indians, including the Nez Perce, that would prepare Indian students for higher education at the university he eventually built in Spokane, the **PRESENT-DAY GONZAGA UNIVERSITY**. Although Cataldo was well regarded, Spalding's reputation was that of an extremely cruel and demanding man, intolerant of the Nimiipu's religion. His wife, Eliza, however, was accepted and honored among the Nez Perce women. Nez Perce Historical Park is built on Spalding's mission site.

Cataldo's **SINGLE-ROOM WHITE CHURCH**, St. Joseph's Mission, is in a grove of trees in a pretty little valley 7 miles south of Lapwai. A shaded spot to rest on a hot day, it's a nice bicycle ride from the Nez Perce National Historical Park at Spalding.

Follow Hwy 95 past Lapwai to the Mission Creek Rd turnoff; 4 miles down the road is St. Joseph's Mission. Open Thurs–Mon, Memorial Day–Labor Day. Guided tours are free. An annual mass, open to the public, is held in the church on the first Sunday of June.

Lolo Trail: *Corridor to Buffalo*

The Nimiipu traveled the Q'ueseyn'ueskit (a Nez Perce word meaning **"TRAIL TO BUFFALO COUNTRY"**) over the mountains to hunt buffalo with the Crow Indians. Now called the Lolo Trail, the deeply embedded route was the **MAIN CORRIDOR TO THE BUFFALO JUMPS** of the Montana Plains where tribes gathered to run buffalo over cliffs and butcher them in an efficient manner. The trail begins in Nez Perce territory, follows the Clearwater River, and passes through traditional Salish territory in Montana's Bitterroot Valley, south of Missoula. Some of the elders from various tribes have good stories to tell about the trail, which was still in use when they were young.

Today you can travel 100 miles along the high divide of the original trail (Forest Service Road 500), which was widened into a narrow, single-lane dirt road in the 1930s. It's treacherous, full of potholes, and clear of snow only from mid-July through late fall. At the highest point in the trail (7,033 feet), you will find one of the many rock mounds where Indians once left **SYMBOLIC MESSAGES**, in the form of feathers, beads, and other objects, for others using the trail.

Highway 12 and Lolo Pass, the main road from Lewiston, Idaho, over the mountains to Missoula, Montana, parallels the Lolo Trail. It follows the Lochsa River and the Middle Fork of the Clearwater, both protected under the Wild and Scenic River system. It's a paved highway and has many pullouts for watching deer, elk, and moose. A surprising number of pedestrian bridges cross the rivers to trailheads.

There are **1,500 MILES OF HIKING TRAILS** along Lolo Pass into Clearwater National Forest's 1.8 million acres, although not all of them are maintained. Elevation is from 1,600 to 7,000 feet, nights are always cool, and the area is covered with snow December through May.

Pick up maps and camping information at Clearwater National Forest headquarters, 12730 Hwy 12, Orofino, ID 83544; (208)476-4541.

Hells Canyon and Snake River: *Seeing Aboriginal Ground*

The Hells Canyon National Recreation Area covers 650,000 acres and has as its centerpiece the deepest river canyon in North America. More than 1,000 miles of trails, some of them in use for centuries, traverse this spectacular region. Although Hells Canyon, the **ABORIGINAL TERRITORY OF THE NIMIIPU**, is a protected canyon, access by jet-boat is common. Jet-boat operators point out trails and several of **112 PICTOGRAPH SITES** on their trips upriver. Vandalism has destroyed many of these cultural heritage sites.

Although the Nimiipu traveled throughout the canyon, hiking can be daunting here. There are drop-off cliffs with steep, sliding rocky sections, poison ivy, ticks, rattlesnakes, and tough weather conditions that range from 112-degree days in summer to snowdrifts in winter. But the payoff makes it worthwhile. Views of bighorn sheep, elk, coyotes, river otters, eagles, and hawks abound in one of the most beautiful stretches of water in the world. You don't have to hike it to see the canyon. You can **FLOAT THE RIVER** with jet-boat outfitters or go upriver for more than 100 miles upstream from Lewiston and Clarkston at the confluence of the Snake and Clearwater Rivers.

For the Nez Perce Tribe's recommendations for river outfitters, call the tribal office; (208)843-2253. (An outfitter using a Nez Perce guide is preferable.) For additional information on recreation in the canyon and adjoining Eagle Cap Wilderness, call Wallowa-Whitman National Forest in Baker, OR, (503)523-6391; Hells Canyon National Recreation Area in Lewiston, ID, (208)743-3648; in Riggins, ID, (208)628-3916; and in Enterprise, OR, (503)426-3151. For information on environmental issues in the canyon, contact Hells Canyon Preservation Council, PO Box 908, Joseph, OR 97846.

The Reservation Loop Road: Commemorating Nez Perce History

The 100-mile loop that encircles the Nez Perce Reservation includes **24 HISTORIC SITES**. From the **NEZ PERCE NATIONAL HISTORICAL PARK** near Lapwai the loop stretches across a sun-drenched plateau, through wheat fields and pine forests, then drops into deep canyons. In early spring, when the wildflowers are blooming among the tall green grass, this is an especially pretty drive.

One site on the route is the **WHITE BIRD BATTLEFIELD OVERLOOK**, which commemorates the opening battle of the Nez Perce War of 1877. At this site, 70 Nez Perce warriors faced more than 100 U.S. soldiers and volunteers. Led by experienced fighters, the Nez Perce, with their well-trained horses, soundly defeated the larger and better-armed force. Knowing that more forces would soon be mounted against them, the Nez Perce moved on to the south fork of the Clearwater River and began their long and bitter journey toward Canada. Today roads encircle the battlefield, allowing visitors to view the grassy ridges and knolls. A 16-mile loop tour around the battlefield begins at milepost 230 on Highway 95, almost 10 miles southwest of Grangeville.

Another important site on the loop tour is the **HEART OF THE MONSTER, THE SACRED CREATION SITE** of the Nimiipu. A mound of stone next to the Clearwater River (near the town of Kamiah), the site includes a shelter with a recording by Nez Perce elder Angus Wilson. In his Native language Wilson narrates one of the many versions of the **TRIBE'S CREATION STORY**.

According to one version of the creation myth, Coyote created the world's animals. A huge monster that lived in the Kamiah area ate all of Coyote's creations for miles around. This angered Coyote, who decided to kill the monster. He allowed himself to be inhaled by the monster, and once inside, cut up its body into small pieces. When the monster's heart was hanging by a thread of tissue, Coyote warned all the little animals to run out of the monster's orifices with its last breath. When Coyote cut the last thread, all the animals escaped, although some of them, such as the rattlesnake, were disfigured by their quick exit from the monster's body. When Coyote emerged, he squeezed the heart, and the drops of blood that fell to the ground

From Highway 94, south of Nez Perce National Historical Park, Route 64 provides a shortcut from the reservation's west side to the eastside town of Kamiah. The road is paved through the wheat fields, then turns to gravel as it descends into the Clearwater canyon with hairpin turns, drop-offs, and no guardrails— but stunning views (beyond your white knuckles gripping the steering wheel).

became the Nimiipu. The monster's heart and liver were left at the spot where he was killed; they were turned to stone and remain at the Nimiipu place of origin. At the interpretive site a trail leads from the parking lot to the fenced Heart of the Monster, with picnic tables under the trees near the Clearwater River.

The Heart of the Monster shelter is 2 miles south of Kamiah on Hwy 12. Open daily, sunrise to sunset. Cultural demonstrations take place at the site Jun–Aug. For more information, contact Nez Perce National Historical Park, PO Box 93, Spalding, ID 83551; (208)843-2261.

HUNTERS OF PREHISTORIC MAMMOTHS

On the Clearwater River, just downstream from the Heart of the Monster, archaeologists recently unearthed the bones of a mammoth. These creatures roamed North America for nearly 2 million years before they became extinct about 11,000 years ago. Archaeological evidence, including bones and spear points uncovered in the dig, indicates ancestors of the Nimiipu hunted mammoths with Clovis-style spear points chipped from stone. Mammoth, water buffalo, and other prehistoric mammal remains were also unearthed during a restoration project in 1994 at nearby Tolo Lake. The artesian lake and wet clay preserved fossil remains that are among the most significant finds in the West. The bones removed from the Tolo Lake excavation are housed at Idaho State University in Pocatello.

Nee-Me-Poo National Historical Trail to Canada

After gold and other metals were discovered in Nez Perce country, the U.S. government negotiated a new treaty with the tribe in 1861. Often called the "steal treaty," it stripped the Nez Perce of the Wallowa and Imnaha Valleys, the Ponderosa Lake area to the south, the Palouse country to the north, the Bitterroot Mountains to the east, and the land at the confluence of the Snake and Clearwater Rivers—the site of the present-day towns of Lewiston and Clarkston. In **ONE OF THE MOST WELL-RECORDED AND POIGNANT EXODUS STORIES IN NORTHWEST HISTORY**, Tuekakas (Old Chief Joseph) in response ripped up his copy of the treaty as well as his Bible, and chiefs Old Joseph, White Bird, Looking Glass, Hushis-Kuate, Tuuhuulhuulzute, Hahtelekin, and others refused to sign or to move from the land. The U.S. military assembled to forcibly remove the Indians. Settlers, assured of their position, fenced the springs and ran their cattle over fields of camas bulbs that had been carefully tended and harvested by the Nez Perce for hundreds of years. With just 30 days to comply before being forcibly relocated to the new reservation, the bands assembled one more time. Emotions ran high. Some young men, furious over the slaughter of family members by whites, left the camp and killed several settlers, setting off the **NEZ PERCE WAR.**

Among those fearing retaliation was Old Joseph's son, Hin-mah-too-yah-latkekht (Young Joseph). With strategists Looking Glass and others, five bands (more than 800 people) of the Nez Perce fled across the Bitterroot Mountains toward safety, planning first to move to hunting grounds in the Bitterroot. They were pursued relentlessly by the U.S. cavalry. Planning to seek asylum with their Crow allies, they were persuaded by the Crows to turn north. Hugh losses were suffered by both the Nimiipu and the cavalry—**MORE THAN 38 SITES MEMORIALIZE THEIR JOURNEY.** The majority who fled were women, children, the elderly and sick, with fewer than 100 warriors and 2,000 horses. For four months across the Bitterroot Mountains (approximately 1,500 miles) toward Canada, the people fought for their lives in more than 20 battles, pursued by the U.S. military. At Big Hole, Montana, there were terrible losses: The remaining Nez Perce surrendered in the Bear's Paw Mountains in northern Montana.

Upon the **SURRENDER OF CHIEF JOSEPH** (the only surviving chief), the Indians were promised safe return to the Northwest. Instead, the remaining Nez Perce were shipped by train to a reservation in Oklahoma, where many subsequently died. More than 150 Nez Perce, including Chief Joseph's wife, escaped to Canada with Chief White Bird. Eventually, some returned to the Nez Perce Reservation. Others, like Chief Joseph, took Colville Chief Moses up on his offer to live on the Colville Reservation in northern Washington.

Today the route is memorialized as the Nee-Me-Poo National Historical Trail. History buffs can trace **THE NEZ PERCE'S ESCAPE ROUTE** as the trail climbs over Lolo Pass, wheels south into present-day Yellowstone National Park, and then swerves north to Bear's Paw Battleground in northwestern Montana, where Chief Joseph ultimately surrendered.

Follow the Nez Perce Trail, by Cheryl Wilfong (Oregon State University Press, 1990), provides a detailed three-in-one guide for the "mainstream, adventurous, or intrepid" traveler, and is packed with historical anecdotes and asides. To order the book, contact the Northwest Interpretive Association, Nez Perce National Historical Park, Rt. 1, Box 100, Spalding, ID 83540; (208)843-2261.

BEAR PAW BATTLEFIELD

Bear Paw Battlefield, about 40 miles south of the U.S.–Canada border, is the site of the last Nez Perce battle and best known as "the place where Chief Joseph surrendered." But it's important to remember that this and other battlefields along the Nez Perce Historic Trail are graveyards where Indian families buried their most beloved—their children, wives, husbands, and grandparents. To understand this more fully, stop at the Blaine County Museum in Chinook, a few miles north of the battlefield (501 Indiana, Chinook, MT (406)357-2590). There you can view a 20-minute multimedia program that brings home to most visitors the true, and often heartwrenching, significance of these sites.

While some people visit the battlefields out of interest in the strategies of the warriors, Indian descendants return to honor those who died. On the anniversary of the surrender at Bear Paw, Nez Perce mourners sit or stand in concentric circles facing a speaker, singer, or spiritual leader. Soldiers of all wars are invited to sit in the inner circle, smoke and pass a sacred pipe, and contemplate the sacrifices of war. All sit in silence as horsemen, dressed in regalia of the last century, ride their Appaloosa mounts four times around the circle, leading a riderless horse that symbolizes those who fell here.

At the Bear Paw Battlefield site, there are no brochures, no visitors centers, no cafes or gift shops. In the shadow of the Bear Paw Mountains, which are covered with snow by late October, the creekbed that snakes through the grasslands and pools here is surrounded by softly rounded hills covered with yellow grass—a place for reflection and contemplation. Please be respectful.

(Havre high school teacher and historian Jim Magera gives private tours of the site, which are approved by the Nez Perce. Contact him at (406)265-1727.)

Big Hole National Battlefield:
Honoring the Nez Perce Flight

One of the most compassionate interpretations of the 1877 Nez Perce flight of 800 people toward Canada is at Big Hole National Battlefield in the Bitterroot Valley. When the Nez Perce began their journey, they headed over the mountains into Montana, where they traditionally spent part of each year hunting and processing buffalo.

Big Hole was a long-used campsite that became the site of one of the worst battles fought as the Nez Perce tried to escape into Canada. Today, in the meadow along the Big Hole River stand the sun-bleached lodgepoles of more than 60 teepees—**AN EVOCATIVE MONUMENT TO THE FALLEN NEZ PERCE** whose remains are buried here. Be sure to ask at the National Park Service interpretive center for a guided tour of the Nez Perce camp, siege area, and howitzer capture site—one that illuminates this tragedy with personal anecdotes from Nez Perce, 7th U.S. Infantry, and Bitterroot Volunteers survivors. Plan to spend about three hours.

Big Hole National Battlefield, 10 miles west of Wisdom, MT, on Hwy 43 (about 115 miles south of Missoula, Montana); (406)689-3155; www.nps.gov/biho. Open daily, year-round.

Chief Joseph Horse Foundation: *Appaloosa Horse Breeding*

One of the great thrills of visiting the Nez Perce Reservation is seeing the Appaloosa horses, with their dappled backs and striped hooves, grazing in a pasture. Imagine these freckled beauties adorned with tinkling bells, brightly colored beadwork, and fringed leather threaded with glass beads. The Nez Perce were known for their skill in breeding strong horses; they were best known for the Appaloosa horse, which they called *mommon*. Named Appaloosa in the 1930s after the Palouse River, the horses were registered as a breed by non-Indian ranchers.

"We bred horses that would be sturdy, sure-footed, good-looking, with strong endurance for racing, that would survive winter—and some happened to have spots," says Allen V. Pinkham Sr., founder of the Chief Joseph Horse Foundation. The nonprofit foundation was created in the 1980s with 14 Appaloosa horses donated by a New Mexico horse rancher and a $15,000 gift from actor Richard Gere; it seeks to reacquaint Nez Perce children with horsemanship. The loss of horses in the Nez Perce culture began with the herd of more than 2,000 that were shot by the U.S. military after the Nez Perce War of 1877. Today the foundation's breeding program is adding the heart-strength of Turkmenistan Akhalteke war horses to the Appaloosa stock. Mares dropped their first foals in the spring of 1995. Visitors can see the **APPALOOSAS DECKED OUT IN BUCKSKIN AND BRIGHT BEADWORK** at a number of Nez Perce events and parades throughout the year.

Several Nez Perce tribal members breed and sell Appaloosas, among them Rudy and Shirley Shebala, (208)926-0858; Bill and Bonnie Ewing, (208)843-7175; Bryce Corlin, (208)843-2134; Carla and Gordy HighEagle, (208)843-2907; Russ Spencer, (208)843-7167; Mario and Claudine Rabago, (208)843-2057; Nancy Wahobin, (208)935-0384; and Jon and Rosa Yearout, (208)843-2452. Best horse souvenir: a $10 black-and-white poster, a reproduction *of an old photograph of an Appaloosa horse in beadwork tack and its rider, available from the Young Horseman Program, PO Box 305, Lapwai, ID 83540; (208)843-7333. Proceeds go to the Chief Joseph Horse Foundation.*

Pocatello: *Shoshone-Bannock Tribe*

The geography of the **SHOSHONE-BANNOCK ANCESTRAL LANDS** alone is impressive. It includes parts of Montana, Idaho, Yellowstone National Park, and northern Utah, Nevada, and California. Today the Shoshone and Bannock Tribes' **FORT HALL RESERVATION** is on fairly flat, dry grasslands on the upper reaches of the Snake River in southeastern Idaho, halfway between Yellowstone National Park and Salt Lake City. The reservation's name, Fort Hall, comes from a fur trading post that was built on the tribe's wintering grounds near the Snake River in the early 1800s. **NINE EMIGRANT TRAILS**, including the Oregon Trail, passed through Fort Hall. If you look closely, today you can still see ruts from the wagons in the tall grass.

The Shoshone and Bannock Tribes were hunters who followed big-game migrations and fished for salmon. When horses were introduced in the early 1700s, the tribes began to travel great distances, pursuing buffalo across the Plains and into New Mexico and Texas. Guns, ammunition, and horses soon gave their armed Blackfeet and Sioux enemies the upper hand, pushing the Shoshone and Bannock back into the Rocky Mountains by the beginning of the nineteenth century.

The Shoshones had long formed alliances with the Cayuse in Eastern Oregon. When the European fur trappers arrived, the Shoshone also formed alliances with the trappers, trading horses for guns to arm themselves against Athabascan and Sioux Indians driven westward from the Plains by settlers.

SACAGAWEA is probably the best-known Shoshone, a member of the Lemhi band. Kidnapped as a child, she was sold or traded to the fur trapper Charbonneau when she was a teenager. She began her mission to lead explorers Lewis and Clark across the Rocky Mountains to the Pacific Ocean shortly before the birth of her son.

The Lewis and Clark expedition of 1805 was followed by fur traders and then by massive pioneer emigration through Shoshone

Chief Pocatello saw his father hanged by white settlers, between the upraised and braced yokes of three wagons, thus fostering his hatred of the white immigrants. Pocatello's band of 450 Northwestern Shoshones was almost totally wiped out at Bear River on January 29, 1863, by a Colonel Conner and his "California volunteers." In the largest military massacre of Indians in U.S. history, even larger than that at Wounded Knee, only seven band members survived.

lands, with disastrous consequences for the fragile desert ecology. Livestock uprooted camas beds; game was hunted almost to extinction; and when settlers put down their roots, land was fenced and entry denied to the Native peoples, who depended on seasonal gathering, hunting, and fishing for their food. Tension mounted with each new encroachment. The removal of Shoshone Indians from areas of land desired by non-Indians resulted in the massacre of more than 250 Shoshones in southeastern Idaho in January 1863. An 1867 presidential executive order established the 1.8-MILLION-ACRE FORT HALL INDIAN RESERVATION, to which the Boise Shoshone were relocated from their western territory. The Fort Bridger Treaty of 1868 confirmed the arrangement, but a survey error reduced the reservation to 1.2 million acres in 1872. The Bannock Wars of 1878 were a final attempt by independent Native hunters to fight for their traditional existence.

From 1885 to 1914 the reservation was cut into allotments of 160 acres to each adult and 80 acres to each child. The Shoshone and Bannock tribes lost half of their reservation, including Lava Hot Springs and what is now the city of Pocatello, through a series of agreements between the tribe and the federal government. Today much of the land is carved into potato fields, Idaho's primary cash crop.

Shoshone-Bannock Tribal Museum

People seem to linger a long time in this small museum near the interstate, perhaps because it has such a personal feel to it. Museum staff, tribal members themselves, seeded the museum's collection with their own FAMILY TREASURES. Here you might meet the granddaughter of the woman you see posed in an 1885 photograph wearing a dress adorned with polished elk teeth. The dress itself hangs nearby too.

The museum's wonderful collection of photographs arose from a call to the Shoshone-Bannock community to comb through their attics for HISTORIC PICTURES. A few of these are formal portraits taken by Benedicte Wrensted, who photographed more than 300 Fort Hall individuals in her Pocatello studio in the late 1800s. The community's photos were copied by the museum, some of them from glass negatives, and hung on the wall. Over the past several years, most of the people in the photographs have been identified by relatives and friends who have wandered into the museum.

Unusual items, such as eagle-bone whistles from past Sun Dances, a willow-frame CRADLEBOARD and water jug, and a BUFFALO-BONE PAINT SET, are on display. Kids go nuts over the STUFFED BUFFALO in the center of the room. A gift shop offers books, beaded items, and other items made on the reservation. A calendar of historic photographs from the Fort Hall Reservation and several posters are on sale.

Shoshone-Bannock Tribal Museum, PO Box 793, Fort Hall, ID 83203; (208)237-9791. The museum is on Simplot Rd, just off I-15, exit 80. Call for hours and admission.

Clothes Horse Trading Post: *Beadwork and Buckskin*

The baby holds her legs in the air, as all infants do, gazing in wonder at the miracle of her own feet enveloped in **BUCKSKIN MOC-CASINS** as soft as velvet, the top hand-stitched with tiny glass beads in a pattern of bright blue flowers. Made of "Indian-tanned" white leather that has been lightly smoked to give it color, the moccasins will hold their sweet campfire smell and vibrant design long after the baby has grown, and even years later after the moccasins have been framed and hung on the wall as art.

More than 300 Shoshone-Bannock men and women produce **HAND-STITCHED GLASS TAPESTRY** in their homes, providing the local tribal store with, literally, a **WALL FULL OF DAZZLING MOCCASINS FOR SALE.** There's **NO OTHER TRADING POST LIKE THIS** in the Pacific Northwest. Many of the moccasins are fully beaded across the top of the foot with florals and geometrics. High-tops, ankle, and slipper styles are made in sizes that range from infant to adult 16, and widths from narrow to wide. Prices range from $25 to $200 a pair, depending on quality of hide and difficulty of the beaded design.

Fully beaded checkbook covers, coin purses, belt buckles, earrings, and headbands are also for sale. The most prized work is the hard-to-find **TRADITIONAL PORCUPINE QUILLWORK**, a technique that predates imported European cut-glass beads. Look also for Edgar Jackson's **COLLECTIBLE BEADWORK**, notable for both its intricate design and its tiny beads. Whimsical buckskin dolls, many of them dressed in beaded regalia and on horseback, are made by the well-known Ottogary family. The store also carries a full line of Western wear, boots, and Western art.

Porcupine quills are gathered by throwing a blanket over the porcupine. Sharp barbs on the quills hook into the blanket, like cactus spines, and pull away from the animal when the blanket is removed. Hollow quills can be dyed, then twisted, flattened, and sewn into intricate patterns to give a garment a textured, luminous look.

Clothes Horse Trading Post, PO Box 848, Fort Hall, ID 83203; (208)237-8433; in the trading post complex off I-15, exit 80. Open 8am–8pm, Mon–Sat; 10 am–6pm, Sun. Call for a color catalog of beadwork; custom orders for beadwork are taken as well.

Annual Shoshone-Bannock Indian Festival

The full moon rises behind the dry hills, crickets are chirping, and in the distance a drumbeat is heard calling hundreds of **INDIAN DANCERS** into the outdoor arena. They are gathered between cars and tepees, tents and campers, putting on the last touches of **FEATHERED AND ELABORATELY BEADED REGALIA**; the youngest dancers, 3 and 4 years old, spontaneously dance in place while they wait to join the dancers already in the circle. There are speeches and prayers, a grand entry that may take up to 2 hours, then dance contests that last until 2 or 3am.

Not everyone watches the dancing. In a nearby building, **TRADITIONAL STICK GAME TOURNAMENTS** are going on, with teams lined up in lawn chairs facing each other, shaking rattles, pounding drums, and singing to distract their opponents as the game's bones change hands. In the dark, children run in all directions, darting between the craft and food booths, laughing, throwing water balloons at each other; the baseball diamond becomes a nighttime playground. A mother unloads a crate of canned pop from the back of her van; her young daughter loads it into two barrels of ice and joyously counts the $58 in the till. Earlier in the day, the grandstand was nearly full for the wild and woolly **ALL-INDIAN RODEO AND INDIAN PONY RELAY RACES**, while 300 pounds of buffalo meat roasted over coals in a pit— a traditional giveaway dinner that includes baked potatoes, chili, and watermelon.

The Annual Shoshone-Bannock Indian Festival is **ONE OF THE LARGEST INDIAN GATHERINGS** in the West, with some 600 of the best dancers in North America competing for nearly $40,000 in prize money. As if this weren't enough, the All-Indian Men's and Women's Sanctioned **SOFTBALL TOURNAMENT** goes on at the same time, with teams competing from all over the country. More than 50 **NATIVE ARTS AND CRAFTS** booths and food concessions circle the grounds.

The Annual Shoshone-Bannock Indian Festival, (208)238-3700, is held Thurs–Sun, the second weekend of August, at the Festival and Rodeo Grounds in Fort Hall. The grounds are off I-15, exit 80, approximately 1 mile west on Simplot Rd. Admission charged at the gate, good for all events. Non-Indians are welcome.

Good Shepherd Mission: *Historic Building*

The little red Episcopal church behind the cemetery on Mission Road was built in 1904 and is on the National Register of Historic Places. The **ORIGINAL CHURCH BELL**, mounted on a small tower outside the church, is rung with a bell cord for Sunday morning services. Inside the church the sun shines through original stained-glass windows;

EAGLE-FEATHER STAFFS are mounted over the altar. The old mission schoolhouse next door, in its original condition except for vinyl-covered floors and a modern kitchen, is available for Episcopal retreats. *Good Shepherd Mission, PO Box 608, Fort Hall, ID 83203; (208)237-9479. It's on Mission Rd; you can't miss it.*

FORT HALL BOARDING SCHOOL SITE

Except for the laundry building and weathered dairy barn, the old government-run Fort Hall boarding school has been torn down. Native children used to chew the bulbs of white death camas to make themselves sick enough to get out of school. One woman who had attended school here as a child remembered the $1 reward for truants, who were brought back with a rope around their necks. The school closed in the mid-1930s. German prisoners of war were housed in the old school buildings during World War II; unmarked graves of German POWs may be found south of the school site.

A colonnade of ancient cottonwoods leads to the site, under the old water tower. A photograph of the school is in the Shoshone-Bannock Tribal Museum.

Other historic buildings, all built by the Fort Hall Indian agency, some of them before the twentieth century, are in a four-square-block area and are still used by the tribe. The old commissary and physician's quarters, a sandstone courthouse, and the superintendent's quarters still stand, as does the old Oregon Shortline railroad depot, moved from its original site. For a tour of the old buildings on the Fort Hall Reservation, call the Shoshone-Bannock Tribal Museum, (208)237-9791.

The Bottoms: *Native Winter Campsites*

The old maps call the Bottoms, a rich river delta in the heart of the reservation, "Indian Wastelands." But the Bottoms is anything but a wasteland. Fed by artesian springs and the Blackfoot, Portneuf, and Snake Rivers, the Bottoms is a **COOL OASIS IN A DESERT LAND-SCAPE**—huge meadows of waist-high grass, nodding sunflowers, tangles of willows and cottonwoods, and clear, cold streams swimming with trout. Slightly lower in elevation than the surrounding benches, the area was a perfect winter camp, where Indians pitched wickiups covered with elk hides for shelter. The wind and snow blew straight across the surrounding benches but drifted only lightly into the Bottoms. The bubbling springs that lace the meadows also kept the ground soft while the desert above froze solid. Except for Lava Hot Springs, 40 miles away, the Bottoms land was the **WARMEST WINTERING PLACE** in the region. The warmth also meant an abundant supply of fish and game—rabbits, antelope, deer, and bison—all through the winter. Because of frozen ground elsewhere, Indians for years buried their dead in the quicksand of the Bottoms. Chief Pocatello (for whom the nearby town of Pocatello is named) was buried here in the late 1800s; weights were attached to his body, and he was lowered into the quicksand.

The Bottoms is loaded with **SHOSHONE ARCHAEOLOGICAL HIS-TORY**. Archaeological evidence supports Shoshone claims that the Bottoms has been a winter camp and gathering place for at least 15,000 years. In the past 200 years, emigrant, freight, and stage roads passed through the Bottoms on the old Indian routes; it was a resting spot on the route of at least nine major emigrant trails from the Midwest.

Fur traders in search of beaver pelts began trapping here in 1810. The **FIRST FUR-TRADING POST**, Fort Hall, was built in the Bottoms in 1834 by Nathaniel Wyeth, and was later an important supply and rest stop for settlers on their way west. Between 1842 and 1852 nearly 200,000 settlers passed through Fort Hall, sometimes 5,000 at a time. Members of the 1843 Great Emigration led by missionary Marcus Whitman passed through here, as did more than 3,000 Mormons on their way to settle what is now Salt Lake City, Utah.

The spot where the trails safely crossed the Snake River is now underwater, flooded with backwater from a dam built at **AMERICAN FALLS** in 1925. The reservoir, rising higher each year, now threatens to flood the Bottoms and the pile of rocks marking the site of the **ORIGINAL FORT HALL TRADING POST**.

A portion of the Bottoms was purchased by the Bureau of Reclamation in 1924 for 15 cents an acre. Today the Bottoms is fenced grazing land for the **TRIBE'S 400 HEAD OF BUFFALO**. It is a haven for wintering birds, and a habitat for bald eagles in cottonwood snags above the Snake River.

Mosquitoes are fierce here in the summer. "No one could ever figure out why the white men erected a year-round, permanent fort there," says Robert "Red" Perry Sr., who was born to a Bannock/Sioux mother on the reservation. Even the missionary Marcus Whitman, in his journals, complained about the ferocity of the mosquitoes in the Bottoms. Wear long-sleeved shirts, jeans, socks with shoes, and plenty of bug repellent when you visit—or use a natural mosquito repellent discovered by the Shoshone: Crush willow branches with a stone and rub the juice on exposed skin.

Access to the Bottoms is restricted. The only way you can enter the area is if you are accompanied by a tribally endorsed tour guide (see Reservation Tours in this section) or purchase a $30-a-day seasonal fishing permit. All others must get permission to enter from the tribal business council. Inquire at the Tribal Fish and Game Department for fishing permits, (208)238-3743, or at the Fort Hall Administrative Office, (208)238-3700.

Old Fort Hall Trading Post: *The Shoshone and the Trappers*

A number of fur-trading companies, attracted by the **LARGE COLONIES OF BEAVERS** living in the marshland, trapped in the Bottoms before Nathaniel Wyeth built his trading post there in 1834. Wyeth, a New England businessman, arrived in the Bottoms in July of that year with $3,000 worth of trade goods. He **ERECTED THE FORT HALL TRADING POST** near the Snake River, a few buildings made of hand-hewn cottonwood, thus challenging the powerful Hudson's Bay Company. Wyeth built a tailor shop to make cotton and wool shirts for the Indians, and he employed Indians to make moccasins and tanned buckskins for the trappers. Hudson's Bay quickly put him out of business, however, and in 1837 Wyeth sold Fort Hall to Hudson's Bay. By 1847, at the peak of emigration, Fort Hall included a two-story store, mill, lumber room, blacksmith, storehouse, dining hall, and a two-story house. But by then most of the **GAME, BEAVERS, AND BUFFALO WERE GONE**; the fragile ecology of the Bottoms had been nearly destroyed by too much hunting and too many people. The Shoshone, who had lived well on seasonal game before the trappers came, were reduced to eating roots. Hudson's Bay had abandoned Fort Hall by the 1850s. By 1864 most of Fort Hall had been torn down and the logs were used to build a stagecoach station.

A **REPLICA OF THE OLD TRADING POST** was established by the Bannock Historical Society, at Ross Park, in nearby Pocatello.

The Oregon Trail Restaurant, a tribally owned cafe, serves buffalo T-bone steak, buffalo burgers, buffalo stew and fry bread, buffalo sausage and eggs, and Indian tacos made with buffalo meat. Just off I-5, exit 80. Open daily, 6am—midnight, year-round. Accommodations are in nearby Pocatello, on I-5. For help with accommodations, contact the Pocatello Chamber of Commerce, 343 W Center St, Pocatello, ID 83204; (208)233-1525.

To visit the Fort Hall Replica, take exit 67 off I-15 to S 5th Ave and the top of Lava Cliffs. In summer the park is open daily, 9am–7pm. Admission fee. For more information, call the Fort Hall Replica, (208)234-7091, or the Bannock County Historical Society, (208)232-7051. The Rotary Rose Garden Visitor Center, at the base of the replica, provides other local information and maps, 2605 S 5th Ave, Pocatello, ID 83204; (208)234-7091.

Reservation Tours: *Native Guides*

ARTIST RUSTY HOUTZ—a bronze sculptor, former professional rodeo cowboy, and movie and television extra (he appeared in the 1950s' *The Tall Man* and numerous episodes of *Bonanza*)—sometimes can be persuaded to give a TOUR OF THE RESERVATION (he's a busy man). Houtz's grandfather was Shoshone, his grandmother Bannock. Short tours include the Bottoms, the springs, several historic buildings and viewpoints, the remaining ruts of the Oregon Trail, and a stop at the tribal museum; longer tours may include a loop drive to Lava Hot Springs and the Bear River massacre site. Arrange tours through the Shoshone-Bannock Tribal Museum, (208)237-9791.

ROBERT "RED" PERRY SR. was born on the reservation to a Bannock-Sioux mother and Irish trapper father. He offers TOURS OF THE BOTTOMS or a drive around the reservation and peppers his tour with personal anecdotes, opinions, and stories. Tours are 2 to 2½ hours long. A second, 4½-hour tour originates at Fort Hall, continues to the old military fort at Lincoln Creek, explores portions of the emigrant trails, including the Oregon Trail, and then circles back to the reservation. Contact Perry at (208)238-0097 or (208)241-0557.

Plummer: *Coeur d'Alene Indian Nation*

The Coeur d'Alene Indian Nation, located south of the resort town of Coeur d'Alene within Idaho's panhandle, occupies a fraction of the tribe's original territory. An arrowhead-shaped piece of land, the reservation includes the edge of the western Rockies, half of Lake Coeur d'Alene, and portions of the fertile Palouse country. French fur traders named the tribe Coeur d'Alene ("heart of an awl"), saying they were the finest traders in the world. The tribe's trade involved yearlong trips to the Pacific coast as well as to the Great Plains to exchange goods. They called themselves Schitsu'umsh, which, in their native Salish language, means "those who are found here."

The Coeur d'Alene Indians lived in LARGE PERMANENT VILLAGES along the Spokane and St. Joe Rivers, near Lake Coeur d'Alene and Hayden Lake and on parts of the large prairie known today as the Palouse country, an area of about 5 million acres. They enjoyed a close relationship with the inland tribes of Canada and the Northwest, sharing a common language and fishing grounds, intermarrying, and attending big trade gatherings and celebrations.

One of the first Catholic missions in the West, the CATALDO MISSION was established on the St. Joe River in the early 1840s. Because of flooding, it was moved to a bluff overlooking the Coeur d'Alene River in 1848. A new church and parish house were erected there and still stand today, both part of **OLD MISSION STATE PARK.**

Silver was discovered in the Idaho panhandle in the 1870s, setting off a frenzy of mining activity. The Coeur d'Alene Indian Reservation, established in 1873, originally included all of Lake Coeur d'Alene. By a series of treaty agreements, however, the reservation was reduced to its present size of 345,000 acres. The tribe is working to reclaim what they have lost, buying back land that is often in high demand. The tribe recently battled a railroad, seven mining companies, and the State of Idaho to successfully reacquire portions of Lake Coeur d'Alene, to enable them to join with the federal government in cleaning up lead, zinc, and cadmium contamination in local lakes and rivers.

In less than a century of mining, at least 72 million tons of waste was discharged into the Coeur d'Alene River watershed and flushed into Lake Coeur d'Alene. Even though most of the heavy metals have sunk to the bottom, and even though Lake Coeur d'Alene may look perfectly clear and lovely, anyone exploring creek beds near the old Kellogg mines east of Coeur d'Alene can readily see the impact of mining.

In addition to the old Cataldo Mission east of Coeur d'Alene, **HISTORIC BUILDINGS** still stand on the reservation, including the old Indian agency office and the girls' living quarters and classrooms at the De Smet Mission. In nearby Rosalia a **BATTLE MONUMENT** marks the spot where Lieutenant Colonel Edward Jo Steptoe and 150 U.S. cavalry soldiers were defeated by local tribes in 1858. Adjacent to the reservation is **STEPTOE BUTTE**, the highest point in the Palouse and one of the most significant sites of the Coeur d'Alene homeland. Now a state park with a road to the top, it offers visitors a breathtaking 360-degree vista from the summit.

Today the **TRIBE'S BENEWAH MEDICAL CENTER** serves 10,000 Indian and non-Indian people in the Coeur d'Alene area and is a national model for rural health care. It includes a wellness center that has an Olympic-sized swimming pool, gymnasium, raquetball courts, and fully equipped fitness center with Jacuzzi, steam, and saunas—all open to the public. The tribe has also partnered with the state to convert the old Union Pacific tracks into

In his popular novel Reservation Blues (Atlantic Monthly Press, 1995), Coeur d'Alene/Spokane tribal member, author, and poet Sherman Alexie places General George Wright in a contemporary setting, as an employee of Cavalry Records. He uses "screaming horse" imagery throughout the book. Alexie referred to Carl P. Schlicke's George Wright: Guardian of the Pacific Coast and Benjamin Manning's Conquest of the Coeur d'Alenes, Spokanes, and Palouses for historical background.

a 72-mile hiking trail from Plummer through the Silver Valley to Mullan on the Idaho-Montana border. Future plans include a resort hotel and an 18-hole championship golf course.

Chatq'ele Interpretive Center: *Exhibiting Coeur d'Alene Traditional Culture*

In 1908 the U.S. Congress carved out 5,505 acres of land and 2,333 acres of lakebed from the Coeur d'Alene Indian Reservation's marsh, woodlands, and open meadows to create **HEYBURN STATE PARK**.

The park includes what is actually four small lakes that pooled together with Lake Coeur d'Alene after a dam was built on the Spokane River. The navigable St. Joe River feeds Lake Coeur d'Alene near Heyburn State Park; the river's swift current and original riverbed are still marked by a line of partly submerged cottonwood trees. You can get a good look at it by hiking the 3-mile **INDIAN CLIFF TRAIL** in the park. Stop at the Chatq'ele Interpretive Center at Rocky Point, east of Plummer, for trail maps of Heyburn State Park. The **INTERPRETIVE CENTER** is located in an old lakefront log lodge, built in 1934 by the Civilian Conservation Corps. A small but lovely display includes unusual **COEUR D'ALENE BUCKSKIN JACKETS AND LEGGINGS** trimmed with white ermine skins, and beadwork created with both European glass beads and older bone beads. There's a "Discovery Corner" for kids. A member of the tribe is on hand to explain Coeur d'Alene traditional culture. Be sure to view the **AWARD-WINNING VIDEO** about the tribe's effort to clean up Lake Coeur d'Alene, *Paradise in Peril*, as well as tapes of storytelling by tribal elders.

For an evocative account of inland Salish tribes (including the Coeur d'Alene) and early Catholic missionaries, read Sacred Encounters: Father De Smet and the Indians of the Rocky Mountain West *(University of Oklahoma Press, 1993). Written by Jacqueline Peterson, with the help of tribal elders, it's filled with archival and contemporary photographs. Available at Old Mission State Park and from most Northwest booksellers.*

Chatq'ele Interpretive Center, Rt 1, Box 139, Plummer, ID 83851; (208)686-1308. From Hwy 95 at Plummer, go east on Hwy 5 for 5 miles to Rocky Point. Watch for signs. The park offers boat launch facilities, beaches, picnic areas, and overnight camping. The park and interpretive center are open summers only. Call to check on fees and dates the park is open.

Annual Stick Game Tournaments: *Traditional Indian Fun*

Around 30 teams gather each year outside the **COEUR D'ALENE CASINO**, on Highway 95 north of Worley, to play "stick game." The sound of singing fills the air as teams sit on the ground, facing each other, under a striped circus tent strung with electric lights.

Each team begins with five counting sticks and a pair of finger-length game pieces made of bone—one marked with colored stripes, the other plain. A team member hides the bones from the opposing team in his or her hands, challenging the other team to guess which hand holds the marked bone. Guess right and you get a counting stick on your side; guess wrong and you lose a stick. The team that acquires all the sticks wins. In the old days, blankets, saddles, baskets, guns, and even horses were used as collateral for bets instead of currency.

As the bones are passed from hand to hand under a scarf, other team members (there can be as many people on a team as a hundred, opposing as few as five or even one) sing family songs and chants in the equivalent of cheering the team at a basketball game. When the game is played at night, by firelight, as it was in the old days, it is even more challenging and memorable.

ANNUAL STICK GAME TOURNAMENTS are held in August at the Coeur d'Alene casino. Teams begin playoff competition on Friday night, continue on Saturday, and play all night through Sunday afternoon. The casino crew serves plenty of coffee. Bystanders can bet on the game. The winning team takes home at least a $10,000 purse. Expect crowds.

The Coeur d'Alene casino is located on I-95, 30 miles south of Coeur d'Alene, near Worley; (800)523-2464. The stick game tournament is held each August; call for dates.

Old Mission State Park: *Historic Cataldo Mission*

The **RESTORED CATALDO MISSION CHURCH** is one of the oldest standing churches in the West and the oldest building in Idaho. Its unique construction alone—thick walls made of woven sticks and grass and plastered with clay mud—sets it apart from other old buildings in the region.

The church and parish house sit on a hill on the old mission grounds, today a state park, above the Coeur d'Alene River. Interstate 90, which cuts through northern Washington, Idaho, and Montana, roars past the mission's still-pastoral setting. Nonetheless, it's easy to imagine the days when the Cataldo Mission was created from what was once wilderness.

The **STATELY GREEK-REVIVAL CHURCH** was designed by Father Anthony Ravalli, a member of Father Pierre John De Smet's Sacred Heart group of missionaries. Under Ravalli's direction, tribal members quarried stones in the mountains and cut trees with an adze, dragging both to the site on carts. A pair of handprints is still visible on an interior wall in a small

The annual Red Bird Memorial Horse Races are tribal member Cliff Sijohn's memorial to his grandfather, Red Bird. Red Bird used to take a string of 25 to 30 horses to Canada each year and race them all summer. The daylong event takes place each fall. Between events there are stick-horse races for all ages. For details, call Cliff Sijohn, (208)686-7402.

room behind the altar. The church's high ceiling is stained blue with juice pressed from huckleberries.

Below the church and parish house, a modern interpretive center has been built into the hillside. An **EXCELLENT NARRATED SLIDE SHOW** tells about the history of the mission, the construction of a military highway close by, and the 1917 flooding of the mission farmland with contaminated waters from the mines. The interpretive center includes a small but exquisite collection of **AUTHENTIC BEADWORK** from the early 1900s, as well as recent **NATIVE ARTWORK**. Pick up a brochure for a self-guided tour of the mission grounds.

Standing inside the spacious church, park rangers, sometimes robed in cassocks, talk about the mission from the viewpoint of an 1840s mission priest. They discuss church furnishings, paintings, and statuary, pointing out details such as the crack in the statue of Mary, which begins at the corner of her eye and, like the trail of a salty teardrop, runs down the front of her robe.

Every August 15, the Coeur d'Alene Tribe sets up tepees on the mission grounds to celebrate the Feast of the Assumption, with a pilgrimage from the mission cemetery to the church for mass. Some of the procession songs have their roots in pre-Christian traditions, as does some of the ceremony that follows. Afterward there is a **TRADITIONAL INDIAN DINNER**, served picnic-style, and drumming, singing, and dancing. The public is invited to attend.

Old Mission State Park, PO Box 30, Cataldo, ID 83810; (208)682-3814. The park is 24 miles east of Coeur d'Alene on I-90. Open daily, year-round. Admission fee.

Coeur d'Alene Administration: *Historic Indian Agency Buildings*

Early twentieth-century Indian agency buildings sit in a cluster on a hill near the tribe's newer **ADMINISTRATION HEADQUARTERS**. The buildings overlook the prairie, with Steptoe Butte in the distance. Woods surround the agency center, and the entire area within a 5-mile radius is a wildlife refuge. In the Joseph Garry Building, you can purchase **BOOKS ABOUT TRIBAL HISTORY** and pick up a **LIST OF INDIAN-OWNED BUSINESSES**, which include grocery stores, a trading post, restaurants, motels, and gift shops.

Coeur d'Alene Tribe Administration, 850 A Street, Rt 1, Box 11 FA, Plummer, ID 83851; (208)686-1800. Open 7:30am–4pm, weekdays. Just south of Plummer, on Hwy 95, take Rt 11 west (it's marked by a sign with an arrowhead on it). Follow Rt 11 uphill several miles, through small farms and woodlands. You may think you're on the wrong road, because it seems such an unlikely spot for the agency to be built, but in the old days the area was accessible via a railroad that stopped on the south side of the hill.

BATTLE OF TOHOTONIMME: HISTORIC SITE

"Remember the Battle," reads the sign at the entrance to Rosalia, Washington, a small town about 17 miles west of the Coeur d'Alene Reservation. Rosalia lies in the shallow, 6-mile-long valley along Pine Creek, next to the hillside. There, in 1858, Lieutenant Colonel Edward J. Steptoe lost a battle against 600 to 1,200 Indians from all over the region, led by the Coeur d'Alene. History books say that Steptoe and his men, surrounded by Indians, made a clever escape over the hillside in the middle of the night. Coeur d'Alene tribal members whose ancestors fought at the Battle of Tohotonimme say that the peace was negotiated with the help of Catholic priests, and that Steptoe and his men were then allowed to leave.

There are different versions of why the skirmish began. Steptoe and his men entered Palouse and Coeur d'Alene territory fully armed, with two howitzers. They were questioned by the Coeur d'Alene about their intent. The battle began after gunshots were fired.

After their surrender, Steptoe and his men returned to Fort Walla Walla on the Columbia River. News of their loss prompted the U.S. army to send in General George Wright, along with armed troops and wagonloads of ammunition, to permanently relocate the Indians to reservations. Wright's tactics for breaking Indian resistance were horrific. He called meetings with important chiefs to discuss peace, but when the chiefs arrived, dressed in ceremonial regalia befitting the occasion, Wright had them hanged. He was also responsible for the destruction of thousands of horses that belonged to the tribes—a loss that effectively crushed the tribes' economy. For extra effect, Wright and his men bludgeoned and shot foals in front of their Indian owners. The slaughter of 800 captured ponies along the Spokane River occurred at milepost 292, on Interstate 90.

Girls' Boarding School:
Mary Immaculate Historic Site

The three-story brick dormitory, one of the few buildings left standing on the historic De Smet Mission grounds, is visible from Highway 95 at De Smet, on the south end of the Coeur d'Alene Reservation. Built in 1919, after two previous structures had burned to the ground, the dormitory is typical of **EARLY 1900S INDIAN BOARDING SCHOOL** dorms. The first floor is all parlors and offices; the second floor contains spacious classrooms and a chapel with the original stations of

You can purchase books about tribal history and pick up a list of Indian-owned businesses, which include grocery stores, a trading post, restaurants, motels, and gift shops, at the new Coeur d'Alene Tribal Administration Center at 850 A Street in Plummer.

the cross still on the walls. Under the sloped eaves of the attic are wide-open dormitories where Indian girls, who were taken away from their families as young as 3 years old, slept in rows of beds. Used as a day school until 1972, the building's classrooms are now home to Lewis & Clark College's extension campus and the tribe's Department of Education. The building, which is on the National Register of Historic Places, is open to the public for tours.

Mary Immaculate Girls' Boarding School. At De Smet, on Hwy 95, take De Smet Rd and turn onto Moctelme (the state's highway department spells it "Mocteline") Rd. Call in advance to arrange a tour of the building, (208)274-2403, ext 2492.

WRITER SHERMAN ALEXIE

Smoke Signals, Coeur d'Alene/Spokane writer Sherman Alexie's humorous and insightful movie about familial relationships, friendship, guilt, and redemption, was filmed on reservation lands of the Coeur d'Alene Indian Nation. Winner at the 1998 Sundance Film Festival, Alexie, whose poetry and prose have been lauded by the New York Times, was finally introduced to mainstream culture when a major distributor picked up the film and it was shown nationwide (now available on video).

A respected poet, novelist, and screenwriter, and winner of many prestigious literary awards, Alexie based Smoke Signals on a short story from his collection The Lone Ranger and Tonto Fistfight in Heaven. In June 1999 The New Yorker selected Alexie as one of 20 writers whose work is the "Future of American Fiction" and printed his short story "The Toughest Indian in the World."

Much of the music in Smoke Signals is composed and sung by Jim Boyd, a Spokane tribal member, professional musician, and longtime friend of Alexie. The soundtrack is available on tape and CD from music stores nationwide.

Steptoe Butte State Park: *Coeur d'Alene Sacred Mountain Site*

Adjoining the Coeur d'Alene Reservation are the rolling hills of the Palouse, some of the most fertile farmland in the world. (The French word *Palouse* means "grass blowing in the wind.") Created during ice-age windstorms, the topsoil here is 32 feet deep. In the heart of the Palouse is solitary Steptoe Butte, the **COEUR D'ALENE'S SACRED MOUNTAIN**, towering more than 1,000 feet above the valley floor. Its peak was a site of meditation, prayer, and ceremony for centuries. The butte, covered with downy grass, is solid rock, 500 million years old. The narrow, paved road to the butte follows tidy wheat fields edged with colorful wildflowers. From the picnic tables sheltered by stubby pines at the foot of the butte, the road spirals to the top, which has been scraped flat and paved for a parking lot. In summer a steady warm wind carries the sweet scent of wild roses, wheat, and dry grass. As the sky darkens, the glow of the city of Spokane lights the sky to the northwest. It is still possible to be alone, with views in all directions, on top of this solitary summit.

The gated road to Steptoe Butte State Park, (509)549-3551, is open from dawn until dusk (or until the gatekeeper shows up to close it). Take Hwy 195 to the town of Steptoe. At Steptoe, turn east on the county road. Drive for 5–7 miles until you see Steptoe Butte Rd. Eight picnic sites. Free.

Bonners Ferry: *Kootenai*

The Kootenai people are geographically split: Part of the tribe lives in Montana (see the Pablo: Flathead section in this chapter); another group lives in Canada; and a third group lives in Idaho. The tribe was separated when Britain and the United States drew the border between Canada and the United States right through the middle of **KOOTENAI ANCESTRAL LANDS**, which stretched from Yellowwood Falls in mid-British Columbia, all the way to Great Falls in Montana, and south to the border of Yellowstone National Park. Today just a few hundred Kootenai people live on a fragment of their **ORIGINAL GROUND IN BONNERS FERRY**, Idaho, a little farming valley in the state's northern panhandle that is surrounded by snowcapped mountains. Only 31 miles from Schweitzer's world-class downhill skiing, Bonners Ferry is also adjacent to the Snow Creek Recreation Area in the Selkirk Mountains, which offers cross-country skiing and snowmobile trails that are maintained throughout the winter.

Surrounded by national forest, the Kootenai living in Bonners Ferry do not have a reservation; they own a **FIRST-RATE HOTEL** on the banks of the Kootenai River, one of Idaho's premier fishing streams. They also raise nearly 20,000 white sturgeon every year in **ONE OF THE MOST UNUSUAL FISH HATCHERIES** in the Northwest.

A Century of Survival, dedicated to "our stubborn, strong-willed, long-suffering ancestors," is a short, lively, easy-to-read, Kafkaesque account of Kootenai history, written and published by the tribe in 1990. Available for $8.95 (including postage and handling) from the Kootenai Tribe, PO Box 1269, Bonners Ferry, ID 83805; (208)267-3519.

Kootenai River Inn: *Tribally Owned Lodging*

The 65-room Best Western Kootenai River Inn is built on the banks of the Kootenai River. The area is gorgeous year-round but is especially so in the fall, when the quaking aspens turn bright yellow against the fresh green of the pines. About 32 miles north of Sandpoint, Idaho, the **HOTEL IS THE JUMP-OFF SPOT** for four seasons of away-from-the-crowds recreation: golf, hiking, whitewater rafting, hunting, fishing, skiing, and snowmobiling—all of which can be arranged through the hotel. The Springs Restaurant and Lounge overlooks the river and is open for breakfast, lunch, and dinner. There is also a 24-hour deli. Use of the indoor pool, sauna, Jacuzzi, steam room, and fitness area is free with your room.

Best Western Kootenai River Inn, 7160 Plaza St, Bonners Ferry, ID 83805; (800)346-5668 or (208)267-8511. Room rates, $80–$225. Open year-round.

Kootenai Tribe Fish Hatchery

The Kootenai Tribe Fish Hatchery is **ONE OF MOST UNUSUAL FISH NURSERY OPERATIONS** in the Pacific Northwest. The hatchery raises **WHITE STURGEON**: big, prehistoric-looking fish that have been landlocked in fresh water since the end of the last ice age, about 10,000 years ago. The female fish first spawn at age 24 and weigh more than 100 pounds; they spawn again every 4 to 6 years.

When brood stock began to dwindle, fishery biologists performed cesareans on the mother fish to remove their eggs. Today egg production is controlled with hormone injections. About 20,000 baby sturgeon are confined and fed in tanks until they're 2 years old and about 16 inches long, at which time they're released into the Kootenai River. The fish are a sight to behold. **VISITORS ARE WELCOME** at the hatchery during business hours (tribal biologists know where all the river's good fishing holes are, for cutthroat trout, kokanee, Dolly Varden trout, and landlocked lingcod).

Kootenai Tribe Fish Hatchery, PO Box 1269, Bonners Ferry, ID 83805; (208)267-3519. Call for directions and best times to visit.

WESTERN MONTANA

Pablo: *Flathead Reservation*

There are several stories about how the Flathead Indian Reservation in Western Montana got its name. One is that fur traders mistakenly thought the Inland Salish people had the same head-shaping custom as the Coast Salish, who shaped their infants' heads with gentle pressure in the cradleboard, "flattening" their foreheads. Perhaps Salish-speaking relatives from the coast were visiting at the time the fur traders showed up in Montana. Another story is that the sign-language motion identifying the Salish was pressing both sides of one's head with one's hands.

Whatever the reason, "Flathead" doesn't accurately describe the handsome Salish or the Kootenai Tribes, who share the **FLATHEAD RESERVATION** in Western Montana. Nor does it remotely begin to describe the beauty of the **MISSION VALLEY**, south of Glacier National Park, which nestles against the impenetrable spine of the Mission Range. The Salish called these mountains the "backbone of the world." The ax-blade peaks of the towering, dark-blue Mission Range define the whole east side of the reservation, which comprises **MORE THAN 1.3 MILLION ACRES**. The glacier-carved valley begins in the south with the hilly grasslands of the **NATIONAL BISON RANGE**, home to hundreds of buffalo, antelope, and elk, flattens into rangeland, and ends in the north at the 28-mile-long Flathead Lake.

Highway 93, a two-lane highway, cuts through the middle of the reservation's Mission Valley, past big-sky cattle ranches, the **POWWOW GROUNDS** at Arlee, the historic **ST. IGNATIUS MISSION**, Ninepipe National Wildlife Refuge, the **PEOPLE'S CENTER AT PABLO**, and the **TRIBALLY OWNED FIRST-CLASS RESORT HOTEL**, KwaTaqNuk, on the south shore of Flathead Lake.

The Salish and Kootenai Tribes originally shared a huge area that stretched from southern British Columbia, northern Idaho, and northern Washington to Western Montana. The 1855 Treaty of Hell's Gate took away most of their land, however, exchanging millions of acres for promises never kept. The tribes ended up with the forested slopes of the Mission Range and the southern half of Flathead Lake (a line was mapped right through the middle of the lake). Some

Kootenais were already living on the western shore of Flathead Lake, on Dayton Creek, and they entered into the treaty agreement in 1855 to keep their land. Their **DESCENDANTS LIVE THERE TO THIS DAY.**

The reservation was divided into allotments by a government act in 1904, 20 years before Native Americans were allowed to vote. Each of the 2,378 tribal members was allowed 80 acres of agricultural land or 160 acres of grazing lands. Unclaimed lands were opened for homesteading and sale. Tribal members who refused to claim their allotments, as a way of saying no to the scheme, were "assigned" land, some of it literally bare rock under a thin layer of soil and grass. Since 1940, the Salish and Kootenai Tribes have been **BUYING BACK LAND** within the reservation that was lost in the early years to homesteaders.

One group of Salish Indians refused to move. **CHIEF CHARLO** held out against settlers in the beautiful Bitterroot Valley, south of Missoula, for 20 years until forced to relocate to the Flathead Reservation. Not one to hang his head, Charlo led his people into the Flathead Reservation settlement of Arlee on horseback, proudly dressed in their finest regalia. But his family says that he was never the same again, embittered by broken promises and the loss of the Bitterroot Valley.

Today about 100 tribal members farm or ranch. Estimated tribal enrollment is about 6,700. The tribe has built an alternative high school, and the **SALISH KOOTENAI COLLEGE** oversees five timber operations; the tribe also has control of the valley's electric service. They have written one of the most stringent water quality and shoreline protection acts in Montana, if not in the United States, to protect Flathead Lake from the impact of unregulated construction. Determined to protect the reservation, the tribe requested a pristine-air designation from the Environmental Protection Agency in 1979; designated the reservation a nuclear-free zone in 1984; and, in 1982, created **ONE OF THE FIRST TRIBAL WILDERNESS AREAS** in the country as part of its commitment to saving habitat.

For their free brochure and map listing 39 sites to visit on the reservation, write Confederated Salish and Kootenai Tribes, PO Box 278, Pablo, MT 59855; (406)675-2700. Free Montana road maps are available from Travel Montana; (800)847-4868 or (406)444-2654.

The People's Center: *Salish-Kootenai Exhibits*

The stone building is built close to the ground, with a copper door that glows in the morning sun and a white-pine arbor encircling the lawn. From the sky the grounds and building resemble an eagle. The People's Center was **CREATED BY SALISH AND KOOTENAI VOLUNTEERS**, who painted the walls, put together the exhibits, and donated family heirlooms. Here the **STORY OF THE SALISH AND KOOTENAI TRIBES** is told by the people themselves, rather than by outsiders. Think of it as the heart of the reservation, thrown open to the public.

At the entrance are **FOUR FLOOR-TO-CEILING CEDAR POLES** on which realistic carvings depict animal and bird tracks and plant and water life. The People's Center includes an interpretive center, gift shop, and a large room for events, cultural classes, and demonstrations. Although the exhibits are labeled, **NATIVE GUIDES** can point out such things as how dried buffalo bladders were worn much like a modern-day fanny pack. **AUDIO TOURS** are provided in the Salish, Pend d'Oreille, and Kootenai languages with English translations. The gift shop sells **NATIVE ART**, with a special emphasis on tribal members' art and work from other Northwest tribes. In addition to fine beadwork, silver jewelry, and antler lamps and chandeliers, the shop also sells locally made T-shirts, books, and audio- and videotapes. The video *WE LIVE IN A CIRCLE*, produced by the Salish Kootenai College Media Center, a 15-minute film shown on request, presents the history of the center and describes the rich culture of the Salish and Kootenai Tribes.

The People's Center, Hwy 93 W, PO Box 278, Pablo, MT 59855; (406)675-0160. The town of Pablo is about 10 miles south of Flathead Lake, on Hwy 93. Call for hours and admission prices.

Colorful "Old West" Trading Posts on the Flathead Reservation

There are four colorful "trading posts" on the Flathead Reservation, all of them on Highway 93. The term comes from the fur-trading posts built throughout the Northwest in the early 1800s when beaver pelts were in high demand.

Modern-day trading posts sell **INDIAN ANTIQUITIES**, new Pendleton blankets and vests, **ARTS AND CRAFTS** (such as new beadwork), contemporary Indian art, and supplies. Some offer tidbits of local history as well. **DOUG ALLARD'S FLATHEAD INDIAN MUSEUM & TRADING POST** (Highway 93, PO Box 460, St. Ignatius; (406)745-2951) displays beautiful old beadwork, as well as portraits of Indian leaders, in a large room adjoining his two-story store.

Preston Miller has moved some of the oldest hand-hewn log buildings on the Flathead Reservation to his trading post, including the 1862 Indian agency building from the town of Jocko and the 1885 Ravalli railroad depot. The historic buildings make his **FOUR WINDS TRADING POST** (Highway 93, PO Box 580, St. Ignatius; (406)745-4336) worth a stop, especially with a guide from the People's Center, who can give you the Indian perspective on the old buildings.

Other trading posts include the **JOCKO RIVER TRADING POST** (Highway 93 N, PO Box 630221, Ravalli; (406)745-3055) and the **POLSON BAY TRADING COMPANY** (320 Main Street, Polson; (406)883-3742).

St. Ignatius Mission National Historic Site:
Built by the Flathead Indians

The narrative posted at St. Ignatius Mission National Historic Site describes several delegations sent by the tribes to bring back the "black robes." Fur traders had brought with them Iroquois trappers who had told of Catholic rituals and beliefs that seemed very similar to Salish and Kootenai spirituality. Narratives say there were "language difficulties," so it is hard to know what exactly the delegations were seeking. Some say it was the power and the "medicine" of the "black robes" that the tribes wanted, and some say that the Jesuits fitted the prophecy of Shining Shirt, a prophet who had seen a vision of men wearing long black dresses and signs of the cross.

The first mission was built in Salish territory by Father Pierre John De Smet on the Bitterroot River, south of Missoula, Montana. In 1854, Jesuit missionaries built a second mission, on a site the Salish called *snieleman*, a word that meant "the surrounded" (because the mission was surrounded by mountains). Their log cabin, sawmill, flour mill, printing press, carpentry shop, and blacksmith's shop were the first in the Mission Valley. The town that developed where the mission was built was named after the church, St. Ignatius. By 1899, with the help of Indians now confined to the Flathead Reservation, the missionaries built a **MASSIVE BRICK CHURCH WITH 58 MURALS** painted on the interior walls. The church still stands, as do several of the small log cabins that were moved next to it (look inside for photographs of the boarding school and gardens). The three-story dormitories of the boarding school, run by the Ursuline Sisters, are gone, however.

To reach St. Ignatius Mission National Historic Site, look for signs on Hwy 93 at the town of St. Ignatius. The church is the largest building around. The church and adjoining log cabins are open daily, year-round.

Native Ed-Ventures: *Guided Tours*

Hire a Native guide for the day. The People's Center offers reservation tours through Native Ed-Ventures, each customized according to visitors' interests. The half-day **"HERITAGE AND HISTORY—FOCUS ON THE ARTS" TOUR**, for example, includes the center, historic St. Ignatius Mission, local galleries, and artists' homes. The **"BEARS, BISON, AND**

BIRDS" tour takes a look at the National Bison Range, the Mission Range, and tribal wilderness areas, with an in-depth explanation of the tribe's efforts to manage its diverse ecosystems in the mountains, meadows, streambanks, and wetlands. The **"POWWOW TOUR"** includes attendance at one of the tribe's special celebrations with a Native guide to explain the songs, dances, and ceremonies and to introduce visitors to dancers and artists. In addition to a number of community events, the tribe hosts two major powwows, the **ARLEE FOURTH OF JULY CELEBRATION AND THE STANDING ARROW POWWOW**, held the third weekend in July. Be prepared to stay late, since most powwows continue until at least midnight. The center also arranges longer tours, including hikes, river floats, and overnight stays with Native families. Visitors can learn firsthand about reservation life from those who live it daily. A daylong exploration of this gorgeous reservation could include time with a mother and her son and an invitation to dance at a powwow. Don't forget to tip your guides; they really earn the money.

Native Ed-Ventures, The People's Center, Hwy 93 W, PO Box 278, Pablo, MT 59855; (800)883-5344 or (406)883-5344.

Flathead Lake and River Cruises: *Native Narration*

Flathead Lake water levels are lowered in the winter to ready the lake basin for glacial runoff in the spring. By mid-June water levels are normal, the lake is clear, and the little (50-passenger) cruise boat, the *KwaTaqNuk Princess*, makes three rounds of the lake a day, through September 30. Cruises are **NARRATED BY THE CAPTAIN OR A TRIBAL MEMBER**. The 1½-hour bay cruise takes visitors through "the narrows," a chain of forested, stepping-stone islands in the glacier-carved lake basin. For a few dollars more, take the 3-hour cruise up to Wildhorse Island, east of the Kootenai town of Elmo. Accessible only by boat, **WILDHORSE ISLAND STATE PARK** is home to wild horses, bighorn sheep, and deer. Twilight cruises leave the dock at 7:30pm daily.

Arrange cruises on the KwaTaqNuk Princess through KwaTaqNuk Resort, 303 Hwy 93 E, Polson, MT 59860; (406)883-2448. Rates are affordable: discounts available for families, seniors, and groups; also available for private charters.

Kerr Dam Vista Point: *Hike to Viewpoint*

Where Kerr Dam now stands was once a spectacular waterfall, considered by the Kootenai Indians as the center of their spiritual world. From the unpaved parking lot, it's some 320 wooden stair steps down to the end of a narrow granite ledge (with a covered shelter perched on the end) overlooking the dam and the dramatic **FLATHEAD RIVER**

GORGE. Built in the 1930s with **INDIAN LABOR**, the dam seems to have grown into the sheer rock walls of the gorge. Despite the concrete and the spillways, this is a breathtaking vista. It's easy to spend an hour with the guides here, admiring the view. Montana Power leases the dam from the Flathead Tribe, sharing hydroelectricity profits with the tribe to the tune of about $12 million a year, and will continue to do so until the lease expires in 2015.

The video series *The Place of the Falling Waters* documents the building of Kerr Dam and how it forever altered the spectacular falls. The series includes interviews with tribal elders, newsreel footage, rare photographs, and aerial footage of the reservation. Produced in 1991 by Salish Kootenai College and Native Voices Public Television Workshop at Montana State University, this set of three 1-hour programs won the Silver Apple Award at the National Educational Film and Video Festival.

Roads to Kerr Dam are unmarked and hard to find. Ask for directions from the People's Center or at the KwaTaqNuk Resort's reception desk. The Place of the Falling Waters video series, which includes three 1-hour programs, is available from Salish Kootenai College, Hwy 93 W, PO Box 117, Pablo, MT 59855; (406)675-4800.

National Bison Range: *Rebuilding Traditional Treasures*

At one time, 30 to 70 million buffalo roamed the Plains, before they were deliberately destroyed by European settlers in an effort to tame the West for farming and cattle ranching. By 1873 only 100 buffalo remained in the wild. That year a Kootenai tribal member, **WALKING COYOTE**, returned to the Flathead Reservation from Musselshell River country with five orphaned calves and began to rebuild the herd. Two white ranchers bought descendants of Walking Coyote's breeding stock, and between 1907 and 1909 three reserves were carved out of Flathead Reservation land by President Theodore Roosevelt and Congress to save the animals from extinction. Today **350 TO 500 BUF-FALO** roam 18,500 fenced acres of the National Bison Range, mostly hilly, dry grasslands on the reservation's south end.

The **WILD GRASSES** that grow on the rocky, arid land are perfectly suited to the buffalo. The native grasses are dryland-adapted: Although most plants grow from their tips, these grasses grow in clumps from the base of their stems and continue to grow after their tops are grazed off. But of course, on the National Bison Range, it's the shaggy beasts that get all the raves, not the slender grass. You may also spot **ANTELOPE**, white-tailed deer, elk, mule deer, **BIGHORN SHEEP**, mountain goats, bears, and **COYOTES**.

Begin at the National Bison Range **VISITORS CENTER** (well marked, off Highway 212), and pick up a map with excellent explanations of how this ecosystem works. Although the area next to Mission Creek on the northern part of the range looks perfect for a picnic, stay in your car and slowly drive the dirt roads; don't walk. Bison can outrun a horse and will charge and gore with their pointed horns. They're especially nasty during the breeding season, from mid-July to August. This is one of the reasons the tribes traditionally preferred to run the buffalo over cliffs to break their necks when slaughtering them for food and hides, instead of facing them head on (see "Buffalo Jump Sites," later in this section).

National Bison Range, 132 Bison Range Rd, Molese, MT 59824; (406)644-2211. The visitors center is off Hwy 212. Look for highway signs directing you to the range.

Ninepipe and Pablo National Wildlife Refuges: *Flathead Conservation Areas*

The Ninepipe and the Pablo National Wildlife Refuges (the **RECREATION AND CONSERVATION AREAS OF THE FLATHEAD RESERVATION**) cover about 4,500 acres of water, marsh, and upland grasses, harboring about 190 species of birds. On the **MIGRATORY FLYWAY**, the refuges are home to 80,000 Canada geese, blue herons, cormorants, redheads, pintails, snow geese, coots, and other waterfowl. Ninepipe refuge is 5 miles south of the town of Ronan. The Pablo refuge is north of the Ninepipe refuge, 3 miles northwest of Pablo. Also see birds at the Nature Conservancy's Safe Harbor Marsh, north of Polson and west of the "narrows" on the west shore of Flathead Lake, visible in the distance from KwaTaqNuk Resort.

The Confederated Salish and Kootenai Tribes provide a free map of the Flathead Reservation's recreation and conservation areas. For more information, contact the Tribal Fish and Game Office, PO Box 278, Pablo, MT 59855; (406)675-2700.

The Ninepipe and Pablo refuge is named after three Ninepipe brothers, well-known singers who used to live on the Flathead Reservation. In the late 1960s, after hearing one of their records, a Canadian woman, whose ardor was kindled by Louis Ninepipe's love songs and flute playing, came to Montana to woo and wed him. Newspapers worldwide carried the story of their courtship, accompanied by their wedding picture. Alas, the bliss didn't last. As the new bride found she had to chop wood day after day, the only flame left burning was the one in the cookstove.

Recreation Areas and Campgrounds: *Tribally Owned and Maintained Zones*

Nine trailheads enter a 93,000-acre **TRIBAL WILDERNESS AREA**, on the west side of the Mission Range, then proceed to more than 100 high-country lakes and ponds, including "kettle lakes," big potholes left by retreating glaciers. Wilderness-area campgrounds, maintained by the tribe, are undeveloped. You must pack in fresh water and pack out garbage. In mid-July, 10,000 acres are closed to the public, when the grizzly bears show up to feed on ladybugs and army cutworm moths above McDonald Lake. Take precautions when camping here at any time of the year.

WHITEWATER stretches of the Flathead River for rafting and river kayaking are accessible from boat ramps below Kerr Dam. Boats with motors (15 horsepower maximum) are allowed on most reservation lakes and the river. All boats must be pulled from Flathead Lake when not in use to protect the water from gas and oil seepage.

Tribal Fish and Game Office, PO Box 278, Pablo, MT 59855; (406)675-2700, ext 595. The tribe's brochure and map, available at the People's Center (see The People's Center in this section), lists 23 state and tribal parks for tent and trailer camping, picnicking, fishing, and wildlife viewing on the reservation's high mountain lakes, wetlands, and streams. All sites are first come, first served. Peak season is Jul–Aug. Campers, fishers, and hunters need to obtain use permits, available at the People's Center, gas stations, and sporting goods stores.

KwaTaqNuk Resort at Flathead Bay:
Tribally Owned Lodging

KwaTaqNuk (pronounced "qua-TUCK-nuck") is Kootenai for "where the water leaves the lake." The KwaTaqNuk Resort is perched on the western shore of Flathead Lake, near the headwaters of the Flathead River. The resort has **ALL THE AMENITIES**: two swimming pools, spa, espresso cart, and 112 spacious guest rooms with balconies offering an astounding view: the ice-capped Glacier Mountains to the north and the Mission Range across the broad windswept, blue-green lake. The small town of Polson, mostly non-Indian owned, is right behind the hotel. Bears occasionally lumber along the waterfront, and a family of mink sometimes slinks into view. Seagulls mingle with bald eagles and osprey over the lake, and migrating tundra swans have been seen in flocks of 800 or more along the shore.

In the summer there may be a tepee on KwaTaqNuk's lawn, referred to with a grin as the "traditional suite" by hotel staff. You can't sleep in the tepee, although blankets and pillows have been found in it on occasion.

Few would guess that this Best Western hotel is tribally owned, except that the captions under the **45 HISTORIC PHOTOGRAPHS** decorating the lobby and public halls actually name the Indians in the pictures and document when and where the photographs were taken. These pictures of the tribal chiefs and leaders were gathered from various museum collections, and all of those pictured were identified by descendants living on the reservation. The hotel's meeting rooms are named after these famous chiefs. Another tip-off about Native ownership: You can order **FRY BREAD** through room service, and it's served with fruit spreads in the dining room. The bright red flag of the Flathead Nation whips in the wind on the flagpole on the hotel lawn.

Guest rooms are large, with roomy tiled baths, classic wicker armchairs, and comfortable beds. All public rooms—including a sun-splashed lounge, dining room, and even the swimming pools—have the same stunning views and decks. The hotel has two gift shops (carrying mostly **WESTERN ART**), a boardwalk along the lake, a full-service marina, excursion and twilight cruises on the tribe's sightseeing boat, and nearby golf and whitewater rafting. Reserve in advance paddleboats, canoes, ski boats, fishing boats, and wind-surfing equipment from Flathead Surf-n-Ski at the hotel's marina.

KwaTaqNuk Resort at Flathead Bay, 303 US Hwy 93 E, Polson, MT 59860; (800)528-1234 or (406)883-3636. Open year-round. Room rates, $98—$128. Peak season is Jul–Aug. Spring and fall travelers are virtually guaranteed rooms with a view (but bring a warm coat; it can snow here in May). Nonsmoking and wheelchair-accessible rooms available, also a conference center and banquet rooms. No charge for kids 16 and under in the same room. For water-sports rentals, contact Flathead Surf-n-Ski, KwaTaqNuk Resort, PO Box 1161, Polson, MT 59860; (800)358-8046 or (406)883-3900.

Char-Koosta News: Tribal Newspaper

Founded in 1957 by tribal leader Walter McDonald, the tribal newspaper *Char-Koosta News* was established to inform the Salish and Kootenai about the consequences of "termination," a Congressional plan to destroy Indian tribes' self-determination and sovereignty. The *Char-Koosta News* is still published weekly by the Confederated Tribes in Pablo and is on newsstands each Friday. The paper's title combines the names of the last two traditional chiefs: Charlo of the Salish Tribe and Koostahtah of the Kootenai Tribe.

Char-Koosta News, PO Box 278, Pablo, MT 59855; (406)675-3000. Call for a complimentary issue and subscription form.

Browning: *Blackfeet Nation*

Montana's 1.5-million-acre Blackfeet Reservation, 13 miles east of Glacier National Park, just south of the Canadian-U.S. border, is **HOME TO 7,500 NATIVE AMERICANS**. The lowest elevation on the reservation is about 3,400 feet; Chiefs Mountain on the Northwest boundary of the reservation reaches 9,000 feet.

Four large bands of Blackfeet shared these **ANCESTRAL LANDS**, covering most of what is now Montana and southern Alberta. In 1830, after epidemics had struck and killed many Blackfeet, their numbers were estimated at 120,000. Blackfeet depended on buffalo for food, clothing, and shelter, living in buffalo-hide–covered tepees that were easily dismantled and moved to new game harvesting areas.

After the Louisiana Purchase, explorers Meriwether Lewis and William Clark surveyed this area, in part to establish the northern boundary of the United States. The Blackfeet were permanently divided when Britain and the United States drew the boundary line across the North American continent right through the middle of Blackfeet ancestral territory.

The Treaty of 1855 formalized the clash of the Blackfeet's semi-nomadic lifestyle with U.S. policy by encouraging white settlement on Indian lands. By 1888 the last of the great herds had been exterminated by whites, and the Blackfeet living in the United States were relegated to a reservation less than 1 percent of the size of their original ancestral homelands.

The Dawes Act divided the reservation into a checkerboard of ownership by allocating sections of land to tribal members and opening the unclaimed lands to homesteaders. By 1900 only about 1,700 Blackfeet remained in the United States.

Today the Blackfeet Nation consists of 15,500 members, with about 7,500 enrolled tribal members living on the reservation. About 1,500 non-Natives live on the reservation. The northern boundary borders the Alberta prairies, the western boundary borders Glacier National Park. To the south is the Two Medicine portion of Lewis and Clark National Forest. The reservation is dotted with dozens of lakes; most of which have been kept in a pristine state with no motorized watercraft allowed. Tribal headquarters are in the town of Browning, a railroad stop on the Burlington Northern–Santa Fe line that parallels Highway 2. The nearest towns are Kalispel, a 2-hour drive west: Great Falls, with a major airport, 125 miles southwest; and Calgary, Alberta, 210 miles north. Visitors to the reservation can learn more about Blackfeet history through the **MUSEUM OF THE PLAINS INDIAN**, take a tour of **HISTORIC SITES**, or attend a **"NATIVE REFLEC-TIONS" PROGRAM IN GLACIER NATIONAL PARK**.

Museum of the Plains Indian

Located on flat grassland just west of Browning, the grounds of the Museum of the Plains Indian are beautified with **COLORFUL PAINTED TEPEES** erected on lodgepoles as well as a monument to **SIGN LAN-**

GUAGE, a trade language developed before white contact to ease communication among the tribal diversity in the Northern Plains region. A permanent exhibition gallery showcases this diversity with displays of **TRADITIONAL NORTHERN PLAINS ART AND ARTIFACTS.** Items of the Arapaho, Assiniboine, Blackfeet, Chippewa, Cree, Crow, Kootenai, Nez Perce, Northern Cheyenne, Pend Orielle, Salish, Shoshone, and the Sioux are exhibited. Authentic Indian clothing (collected in the 1800s) is dressed on life-size mannequins. A five-screen **MULTIMEDIA PRESENTATION** about the evolution of Indian culture in the Northern Plains (*Winds of Change*, narrated by Vincent Price and produced by Montana State University at Bozeman) accompanies the exhibits.

Held every year in mid-July, the North American Indian Days is one of the largest Native gatherings in the United States, bringing together U.S. and Canadian tribes in campers, RVs, and tepees for four days of parades, powwows, traditional dances, bone games, and baseball. For more information, call the North American Indian Days Committee, Blackfeet Tribal Council; (406)338-7276.

In addition to the historical exhibits, the museum hosts major **TRAVELING ART EXHIBITIONS,** with accompanying catalogs. Changing galleries introduce aspects of contemporary Native design and remind visitors that Indians continue to produce art; these shows are organized in cooperation with the Northern Plains Indian Crafts Association. Native artists are featured in one-person shows throughout the year, and their work is sold in the museum. Native performance artists and writers also are introduced here. **ART DEMONSTRATIONS** are usually held in conjunction with major exhibitions.

The museum is administered by the **INDIAN ARTS AND CRAFTS BOARD,** established in 1935 as an independent agency of the U.S. Department of the Interior. The Indian Arts and Crafts Board also administers the Sioux Indian Museum in Rapid City, South Dakota, and the Southern Plains Indian Museum in Anadarko, Oklahoma. All three museums interpret Plains Indian culture. The primary purpose of the Indian Arts and Crafts Board is to promote Native art and discourage its misrepresentation by publishing a source directory and allowing **ONLY NATIVE AMERICAN-MADE ART AND CRAFTS** in the museum.

Museum of the Plains Indian, PO Box 410, Browning, MT 59417; (406)338-2230. Hwy 89, west of Browning. Open daily, Jun 1–Oct 1; weekends only, Oct 2–May 31. Call for hours. Admission. Tours are available by appointment only.

Lodgepole Gallery and Tipi Camp: *Blackfeet Art and Culture*

Blackfeet tribal member Darrell Norman offers travelers an opportunity to stay on his 200-acre horse ranch on the Blackfeet Reservation. At the Lodgepole Gallery and Tipi Camp, camp in

BLACKFEET-STYLE CANVAS TEPEES, take GUIDED TRIPS TO HISTORIC BLACKFEET SITES, enjoy informal STORYTELLING FROM TRIBAL ELDERS, and try your hand at TRADITIONAL ARTS AND CRAFTS. Norman is one of 20 to 30 people on the reservation to have a painted tepee; the designs are inspired from dreams or visions. Norman's is painted with crow images and is used for ceremonies.

Horses grazing on the ranch are descendants of those bred in the early 1700s by the Blackfeet from stock brought to North America by the Spanish. Small and fast, most SPANISH MUSTANGS were replaced with draft horses when federal policy divided the reservation into lots and tried to force the Indians to farm. Only about 2,200 Spanish mustangs have been registered in the United States since 1957; about 120 of those animals, bred from only 8 original horses, form the core of the new Blackfeet herd at Norman's ranch. Early risers can help Norman's partner and herd manager Bob Black Bull feed these stunning animals.

Curly Bear Wagner offers a 12-day tour, four times a year, through sacred and historical Blackfeet sites. The tour begins in Pipestone, Minnesota, at an ancient pictograph site. It then visits the Badlands in South Dakota, Montana's Black Hills and Bear Butte, and Wyoming's Devil's Tower, Medicine Wheel, and Cody Museum. In southeastern Montana, the group visits the Little Big Horn Battlefield,, the Museum of the Rockies, the Montana History Museum, and the Lewis and Clark Interpretive Center. The tour concludes with Wagner's day tour of Blackfeet historical sites in the reservation and an overnight stay at Lodgepole Gallery and Tipi Camp.

Norman, whose Blackfeet name is Ee-Nees-Too-Wah-See (Growing Like a Buffalo), has been initiated into the Blackfeet's traditional Thunder Pipe Society. A third partner, Curly Bear Wagner, is a Blackfeet tribal member who leads tours on the reservation.

The ranch's gallery offers BLACKFEET TRADITIONAL AND CONTEMPORARY ARTS AND CRAFTS. Meals (available at extra charge) are served buffet style and include such TRADITIONAL FOODS as buffalo ribs cooked with wild onions dug from the prairie.

Lodgepole Gallery and Tipi Camp, PO Box 1832, Browning, MT 59417; (406)338-2787. Tepee camping, $40 per tepee plus $10 per person; meals $34 per day per person, including traditional meal. Historic tours and craft workshops by advance arrangement only. No showers or bathing facilities are at the camp. Visitors may wish to bring their own sleeping bags.

Blackfeet Historical Site Tours: Blackfeet Guides

These excellent half- or full-day tours are offered by Curly Bear Wagner, a Blackfeet tribal member and historian. Tours begin at the Museum of the Plains Indian in Browning, on the Blackfeet Reservation, where Wagner INTERPRETS THE COLLECTION from the Blackfeet perspective. The tour continues into Blackfeet territory to visit such historic sites as the spot on Two Medicine River where the Lewis and Clark expedition met with the Blackfeet in 1802 and the Holy Family Mission, constructed in 1898 by Jesuits. Visitors explore **BLACKFEET TRA-DITIONAL CULTURE** by looking at tepee rings, a buffalo jump (where buffalo were slaughtered by herding them over a cliff to the butchering ground below), and sites of **CEREMONIAL SUN DANCES**.

Wagner also addresses contemporary Blackfeet culture and U.S. federal Indian policy with a visit to the historical Indian agency site, near present-day Browning, which operated from 1880 to 1895. He visits **GHOST RIDGE** and tells the poignant story about the starvation winter of 1883, when provisions were not delivered to the Blackfeet who had been forced to give up their own traditional food-gathering and hunting practices. The tour also explores the burial grounds of Blackfeet remains recovered in 1989 from the Smithsonian Institution and Chicago's Field Museum.

Full day tours include Badger Creek and the Old North Trail, an overland route used generations ago by indigenous people that began in the Bering Strait and continued south all the way to South America. Badger Creek is also the site where the American Fur Trading Company set up camp and a trading post in the early 1800s. Visitors hike with Wagner to a clearing on 9,000-foot Chief's Mountain, a Blackfeet sacred site, then head across the Canadian border to the UNESCO World Heritage Site of the **HEAD-SMASHED-IN BUFFALO JUMP**, where for 5,500 years indigenous peoples would run herds off cliff ledges to their deaths and for processing meat, hides, and bones.

Blackfeet Historical Site Tours, PO Box 2038, Browning, MT; (406)338-2058. Tours are scheduled from May–Sept. Contact owner Curly Bear Wagner to arrange tours during the rest of the year. Full-day tours include lunch. Call for prices.

Native Cultural Programs at Glacier National Park

Popular **BLACKFEET BALLADEER JACK GLADSTONE** teaches about **BLACKFEET MYTHOLOGY AND HISTORY** through songs and stories each summer at Glacier National Park headquarters. His lively programs, "Native Reflections," and "Native American Speaks" elucidate the Blackfeet historical experience. Gladstone's lineage is Blackfeet and Scot (his great-grandfather came west with the British Hudson's Bay Company). In his retinue of songs is **"HUDSON BAY BLUES,"** about the fur-trading company's arrival in Blackfeet country in 1793 and the trading post it set up with "flintlocks, wool socks, coffee beans, denim jeans." He continues, singing that this mercantilism got the Indians ready for today's shopping: "Now we've got Spandex, Gore-Tex, Nike Airs, Gummi Bears, ceiling fans, frying pans, turkey, veal, shrimp, or Spam. Keyboards to surf the Net on a tidal wave of debt."

Glacier National Park, PO Box 129, West Glacier, MT 59936; (406)888-7800 (select "Park Information" from the automated phone menu); or contact Jack Gladstone directly through Hawkstone Productions, PO Box 7626, Kalispell, MT 59904; (800)735-2965.

Lewis and Clark Trail Interpretive Center: *Documenting the Original Indian Routes*

Built on a cliff overlooking the great falls of the Missouri River, the Lewis and Clark National Historic Trail Interpretive Center devotes a whole floor to the Indian **TRIBES WHO ORIGINALLY SETTLED THE ENTIRE LENGTH OF THE TRAIL** (after all, explorers Lewis and Clark followed established Indian routes between villages, where they were hosted during their journey). Tribes helped assemble these exhibits, which include walk-throughs of the **TRADITIONAL HOUSES** of Mandan and Hidatasa, Otoes, Blackfeet, Shoshone, Nez Perce, and Chinook. In the summer there are different styles of teepees and demonstrations outside on the river banks.

Lewis and Clark National Historic Trail Interpretive Center, 4201 Giant Springs Rd, Great Falls, MT 59403; (406)727-8733; www.corpsofdiscovery.org. Open year-round. Admission fee.

Russell Museum: *Plains Indian Art and Artifacts*

Artist C. M. Russell, who painted and sculpted Western scenes and people at the turn of the 20th century, was friends with many Blackfeet, Gros Ventre, and other Plains Indians. Many of them gave Russell all sorts of beautiful **BEADED TAPESTRY, ARTICLES OF CLOTHING, MOCCASINS, BONE AND SHELL JEWELRY, TOYS, AND PIPES**, and also posed for him in his Great Falls log cabin studio. The studio still stands, now filled with Russell's personal collection of Plains Indian art and artifacts (which also includes Tlingit and Nuu-Cha-Nulth baskets, a Chehalis woven fiber bag, and Hopi and Navajo items). The studio also houses the Mrs. J. A. Kelly Collection of **INDIAN ARTIFACTS**. It is open to the public, as is an adjoining museum filled with Russell's own art.

C. M. Russell Museum Complex, 400 13th St N, Great Falls, MT; (406)727-8787; open year-round.

Buffalo Jump Sites

For thousands of years the Northern Plains Indians hunted buffalo by driving them over cliffs (buffalo jumps) to the butchering grounds below. Buffalo meat, bone, and hide were used for food, clothing, shelter, blankets, tools, and even musical instruments. One of more than 300 bison kill sites in Montana, **ULM PISHKUN** at one time was enormous; a mile-long corridor built to herd buffalo straight to the cliff's edge. Today the site is marked by an **INTERPRETIVE CENTER DEDICATED TO BUFFALO CULTURE**—a collaborative effort between the nine tribes of Montana, archeologists, historians, and Montana Fish, Wildlife, and Parks—to explain the nature of the beast and its importance to the Plains people's survival.

The site is about 130 southeast of Browning; take I-5, the park is 12 miles west of Great Falls. PO Box 109, Ulm, MT 59485; (406)866-2217. Open 10am–6pm, Memorial Day–Sept. 30, or by appointment. Another such jump, Head-Smashed-In Buffalo Jump (protected as a UNESCO World Heritage Site) is just across the border from Browning, near Fort Macleod, Alberta; (403)553-2731; www.head-smashed-in.com. The interpretive center is 18 miles west of Fort Macleod. Open daily, 9am–5pm, with extended hours during summer.

APPENDIXES

Sacred Ceremonies and Sites

Because Native peoples welcome visitors so warmly, sharing their traditional stories, songs, dances, and foods, visitors are sometimes surprised to learn that certain lands or religious ceremonies are closed to them. But as in any religion, Native ceremonies, symbols, and places are sacred, and are not to be shared with strangers in a casual way. Nor is sharing intended to deepen the pockets of outsiders, who pretend to sell Native spirituality to the general public. Spiritual teaching is not for sale; when the time is right, it is given without charge. Your respect and consideration regarding this are deeply appreciated.

There is another reason that tribes are cautious with their spiritual teachings. During the late 1800s and early 1900s, the federal government vigorously suppressed Native religions and ceremonies. Regulations were passed that banned all practices, including dancing, singing, burial customs, sharing wealth with family and tribal members, and holding gatherings off the reservation. During this time, religious practices had to be conducted in secret. The fear still exists that those days may return.

In addition to protecting the sacredness of their religious ceremonies, Native peoples have tried—often in vain—to protect sacred grounds. However, during the past century, countless sacred sites— honored by more than 500 generations of tribal peoples—have been desecrated by everything from strip mining to building construction. Some sites are unknowingly desecrated by hikers or campers who stumble onto a site and want to take home a souvenir. However, those "souvenirs" are usually important religious items meant to remain at a specific place, or are funerary items meant to stay with the deceased. Archaeologists, driven to learn what they could about Native peoples, have for years failed to consult with the tribes or with family members before removing items that had been deliberately placed. Perhaps the most painful desecration of all has been the casual removal of the dead from family graves.

If you should ever find remains, petroglyphs, or other items, take note of where you found them—but do not remove them. Alert the nearest tribe and the state historic preservation office. Looting on federal or tribal lands is a crime. When a tribe is willing to share historic sites and cultural areas, we have included them in this book. You can also contact each tribe's cultural committee, which considers requests for information (see the list of tribal offices in this appendix).

For more information about historic sites, battlefields, and monuments, we recommend George Cantor's *North American Indian Landmarks: A Traveler's Guide* (Gale Research, 1993), or David Hurst Thomas's *Exploring Ancient Native America: An Archaeological Guide* (Macmillan, 1994). Both books include contributions by Cheyenne writer/poet Suzan Shown Harjo, who heads The Morning Star Institute, a cultural and arts advocacy organization in Washington, D.C. Harjo's well-known poem *Sacred Ground* follows; Harjo rewrote it especially for this book, creating new verses about Northwest sacred sites.

Powwows

The word *powwow* comes from the Native peoples of the Northern Woodlands. Named after their spiritual gatherings of medicine people, powwows were a time for healing and prayer. In later years, Europeans witnessing powwows wrongly concluded that the gatherings were merely social events. Peoples of the Northwest held similar gatherings for spiritual, social, and economic reasons. Through large gatherings, individuals sought marriage partners from other tribes, and trade was conducted up and down the coast and across the continent.

Contemporary powwows

Powwows and celebrations are still held today throughout the Northwest. They present a wonderful opportunity for cultural exchange. Most powwows are open to the public. Some are huge events. A recent powwow in Vancouver, B.C., for example, drew several drum groups, more than 600 dancers, and over 20,000 spectators. A powwow can last for a few hours, all night, or for as long as two weeks. Powwows are alcohol- and drug-free.

Powwows are usually held in outdoor powwow arbors; sometimes they take place in gymnasiums or ballrooms. Today's powwows still mirror the past and include a feast provided by the hosts for the honored guests. At the Shoshone-Bannock Festival in Idaho, or the Arlee Powwow in Montana, the community will most often host a buffalo feast; at the Treaty Day Celebrations along the Columbia River or a powwow in the Puget Sound area, you'll be offered a salmon dinner.

Today, powwows are still spiritual events. Special prayers are made to the creator, with thanks for all that's been given. The people ask for blessings for the powwow grounds and dancers. Special ceremonies are conducted for those dancers returning after a prolonged absence due to a death in the family. There are honoring songs and special dances offered for veterans, and memorials for loved ones, name-givings, giveaways, or whenever an eagle feather drops in the arena.

During these ceremonies, be respectful of the silence and stand when others do. For example, everyone stands during the "Grand Entry" and "Honor Dances," to pay respect to the flags and the dancers. If you have questions, wait until after the ceremony to ask them. There is usually an information booth or stand where powwow committee members are available to answer your questions and provide directions.

Traditional games, sometimes called hand game, stick game, or bone game, are played at all hours in arbors, tents, or other covered buildings. Canoe races, rodeos, horse races, and baseball tournaments often accompany the dances. Vendors selling traditional and contemporary arts and crafts, shawls, blankets, music tapes, and food are reminiscent of the trade that was prevalent in historic gatherings.

Most powwows are inter-tribal, with dancers and drum groups from throughout the United States and Canada. In recent years, the larger powwows have offered thousands of dollars in prize money to the dancers and drum groups.

The Dancers

The drum is the center of the powwow, the heartbeat of the nations, drawing the people together. Dancers fill the arena during the inter-tribal dances, from the smallest child able to bounce to the rhythm, to the grandmothers and aunties dressed in intricately beaded buckskin dresses with fringe that gracefully sways to each drum beat.

Each tribe has its own traditional dances and songs. These dances are rarely performed during contemporary powwows; they are held for special ceremonies and celebrations. The dances you'll see at a contemporary powwow are adapted from the Plains Indians and shared by tribes throughout the United States.

A favorite of the audience, because of their fast steps and swift turns are the fancy dancers, whose colorful outfits may be elaborately beaded and adorned with feather bustles. Traditional dancers, the proud bearers of culture, wear prized heirlooms, such as eagle feathers, that may have been passed down for generations. Their outfits are a strong contrast to contemporary fancy dancers, who lean toward bright neon colors, the better to catch the eye of the judges. The grass dancers' outfits, fringed with yarn and ribbons, resemble the graceful swaying motion of the prairie grass.

Shawl dancers wear a long-fringed shawls over beaded or ribbon dresses; their dances are said to be inspired by the butterfly, moth, hummingbird, and other small birds. Jingle dresses are adorned with hundreds of cone-shaped bells made from tobacco can lids; each bell is said to represent a prayer to the creator.

The dance area must be respected. Do not enter it unless the master of ceremonies invites you with a call for an "inter-tribal" or "round dance." The round dance, sometimes called a "friendship dance," is performed by facing the center of the arena in a large circle. Follow the dancer beside you.

Powwow Etiquette

At the Peoples' Center in Pablo, Montana, guides are available to help explain how the powwow works. They introduce the visitors to dancers and artists. Many other tribes are following suit. If guides aren't available, you need to know that there are a number of customs and ceremonies that may occur.

- Powwows are like large extended family gatherings. Friends and families make plans each year to meet at different gatherings; many have attended the same gatherings for generations. Families may bring their tepees, with the local hosts providing the tepee poles. Never enter a tepee without an invitation; these are private homes during the powwow.

- Chairs surrounding the ring and the front seats of grandstands are reserved for elders and families of the dancers. Out of respect for the elders and dancers, do not stand in front of them, or sit in their chairs.

- Many powwows do not have seating. Bring along a lawn chair or blanket, but do not put them in front of the elders' seats.

- Casual street clothes are appropriate attire for spectators (jeans and T-shirts are okay, suggestive clothing is considered disrespectful). Women entering the dance ring should wear a shawl around their shoulders.

- It's generally acceptable to take photographs or videos of dancers inside the dance area for your personal use, but you should ask permission from the master of ceremonies or staff beforehand. Always ask permission before taking any individual's photograph outside the dance circle. Never publish a photo without permission of the dancer.

- Don't be offended or upset if someone does not respond to you. If you ask a question about something that a vendor or a dancer doesn't feel you need to know, they may just ignore the question. Silence is often considered more polite than a negative response or a refusal of a request.

Calendar of Events

The following is a list of some of the larger gatherings held in the Northwest. Some are called "powwows," some are called "celebrations." No matter what they are called, the public is welcome to attend. Call ahead for the exact dates and times, which often vary from year to year. Don't hesitate to ask questions if you're not sure what to wear, how to act, what to bring, or whether cash donations are needed.

Each tribe holds other community events as well. If you are planning to be on or near a reservation, call the tribe and ask whether any events are scheduled that are open to the public. Colleges and universities in major Northwest cities often have urban Indian organizations that sponsor powwows and events as well.

Idaho and Montana

January–March

Annual Native American Art Association Show, Great Falls, MT; (406)791-2212. Powwow and parade.

April–June

Annual Shoshone-Bannock Hand/Stick Games Tourney, Fort Hall Reservation, Fort Hall, ID; (208)238-8821.

Chief Joseph & Warriors Memorial Pow Wow, Nez Perce Reservation, Lapwai, ID; (208)843-2253.

Annual Arlee 4th of July Celebration, Flathead Reservation, Arlee, MT; (406)675-0160, (406)676-5280, or (406)675- 2700.

July–September

Shoshone-Bannock Indian Festival, Fort Hall Reservation, Fort Hall, ID; (800)497-4231 or (208)237-8774. Four-day festival with parade, powwow, rodeo, art exhibition, buffalo feast, arts and crafts.

Nee-Mee-Poo Sapatqayn and Cultural Days, Nez Perce Reservation, Spalding, ID; (208)843-2261. Horse parade, cultural demonstrations, speakers, drumming and dancing, arts and crafts.

Standing Arrow Pow Wow, Flathead Reservation, Elmo, MT; (406)675-0160.

Chief Looking Glass Pow Wow, Nez Perce Reservation, Kamiah, ID; (208)935-0716.

October–December

Reservation-wide Championship Wardancing, Flathead Reservation, St. Ignatius, MT; (406)675-0160.

Thanksgiving Day Pow Wow, Salish and Kootenai Nations, Flathead Reservation, St. Ignatius, MT; (406)675-2700.

Four Nations Pow Wow, Nez Perce County Fair Grounds, Lewiston, ID; (208)843-2253.

Oregon and Washington (Eastern): Columbia River Basin

January–March

Lincoln's Day Pow Wow, Warm Springs Reservation, Simnasho Longhouse, Simnasho, OR; (541)553-1161.

Speelyi Mi Arts & Crafts Fair, Yakama Reservation, Yakima, WA; (509)865-5121. Traditional exhibits, art show, daily entertainment.

Annual Father's Day Fishing Derby at Indian Lake, Umatilla Reservation, Pilot Rock, OR; (503)276-3873.

Washington's Birthday Pow Wow, Yakama Reservation, Toppenish, WA; (509)865-5121.

April–June

Pi-Ume-Sha Treaty Days Powwow, Warm Springs Reservation, Warm Springs, OR; (541)553-1161. All-Indian rodeo, endurance horse race, softball tourney, fun run, golf tourney.

Root Feast & Rodeo, Warm Springs Reservation, Warm Springs and Simnasho, OR; (541)553-1161. Traditional foods and ceremonies.

Annual Memorial Day Weekend "Open Jackpot Rodeo," Yakama Reservation, White Swan, WA; (509)848-3329.

Treaty Days Tinowit International Pow Wow and White Swan Annual All-Indian Rodeo, Yakima and White Swan, WA; (509)865-5121.

All-Indian Rodeo, Tygh Valley, OR; (541)483-2238. Western States Indian Rodeo Association–sanctioned rodeo, parade, helicopter rides, pony rides, western dances, fun run, arts and crafts, baseball tourney, Buckaroo Breakfast.

Eagle Spirit Father's Day Celebration, Yakama Indian Nation, White Swan, WA; (509)877-6754 or (509)848-3415. Camping, concessions, arts and crafts vendors, powwow, traditional gaming.

Annual 10-Day Encampment, Yakama Indian Nation, White Swan, WA; (509)865-5121.

Celico Wy-Am Salmon Feast, Celilo Village, OR; (509)848-3461.

Root Feast Celebration, Umatilla Reservation, Mission, OR; (541)276-3165.

July–September

Omak Stampede and Suicide Race, Colville Reservation, Omak, WA; (800)933-6625. Second weekend in August. PRCA–sanctioned rodeo with top stars, Native American encampment, world-famous race.

Spokane Falls Northwest Indian Encampment & Pow Wow, Riverfront Park, Spokane, WA; (509)535-0866. Every August. Dancing contest, Indian art auction, arts and crafts vendors, exhibits, modern dances, arcade.

Salish Fair and Buffalo Barbecue, Kalispel Tribe, Usk, WA; (509)445-1178. Dance competition, Native foods, arts and crafts.

Pendleton Round Up and Rodeo, Pendleton, OR; (800)524-2984. Happy Canyon Pageant, Native American encampment, Indian art auction, arts and crafts vendors, parade, rodeo.

Annual Golden Eagle Pow Wow, Yakama Indian Nation, Toppenish, WA; (509)865- 5121 (ask for AAOA).

Eagle Spirit Celebration, Yakama Reservation, White Swan, WA; (509)865-5121.

Spokane Indian Days, Tribal Fairgrounds, Wellpinit, WA; (509)258-4060.

October–December

Mid-Columbia River Pow Wow, Celilo Village, OR; (509)848-3461.

Restoration Celebration and Powwow, Siletz Reservation, OR; (541)444-2532.

Oregon (Western) and Northern California

April–June

Memorial Day Rodeo & Powwow, Klamath Tribe, Klamath Falls, OR; (800)524-9787.

July–September

Hoopa All-Indian Rodeo, Rodeo Grounds, Hoopa, CA; (916)625-4227. Western States Indian Rodeo Association–sanctioned rodeo, arts and crafts, dances.

Nesika Illahee Pow Wow, Confederated Tribes of the Siletz, Government Hill, OR; (800)922-1399 or (503)444-2532. Second week in August.

Hupa Tribe's Annual Sovereign Day Celebration, Hoopa, CA; (916)625-4211.

Grand Ronde Pow Wow, Pow Wow Grounds, Grand Ronde, OR; (800)422-0232.

All-Indian Rodeo and Barbecue, Klamath Tribe, Chiloquin, OR; (800)524-9787.

Klamath Treaty Days Celebration, Chiloquin, OR; (503)783-2005.

Washington (Western): Olympic Peninsula/Puget Sound

April–June

Chief Tahola Days, Quinault Indian Nation, Tahola, WA; (360)276-8211. Canoe races, baseball tourney, arts and crafts, food.

Annual Stommish Water Festival, Lummi Reservation, Bellingham, WA; (360)384-1489. War canoe races, footraces, tugs-of-war, traditional dancing, salmon barbecue, traditional bone game tournament, arts and crafts.

Sa'Heh'Wa'Mish Powwow and Art Fair, Squaxin Island Tribe, Mason County Fairgrounds, Shelton, WA; (206)426-9781. Traditional salmon bake, arts and crafts, entertainment.

Annual Native American Art Fair, Suquamish Tribal Center, Suquamish, WA; (360)598- 3311. Artists' displays and sales, Native foods.

Drummers Jam, Suquamish Tribe, Indianola, WA; (360)598-3311. Powwow drummers and dancers, arts and crafts; camping available.

Sharing of the Culture Annual Art Sale, Lummi Nation and Allied Arts of Whatcom County, Bellingham, WA; (360)384-2338.

July–September

Chief Seattle Days, Suquamish Tribe, Suquamish, WA; (206)598-3311. Annual celebration in honor of Chief Seattle, held annually since 1911. Memorial service, powwow, war canoe races, salmon bake, arts and crafts, dances, and entertainment.

Makah Days Celebration, Makah Reservation, Neah Bay, WA; (360)645-2201. Canoe races, parade, salmon bake, arts and crafts fair, dances, fireworks, traditional bone game tourney.

Annual Seafair Indian Days, Daybreak Star Indian Cultural Center, Discovery Park, Seattle, WA; (206)285-4425. Powwow, arts and crafts, salmon bake; camping available.

Annual Salmon Homecoming Celebration, Seattle, WA; (206)386-4320. Sponsored by Northwest tribes, Northwest Indian Fisheries, and City of Seattle. Four days of ceremonies, storytelling, forums, a powwow, and music to honor the salmon.

Muckleshoot Annual Pow Wow, Auburn, WA; (206)939-3311.

Puyallup Tribe Annual Pow Wow and Salmon Bake, Tacoma, WA; (206)597-6200.

October–December

Washington Indian Nations Art Celebration, Bellevue, WA; (206)665-1925.

Buying Native Art

Native art reflects each tribe's unique artistic heritage—whether it's the soft Wasco sally bags woven of wild grasses; the Tlingit, Haida, and Tsimshian totem poles carved from towering cedar trees; or the intricate glass beadwork of the Shoshone, adapted from the decoration of ceremonial regalia with dyed porcupine quills, elk teeth, and beads made of bone. Native artists draw inspiration from a continuity of culture. Even the most modern Native art is often guided by custom and culture. An Eagle Clan Tlingit artist would not carve the story of the Raven Clan without special permission. A basketmaker would not weave another family's designs without their approval.

The most important guideline to follow in purchasing Native art—especially for those who want something more than a simple souvenir—is to ensure the item's authenticity. When buying art from a gallery or a vendor, ask who made the item and what the artist's tribal affiliation is. A good gallery knows its artists or can get information about them; the best galleries mark each piece with the name of the artist and the tribal affiliation. If the sellers don't know who made the piece, there's a chance it is not Indian-made. Ask for information in writing. Many shops provide certificates of authenticity—even for the smallest items. If you're still not sure, call the tribe and ask. Every tribe has an enrollment office that keeps track of each of its members.

Don't be fooled by works marked "Indian-style," or "in the tradition of," or labels that describe the artist as having "Indian heritage." These descriptions are often used to get around federal and tribal laws. (The Indian Arts and Crafts Act protects buyers from imitations. The law provides stiff fines for those caught selling or promoting products as Indian-made if they are not.) No one can blame non-Native artists who are drawn to Native images and art—the bold forms and intricate design would capture any artist's imagination. In fact, some non-Natives have taught Natives traditional skills. However, these works, no matter how good, are only replicas of the real thing. Non-Indian artists with integrity do not claim that their work is authentic.

Some other guidelines for buying Native art:

- Remember that the ability to determine quality comes with time and observation. The more examples you see, the more you will appreciate the distinctions. At first, all totems and masks may look the same. After a while you can tell the differences in style and artist's work. Some galleries provide free printed materials that explain the art forms, or have reprints of articles about artists and motifs. Or ask the gallery to recommend a book on the topic.

- If you are going to invest in a major piece of art, buy a few books or magazines to learn what to look for. *Native Peoples, Indian Artist,* and *American Indian Art* magazines have articles on Native arts and cultures.

- Instead of relying on galleries, buy Native art from the artists themselves—at powwows, art markets, or special events. Don't be surprised if the artist is reserved. Artists are not always used to selling their work, and feel more comfortable discussing how a piece is made or how they learned their craft than trying to sell it.

- Don't be surprised by innovation and contemporary styles. Remember that culture is a living thing. Some of the jewelers and painters in the Northwest attended the Institute of American Indian Art in Santa Fe and have been influenced by the styles of the Southwest. Keep in mind that there's no such thing as "Indian art"—only art in whatever traditional or contemporary form that is produced by an American Indian, First Nations, or Alaska Native artist.

Traditional Gaming and Casinos

From modest bingo halls to lavish Las Vegas-style casinos, Indian tribes offer a full range of attractions for those who wish to court Lady Luck Indian style. Whether or not you are a gambler, you'll take a certain risk walking through these doors—you may have to challenge your attitudes and preconceptions of modern Indian people.

Visit, for example, the Wild Horse Gaming Center in Umatilla, Oregon. Created by Disneyland stagehands, its whimsical Western setting is clearly a place to drop your attitudes, along with your wallet, and have some fun. The Jamestown S'Klallam's Seven Cedars Casino in Washington, with its totems, grand longhouse-style entry, and immense cedar beams, opens into a first-class gallery featuring some of the finest artists from the Northwest. The Indian Head Gaming Center at Warm Springs, Oregon, has made major purchases of oil paintings and masks from Northwest Indian artists, and had the tribe's clothing factory design and produce the uniforms for their personnel. The Indian casinos will go out of their way to make you feel welcome—they provide classes for new players, handouts explaining the activities, and friendly employees to show you how to play even the most complicated games.

Participating in games of chance and skill is nothing new for Native tribes. For centuries, such competitions have been a serious sport for them, and the pot was worth much more than mere money. The Iroquois played lacrosse to settle land disputes with other tribes (much more civilized than war). Horse races were held throughout the Northwest, helping redistribute wealth as well as settle disputes. When Lewis and Clark came to the Northwest, they were dismayed by the amount of time Native peoples spent on social and recreational activities, ceremonies, dances, and gaming. Today, however, economists consider the amount of time spent on family and recreation a sign of an advanced civilization. Indeed, our ideas of play have come a long way.

In a strange twist of fate, the treaties that removed Indians from their traditional lands also protected their rights on the reservation to which they were assigned. Those treaties have given the tribes a competitive advantage in the business of gaming. In the 1980s, when the Cabazon Tribe in California decided to allow gambling on their reservation, nearby casinos were up in arms. The state of California took the tribe to court. The case went all the way to the U.S. Supreme Court, which declared that tribes were sovereign and had the same rights as any other government (or state) to allow gaming. Congress, in its response to the outcry, passed additional legislation that allows states a process with which to negotiate with tribes about instituting gambling.

Using games of chance as an economic option is not unique to the tribes. States such as Nevada and New Jersey have done the same; many churches raise funds from casino nights and bingo halls. And just as the states and churches use the money for the benefit of their constituents, the tribes use the money raised through the casinos to address the problems of poverty and unemployment on their reservations. For example, the Tulalip Tribe in Washington, which opened gaming operations in 1991, has seen unemployment on its reservation drop from 65 to 10 percent. They have also used proceeds to establish an elder-care facility.

So, when you visit an Indian gaming center, you're doing far more than courting Lady Luck. As one casino player said, "This is my way of donating money to the Indians, and having some fun while doing it." At many centers, you can buy Native art, learn a little about the tribe's culture, and enjoy a good meal—as well as have some fun. Some casinos (such as the one at Coeur d'Alene, Idaho) even host traditional Native games, such as hand-game tournaments, so you can see how it was all done in the past.

Casinos

California: Northern

ELK VALLEY CASINO, Elk Valley Rancheria, 2500 Howland Hill Rd, Crescent City, CA 95531; (888)574-2744 or (707)464-1020. Bingo, video slots, blackjack, poker, keno machines, and others. Cafe (open 24 hours. Open daily, 24 hours. No alcohol.

LUCKY BEAR CASINO, Hupa Tribe, Hwy 96, Hoopa, CA 95546; (530)625-4048. Video slots. Open 10am–midnight, Sun–Thurs, 10am–2am Fri. and Sat.

LUCKY SEVEN CASINO, Tolowa Rancheria, Hwy 101, 350 N. Indian Rd., Smith River, CA 95567; (707)487-7777. Video slots now, table games when new facility is built. Restaurant planned. Open 24 hours a day, daily.

Idaho

CLEARWATER CASINO, Nez Perce Tribe, 7463 N and S Highway, Lewiston, ID 83501; (877)678-7423 or 208 746-0723; four miles east of Lewiston on Hwy 12/95. Video slots; bingo, off-track betting. Snack bar with steak grill. Open daily, 24 hours a day.

COEUR D'ALENE TRIBAL BINGO/CASINO, Coeur d'Alene Tribe, Junction of Hwy 58 and US 95, Worley, ID 83876; (800)523-2464 or (208)686-0248. About 30 minutes south of the resort town of Coeur d'Alene. Video slots, pull-tabs; bingo Fri–Sun; stick game tournaments in summer. High Mountain Steak House, open daily for breakfast, lunch dinner. Hotel opens 2001; gift shop; open daily, 24 hours a day.

KOOTENAI TRIBAL CASINO, Kootenai Tribe, Kootenai River Inn, Hwy 95, Bonners Ferry, ID 83805; (800)346-5668 or (208)267-8511. Video slots; bingo Wed, Fri–Sun. Restaurant, 48-room resort hotel overlooking the Kootenai River, pool, spa. Open daily, 24 hours a day.

SHOSHONE-BANNOCK GAMING, Shoshone-Bannock Tribe, I-5, Exit 80, Fort Hall, ID 83203; (800)497-4231. A few miles north of Pocatello, halfway between Salt Lake City, Utah, and Yellowstone National Park, on the Fort Hall Shoshone-Bannock Reservation. Pull-tabs; bingo Tues and Fri.–Sun. Concession stand, nearby restaurant and trading post with Native beadwork for sale. Open 8am–midnight weekdays, 24-hours weekends.

Oregon

CHINOOK WINDS GAMING AND CONVENTION CENTER, Confederated Tribes of Siletz Indians, 1777 NW 44th, Lincoln City, OR 97367; (800)863-3314. Watch for signs from Hwy 101 in Lincoln City. Casino and convention center overlooks Pacific Ocean. Video slots, card tables (blackjack, poker), craps, roulette. Rogue River Restaurant and Lounge, and buffet; accommodations nearby. 2,000-seat auditorium for headliner entertainment. Open daily, 24 hours a day.

INDIANHEAD CASINO, Confederated Tribes of the Warm Springs Reservation, 823 Hwy 8, Warm Springs, OR 97761; (800)238-6946 or (541)553-6122. At KahNeeTa Resort. Video slots, card tables (blackjack, poker). Delicatessen on site; full-service resort with restaurants, accommodations, swimming, horseback riding, golf course. Open 10am–2am daily. Longer hours summer months.

KLA-MO-YA CASINO, Klamath Tribes, 34333 Hwy 97 N, Chiloquin, OR 97624; (888)552-6692 or (541)783-7529. Video slots, card tables (poker, blackjack). Deli, all you can eat buffet, children's arcade. Gift shop. Open 9am–midnight Sun–Thurs, until 2am Fri and Sat nights; longer hours summers.

THE MILL CASINO HOTEL, Coquille Tribe, 3201 Tremont, North Bend, OR 97459; (800)953-4800 or (541)756-8800. A $20 million remodel of a mill building on the Coos Bay waterfront. Video slots, blackjack, poker, bingo, roulette, craps. Sports bar, arcade. Bayfront dining in the Plank House Restaurant. Adjoining 3-story waterfront hotel. Convention facilities. Golf packages available. Headliner entertainment and special events. Open daily, 24 hours a day.

THE OLD CAMP CASINO, Burns-Paiute Tribe, 2205 W Monroe, Burns, OR 97720. Off Hwy 20. (888)343-7568 or (541)573-1500. Blackjack, bingo, poker, video slots. Fine dining. Open 11am–11pm weekdays; 11am–2am Friday; 9am-2am Sat. Longer hours in the summer.

SEVEN FEATHERS HOTEL & CASINO RESORT, Cow Creek Band of Umpqua, 146 Chief Miwaleta Lane, Canyonville, OR 97417; (800)548-8461. Off I-5, exit 99. Video slots, bingo, keno and card tables (blackjack, poker), roulette, craps and other games. The Camas Room for fine dining; Cow Creek Restaurant (open 24 hours); Scoops Ice Cream Parlour; 150-room hotel with indoor pool, spa, saunas. Live cabaret shows in Casino Cabaret, Tues–Sun, twice daily. Open daily, 24 hours a day.

SPIRIT MOUNTAIN CASINO AND SPIRIT MOUNTAIN LODGE, Confederated Tribes of Grand Ronde, 27100 SW Salmon River Hwy (Hwy 18), PO Box 39, Grand Ronde, OR 97347; (800)760-7977 or (503)879-2350. Thirty minutes from Salem, McMinnville, and Lincoln City. Video slot machines, card tables (blackjack, poker), roulette, craps, and other games, off-track betting, keno, bingo. Children's Play World (daycare), arcade for older children; non-smoking casino; Legends Restaurant and Lounge, Coyote Buffet, Starbucks, Elk Horn cafe and Rock Creek Court deli;1100-seat concert hall, headline entertainment. Spirit Mountain Outfitters gift shop. Open daily, 24 hours a day.

WILDHORSE CASINO RESORT, Confederated Tribes of Umatilla Indians, 72777 Hwy 331, Pendleton, OR 97801; (800)654-9453 or (503)278-2274. A few miles east of Pendleton, off I-84. Video slots, off-track betting, live keno, bingo, card tables (blackjack, poker). Snack bar, Wildhorse Casino restaurant; 100-room Wildhorse Hotel with indoor pool, spa; RV park, 18-hole championship golf course. Adjoining museum. Open daily, 24 hours a day.

Washington: Eastern

COULEE DAM CASINO, Confederated Tribes of the Colville Reservation, 515 Birch St, Coulee Dam, WA 99116; (800)556-7492 or (509)633-0766. Pull-tabs, slots, live keno, bingo, blackjack. Snack bar, gift shop with Native art and souvenirs. Open daily, 10am–midnight weekdays and Sun, 10am–2am Fri–Sat.

DOUBLE EAGLE CASINO, Spokane Tribe, 2539 Smith Rd, Chewela, WA 99109; (509)935-4406. Blackjack, slots, roulette, Double Eagle Casino Cafe. 9am–1am Mon–Thurs; Fri and Sat, 24 hours.

MILL BAY CASINO, Confederated Tribes of the Colville Reservation, 455 E Wapato Lake Rd, Mansen, WA 98831; (800)648-2946 or (509)687-2102. Overlooking Lake Chelan. Slots, pull-tabs, card tables (blackjack, craps, roulette). Coyote Cafe and a deli, gift shop. Open daily, 24 hours a day.

OKANAGAN BINGO-CASINO, Confederated Tribes of the Colville Reservation, 41 Appleway Rd, Okanagan WA 98840; (800)559-4643 or (509)422-4646. Off Hwy 97, just south of Omak, overlooking the Okanagan River. Video poker, bingo (Fri–Tues), pull-tabs, blackjack, craps. Deli, gift shop. Open weekdays 10am-12am Sun–Thurs, 10am–2am Fri–Sat. Open one hour earlier in the summer.

SPOKANE INDIAN BINGO AND CASINO, Spokane Tribe, Hwy 395, Smith Rd, Chewelah, WA 99109; (800)322-2788 or (509)935-6167. Slots, card blackjack, craps, roulette, pull-tabs. Bingo Sat, Sun, and Tues. Mistequa Cafe. Open 9am–2 pm daily.

TWO RIVERS CASINO AND MARINA, Spokane Tribe, 6828-B Hwy 25 S, Davenport, WA 99122; (800)722-4031 or (509)722-4000. Overlooks Lake Roosevelt (the Columbia River). Blackjack, craps, roulette, video slots. Cafe. Hotel in the works; adjoins RV park, marina, and tent campground. 9am–1 pm Mon–Thurs, 24-hours Fri and Sat.

THE YAKAMA NATION LEGENDS CASINO, Confederated Tribes and Bands of the Yakama Indian Nation, 580 Fort Rd, Toppenish, WA 98948; (877)726-6311. Off Hwy 97, across the road from the tribal center. Video slots, card tables (poker tournaments and other games), craps, roulette; bingo, keno. Mountain View buffet, Legend's Deli. Headliner entertainment in the bingo hall (seats 1100 concert style), daycare. Alcohol free. 10am–3am daily.

Washington: Olympic Peninsula and Pacific Coast

CHINOOK INDIAN BINGO, Chinook Tribe, 10th and North Pacific, Long Beach, WA 98584; (360)642-4650. On the Long Beach Peninsula, off Hwy. 103, on the southern Washington coast. Non-smoking area, restaurant. Open Sat–Mon, 10am–11pm. Games start at noon and 6pm.

LUCKY EAGLE CASINO, Chehalis Tribe, 12888 188th St SW, Rochester, WA 98579; (800)720-1788 or (360)273-2000. Watch for exit signs on I-5, between Centralia and Olympia, to the Chehalis Reservation; the reservation is off Hwy.12, a few miles past the town of Rochester. Video slots, (card tables), craps, blackjack, poker, roulette, and other games. The Golden Eagle Restaurant, Tomahawk sports lounge, deli. Live boxing matches monthly, comedy, live radio broadcasts. Open 10am–4am weekdays, Fri–Sat. open 10am–6am.

SEVEN CEDARS CASINO, Jamestown S'Klallam Tribe, 270756 Hwy 101, Sequim, WA 98382; (800)4lucky7 or (360)683-7777. Near Sequim Bay on the Strait of Juan de Fuca; casino is built in the style of a longhouse, with seven hand-carved totem poles outside. Slots, all the table games, roulette, poker, bingo. The Salish Room (seafood buffet Fri and Sat), and Totem Lounge. Native fine-art gallery shop. Open at noon 'til 1am or 3am, daily.

STILLWATER BAY BINGO AND CASINO, Shoalwater Bay Tribe, 4112 Hwy 105, Tokeland, WA 98590; (888)332-2048 or (360)267-2048. Bingo machines, blackjack and poker, video slots. Full service deli. Friday TGIF free food and live music. Open daily.

Washington: Puget Sound Area

CLEARWATER CASINO AND BINGO HALL, Suquamish Tribe, 15347 Suquamish Wy, Suquamish, WA 98392; (800)375-6073 or (360)598-3399. Off Hwy. 305, on the north side of the Agate Pass bridge. Facility is decorated with Northwest Coast art. Bingo, video bingo, pull-tabs, slots, card games, keno. Buffet for lunch and dinner. Snack bar. The Bar lounge features various entertainment. Open 11am–2am Sun–Thurs; 11am–4am Fri–Sat.

EMERALD QUEEN CASINO, Puyallup Tribe, 2102 Alexander Ave., Tacoma, WA 98421; (888)831-7655 or (253) 594-7777. Boat and shoreside, nightclub top floor for dancing. Blackjack, roulette, pull-tabs, card games, keno, craps, video slots, video bingo and other games. Three story river paddlewheel moored on the Tacoma waterfront. Exit 137 from I-5, right on 54th Ave N, left on Hwy 509, right on Alexander. 1800-seat auditorium on the shoreline for live headliner entertainment. Lafayette's fine dining and buffet; snack bars, Sub Club deli. Beer Garden Bar up top, Big Reub's lounge, Bourbon St. Bar, Royal St Bar. Gift shop. Open 10am to 6am daily.

LITTLE CREEK CASINO, Squaxin Island Tribe, West 91, Hwy 108, Shelton, WA 98584; (800)667-7711 or (360)427-7711. Opposite the entrance to the Squaxin Island Reservation, south of Shelton, off Hwy. 101. Roulette, craps, blackjack, poker, slots, pull-tabs; bingo Sun–Thurs. Live entertainment. Legends Fine Dining, Creekside Cafe. Gift shop. Open daily 10am–4am Sun–Thurs; Fri and Sat. 10am–6am.

MUCKLESHOOT CASINO AND BINGO, Muckleshoot Tribe, 2402 Auburn Wy S, Auburn, WA 98002; (800)804-4944 or (253)804-4444. Craps, roulette, Pai Gow, mini-baccarat, blackjack, poker, live keno, pull-tabs, off-track betting; bingo daily, (253)735-2404. The Kookaburra's Restaurant, Island Deli, Pisces Buffet. Club Galaxy showroom seats 250 for live entertainment. Gift shop featuring local artists. Open 10am–6am daily.

NOOKSACK RIVER CASINO, Nooksack Tribe, 5048 Mount Baker Hwy, Deming, WA 98244; (360)592-5472. Craps, roulette, blackjack, poker, Pai Gow, slots, keno, mega-bingo, pull-tabs. Paradise Buffet: All You Can Eat buffet with Asian dishes, North Fork Bar and Grill. Sunset lounge with live entertainment on weekends; champagne brunch Sun, gift shop with Native art. Open 10am–3am Sun–Thurs, 10am–5am Fri–Sat.

PUYALLUP BINGO PALACE, Puyallup Tribe, 2002 E 28th, Tacoma, WA 98513; (253)383-1572. Three bingo sessions daily. Concession stand with breakfast, lunch, dinner, food court, gift shop with Indian art. Call for hours.

RED WIND CASINO, Nisqually Tribe, 12819 Yelm Hwy SE, Olympia, WA 98513; (360)412-5000. Exit 111 off I-5 offskirts of Lacey. Slots, card games include blackjack, roulette, craps. Blue Camas Cafe (steaks, pasta, burgers). Gift shop featuring local and Southwestern fine Indian art. Open 10am–4am daily.

SKAGIT VALLEY CASINO RESORT, Upper Skagit Tribe, 5984 N. Darrk Lane, Bow, WA 98232-8631; (877)275-2448 or (360)724-7777. From I-5, take the Bow Hill exit. Its tower and lights make the casino visible from the exit. Slots, blackjack, roulette, craps, baccarat, live keno, poker, video bingo, craps. Club card services, The Fresh Market Buffet and Moon

Beach Grill Restaurant, Northern Lights Deli, nightly entertainment in the lounge Thurs–Sat; gift shop with Native art and souvenirs. Open daily, Sun–Thurs. 9am–3am; Fri–Sat. 9am–5am. Table games open at 11 am.

Swinomish Casino and Bingo, Swinomish Tribe, 12885 Casino Dr, Anacortes, WA 98221; (360)293-2691. Just off Hwy. 20, north of the bridge over the Swinomish Channel, east of Anacortes. Blackjack, poker, craps, roulette, Pai Gow, poker, red dog, slots, pull-tabs. Bingo in a non-smoking and smoking room), matinees and evening with deli table service. Totems Two Salmon Cafe, buffet. Deli. Gift shop. Small arcade for children. Open 11am–4am Sun–Thurs, 11am–6am Fri and Sat. Live comedy and music on weekends, cabaret.

Tulalip Casino, Tulalip Tribe, 6410 33rd Ave NE, Marysville, WA 98271; (888)272-1111 or (360)651-1111. Just off I-5 at Marysville, north of Everett. Slots, blackjack, roulette, craps, poker and other card games, keno, pull-tabs; bingo daily. Prince of Whales Restaurant, deli, gift shop. Open 10am–6am daily.

Tribal Administrative Offices

An Indian government may be referred to as a band, a tribe, or a confederation. The smallest unit, a band, usually refers to a family unit or a small group of people who lived together on their original lands. A tribe may include several bands of people who have the same language and culture. A confederation is made up of several tribes and bands who were moved to a reservation that is not in their original territory. An example of a confederation is the Yakama Nation, which is made up of 14 tribes and bands. Sometimes this nomenclature gets confusing, as when the Confederated Tribes of the Yakama Nation are simply referred to as the Yakama Tribe. The important thing to remember is that bands, tribes, and confederations have a special relationship with the U.S. government. They are nations within a nation, and have signed treaty agreements with the United States that are legal and binding. The following is a list of tribal offices in the Northwest (except for those in British Columbia). All tribes have a governing body, which might include hereditary chiefs or elected officials or a combination of both. Tribes also have an administrative body that makes government, economic, and resource decisions for their people.

California

Hoopa Valley Tribe
PO Box 1348
Hoopa, CA 95546
(916)625-4211

Idaho

Coeur d'Alene Tribe
Tribal Headquarters
Po Box 408
Plummer, ID 83851
(208)686-1800

Kootenai Tribe of Idaho
PO Box 1269
Bonners Ferry, ID 83805
(208)267-5223

Nez Perce Tribe
PO Box 305
Lapwai, ID 83540
(208)843-2253

NORTHWESTERN BAND OF SHOSHONI
427 North Main, Suite 101
Pocatello, ID 83204
(208)478-5712

SHOSHONE-BANNOCK TRIBES
OF THE FORT HALL RESERVATION
PO Box 306
Fort Hall, ID 83203
(208)238-3700

Montana

CONFEDERATED TRIBES OF
SALISH & KOOTENAI
PO Box 278
Pablo, MT 59855
(406)675-2700

Oregon

BURNS-PAIUTE TRIBE
HC 71 100 Pa Si Go St
Burns, OR 97720
(541)573-2088

CONFEDERATED TRIBES OF COOS,
LOWER UMPQUA & SIUSLAW
338 Wallace Ave.
Coos Bay, OR 97420
(503)267-5454

CONFEDERATED TRIBES OF
GRAND RONDE
9615 Grand Ronde Rd
Grand Ronde, OR 97347
(800)422-0232

CONFEDERATED TRIBES OF
SILETZ INDIANS
PO Box 549
Siletz, OR 97380
(541)444-2532

CONFEDERATED TRIBES OF THE
UMATILLA INDIAN RESERVATION
PO Box 638
Pendleton, OR 97801
(541)276-3165

CONFEDERATED TRIBES OF
WARM SPRINGS
PO Box 1299
Warm Springs, OR 97761
(541)553-3257

COQUILLE INDIAN TRIBE
PO Box 783

North Bend, OR 97459
(541)756-0904

COW CREEK BAND OF UMPQUA
2317 NE Stephens St., Ste. 100
Roseburg, OR 97470
(541)672-9405

KLAMATH TRIBES
PO Box 436
Chiloquin, OR 97624
(541)783-2219

Washington

CHEHALIS TRIBE
PO Box 536
Oakville, WA 98568
(360)273-5911

CHINOOK TRIBE
PO Box 228
Chinook, WA 98614
(360)777-8303

CONFEDERATED TRIBES OF COLVILLE
PO Box 150
Nespelem, WA 99155
(509)634-8883

YAKAMA INDIAN NATION
PO Box 151
Toppenish, WA 98948
(509)865-5121

COWLITZ TRIBE
PO Box 2547
Longview, WA 98632
(360)577-8140

DUWAMISH TRIBE
140 Rainier Ave S, #7
Renton, WA 98055
(206)226-5185

HOH TRIBE
2464 Lower Hoh Rd.
Forks, WA 98331
(360)374-6139

JAMESTOWN S'KLALLAM TRIBE
1033 Old Blyn Hwy
Sequim, WA 98382
(360)683-1109

KALISPEL TRIBE
PO Box 39
Usk, WA 99180
(509)445-1147

LOWER ELWHA S'KLALLAM TRIBE
2851 Lower Elwha Rd
Port Angeles, WA 98362
(360)452-8471

LUMMI INDIAN NATION
2616 Kwina Rd
Bellingham, WA 98226
(360)384-2229

MAKAH TRIBE
PO Box 115
Neah Bay, WA 98357
(360)645-2201

MUCKLESHOOT INDIAN TRIBE
39015 172nd Ave SE
Auburn, WA 98002
(206)939-3311

NISQUALLY TRIBE
4820 She-Nah-Num Dr SE
Olympia, WA 98513
(206)456-5221

NOOKSACK INDIAN TRIBE
PO Box 157
Deming, WA 98244
(360)592-3210

PORT GAMBLE S'KLALLAM TRIBE
31912 Little Boston Rd NE
Kingston, WA 98346
(360)297-2646

PUYALLUP TRIBE
2002 E 28th St
Tacoma, WA 98404
(253)573-7800

QUILEUTE TRIBE
PO Box 279
La Push, WA 98350
(360)374-6163

QUINAULT INDIAN NATION
PO Box 189
Taholah, WA 98587
(360)276-8211

SAMISH TRIBE
PO Box 217
Anacortes, WA 98221
(360)293-6404

SAUK-SUIATTLE TRIBE
5318 Chief Brown Lane
Darrington, WA 98241
(360)436-0131

SHOALWATER BAY TRIBE
PO Box 130
Tokeland, WA 98590
(206)267-6766

SKOKOMISH TRIBE
N 80 Tribal Center Rd
Shelton, WA 98584
(360)426-4232

SNOHOMISH TRIBE
144 Railroad Ave. Suite 201
Edmonds, WA 98020
(425)744-1855

SNOQUALMIE TRIBE
PO Box 670
Fall City, WA 98024
(425)222-6900

SPOKANE TRIBE
PO Box 100
Wellpinit, WA 99040
(509)258-4581

SQUAXIN ISLAND TRIBE
SE 70 Squaxin Lane
Shelton, WA 98584
(206)426-9781

STEILACOOM TRIBE
PO Box 88419
Steilacoom, WA 98388
(253)584-6308

STILLAQUAMISH TRIBE
PO Box 277
Arlington, WA 98223
(360)652-7362

SUQUAMISH TRIBE
PO Box 498
Suquamish, WA 98392
(360)598-3311

SWINOMISH TRIBE
PO Box 817
La Conner, WA 98104
(360)466-3163

TULALIP TRIBES
6700 Totem Beach Rd
Marysville, WA 98270
(360)651-4000

UPPER SKAGIT TRIBE
2284 Community Plaza Way
Sedro Woolley, WA 98284
(360)856-5501

INDEX

U–V

MEET ALASKA'S NATIVE PEOPLES

Inupiat

Athabascan

Yupik Aleut

Alutiiq

Tlingit

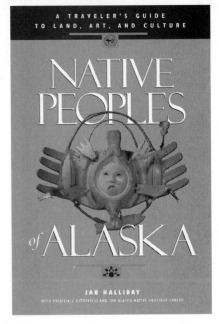

A TRAVELER'S GUIDE
TO LAND, ART, AND CULTURE

NATIVE PEOPLES of ALASKA

JAN HALLIDAY
WITH PATRICIA J. PETRIVELLI AND THE ALASKA NATIVE HERITAGE CENTER

Native Peoples of Alaska
A Traveler's Guide to Land,
Art, and Culture

Jan Halliday with **Partricia J. Petrivelli**
and **The Alaska Native Heritage Center**

Paperback, $17.95 • ISBN 1-57061-100-9
320 pages, includes detailed maps

• From popular destinations to
new discoveries, here are over
500 recommendations for
discovering Native Alaska.

• Clear directions on how to get
to all destinations, with complete information about air
travel, ferries, cruise ships, and
charters.

• Extensive descriptions of
authentic arts and crafts galleries, artists, and museums.

• Native-owned visitor services,
including lodgings, tours,
wilderness adventures, fishing
charters, and river trips.

"As you explore the vast wilderness of
Alaska, take time to meet some of
the native people. . . . Whether
you're interested in viewing totemic
art, purchasing beaded moccasins,
enjoying a tribal salmon bake or
sightseeing with insiders, this is the
book for you."
—*Coast to Coast* magazine

"What makes this book so special
are the people we meet, from Barrow
to Ketchikan. By giving us both
faces and facts, *Native Peoples of Alaska*
heralds a welcome new genre of
travel guidebook—one that's both
passionate and comprehensive."
—Ben Marks, Senior Editor, Travel,
Sunset magazine

SASQUATCH BOOKS
www.SasquatchBooks.com

Available at bookstores everywhere. To order, call 800-775-0817 or order online at www.SasquatchBooks.com